To The Sea

To The Sea

A History and Tour Guide of Sherman's March

JIM MILES

RUTLEDGE HILL PRESS
Nashville, Tennessee

Copyright © 1989 by Jim Miles

Published in Nashville, Tennessee, by Rutledge Hill Press, Inc., 513 Third Avenue South, Nashville, Tennessee 37210

Typography by Bailey Typography, Inc.
Drawings by Tonya Pitkin Presley, Studio III Productions
Unless noted differently, photographs are by the author.

Library of Congress Cataloging-in-Publication Data

Miles, Jim.
    To the sea : a history and tour guide of Sherman's march / Jim Miles.
       p.   cm.
    Includes bibliographical references.
    ISBN 1-55853-047-9
    1. Sherman's March to the Sea. 2. Georgia—History—Civil War, 1861–1865—Battlefields—Guide-books. 3. Georgia—Description and travel—1981—Guide-books. 4. Historic sites—Georgia—Guide -books. 5. South Carolina—Description and travel—1981—Guide -books. 6. Historic sites—South Carolina—Guide-books. 7. United States—History—Civil War, 1861–1865—Battlefields—Guide-books. I. Title.
E476.69.M54   1989   89-24232
973.7'378—dc20   CIP

Printed in the United States of America
1 2 3 4 5 6 7 8 — 95 94 93 92 91 90 89

Introduction

In November 1864, General William T. Sherman burned Atlanta and took an army of eighty thousand hardened Union veterans on a campaign that became famous as The March. When they reached Savannah a month later, an ugly scar that measured three hundred miles long and sixty miles wide was burned across Georgia.

Sherman crushed the economic heart out of the Confederacy. His men destroyed factories, mills, and agricultural produce. Thousands of civilians, mostly women, children, and the elderly, were left hungry, destitute, and sometimes homeless.

"Total War" had been created, and it was successful. Confederate armies starved. Military supplies could not be replenished, and rebel soldiers deserted by the score to return home and care for their families.

Soon after Sherman unleashed his forces on the Carolinas, the Confederacy collapsed, ending the bloodiest war in American history.

Sherman's March to the Sea. The phrase evokes powerful images for all Americans. To people of the North it was a triumphal procession in which right prevailed and an evil rebellion and institution were destroyed. To the South, it was the ultimate cruelty—a cowardly war against innocent civilians, an act so despicable that it took Georgia one hundred years to recover economically. A scar still remains on the southern psyche.

This is the story of the March to the Sea, the reasons behind Sherman's controversial decision to wage war against civilians and how that campaign was executed; and it is the story of the people who were involved in the March. There are terrified citizens who lose every morsel of food and valiant women who stoutly defend their homes and families against loss and insult. There are soldiers of all stripes, from savage men who steal, burn, rape, and kill with no compunction, and gallant warriors who defy the mob mentality to shield Georgia's innocents. There are brilliant Union commanders, bewildered southern officials, and brave fighting men in both blue and gray. This was the March. ■

Touring the March to the Sea

Today it is a simple matter to reach Savannah from Atlanta. It is a five-hour journey by automobile, south from Atlanta to Macon on I-75 and east from Macon to Savannah on I-16.

Thus it is hard to appreciate the magnitude of the March to the Sea. Sherman's soldiers, tramping over primitive dirt tracks, took a month to reach Savannah, passing through dozens of cities and towns and terrifying thousands of civilians. While inventing a new form of war, they set the Georgia economy back one hundred years.

It is important to remember how this campaign was executed and that those Georgians were ordinary citizens of their day. The only way to understand the military maneuvering and the plight of the civilians is to trace Sherman's path.

Sherman's army marched in two wings, with each wing taking two different roads. Our tour is organized to follow the major events of each wing and to highlight the fascinating variety of historic features found in central and eastern Georgia.

To follow this tour means striking out from the interstate highways and exploring what is becoming known as the "other Georgia," the less developed hinterlands found outside Atlanta and other major cities. This is small town, pickup truck country, where church and family are still the centers of life. A region of farmers and factories, it is a land where people you pass on the road will nod or wave, an America that is vanishing. Its passing should be mourned.

The driving tour to historic sites has been exhaustively researched; but readers should bear in mind that highways and streets are occasionally altered, and names and designated numbers of roads are often changed. That is why we have included written directions, mileage, and maps. These should enable you to circumvent any changes that might be made in the tour route in coming years. Also, remember that odometers can vary considerably. Our 1.1 might be your 1.2, so please take this into account. When in doubt about your location, don't hesitate to ask local residents for directions. While preparing these guides, we were frequently "misplaced."

For safety's sake it is obviously best to tour the March to the Sea with a companion. While one drives, the other can read and direct. It is also advisable to read the touring information before starting to drive. Familiarizing yourself with the tour will enable you to choose the sites you would like to visit beforehand.

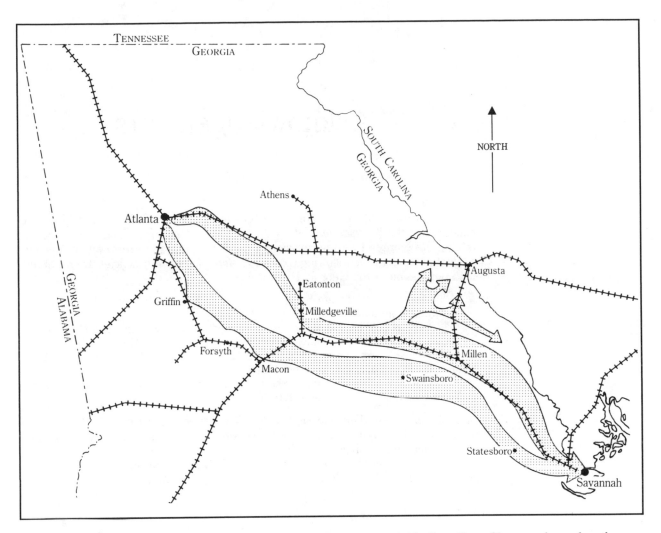

Map 1: Sherman's army marched in two wings; the Left Wing, commanded by Gen. Henry Slocum, advanced on the northern flank, and the Right Wing, commanded by Gen. O. O. Howard, advanced to the south.

By all means, be respectful of private property; do not trespass on land or call on the residents of a private historic home. It is extremely difficult to live in or on a part of history. There are too many vandals and arsonists around to be tolerant toward uninvited visitors. Fortunately, many historic homes are open as part of community tours around Christmas and during the spring. Check calendars of events for specific dates. ■

Acknowledgements

Quotations from "Major Connolly's Letters to His Wife: 1862–1865," which first appeared in the *Transactions of the Illinois State Historical Society,* volume 35 (1926), are reprinted with permission of the Illinois Historic Preservation Agency.

Quotations from the following *Georgia Historical Quarterly* articles are reprinted with permission of the Georgia Historical Society:

"Letter of a Confederate Surgeon on Sherman's Occupation of Milledgeville." Volume 32 (September 1848), pages 231–32.

"Fanny Cohen's Journal of Sherman's Occupation of Savannah," edited by Dr. Spencer Bidwell King. Volume 41 (December, 1957), pages 407–16.

"A Yankee Views the Agony of Savannah," edited by Frank Otto Gatell." Volume 43 (December, 1959), pages 428–31.

"The John Van Huzen Diary of Sherman's March from Atlanta to Hilton Head." Volume 53 (June, 1969), pages 220–40.

Quotations from *With Sherman to the Sea,* edited by Oscar Osburn Winther, copyright © 1943 by Louisiana State University Press, are reprinted by permission of Louisiana State University Press.

Quotations from *Marching with Sherman: Passages from the Letters and Campaign Diaries of Henry Hitchcock,* edited by M.A. DeWolfe Howe, are reprinted with permission of Yale University Press.

Contents

To The Sea

Atlanta

While planning the March to the Sea, Sherman visited this Union fort constructed to defend against Hood.
[LIBRARY OF CONGRESS]

CHAPTER 1

"I Can Make Georgia Howl"

I n early September 1864, William T. Sherman enjoyed the adoration of the entire North. In four months he had successfully led 120,000 soldiers across one hundred miles of hostile territory, survived numerous battles and countless skirmishes, inflicted terrible punishment on a Confederate army, and occupied the second most important city in the South—Atlanta, Georgia. Any military figure would have accepted that as the pinnacle of a brilliant career, and few Americans could imagine greater success on the battlefield. But the War was not yet won, and Sherman's mind worked relentlessly on a plan that would bring the Confederacy to its knees.

At Jonesboro on September 1, 1864, Sherman's forces brushed away a Confederate effort to prevent the destruction of Atlanta's last railroad. This vital city, the transportation and manufacturing center of the South, was isolated. That night Confederate General John B. Hood destroyed enormous stores of supplies he could not remove and evacuated the Army of Tennessee south to Lovejoy.

As Sherman cautiously probed the hastily erected, but formidable, Rebel works at Lovejoy, a part of his army marched into Atlanta and received its surrender from Mayor James M. Calhoun. On September 3 Sherman led his triumphant soldiers into Atlanta and wired President Abraham Lincoln, "So Atlanta is ours, and fairly won." The Atlanta Campaign, which had cost 35,000 Confederate casualties and 31,000 of Sherman's men, was concluded.

Sherman's victory was heralded as the most brilliant military campaign in history. The general was compared to Napoleon and Frederick the Great, and his name was mentioned prominently as a future presidential candidate. The news of Atlanta's fall was received in the North with great joy, leading Lincoln to declare a day of thanksgiving. It was a feat worth celebrating, yet the victory was incomplete. Hood's army was still intact, and in Virginia U. S. Grant had absorbed staggering casualties in an unsuccessful summer-long campaign to crush Robert E. Lee and the nearly invincible Army of Northern Virginia. Perhaps most important of all, the heartland of the Confederacy still produced large amounts of food and munitions to supply its armies, and the will of the southern people to prosecute the war seemed undeterred by this reversal.

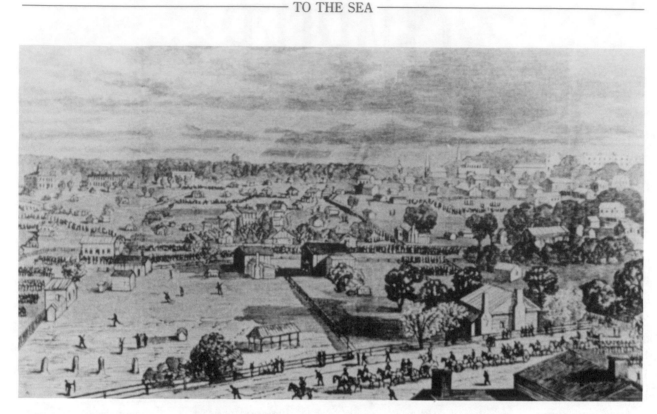

Union troops triumphantly enter Atlanta in September 1864.

In Sherman's mind, the fall of Atlanta was the first step in bringing the Civil War to a victorious conclusion. As his men rested in the occupied city, the fiery military genius pondered his next move.

While Sherman was formulating his plan, there was plenty of work for his men to do in Atlanta. The Confederate defenses were too extensive for the Federals to hold, and military engineers constricted the line to a strong, compact series of artillery forts connected by well-protected infantry trenches. Soldiers scavenged materials from shell-damaged or deserted structures and set about building comfortable quarters for their stay. Abundant provisions flowed south from Chattanooga down the railroad. Bars and games of chance proliferated as the army enjoyed a "protracted jubilee" over the victory, wrote a soldier from Illinois. "All were happy and smiling from the commander-in-chief to the humblest private in the ranks." Sherman concurred, stating, "We felt perfectly at home." Military bands were soon performing regularly, and the headquarters press printed programs for amateur theatrical productions.

On September 8 Sherman announced a controversial decision. "The city of Atlanta," he declared, "being exclusively required for warlike purposes, will at once be evacuated by all except the armies of the United States." At the time of Atlanta's surrender, the city had a civilian population of 22,000–30,000.

Because Sherman refused to be burdened with feeding and guarding Atlanta's remaining population, and since he could not protect them if hostilities erupted again, all civilians would have to leave. Those who so desired would be sent north, and some chose that option. The remainder would be delivered to the Confederate lines at Lovejoy.

Sherman anticipated the anguished cries of protest that this policy would provoke. "If the people raise a howl against my barbarity or cruelty," he informed a superior, "I will answer that war is war and not popularity seeking."

Mayor Calhoun of Atlanta opened the howling, pointing out that winter was rapidly approaching. Atlanta's population, consisting of women and children and the sick and aged, could not be expected to survive the proposed dislocation. The act was "appalling and heartrending," he informed Sherman, whose reply was firm:

> You can not qualify war in harsher terms than I will. War is cruelty and you cannot refine it. . . . You might as well appeal against the thunder storm as against these terrible hardships of war. . . . But, my dear sirs, when peace does come, you may call on me for any thing. Then will I share with you the last cracker, and watch with you to shield your homes and families against danger from every quarter.
>
> Now you must go, and take with you your old and feeble, feed and nurse them, and build for them, in more quiet places, proper habitations to shield them against the weather until the mad passions of men cool down and allow the Union and peace once more to settle over your old homes at Atlanta.

Hood assaulted Sherman's decision as he would have an enemy army. This "studied and ingenious cruelty" was unprecedented in war, he thundered. "In the name of God and humanity, I protest."

Sherman was in no mood to accept such criticism quietly. "In the name of common sense," the Union general answered, "I ask you not to appeal to a just God in such a sacrilegious manner." He blamed Southerners for plunging the nation into "a dark and cruel war. If we must be enemies, let us be men and fight it out as we propose to do, and not deal in such hypocritical appeals to God and humanity. God will judge us in due time, and he will pronounce whether it be more humane to fight with a town full of women and the families of a brave people at our backs, or to remove them to places of safety among their own friends."

This acrimonious exchange continued for two days, but Hood had no choice but to accept a truce for the transfer of Atlanta's noncombatants. Federal trains and one hundred six-mule team wagons transferred the people to Rough and Ready, and Confederates escorted them across fifteen miles of destroyed railroad track to Lovejoy. Over 1,600 people, 446 families by count, found crude shelter in south Georgia.

A northern newspaper correspondent was touched by the scenes he witnessed as Atlanta's people were forced to leave their homes: "Old age and tottering infants huddled together, awaiting their chance of escape," he wrote. The elderly, children, and women "cast many a long lingering look at their once happy home, which they were now about to abandon, perhaps

Atlanta's civilians pack their property aboard U.S. Army wagons for transportation to Confederate lines at Rough and Ready. [HARPER'S WEEKLY]

forever." He was disgusted to see officers extorting money from people who wanted a seat on a northbound train, even wounded soldiers. Many homes were looted the moment residents were out of sight.

Mary Gay was on hand when the refugees were deposited at Rough and Ready, "dumped upon the cold ground without shelter," in a chilling rain with no food or medical care. These civilians were "aged grandmothers upon the verge of the grave, tender girls in the first bloom of young womanhood, and little babes not three days old in the arms of sick mothers." The refugees brought their pots, furniture, and whatever else they could secure to the tops of the cars and wagons. Most had little but clothing, and they now found themselves "thrown out upon the cold charity of the world." The act of one beautiful southern girl impressed Gay and the Union guards alike. Leaving the train, she knelt and kissed the unconquered earth. A Federal officer asked Gay for an introduction—"I would offer her the devotion of my life," he swore—but the offer was rejected.

"We will fight you to the death," Hood threatened when the transfer was over. "Better die a thousand deaths than submit to live under you. . . ."

The charges of cruelty, and perhaps the perceived necessity of expelling innocents, led Sherman to justify himself to a visiting clergyman: "I have made war vindictively; war is war, and you can make nothing else of it. But Hood knows as well as anyone that I'm not brutal or inhuman."

Captain George W. Pepper, a war correspondent, walked the quiet streets of the city after the mass deportation. "Here are the luxurious homes, now the scenes of no domestic joys," he wrote, "stately warehouses, where no wealthy men congregate, beautiful temples where resound no more the organ's swell or the notes of praise."

With Atlanta's occupation secured, Sherman turned his attention to his next maneuver. He was deep in hostile territory and supplied by a fragile railroad that stretched three hundred miles to Nashville. The rails could be easily cut by the aggressive Confederate cavalry, and the energetic, offensively oriented Hood was not likely to remain idle for long. "I've got my wedge pretty deep," Sherman remarked, "and must look out I don't get my fingers pinched."

Sherman would have to continue military operations, but in which quarter? Before leaving Chattanooga in the spring, Sherman had been asked about his operations after Atlanta. "Salt water," he had muttered. "Salt water."

On September 4, Sherman wrote Army Chief of Staff General Henry Halleck about this subject. Sherman said there were no military objectives south of Atlanta until Macon, a hundred miles away. He suggested that while Federal forces surrounding Mobile marched north to Montgomery and Selma, he could move through LaGrange and West Point. The two parties could combine to capture Columbus, opening the Chattahoochee and Apalachicola rivers to Federal traffic.

On September 10 Sherman expressed the belief that he could capture Milledgeville, then turn on Macon or Augusta and "sweep the whole State of Georgia," but he warned against venturing far from his base of supplies in Atlanta.

The Man Who Made War Hell ■ William T. Sherman

[LIBRARY OF CONGRESS]

Sherman, considered to be one of the greatest generals in American history, definitely had one of the country's most unusual military minds. Named Tecumseh at birth for the famous Indian warrior, William was added by his adoptive parents, whose daughter, Ellen, he later married.

Weary of trying to earn a living in the military, Sherman entered civilian life in 1853 and failed miserably in business. He seemed to have found his niche as commandant of a military school, which would become Louisiana State University, when the Civil War began. Sherman rejected a Confederate commission, one of the few offered a native Northerner, and rejoined the U. S. Army.

Sherman's volatile temper and absolute contempt for a free press embroiled him in conflicts that almost led to his dismissal. The general actually considered suicide, but his star began to rise when he assisted Grant in the capture of Vicksburg. After the pair relieved the Confederate siege of Chattanooga, Grant left his trusted friend in charge of the Western armies.

Sherman's brilliant maneuvering won him Atlanta, and his virtually unopposed March to Savannah and through the Carolinas was a stroke of genius that pierced the hollow shell of an exhausted Confederacy. Paradoxically, when that devastating campaign was over, Sherman was harshly censored by Congress for granting generous terms to surrendering Confederates.

After the War, Sherman refused to challenge Grant for the Presidency, and he continued to resist the temptation of political office for the rest of his life. He remained in the army until 1883. To the North, Sherman was a conquering hero; to the South, evil incarnate. To all, he was a temperamental, unpredictable military phenomenon. ■

Union soldiers in Atlanta rejoice after being paid.

By September 20 Sherman was definitely considering the eastern seaboard as his next objective. If a base of operations on the Atlantic coast were secured for him, "I would not hesitate to cross the State of Georgia with sixty thousand men," he informed Grant, who as General-in-Chief of the Armies was his superior, "hauling some stores and depending on the country for the balance." As he had done before starting for Atlanta, Sherman studied prewar census reports from each Georgia county (Grant had said of Sherman, "He bones all the time when he is awake"), concentrating on the agricultural production of each. By this means he could determine if his army could survive. "Where a million of people find subsistence, my army won't starve," he concluded.

On October 1 Sherman proposed to Grant that the defense of Tennessee be left to his most experienced general, George Thomas. Sherman would "destroy Atlanta, and then march across Georgia to Savannah and Charleston, breaking [rail]roads and doing irreparable damage." He recognized the dangers inherent in such an undertaking, adding that "in a country like Georgia, with few roads, [and] innumerable streams," an inferior force could delay and harass his army into impotence. Still, he felt confident the Rebels were incapable of impeding the movement.

After the railroad was wrecked in Tennessee by the legendary Confederate raider Nathan Bedford Forrest on October 9, Sherman declared it "a physical impossibility to protect the roads" and asked Grant to be "turned loose." Sherman had managed to stockpile a herd of eight thousand cattle and three million bread rations, and he suggested that the railroad from

Chattanooga to Atlanta be destroyed; then he would "strike out with our wagons for Milledgeville, Millen, and Savannah. Until we can repopulate Georgia [with loyal citizens], it is useless for us to occupy it; but the utter destruction of its roads, houses, and people will cripple their military resources. . . . I can make this march, and make Georgia howl." Such an act would destroy "the possibility of Southern independence. They may stand the fall of Richmond, but not of all Georgia. We cannot remain on the defensive," he concluded.

Sherman proposed to "send back all my wounded and unserviceable men and, with my effective army, move through Georgia, smashing things to the sea."

Grant gave Sherman a sign of encouragement on October 12. "On reflection I think better of your proposition," he telegraphed.

In a message to Halleck on October 19, Sherman indicated that Grant preferred that he march to Savannah, while Halleck favored a move into Alabama. "Therefore, when you hear I am off, have lookouts at Morris Island, South Carolina, Ossabaw Sound, Georgia, and Pensacola and Mobile bays. . . . This movement is not purely military or strategic, but it illustrates the vulnerability of the South. They don't know what war means."

On the following day Sherman outlined his options and concluded, "By this [march] I propose to demonstrate the vulnerability of the South and make its inhabitants feel that war and individual ruin are synonymous terms." He continued this philosophy on October 22 to Grant:

This may not be war, but rather statesmanship; nevertheless, it is overwhelming to my mind that there are thousands of people abroad and in the South, who will reason thus, if the North can march an army right through the South, it is proof positive that the North can prevail in this contest, leaving only open the question of its willingness to use that power.

Summarizing the campaign possibilities to Grant, Sherman estimated that a move to the Atlantic would destroy Confederate communications and transportation. He would then be in a position to reinforce Grant in the campaign against Lee. A move to the Apalachicola River through the Flint River valley would be the safest maneuver. It might result in the liberation of Federal soldiers held at the notorious prison camp at Andersonville and could result in the destruction of 400,000 bales of cotton around Albany. The third option, to Columbus and Montgomery, then Mobile or Pensacola, would result in Mobile's capture. Sherman's preference was to "move via Macon and Millen to Savannah."

While this exchange was in progress, Hood made his move. After being denied reinforcements, which did not exist at this late date in the Confederacy, Hood was granted permission by officials in Richmond to move the Union prisoners at Andersonville out of Sherman's reach. Then he shifted his 35,000 remaining soldiers northwest from Lovejoy to Palmetto. The Confederate general intended to strike north and destroy Sherman's railroad lifeline into Tennessee and capture isolated garrisons. He planned to destroy any Union troops sent to pursue him, and perhaps plant the Confederate

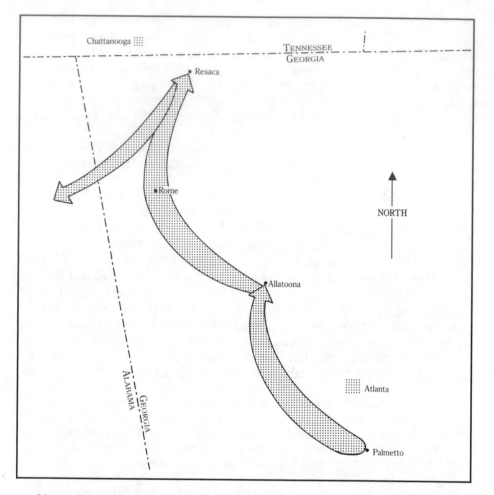

Map 2: Desperate to regain the offensive, Hood marched his army through northern Georgia, retreating from conflicts at Allatoona on October 3 and at Resaca on October 17.

banner on the shores of the Ohio River. Hood was nothing if not ambitious. "Sherman is weaker now than he will be in the future," he noted, "and I as strong as I can expect to be." Now was the time to strike.

Having lost 21,000 men and the city of Atlanta during the summer, Hood was launching a desperate offensive to regain the initiative. Since he refused to accept any responsibility for his recent reverses, a future operation seemed doomed to repeat earlier mistakes. "According to all human calculations," he had written Confederate President Jefferson Davis, "we should have saved Atlanta had the officers and men of the army done what was expected of them." His army had been gutted by heavy desertions in recent weeks, and his men were poorly supplied. Equipment and munitions were at a preminum, and many of the ragged men were barefooted. Only a bold stroke could hold such an army together.

Davis seemed to share that belief. After Atlanta was lost, he wrote, "I think Atlanta can be recovered, that Sherman's army can be driven out of Georgia, perhaps utterly destroyed." Through Governor Joseph Brown's brother, Davis suggested that Sherman's ruin would be helped if the Governor would raise another ten-thousand-man militia among the men exempted from military service. In response, Brown declared the war emergency in Georgia over, withdrew his militia from Hood's service, and sent them home on a harvest furlough. Davis considered this a treasonous move.

On September 25 Davis arrived at Palmetto to rally the troops and confer with Hood. "Be of good cheer," Davis advised the men, "for within a short while your faces will be turned homeward and your feet pressing the soil of Tennessee." The President's remarks were met with cheers from some, but many cried, "Johnston! Give us back old Joe," a reference to their former commanding general, Joseph E. Johnston, a popular leader who had not needlessly sacrificed his men in poorly executed battles, which seemed to be Hood's legacy.

Davis's revelation of Hood's intentions was fully covered in southern newspapers, providing Sherman with adequate notice of Confederate plans. "To be forewarned was to be forearmed," he noted. Sherman added that Davis must have "lost all sense and reason" to give away valuable military intelligence so freely.

Before leaving Palmetto for Macon and another round of injudicious speechmaking, Davis agreed to transfer one of Hood's corps commanders,

Hood's Fate

When Sherman began his bold, unopposed March through the heart of the Deep South, John B. Hood was still preparing to invade Tennessee with the last Confederate soldiers available to defend the region.

Bad weather delayed Hood until November 21, but then he moved swiftly from Florence, Alabama, with 38,000 men and 108 cannon. Union General John M. Schofield's thirty-thousand-man force was caught by surprise, and the Yankees found themselves cut off at Spring Hill, Tennessee. Certain that an attack in the morning would destroy Schofield, Hood settled down for the night of November 30. Incredibly, in the darkness Schofield's army crept through the midst of the sleeping Army of Tennessee and established a position at Franklin.

Although he had ignored reports of Federal movements during the night, Hood lashed out at everyone in the Rebel army for allowing Schofield to escape and ordered his army to pursue rapidly. He soon found the Federals entrenched on a high ridge with two miles of open fields at their front.

Without waiting for his artillery or a third of the army to arrive, Hood launched an assault. His men complied with accustomed vigor. After they swarmed furiously over the center of the Union line, savage hand-to-hand fighting erupted. Union reinforcements restored their perimeter, and the battle became a slaughter. At Franklin, Hood lost seven thousand men; six of the dead were generals. Schofield's casualties were 2,200 killed, wounded, and captured.

Schofield withdrew to Nashville, which was defended by General George Thomas, the Union's faithful "Rock." He had fifty thousand men manning substantial fortifications.

When Hood arrived at Nashville, his force consisted of 23,000 men. These scarecrows in gray were hungry and barefooted as they stood on an inch of ice that covered the ground. The very idea seems ludicrous, but Hood invested the city. The Union works stretched for ten miles and defended eight major roads; Hood's line was only four miles in length and covered four roads. The Confederate flanks were ripe for turning.

"Old Slow Trot" Thomas deliberately built up his strength, a lengthy process that nearly led Grant to remove him; but on December 15 he attacked. The Federals feinted on Hood's left flank and struck the right flank a devastating blow that swept the Confederates back two miles. Somehow the Rebels threw up a second line, but on the following day a Union column got into Hood's rear and the Army of Tennessee collapsed. Broken troops streamed south as Confederate General Stephen D. Lee stood by the roadside and cried out, "Rally, men! Rally! For God's sake, rally! This is the place for brave men to die!"

Thomas had lost 3,000 men, Hood 6,400 of the South's fast dwindling soldiers. The Confederates struggled south into Alabama in a bitter winter retreat, hounded by Federal cavalry. It was the worst defeat ever inflicted on a Confederate army.

In January 1861 Hood asked Jefferson Davis to relieve him of command. When Joseph Johnston returned, by order of Robert E. Lee over Davis's objections, the once great Army of Tennessee had virtually ceased to exist. ∎

William J. Hardee, who was blamed by Hood for all the recent Confederate reverses. Hardee was assigned to command the Department of South Carolina, Georgia, and Florida, with headquarters in Charleston.

By October 4 the Confederates had crossed the Chattahoochee, bypassed Marietta, and destroyed nine miles of track around Big Shanty and Acworth. Sherman could not ignore this threat to his supply line. He left 12,000 soldiers to guard Atlanta and led 65,000 men out of the city to pursue Hood. On October 5 Sherman rode to the summit of Kennesaw Mountain, where his troops had been soundly defeated the previous June, and watched a distant battle at Allatoona. After a savage fight, the Confederates were repulsed.

Hood established a position at Dallas, then disappeared into the rugged country of North Georgia, covering up to twenty miles a day. Sherman was temporarily alarmed that Hood might be doubling back to attack Atlanta, but

The last train filled with Atlanta's citizens and their belongings prepares to leave the city after Sherman's ordered evacuation. [LIBRARY OF CONGRESS]

the unpredictable Rebel soon appeared farther north at Resaca, scene of yet another earlier encounter in the Atlanta Campaign. The Confederates destroyed twelve miles of track but failed to capture a Federal garrison that occupied a blockhouse, then continued north to subdue Union detachments at Dalton and Tunnel Hill. When Sherman approached, Hood returned south to Resaca and marched west through Snake Creek Gap.

Hood established a strong defensive position at LaFayette. When Sherman arrived on October 17 and deployed his forces to give battle, the Confederates again withdrew, this time west into Alabama. Sherman angrily followed the fast moving Hood, complaining that his opponent's activity was "inexplicable by any common-sense theory." This meaningless ramble through the South was delaying his own offensive plans.

Sherman finally determined that it was not possible to corner Hood and force a fight, stating, "It was clear to me that he had no intention to meet us in open battle." He added, "No single army can catch Hood." Sherman wrote to Thomas, "To pursue Hood is folly, for he can twist and turn like a fox and wear out any army in pursuit; to continue to occupy long lines of railroads simply exposes our small detachments to be picked up in detail and forces men to make counter-marches to protect lines of communication."

"If he [Hood] will go to the Ohio River, I will give him rations," Sherman declared, concluding, "Let him go north. My business is down South."

Sherman had earlier sent Thomas to command Federal troops in Nashville in case Hood should invade that state. He now dispatched additional troops, giving Thomas a total of seventy thousand men, twice Hood's strength. Having provided for any situation that Hood might precipitate, Sherman turned to his own scheme.

In early November Sherman received official permission to proceed with plans to abandon his base of supply and march cross-country to Savannah. Realizing that a continued pursuit of Hood was pointless and would negate the gains of the Atlanta Campaign, Grant wrote, "I say then, go as you propose." Grant had convinced Lincoln of the plan's wisdom, saying, "Sherman's proposal is the best that can be adopted." He also reminded the Chief Executive that no one was so good at maneuver as Sherman. The army's Chief of Staff telegraphed Sherman, "Whatever results, you have the confidence and support of the Government."

Sherman moved rapidly to implement his plan. Establishing his headquarters at Kingston, Georgia, Sherman sent every unnecessary article north to Chattanooga on a nearly continuous stream of trains. Some of the garrison troops who had protected the railroad were sent to Tennessee, along with any man declared physically unfit by an army doctor. Major George Ward Nichols, aide-de-camp to Sherman, noted, "The sick and wounded, non-combatants, the machinery, extra baggage, tents, wagons, artillery, ammunition stores, every person and every thing not needed in the future campaign were sent back to Chattanooga. The army was stripped for fighting and marching."

On November 13 this operation was completed. Nichols wrote, "Yesterday the last train of cars whirled rapidly past the troops moving south, speeding, over bridges and into the woods as if they feared they might be left helpless in the deserted land." The railroad was destroyed and the telegraph lines severed. Sherman, having received a final message from Thomas, responded, "Dispatch received. All right." Sherman could not be recalled now.

An extraordinary event was in the making. A Confederate army had left a destructive Federal force deep in southern territory without opposition. Hood marched into Tennessee, hoping to recapture not only the Volunteer State but also Kentucky; but Sherman was left free to plow through the unprotected heart of the South.

Secrets are rarely kept for long in an army. Private Theodore Upson confided in his diary, "There are rumors that we are to cut loose and march south to the ocean." ∎

CHAPTER 2

"Ruin, Universal Ruin"

With the final decision made to march for the coast, Sherman attended to the details of the campaign. His first chore was to eliminate Atlanta as a manufacturing and transportation center. Any usable railroad or war material that Hood had left intact, and public buildings and property, would have to be destroyed. Atlanta would certainly be reoccupied by Confederate forces after he departed, and Sherman would not allow the city to be useful in any military capacity.

Sherman delayed this destruction until his planned return to the city on November 15, but rumors of the army's imminent departure had spread throughout the ranks. Soldiers consumed every ounce of liquor they could find, and drunken men soon began practicing the art of arson on deserted homes in the city. A block was burned on November 11, and more structures were torched each night.

Activities by withdrawing Federals in northern Georgia provided an ominous omen for Atlanta's treatment. As a Union officer traveled north to Chattanooga, he paused at Dalton and was surprised by the condition of the city. "Dalton has been almost destroyed by the different armies which have been in it," he wrote. "Houses have been torn down, many being first stripped of the clapboarding to make bunks, etc., for the soldiers, and the remainder gradually destroyed for firewood and the like. It was manifestly a pretty town once, and in a beautiful situation."

The organized destruction in preparation to abandoning Atlanta began in Rome, which had been occupied since May. On November 4 General John Corse received orders from Sherman to prepare his troops to leave the city. Before departing, he was to "destroy in the most effective manner, by fire, or otherwise, all bridges, warehouses, and buildings, especially adapted to armed use, lumber and timber." Any items that could not be transported to Union-held territory would also be destroyed.

On November 10 Sherman telegraphed orders to destroy Rome. That night Corse started his devil's work. Two railroad depots, a grist mill, a cotton warehouse, a hotel, a bank, and most of the business district were burned. The Nobel Foundry, an important Confederate facility, was leveled by explosive charges.

"Never had a scene of such wantonness and misery been presented to Rome," wrote Charles B. Battey, Jr. "Dry goods boxes and trash were piled high in stores and set off, and the crackling of the timbers furnished a melancholy echo to the wails of women and children. Soldiers ran from place to place with firebrands in their hands, setting the places designated here, and perfectly harmless places there. Necessarily the stores and shops next to the condemned improvements went up in smoke. With hundreds of bayonets bristling, the forty steadfast male Romans (all that remained in the city) could do nothing but watch and allow their souls to fill with regret."

"Only isolated structures escaped," he continued, "until there was no place much to do business, and less business to do than places. A livery stable caught, and the odor of burning horseflesh could be detected for several blocks. The whinnies of the horses told of their awful plight."

A number of homes were burned, some accidentally by flying embers and some torched deliberately by vindictive soldiers.

"The night the town was burned I was all alone, except for my little children," a woman wrote her husband in Alabama. "I cannot describe my feelings. I did not know what to do, so I went to washing, and washed two or three dozen pieces. . . . I passed the night away somehow and am still alive."

The Federals marched out early the following morning, leaving a city of smouldering ruins and free-standing chimneys in what Union General Jacob Cox had called "one of the pleasantest towns we have found in the South." Two days later a resident described that same city: "The streets were entirely deserted. Everything was as still and quiet as if no war was in progress. The business section was dead."

From all across northern Georgia, columns of men marched toward Atlanta. They destroyed their protective stockades, the railroad they had guarded for six months, and any unfortunate town that happened to be on their route of march. "Behind us we leave a track of smoke and fire," Nichols recorded.

On November 13 Federal troops rampaged through Acworth. Major James Connolly was present and tried to prevent its destruction, but he gave up the effort when he saw the extent of the arson. A few homes occupied by "'war widows' and their families" were saved, "but all the rest of the town went up in smoke," leaving the town "a heap of ruins. It is evident that our soldiers were determined to burn, plunder, and destroy everything in their way on this march. If we are to continue our devastations as we began today, I don't want to be captured on this trip, for I expect every man of us the rebels capture will get a 'stout rope and a short shrift.'"

Major Henry Hitchcock, newly arrived on Sherman's staff to handle the general's growing correspondence, was similarly disturbed as he rode on November 13 with Sherman's staff to Marietta. There he saw "columns of black smoke and lurid flame—terrible commentary on this display and its real meaning." Sherman told Hitchcock that soldiers had burned Marietta without authorization, but guards posted to protect the town had been unable to prevent it. The commanding general then amused himself by reviewing his cavalry, led by General Judson Kilpatrick. "Splendid sight," Hitchcock thought as Sherman rode past the entire line of five thousand cavalrymen, "and uproarious cheers from men; he got excited, waved hat,

Before leaving Atlanta, Union troops remove iron and ties from a roadbed. The ties were burned, and the rails were heated and twisted around trees and poles.

etc. Then took position and whole command filed by at trot—thought they never would get done."

Passing through the town later, Connolly recorded, "When we reached Marietta we found that all the business part of town was burned by Kilpatrick's cavalry last night."

"All the principal buildings around the public square in this town were burning as we passed," added a Federal colonel. "General Sherman was standing looking on."

A soldier marching to Atlanta, seeing smoke and flames from the burning Chattahoochee River bridges, remarked, "I believe Sherman has set the river on fire."

"Reckon not," answered a companion. "If he has, it's all right." The indifference he expressed would lead to indiscriminate destruction throughout Georgia.

Hitchcock, who had joined Sherman at Kingston, determined to keep a detailed journal of his activities in the army. He proved to be a keen observer. Because Hitchcock spent most of his time near Sherman and wrote as events occurred, his writings became the most reliable account of the March.

Sherman had taken Hitchcock into his confidence concerning the nature of

19

the coming mission. "It's a big game, but I can do it," he said, "I *know* I can do it," and Hitchcock certainly believed him. "You may be sure of one thing—that what he says he can do, he *can.*" Hitchcock was immediately convinced of Sherman's ability, noting that his intelligence was the "sort of power which a flash of lightning suggests," clear, intense, and rapid.

The commanding general and his staff had left Kingston early on November 12. Passing through Cartersville, they watched the last three trains from Atlanta cross the Etowah River. After they rode twenty miles, they camped near Allatoona for a supper of milk, butter, and hardboiled eggs. On November 13 the staff rode through the abandoned fortifications at Kennesaw Mountain—"Such lines as rebs had," Hitchcock noted. The party continued to Marietta.

On November 14 Sherman rode on into Atlanta, a distance of twenty miles, and shared with the new men points of interest along the way. The route was clogged by marching columns of men, who instantly recognized their commander and "whisper name along ranks, and watch movements. No cheers from *vets*—he don't like it," Hitchcock had discovered.

Every foot of the railroad along the route had been destroyed. The ties were burned, and nine out of ten rails were bent. Sherman proudly boasted that the Confederates could only produce rails in Richmond now that he had captured Atlanta.

Hitchcock crossed the Chattahoochee on a wagon bridge; the railroad bridge had been destroyed earlier in the day. He rode to headquarters at the Lyon House, a fine, two-story brick home located on high ground. Hitchcock was excited by the prospect of his first military adventure. "We start tomorrow for the seashore," he wrote.

Two days before the demolition began, Nichols recorded in his journal:

Atlanta is entirely deserted by human beings, excepting a few soldiers. The houses are vacant; there is no trade or traffic of any kind; the streets are empty. Beautiful roses bloom in the gardens of fine houses, but a terrible stillness and solitude cover all, depressing the hearts even of those who are glad to destroy it. In the peaceful homes of the North there can be no conception how these people have suffered for their crimes.

During Sherman's absence, his chief engineer, Captain Orlando Poe, had been permitted to play with his new invention. It was a battering ram that consisted of a twenty-one-foot long iron bar, swinging on chains from a ten-foot high wooden brace. With this fiendish device he demolished stone and brick buildings, including the railroad station, factories, warehouses, and Atlanta's huge stone roundhouse. "Perfect smash," Hitchcock wrote of the depot after Poe was finished with it. Excess wagons, mattresses, and other flammable materials were placed in buildings, ready for ignition, and explosives were placed under more substantial structures.

"He [Poe] had a large force at work," wrote Sherman, and "had leveled the great depot, round-house and the machine shops of the Georgia Railroad, and had applied fire to the wreck. One of these machine shops had been used by the rebels as an arsenal, and in it were stored piles of shot and shell, some of which proved to be loaded, and that night was made hideous by the bursting of shells, whose fragments came uncomfortably near Judge Lyon's house, in which I was quartered."

"The stone depot had been previously mined," wrote Captain J. C. Van Duzer, a telegraph operator, "and packages of powder buried under its walls. The object I suppose is to set the woodwork on fire as soon as we leave and let the powder do what we left undone."

To prevent arson, soldiers on provost duty were instructed "to protect from accidental or wanton fire and destruction all buildings not designated to be destroyed."

In the late afternoon gloom of November 15, the authorized fires were set. First the iron foundry, valued at half a million dollars, was destroyed, then an oil refinery was torched. That was followed by a warehouse, the depot area, and the remains of Hood's arsenal. As the wind picked up, these intense fires raged out of control and spread to other buildings. Shells buried in the ruins of the arsenal exploded, raining dangerous shrapnel and burning debris across the city. Smoke billowed toward the sky as buildings, built primarily of dry southern pine, exploded into flame. The sinking sun was obscured by a pall of smoke, and the air grew oppressive under the suffocating clouds.

Hitchcock watched the spectacle from a headquarters window, where Sherman remarked that the fire could probably be seen from Griffin, forty miles to the south. Hitchcock saw "immense and raging fires lighting up whole heavens—first bursts of smoke, dense, black volumes, then tongues of flame, then huge waves of fire roll up into the sky; presently the skeletons of great warehouses stand out in relief against sheets of roaring, blazing, furious flames—then the angry waves roll less high, and are of a deeper color, then sink and cease. . . . Now and then are heavy explosions, and as one fire sinks, another rises, further along the horizon." It was a sight that was "lurid, angry, dreadful to look upon."

Sherman had previously explained to Hitchcock why the city had to be utterly destroyed:

> "This city has done more and contributed probably more to carry on and sustain the war than any other, save perhaps Richmond," he said. "We have been fighting *Atlanta* all the time, in the past: have been capturing guns, wagons, etc., etc., marked *Atlanta* and made here, all the time: and now since they have been doing so much to destroy us and our Government we have to destroy them, at least enough to prevent any more of that."

"The heart was burning out of beautiful Atlanta," wrote a reporter for the New York *Herald*, David Conyngham.

> The air was resonant with explosions, while flames were mounting to the sky from burning depots and factories all over the city . . . men were cheering and singing patriotic songs, and fairly revelling in the excitement and novelty of the situation.
>
> A stone warehouse was blown up by a mine. Quartermasters ran away, leaving large stores behind. The men plunged into the houses, broke windows

and doors with their muskets, dragging out armfuls of clothes, tobacco, and whiskey, which was more welcome than all the rest. The men dressed themselves in new clothes, and then flung the rest into the fire.

The streets were now in one fierce sheet of flame; houses were falling on all sides, and fiery flakes of cinders were whirled about. Occasionally shells exploded, and excited men rushed through the choking atmosphere, and hurried away from the city of ruins.

The burning city displayed a unique beauty as Conyngham marched out later that night.

At a distance the city seemed overshadowed by a cloud of black smoke, through which, now and then, darted a gushing flame of fire, or projectiles hurled from the burning ruin.

The sun looked, through the hazy cloud, like a blood-red ball of fire, and the air, for miles around, felt oppressive and intolerant. . . . The "Gate City" was a thing of the past.

Colonel Adin Underwood, who watched the spectacle with his Massachusetts infantry, remembered the night as "one to be remembered":

No darkness—in place of it a great glare of light from acres of burning buildings. This strange light, and the roaring of the flames that licked up everything habitable, the intermittent explosions of powder, stored ammo, and projectiles, streams of fire that shot up here and there from heaps of cotton bales and oil factories, the crash of falling buildings, and the change, as if by a turn of the kaleidoscope, of strong walls and proud structures into heaps of desolation; all this made a dreadful picture of the havoc of war, and of its unrelenting horrors.

As the band was playing in the theater that night, the flaming red light from the approaching fire which flooded the building, the roar of the flames and the noises of the intermittent explosions added scenic effects which were not down in the bills, and will never be forgotten. And when later in the night it serenaded Sherman and played in the light of the flames "John Brown's Soul Goes Marching On," the members must have appeared to the crestfallen civilians like so many Neroes fiddling with delight at the burning of Rome. It seemed like a demoniacal triumph over the fate of the city that had so long defied Sherman's armies.

W. C. Johnson marched through the city as the fire raged. "The writer can never forget the awfully grand sight witnessed here to-night, of the burning of the city," he wrote in his diary. "It appears as an ocean of fire as we look down upon the great volumes of fire and smoke, the ruinous flares leaping from building to building, and leaving nothing but the smouldering ruins of this once beautiful city. Surely the terrors of war are being fearfully felt, and demonstrated, in this sunny south country—a desolate country indeed."

An officer who dodged falling debris as he negotiated the dangerous streets of Atlanta added, "All the pictures and verbal descriptions of hell I have ever seen never gave me half so vivid an idea of it as did this flame-

The city of Atlanta is reduced to ruin by a raging inferno.

wrapped city tonight."

"We have utterly destroyed Atlanta," Upson wrote in his journal. "I don't think any people will want to try and live there now. It is pretty tough to rout people out of their homes in this way, but it is war."

The flames enabled men two miles distant to read letters received from faraway sweethearts. One doctor marching ten miles away swore he could read his watch by the glow. The fire finally died down around midnight, but then looters and arsonists descended upon the city's residential areas. Soldiers broke into houses, stole such items as suited their fancy, then torched the homes. Army stores were looted, and thousands of windows were shattered for the thrill of the crashing sound. Men "shouted and danced and sang while pillar and roof and dome sank into one common ruin," a witness remembered.

A sergeant from Michigan was about to torch a home when "a little girl about ten years old came to me and said, 'Mr. Soldier you would not burn our home, would you? If you do where are we going to live,' and she looked into my face with such a pleading look that I could not have the heart to fire the place so I dropped the torch and walked away." Most of the men were not so compassionate.

"This is the penalty of rebellion," Captain Pepper would write. "Heaven and earth both agree in decreeing a terrible punishment to those perdisious [*sic.*] wretches who concocted this wasting and desolating war."

"It was hard to restrain the soldiers from burning [the city] down," wrote Conyngham, particularly those men who "expected to get some booty under cover of the fire."

The commander of the Provost Guard thought his men did all they could to stop the arson. Unfortunately, "the excitement of so great a conflagration was almost overpowering," especially for troops from northern Georgia who had been torching towns for nearly a week. Captain Poe believed most of the destruction had been accomplished "by lawless persons, who, by sneaking around in blind alleys, succeeded in firing many houses which it was not intended to touch."

Some officers were disgusted by the activity. "This destruction of private property in Atlanta was entirely unnecessary and therefore a disgraceful piece of business," blustered one witness. "The cruelties practiced on this campaign toward citizens have been enough to blast a more sacred cause than ours. We hardly deserve success."

Hitchcock saw the results in a more personal manner. "Doubtless it will be death to those of us who may fall into their [Rebel] hands."

Some blamed Sherman for not exercising sufficient control over his men. On this occasion at least, Sherman had taken to the streets to organize parties to extinguish unauthorized fires, but the conflagration was beyond control. Atlanta burned throughout the night and smouldered for days. The smoke was visible for twenty miles, and the stench of burned buildings, meat, bedding, and a hundred other scorched items, was evident almost as far.

"Atlanta, Night of the 15th November," Nichols wrote.

A grand and awful spectacle is presented to the beholder in this beautiful city, now in flames. The heaven is one expanse of lurid fire; the air is filled with flying, burning cinders; buildings covering two hundred acres are in ruins or in flames; every instant there is the sharp detonation or the smothered booming sound of exploding shells and powder concealed in the buildings, and then the sparks and flame shoot away up into the black red roof, scattering cinders far and wide.

    To-night I heard the really fine band of the Thirty-third Massachusetts playing "John Brown's Soul Goes Marching On," by the light of the burning buildings. I have never heard that noble anthem when it was so grand, so solemn, so inspiring.

Others were touched by the same combination of grand music and awe-inspiring destruction. "Quite a feature tonight was a serenade," wrote Hitchcock. "Always will the Miserere in *Trovatore* carry me back to this night's scenes and sounds."

Captain Pepper recorded his impressions while leaving Atlanta that night.

Clouds of smoke, as we passed through, were bursting from several princely mansions. In the solemn starlight we could see the billows of smoke rolling up from the city of Atlanta. Such clouds of smoke, and vast sheets of flame, mortal eye has seldom seen. The whole region for miles was lighted up with a strange and indescribable glare.

Of the destructive fire, Sherman believed it did not "reach the great mass of dwelling-houses."

Atlanta's railroad roadhouse after its destruction by explosives just before Union troops abandoned the city. [LIBRARY OF CONGRESS]

The sun rose to shine darkly through a shroud of smoke that hung over the city. Over two hundred acres of formerly thriving city had been reduced to ashes. Poe estimated that thirty-seven percent of the city had been destroyed, but that was a charitable estimate. The commercial and industrial areas were total losses. Only 400 of 4,500 businesses and homes escaped damage. In response to the persistence of Father Thomas O'Reilly, an Irish-born priest who had unselfishly ministered to wounded soldiers of both armies, the Church of the Immaculate Conception and a cluster of other churches and city hall were spared. Soldiers on duty there took their jobs of protection seriously. Hitchcock said the sentries made him leave the sidewalk and walk in the street past the quiet sector.

One of the few public buildings spared was the Medical College, saved by the subterfuge of Dr. Peter Paul Noel D'Alvigny, a Confederate surgeon. He had been notified that the hospital would be torched and all the patients had been safely removed. When a Federal demolition crew entered the first floor, proceeded to break up the furniture and beds, and added straw to the debris for easy ignition, Dr. D'Alvigny placed his orderlies in bed on the second floor.

As the Yanks set their fire, the doctor ran downstairs, exclaiming that the hospital had not been evacuated. "Nonsense," growled the officer in charge. "I have been told to destroy this building, and all the patients were to have been evacuated hours ago."

"Come see for yourself," an apparently anguished D'Alvigny exclaimed. Entering the upstairs ward, the Union officer witnessed men writhing in feinted pain and moaning from imaginary wounds and fevers. The Federal rushed downstairs and helped his men extinguish the fire. "Remove those patients," he sternly ordered the doctor, "we'll be back before dawn." In the excitement surrounding Atlanta's demise, the hospital was overlooked.

A few civilians had managed to remain in the doomed city. For them the night was an endless terror. "Oh, what a night!" cried Carrie Berry. "It looked like the whole town was on fire." She sat up all night to prevent her home from being burned. "They [Federal soldiers] behaved very badly . . . nobody knows what we have suffered." Structures continued to burn throughout the next day as frightened citizens cowered in their homes, fearful of the approaching night, "because we do not know what moment that they will set our house on fire," Berry noted.

Nobel Williams and other Atlantans saw "their own beloved city was enveloped on all sides in a seething mass of smoke and flame, madly curling upward to the blue skies above, and leaving behind only blackened ruins and heaps of ashes."

The house of a "Dr. C" survived, but the intensity of surrounding blazes drew out the rosin in his front door. He survived in a circle of "fire, smoke, and heat."

The grim ruins were surrounded by the debris of three major battlefields, where Atlanta's fate had been determined in the summer. Hundreds of decaying animal carcasses still lay scattered across the landscape. They were joined by an estimated three thousand exhausted horses and scrawny cattle that had been killed with axe blows and abandoned to rot in Atlanta's ruins. "The whole country is full of dead horses and mules, and the ditches full of stagnant water," wrote Lizzie Perkerson.

When Sherman departed, the city was invaded by scavengers from across northern Georgia, desperate people from up to one hundred miles away. They completed the looting by hauling away from the ruins iron, coffee, sugar, salt, and any other useful items they could find. For a few weeks the city was dominated by thousands of dogs, abandoned pets who roamed in wild packs. "Man's best friend had reverted to wolfish tendencies," wrote a woman. One of the few sounds in the abandoned city was the "distant baying of dogs, dangerous dogs." The city was also invaded by cats of all sizes who were "ready to devour the scanty food" left to the people.

A week after Sherman left Atlanta, Governor Joseph E. Brown dispatched Militia General W. P. Howard to survey the city. He reported every factory, business, school, and 3,200 houses that had been destroyed within the city. An estimated 1,800 additional houses had been torched in surrounding areas. The only useful items that remained were bricks, brass, and copper. Even the flanges of wheels on rail cars had been broken. "In short," Howard wrote, "every species of machinery that was not destroyed by fire was most ingeniously broken and made worthless in its original form."

Of Atlanta's formerly abundant shade trees, two thirds had been cut down for use as firewood or building shacks during the Union occupation. "The suburbs present to the eye one vast, naked, ruined, deserted camp," the general reported.

Howard was appalled by the destruction visited upon Oakland Cemetery, where horses had grazed on ornamental shrubs. "The ornaments of graves, such as marble lambs, miniature statuary, souvenirs of departed little ones are broken and scattered abroad," Howard continued. "The crowning act of all their wickedness and villainy was committed by our ungodly foe in removing the dead from the vaults in the cemetery, and robbing the coffins of the silver name plates . . . and depositing their own dead in the vaults."

Howard estimated that a million dollars' worth of usable material had been appropriated by civilian looters after Sherman left the city.

> There were about 250 wagons in the city on my arrival, loading with pilfered plunder; pianos, mirrors, furniture of all kinds, iron, hides without number, and an incalculable amount of other things, very valuable at the present time. This exportation of stolen property had been going on ever since the place had been abandoned by the enemy. Bushwhackers, robbers, and deserters, and citizens from the surrounding country for a distance of fifty miles have been engaged in this dirty work.
>
> Many of the finest houses mysteriously left unburned are filled with the finest furniture, carpets, pianoes, mirrors, etc., and occupied by parties, who six months ago lived in humble style. About fifty families remained during the occupancy of the city by the enemy and about the same number have returned since its abandonment.

An Augusta newspaper reporter found a "country cousin" hauling a piano through a street with a rope. She was taking this "pretty table to my home," the woman explained.

An Atlanta newspaper, the *Daily Intelligencer,* had departed the besieged city for Macon the previous summer. It shortly returned and described the state of Atlanta's railroads:

> [They] are destroyed in the completest manner by burning the cross ties and bending and twisting the iron. . . . The piles of cross ties are so numerous and spread out to such an extent as to remind one of the ocean when its waves are raised by a brisk wind. It is an ocean of ruins.
>
> The stillness of the grave for weeks reigned over this once bustling, noisy city. No whistle from railroad engines, no crowing of cocks, no grunting of hogs, no braying of mules, no lowing of cows, no whirring of machinery, no sound of the hammer and saw—nothing but the howling of dogs was heard in our midst.
>
> Profound silence reigned in our streets . . . no children in the streets, no drays, no wagons, no glorious sound of the Gospel in the churches; the theater was hushed in the silence of death. Ruin, universal ruin, was the exclamation of all.

The newspaper related the history of Atlanta to determine what had brought about this sad state.

Twenty-five years ago and the site which Atlanta, the 'Gate City' of the South, occupies was a forest, which but a few years atecedent to that period was the abode of the red man. . . . Then was developed that great system of railroads.

War came, and still Atlanta was a progressive city. Population and wealth, until the Spring of the present year, literally poured into it. . . . As a Commercial Depot, it was in advance of any city in the adjoining states. As a Financial Mart, she rivaled her most prosperous sister cities of the South.

To the enemy it became a prize coveted as much as Richmond . . . almost superhuman efforts made, alas! too successfully made, to capture and possess it . . . and then amid the glare of its thousands of burning tenements, the flames rising so as to light the country for miles and miles. . . . So much now only for the past of Atlanta . . . We must next turn to the *present*.

A city destroyed by *fire*! . . . This will be the nucleus, the corner stone, the foundation as it were upon which the city will again be restored. The energy for which her citizens have been distinguished has already begun to manifest itself. But so much for the *past* and *present* of Atlanta. Let us now look to its *future!*

That which built Atlanta and made it a flourishing city will again restore it, purified, we trust, in many particulars by the fiery ordeal through which it has passed.

The people of Atlanta soon started to return. Numerous residents, turned out of their homes two months earlier, trudged back into the city. They salvaged what remained, mostly bricks and tin, and started to rebuild. A month after Sherman departed, the people of Atlanta had elected a mayor and restored mail service. The *Daily Intelligencer* was being published. The railroads were repaired, and trains brought supplies into the devastated city. Industry was rebuilt. Atlanta was indeed destined to rise, Phoenix-like, from the ashes of defeat.

The fate of eastern Georgia would be different. ∎

CHAPTER 3

"Ready for a Meal or a Fight"

At daybreak on the morning of November 16, Sherman mounted his favorite horse, a fast walker named Sam, and rode east from his Atlanta headquarters.

The army he was sending from the city was radically changed from the one with which he had invaded Georgia seven months earlier. Then he commanded three armies: the massive Army of the Cumberland, commanded by George Thomas; the Army of the Tennessee, led by James B. McPherson until his death at the battle of Atlanta, and afterwards by O. O. Howard; the small Army of the Ohio, under John Schofield; as well as a cavalry corps led by Judson Kilpatrick. His strength peaked during that campaign at 120,000.

Thomas, many of his men, and Schofield's complete army were now in Tennessee to contain Hood. Sherman retained 62,000 men, arguably the best soldiers in the service of the United States. The infantry was divided into four corps, with two corps in each of two armies. These armies were commonly called wings during the sweep through Georgia. Three divisions constituted a corps.

The Left Wing, which advanced on the northern flank, was composed of the 14th and 20th Corps from the venerable Army of the Cumberland. During the March, it adopted the name Army of Georgia, which never set well with most Georgians. The wing was commanded by Henry Slocum; the 14th Corps was led by a general with the unlikely name of Jefferson Davis; the 20th by Alpheus S. Williams.

The Right Wing, to the south, was the reorganized Army of the Tennessee, which was still commanded by O. O. Howard. Its 15th Corps was commanded by Peter J. Osterhaus, while Francis P. Blair led the 17th Corps.

Judson Kilpatrick had been wounded early in the Atlanta Campaign at Resaca. He had returned to his home in New York to recuperate, and now was ready to lead Sherman to the coast. The flamboyant cavalryman led five thousand cavalrymen to screen the infantry and to scout for the army.

An additional two thousand men rode with the artillery trains, which consisted of sixty-five cannon. They had two hundred rounds per gun. Each piece was pulled by eight horses.

The Teacher General ■ Henry W. Slocum

Slocum's first career, which lasted only three years, was teaching; but in 1848 he secured an appointment to West Point. This native New Yorker, who was born in 1822, remained in the army four years, then left to practice law.

As war clouds gathered in 1861, Slocum offered his services to the Union. Wounded at First Manassas, he covered the Federal retreat from Second Manassas. His unit suffered heavy losses at Chancellorsville, then helped hold the line at Gettysburg.

In late 1863 Slocum was transferred to the Vicksburg Military District. In July 1864, after Joseph Hooker angrily resigned his commission because he was not promoted to lead the Army of the Tennessee, Slocum was given command of his corps. Slocum's men were the first to enter the captured city of Atlanta.

Slocum led the Left Wing, which officially became the Army of Georgia, on the March to the Sea and through the Carolinas. After the war, he entered politics and won three terms to the House of Representatives. ■

[LIBRARY OF CONGRESS]

Sherman took 2,500 supply wagons, each drawn by six mules. His six hundred ambulances were each pulled by two horses. Every column had a wagon train that carried pontoons for bridging the numerous rivers in east Georgia. The expedition was encumbered by a total of 25,000 horses and mules and a herd of 10,000 cattle.

The wagons carried 1,200,000 rations of hardtack, and enough pork, coffee, salt, and sugar to last forty days. The animals had five days' forage, enough to clear the ravaged region surrounding Atlanta. Also stored in the wagons were two hundred rounds of ammunition for each soldier. They carried forty rounds in cartridge boxes, and many men kept another twenty in their pockets. Food could be replenished on the March, but there would be no more ammunition until they reached the coast.

"Probably never were wagons of an army more completely loaded with only the essentials required for a campaign," Private Rice Bull noted. The personal possessions of even officers were stripped to a minimum. Sherman was one of the lightest travelers. His staff consisted of five men, and he kept pertinent correspondence in his pockets, which were frequently emptied. In his saddlebags he carried a change of underwear, cigars, and a flask of whiskey.

To provide for obtaining food during the campaign, on November 9 Sherman had issued Special Orders No. 120. Section Four outlined the process by which foragers would feed the men.

"The army will forage liberally on the country during the march," the fateful orders read. Only authorized foraging parties under the command of "discreet" officers would be allowed to obtain provisions. Soldiers were admonished not to "enter the dwellings of the inhabitants, or commit any trespass."

Policies of destruction were laid down in Section Five. Only corps commanders, four generals, and presumably Sherman, Slocum, and Howard, could officially authorize the destruction of mills, houses, and other property. In areas where no opposition to the Federal advance was encountered, there should be "no destruction of such property . . . permitted," but bushwhacking should be met with "a devastation more or less relentless, according to the measure of such hostility."

Article Six dealt with the confiscation of horses, mules, and wagons. Such items could be taken "freely and without limit," although a distinction should be made between "the rich, who are usually hostile, and the poor and industrious, usually neutral or friendly."

"In all foraging," Sherman concluded, "the parties engaged will refrain from abusing or threatening language . . . and they will endeavor to leave with each family a reasonable portion for their maintenance."

The chances that this orderly system of foraging would succeed was in serious doubt from the start of the March. When Atlanta's population was deposited at Rough and Ready in mid-September, Hood had sent the following message to Governor Brown: "The enemy having robbed the people in the vicinity of Jonesborough, I have about 1,000 applications daily for rations for persons in that quarter. I cannot subsist them. Can you not make ar-

Union troops stream out of Atlanta in mid-November 1864, as the city smoulders behind them. [BATTLES AND LEADERS]

ments and send food for them?"

During a period in which the Federal army was being bountifully supplied by rail, soldiers cleaned the region south of Atlanta of all food and forage. The residents and refugees were facing starvation.

When Hood started north in October and damaged the railroad at several locations, Federal generals dispatched their soldiers into the surrounding countryside. They were to gather all the food for men and fodder for horses, mules, and cattle, that could be located. On October 21 several brigades from the 20th Corps spent four days stripping the area around Decatur. A single brigade reported its share as 30,000 bushels of corn, 55,000 pounds of fodder, and "large quantities of provisions which were captured by the men and no record kept of the amount." The raid, which was protected from Confederate cavalry by a massive force of four infantry brigades and two artillery batteries, brought in eight hundred wagons filled with corn.

Another expedition of 733 wagons netted 11,000 bushels of corn and "a considerable quantity of fresh beef, fresh pork, poultry, sweet potatoes, and other species of provisions." A fourth effort near Lawrenceville located only six thousand bushels of corn, which was hauled in three hundred wagons, but the official report contained an ominous note. The raid, it said, produced "the usual amount of provisions and other promiscuous articles." The soldiers were entering and looting private residences.

The foraging expeditions gathered nearly 2,000,000 pounds of corn and 140,000 pounds of fodder—a total of 2,600 wagon loads. This haul was just for the subsistence of the garrison left to protect Atlanta. The troops chasing Hood in northern Georgia and Alabama were faring just as well, as Sherman revealed in a letter to Slocum on October 23. "We find abundance of corn and potatoes out here, and enjoy them much. They cost nothing a bushel. If Georgia can afford to break our railroads, she can afford to feed us. Please preach this doctrine to men who go forth, and are likely to spread it."

Troops protecting Rome cleared the surrounding valleys of their rich stores of crops. From a plantation in Chattooga County in mid-October, Mrs. Naomi Bales wrote: "Again our home was pillaged from foundation to attic. Large army wagons were loaded to the brim with corn, fodder, and wheat; cows and hogs were driven off or shot, smokehouses stripped, pantries cleaned of every movable article, and such as could not be carried off was broken or damaged."

Union soldiers destroyed everything they could not carry and departed, but then arrived what Bales called the "wagon dogs." Bales and her sister were locked in a room while men went through bureaus, wardrobes, and mattresses. The Federals finally threatened to strip search the women, but did not carry out that particular outrage. That was fortunate because "I had several thousand dollars in Confederate money in a bustle around my waist," Mrs. Bales revealed, "and my small amount of jewelry and a few keepsakes in huge pockets under my hoops." Her sister had sewn pockets beneath her hoops and secreted her jewelry and the family flatware.

For a month the Bales "literally lived from hand to mouth. We picked up scraps of potatoes left in the fields, small scattered turnips and meat from the carcasses left by the Yankees and dragged in by the negroes. The new corn left was sufficiently soft to be grated on graters constructed from mutilated tinware."

Eastern Georgia could expect similar behavior.

The wings would advance on two routes, separated by twenty to forty miles. Each corps would march on a different road. This dispersion served several useful purposes. By avoiding congestion, the army could advance more quickly, and it would allow a larger area for each corps to forage for food. The policy would also result in a broad swath of devastation across the center of Georgia that would measure sixty miles wide and three hundred miles long.

Militarily, the divergent columns would serve to confuse the Confederates. The southern wing would advance south to threaten Macon, while the northern wing feinted on Augusta. The Confederates would be forced to split their paltry strength between the two cities, and Sherman intended to ignore them both. He would concentrate his forces around Milledgeville, the state capital, and sweep on toward Savannah, which would be occupied as a base for rest and resupply.

The soldiers who trooped out of the ruined city were tough and robust. These lean combat veterans were young; few had been eligible to vote in the recent presidential election. There were a few green recruits, but they learned quickly through necessity. Of 218 regiments, 185 were composed of bronzed western farmers, mainly from Ohio, like Sherman, or Illinois and Indiana. They had fought, usually victoriously, in Missouri, Arkansas, Kentucky, Tennessee, Mississippi, and Georgia. They had seen, and often contributed to, the death and destruction found on a dozen Civil War battlefields—Pea Ridge, Fort Henry and Fort Donelson, Shiloh, Vicksburg, Perryville, Stone's River, Chickamauga, Missionary Ridge, and various conflicts around Atlanta. These independent men prided themselves on being undisciplined in the ranks, tough on the march, and nearly invincible in battle.

The 20th Corps hailed from the eastern Army of the Potomac. They had been transferred west to help lift the Confederate siege of Chattanooga a year earlier. These soldiers had fought valiantly, but with little success, at First Manasses, in the Valley against Stonewall Jackson, at Antietam, Fredericksburg, Chancellorsville, and Gettysburg. Highly disciplined and pretty on parade, they were subjected to constant verbal abuse from their western comrades. Despite the taunting, when the lead started to fly, east and west knew they could depend on each other's combat skills.

What had made this Western army successful while Union forces floundered in Virginia was leadership. Sherman had managed to weed out his burdensome political appointees and incompetent regular army officers. Those who remained were young, talented, and largely self-educated in military matters. Many had risen from the enlisted ranks and were therefore more concerned with the welfare of the common soldier. Unfortunately, however, this familiarity often led to lax discipline.

For this campaign, the infantry traveled even lighter than usual. Each man carried his rifle and ammunition, a rubber poncho and blanket, haversack, canteen, tin cup, and eating utensils. Three men constituted a mess. They slept together in one tent, and at reveille one fetched water, the second cooked breakfast, and the third packed their gear. Each regiment had pack mules that carried the cooking and camping equipment, and food was brought in daily by foragers. When that was scarce, rations were secured from supply wagons.

This army seemed destined for success. "We have weeded out all the sick, feeble ones, and all the faint-hearted ones," Upson wrote, "and all the boys are ready for a meal or a fight, and don't seem to care which it is. . . . Such an army as we have I doubt if ever was got together before."

Oakey concurred with this sentiment. "The army was reduced, one might say, to its fighting weight," he wrote, "no man being retained who was not capable of a long march." Sherman believed all the men were "able bodied, experienced soldiers, well armed, equipped, and provided . . . with all the essentials of life, strength, and vigorous action," and so it proved. As the March continued into the Carolinas, Confederate General Joseph E. Johnston said, "There has been no such army since the days of Julius Caesar."

In one of his last messages north, Sherman requested the Navy prepare a base for him on the Atlantic Coast. They should look for him around Christmas between Hilton Head, South Carolina, and Savannah, Georgia. He cautioned Grant, and his wife Ellen, not to expect any reports of his movements until his destination had been reached. A number of northern newsmen and artists accompanied the Federal columns, but there would be no facilities for transmitting a story. Check the Rebel papers, Sherman advised, but read between the lines. The Confederates had never failed to keep the people informed, even if only in a distorted version of the truth.

The March would prove to be a radical departure from traditional military strategy. Instead of attacking an enemy army, Sherman intended to advance three hundred miles through hostile but undefended territory without a base of supply. Back in May, Grant had instructed Sherman to attempt the destruction of the Confederate Army of Tennessee and to advance into Georgia, breaking up the country as much as possible. Georgia's interior was the Confederate breadbasket, and Sherman intended to destroy it. Such an act would demoralize both the people of Georgia and civilians throughout the entire South. It would prove, as Sherman stated, that the Confederacy was a hollow shell that could be easily pierced.

Sherman believed the people of the South, particularly the planter class, bore a "collective responsibility" for the Civil War. "The entire South, man, woman, and child, is against us," he observed. They must be defeated to bring a successful conclusion to the terrible War.

Sherman had first put forth this disturbing idea in a letter he penned in 1863. In European conflicts, Sherman wrote, wars were fought between kings. Noncombatants and their property were generally left undisturbed. In this war the southern people had allowed themselves to be deluded. They must bear the blame—and the resultant punishment.

"Three years ago, by a little reflection and patience," he stated, "they could have had a hundred years of peace and prosperity, but they preferred war; very well." A year ago, he continued, they could have saved their slaves, "but now it is too late. All the powers of earth cannot restore to them their slaves, any more than their dead grandfathers." Next year, "their lands will be taken; for in war we can take them, and rightfully, too." He raised the possibility of dispossessing the citizens of occupied areas from their lands, which would be given to those loyal to the United States. In yet another year, Sherman thundered, Southerners "may beg in vain for their lives."

> To those who submit to the rightful law and authority, all gentleness and forbearance; but to the petulant and persistent secessionists, why, death is mercy, and the quicker he or she is disposed of the better. Satan and the rebellious saints of Heaven were allowed a continuous existence in hell merely to swell their just punishment. To such as would rebel against a Government so mild and just as ours was in peace, a punishment equal would not be unjust.

Sherman sent a copy of the letter to his brother, U.S. Senator John Sherman, with hopes that it would be published throughout the South. The only harm to the general would be if southern newspapers branded him "as the prince of barbarians." He hoped the missive would find its way into the hands of civilians who lived in the path of his future operations. "Read to them this letter," he advised, "and let them use it so as to prepare them for my coming." It seemed to be a letter written directly to Georgians.

Sherman's treatment of southern civilians had become apparent before the fall of Vicksburg, a full year earlier. After brushing off a feeble Confederate defense of Jackson, the Mississippi capital, in May 1863, Sherman's troops thoroughly looted homes and shops and burned much of the city.

In July Vicksburg was captured, and in the fall Sherman had helped relieve the siege of Chattanooga. By February 1864, he had returned to Vicksburg and planned a raid that seems to have been practice for the March to Savannah. He hoped to abandon his base of supply and advance on Mobile through Meridian, Mississippi. He would subsist his men off the land.

Sherman's troops started the raid by burning Jackson for the third time. They arrived at Meridian to find twelve million dollars worth of equipment and supplies evacuated. Sherman was angry that the Confederates had dared to take such a precautionary measure. He decided to exact revenge on Meridian's civilians. "For five days," he wrote, "ten thousand men worked hard and with a will in that work of destruction, with axes, crowbars, sledges, clawbars, and with fire, and I have no hesitation in pronouncing the work as well done. Meridian, with its depots, storehouses, arsenal, hospitals, offices, hotels, and cantonments, no longer exists."

Lack of cavalry support forced Sherman to return to Vicksburg, but he had destroyed ten thousand bales of cotton, burned two million bushels of corn, and inflicted five million dollars damage, three fourths of it to private property. At Meridian, Sherman displayed "a sinister zeal for destroying southern property," historian Bruce Catton wrote.

While occupying Atlanta, this streak reasserted itself in an even more vicious style. It started while Sherman was chasing Hood and the Federal army was living off the land. Confederate cavalry was harassing isolated Union garrisons that had been left to guard the railroad. Sherman's response to these attacks, which were executed by recognized units of the Confederate army, was as chilling a precursor for the civilians in eastern Georgia and the Carolinas as the foraging and looting had been.

Concerned by attacks on the railroad north of Cartersville, Sherman wrote the Federal commander of the region, General Lewis D. Watkins:

> Cannot you send over about Fairmount and Adairsville, burn ten or twelve houses of known secessionists, kill a few at random, and let them know that it will be repeated every time a train is fired on from Resaca to Kingston?

The suggestion that innocent civilians be summarily executed for military action by Confederate soldiers was extraordinary, but it was only the beginning. On October 30 John E. Smith, commander of the 15th Corps, ordered his Ohio cavalry to Canton, where "you will permit the citizens to remove what they desire and burn the town." He would then proceed to Cassville, which would receive the same treatment. Smith ordered three houses in Cartersville destroyed that day.

Several days later, Sherman prepared an arrest list for men "who are said

The Political General ■ Alpheus S. Williams

Williams was born in 1810 in Connecticut and graduated from Yale. After extensive travel, he settled in Detroit and won various political offices. He became a lieutenant colonel of Michigan militia during the Mexican War and made brigadier general in 1861.

He served in the Shenandoah Valley against Stonewall Jackson and fought at Cedar Mountain, Chancellorsville, and Gettysburg. He traveled west with the 20th Corps after the Union disaster at Chickamauga and commanded a division in the Army of the Cumberland during the Atlanta Campaign. On the March he led the 20th Corps.

Williams was never promoted to major general and did not long retain command of a corps, probably because he was not "regular army." After the Civil War, he returned to politics and won two terms to the United States House of Representatives. ■

[LIBRARY OF CONGRESS]

35

to be more or less implicated with the guerillas." Two houses were burned, one blown up, and a number of civilians arrested.

Left homeless during a period of freezing rain, many people, mainly women, children, and the elderly, wandered across north Georgia in search of shelter. After dark on November 12, some desperate civilians attempted to board a Union train for transportation to safety. A Federal soldier wrote, "All assisted in keeping them off." Beaten away by the butts of rifles, the refugees continued their wandering through a desolate region.

Corse, the garrison commander at Rome, asked permission to punish some pesky Texas cavalry by burning three communities: Cedartown, Van Wert, and Buchanan. Fortunately, even Sherman thought that action would be premature. He told Corse to "wait a little."

To curb cavalry attacks, which he termed "guerilla activity," Sherman authorized Watkins to "arrest some six or eight citizens known or supposed to be hostile. Let one or two go free to carry word to the guerilla band that you give them forty-eight hour's notice that unless all the men of ours picked up by them in the past two days are returned, Kingston, Cassville, and Cartersville will be burned, as also the houses of those arrested."

When seven foragers were captured in the same vicinity, Sherman sent a regiment to "seize some citizens, and send on to inform the enemy he must bring those men and all others captured in same manner back at once. They must be returned by tomorrow noon, else the regiment will burn a dozen houses in retaliation."

One man caught in the dragnet was to be "kept in confinement beyond a possibility of escape during the war." Others were sent to Chattanooga "to be imprisoned and held as hostages" for thirty-one soldiers who had been "unlawfully captured and made prisoners."

A climate of terror had definitely fallen over any area that might come under control of Sherman and his hardened soldiers.

Everyone except Sherman and his soldiers seemed to harbor severe reservations about the wisdom of the March. President Lincoln remained preoccupied throughout its duration, apologizing for ignoring one visitor by saying, "Excuse me for not noting you. I was thinking of a man down South." When Senator John Sherman asked the President what news there was of the March, Lincoln replied, "I know the hole he went in at, but I can't tell you the hole he will come out of."

British military experts, who closely scrutinized Confederate and Federal moves throughout the Civil War, were skeptical of Sherman's chances of success. "He has done either one of the most brilliant or one of the most foolish things ever performed by a military leader," the respected British *Army and Navy Gazette* stated. The London *Herald* noted that Sherman, the hero of Atlanta, would be "the scoff of mankind, and the humiliation of the United States for all time" if his plan failed. If it was successful, his name would be engraved on the tablets of history. The *Herald* applauded Sherman's idea, calling it "sublime audacity" that would be a "most tremendous disaster or a world triumph." If successful in this endeavor, the London *Times* believed "General Sherman will undoubtedly be entitled to the honor of having added a fresh chapter to the history and practice of warfare." But the *Times* warned it would "be strange indeed" if, after reaching Savannah after such a difficult journey, the Union army was in shape to storm "a town so well fortified and so strenuously defended."

Sherman's preparations could not escape scrutiny in the South. The destruction of the railroad between Atlanta and Chattanooga was proof of an imminent movement. Southern newspaper editors were convinced Sherman had found himself beset by troubles deep in enemy territory. "God has put a hook in Sherman's nose," railed a Richmond preacher, "and is leading him to destruction."

"Instead of overwhelming the State at his ease, as he has proudly boasted," one paper boldly proclaimed, "he will be fortunate if he succeeds in making good his escape."

"If Sherman can do all this with the force at his command," editorialized the Richmond *Whig,* "then he is a much greater commander than we take him to be, and the Georgians are a much tamer people than they have credit for being." While paying homage to Sherman's military skills, "we venture to predict that he has been woefully outgeneraled this time."

The London *Post* shared this view. "It will be the fault of the people inhabiting those countries if his army is not utterly destroyed long before it shall have reached" the coast.

Sherman's advance was a retreat, southern editors and the Confederate government claimed. An enraged southern populace—women, grandfathers, and children—would rise up in a guerilla movement to oppose and destroy Sherman in Georgia's swamps. The Federals would be annihilated in Georgia's interior, like Napoleon in the winter retreat from Moscow. "Who is to furnish the snow for this Moscow retreat?" Sherman quipped while reading one southern paper.

A New York *Times* editorial called the March "dramatic and exciting" and believed it might be "the most remarkable military achievement of the war." They felt the March was unique "in modern military history" and likened it to Cortez's burning his ships and "plunging into the darkness of an enemy's territory, burning their shelter behind them . . . never to be heard of more till the enemy reports to us victory or disaster."

"Old Sherman's got the big head now," said one of his confident soldiers. "He's captured Atlanta and thinks he can go wherever he pleases." His men were more than willing to follow. "They stepped high and long," was how a Wisconsin soldier described the army's departure; "they sang and made merry, and could not for the life of them see why the glorious march had not begun a long time before."

One Illinois soldier was apprehensive about "marching out into a great unknown," where they might "leave their bones in a strange and unfriendly land forever."

It was 7:00 A.M. when Sherman turned east toward Decatur. He was distinctive in his shapeless hat, a pair of low-cut civilian shoes in place of boots, and his characteristic cigar that was constantly rolled between his teeth. Sherman paused at Bald Hill, which in the July heat had been the focal point of the fiercest battle for Atlanta. Formidable earthworks, now abandoned, scarred the land. The debris of battle remained to litter the ground.

The Union General Who Owned Slaves ∎ Francis P. Blair

Blair was born in 1821 and graduated from Princeton University, then studied law at Transylvania College in Kentucky. He settled in Missouri and served two terms in the United States House of Representatives. Although he owned slaves, Blair fought against the extension of slavery into the territories.

Leaving Congress in 1863, he entered the army as a major general and fought at Vicksburg, then commanded the 17th Corps during the March to the Sea. Sherman considered Blair a good friend and praised his service.

Following the Civil War, Blair returned to politics. He was Horatio Seymour's Vice-Presidental candidate on the Democratic ticket in 1868. They lost heavily to a Republican slate led by U. S. Grant. Blair served briefly in the U.S. Senate before his death in 1875. ∎

[LIBRARY OF CONGRESS]

Graves of his men killed in the terrible struggle were scattered across the hill, marked now by simple boards that had names etched on them. Sherman could see the spot where McPherson, a man he loved like a son, had died.

"Behind us lay Atlanta," Sherman wrote ten years after the War, "smouldering and in ruins, the black smoke rising high in the air and hanging like a pall over the ruined city."

From this vantage point, Sherman could see both of his wings exiting the burned city.

He continued:

> Away off in the distance, on the McDonough road, was the rear of Howard's column, the gun-barrels glistening in the sun, the white-topped wagons stretching away to the south; and right before us the Fourteenth Corps, marching steadily and rapidly, with a cheery look and swinging pace, that made light of the thousand miles that lay between us and Richmond. Some band, by accident, struck up the anthem of "John Brown's Soul Goes Marching On"; the men caught up the strain, and never before or since have I heard the chorus of "Glory, glory, hallelujah!" done with more spirit, or in better harmony of time and place.
>
> Then we turned our horses' heads to the east; Atlanta was soon lost behind the screen of trees, and became a thing of the past. Around it clings many a thought of desperate battle, of hope and fear, that now seem like the memory of a dream. The day was extremely beautiful, clear sunlight, with bracing air, and an unusual feeling of exhilaration seemed to pervade all minds—a feeling of something to come, vague and undefined, still full of venture and intense interest. Even the common soldiers caught the inspiration, and many a group called out to me as I worked my way past them, "Uncle Billy, I guess Grant is waiting for us at Richmond!"

That statement typified the "devil-may-care" philosophy that infected Sherman's army at the start of its adventure. They believed, with few reservations, that Sherman would lead them in a campaign that would result in total victory.

Thinking of Hood marching into Tennessee at this moment, as he left for the Atlantic Ocean, Sherman considered that the general who was right would likely end the war. "Two hostile armies, marching in opposite directions, each in the full belief that it was achieving a final and conclusive result in a great war," he wrote. That determination would be made within six weeks. ▪

The Left Wing

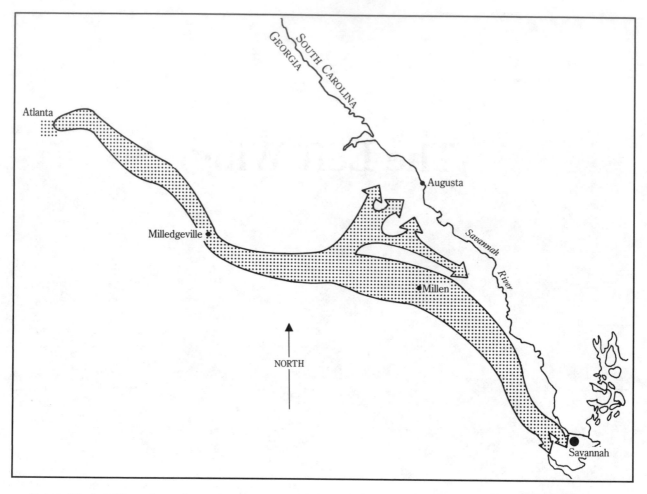

Map 3: The Left Wing advanced west from Decatur to Milledgeville, made a diversionary calvary feint at Augusta, and marched on to Savannah.

CHAPTER 4

"The Time of Trial Has Come"

Sherman accompanied the Left Wing's 14th Corps, the last Union troops to leave Atlanta, out of the city. After resting at a house for half an hour, his party passed through Decatur at noon. They saw few civilians on the route.

"Weather fine for marching," Hitchcock wrote at 7:00 A.M. Glancing behind, he saw "clouds of heavy smoke rise and lay like pall over doomed city." He recorded a curious incident. "Fellow very drunk, sitting on ground as we passed troops . . . cursed General loudly . . . General rode quietly by him, not 10 feet off—heard all—no notice."

"Leaving the burning, smouldering ruins of the once flourishing city of Atlanta in our rear," W. C. Johnson wrote, "we lose sight of them." He found it an "interesting as well as a magnificent sight to witness the large body of troops moving out on the different roads for what promises to be a great raid through the enemy's country." Being separated from a base of supply and communication, and far removed from friendly help, held no terror for him. He had "full confidence in our commanding general." Telegrapher John Van Duzen echoed that thought. "We start . . . for the seashore. Perhaps the rebs will be puzzled to guess where the blow will fall."

Lizzie Perkerson watched the troops plod past her home all day. After the column was gone, she "felt free as a bird turned out of a cage." The last soldiers confidently said they "were going to play smash with the Confederacy, just going to sweep it out at one lick."

Decatur had been battered during the summer when Federal cavalry fought fiercely to prevent Confederate horsemen under Joseph Wheeler from destroying an extensive Union wagon train. Federal raiders and foragers had since devastated the region. Sherman called the city "a dilapidated village" consisting of a few homes and a courthouse. An enlisted man, Private Rice Bull, noticed that it showed the "dire effects of war."

A local woman described her community as a "war stricken section of country where stood chimneys only, standing amid ruins." The area was so deserted that the "solitude was terrifying."

Bull had departed Atlanta at 4:00 A.M. and occasionally glanced back to see "smoke and flames of burning buildings rise to the sky." Black columns

A seemingly endless column of soldiers and wagons tramp east from the destroyed city of Atlanta. [HARPER'S WEEKLY]

of smoke were visible throughout the day as the city was obscured by a pall of smoke.

Decatur's trial had not yet ended. Sherman's men burned mills and gins between Atlanta and Decatur and spared few homes. Martha Amanda Quillen calculated the rate of Federal advance by the appearance of smoke on the horizon as buildings were fired. "As far as the eye could reach," two to three miles, she believed, "the lurid flames of burning buildings lit up the heavens."

Homes of friends were burned, and Quillen heard the "wild shout" of soldiers as they approached. Fortunately, Federal officers established headquarters in her home, which was spared, and a rearguard camped in the city for several hours. They frightened women and children with their loud, coarse language, and some soldiers burned homes that other Federals fought to save. Marching out of town in a freezing, pre-dawn rain, a private recorded, "We would have frozen, if the fence on both sides of our route had not been fired and burned by those ahead of us." The intense heat forced wagons to leave the road and advance through fields.

Sherman continued through the rolling, wooded countryside, passing seemingly endless columns of wagons and marching soldiers. Hitchcock described Sherman as quiet, but responsive to questions. The general stopped at a house six miles east of Decatur and took a two-hour nap. There an old man claimed he had opposed the war. "Mighty few of the people about here were in favor of the war," Hitchcock wrote, "but their leaders told them they ought to do so and so, and they done it."

Sherman spent a fitful first night on the March near Lithonia, a village of three hundred. He gazed upon Stone Mountain, an enormous granite monolith that Major James A. Connolly called "one of the great natural curiosities of this continent." Bull considered it unique, a "big round stone as smooth as a paving block without any vegetation or trees on its surface." Sherman was impressed by the Union camp. He likened the glowing fires that pierced the darkness for miles around to a political torch light parade, only these torches were "burning houses, outbuildings, and fences." That fact did not seem to disturb him.

The destructive work had certainly begun. Soldiers ripped up the railroad and burned Lithonia's depot, railroad property, and a few additional homes. The soldiers were well fed, as Captain Pepper noted "food in gardens, food in cellars, stock in fields, stock in barns, poultry everywhere, appears in the distance, disappears in the presence, and was borne away upon the knapsacks and bayonets of thousands of soldiers."

Thomas Maguire's Promised Land plantation was near Stone Mountain. As he watched the ominous smoke rising from Atlanta on the previous day, he wrote, "We are now waiting for the worst to come." On November 16 Yankees camped all about his home. "At every side hogs and sheep are being shot down and skinned to regale the Yankee palates," he wrote. Maguire spent the night in the woods, returning home the next day to find "great destruction of property. Gin house and screw burned, stables and barn all in ashes, fencing burned and destruction visible all around. The carriage and big wagon burned up, corn and potatoes gone, horse and steers gone, sheep, chickens, and geese, also syrup boiler damaged, one barrel of syrup burned, saddles and bridles the same." His corn cribs, gin, and piles of straw still smouldered. Cotton bales had been slashed and laid out for use as beds by the soldiers. "The destruction of Jerusalem on a small scale," Maguire concluded.

In the morning a Federal signal team climbed a granite outcropping near Lithonia, a smaller version of Stone Mountain. They reported Atlanta was still burning. Bull saw the smoke, too, and found it a "grand but sorrowful sight; the homes of thousands of people, most of whom were innocent of any wrong doing, were being destroyed."

The commanding general had been up early on November 17 to personally supervise the railroad and building destruction in Lithonia. Long lines of men, using tools developed by engineer Poe, tore rails, ties and all, from the grade. The ties were stacked into waist-high piles and torched, then the centers of the rails were placed over the fire. When the rails were red hot, they were rendered useless by bending them around telegraph poles or trees. These became famous as "Sherman's neckties." Certain groups of soldiers who took particular pride in their work periodically left rails twisted into the letters U and S, to remind the people of their sin of rebellion.

The Federals passed through Conyers, a village of five hundred inhabitants that was described by the invaders as "a perfect garden." "Whites look sullen," Hitchcock wrote of their passage, "darkies pleased." Connolly and a friend, a captain who was a fine piano player, decided to enjoy some music while waiting for the railroad to be destroyed through Conyers. Knocking at a house, they found a "grey-headed . . . ministerial looking old Rebel," whose daughter had a piano. The captain sat at the instrument and proceeded to play the "Star-Spangled Banner" and other selections, including "Dixie." The old man and several women looked on in amazement. They

43

never thought that a "rough, vulgar, brutal Yankee" could play such beautiful music. The men enjoyed an excellent conversation, but the women seemed extremely discomfited, though they struggled "to appear composed."

Finished with the improvised concert, Connolly and the captain rode on four miles to a plantation owned by a Mr. Zachry. Slaves claimed the man had received a captured United States flag from his son, a Confederate colonel in Virginia, but Zachry denied possessing such a flag. Thorough searches proved fruitless; but when soldiers prepared to burn his house, the elderly man produced the banner. This act saved his home, but little else, from destruction.

In Conyers the Yankees encountered an exhausted refugee, an old woman who had fled before Federal advances six times in three years, beginning in Kentucky. "I don't care where you go next," she told a soldier. "I'm done running. I'm going to let you go first, maybe I'll follow."

John Van Duzer caught a glimpse of Slocum's wagon train in the distance. It was not the only evidence of the other wing's progress, which "long columns of smoke for miles along the route will testify." His unit made slow progress but found the foraging grand. "We are now beginning to realize some of the pleasures attending a raid. I have just feasted upon one of the best meals it has been my fortune to partake of since I left home."

Sherman stopped by the Conyers home of Mrs. Scott to read recent Augusta newspapers. The editor predicted Sherman's imminent destruction, but the general was pleased to learn that his plans and direction of travel had not yet been determined. He also learned that the legislature was still in session at Milledgeville.

After fifteen miles of travel, Sherman camped on the slope of a large field. Stretching to the horizon along the railroad in both directions were fires as ties were burned and rails bent. Hitchcock noticed that the railroad in this region seemed new, and the country supported fine farms. While he packed pine boughs beneath a blanket for use as a mattress, Sherman sent for a local man to question about local roads. "Don't want white man," he specified, believing them to be unreliable.

A bright, elderly man was procured, and he talked with Sherman for a long while. "When the Yanks far off," the slave confided, "our people [white] very brave—women and children whip 'em—but come close and then how they do get up and *dust*."

The mighty army surged through Covington. Nine miles east they came to a large plantation operated by Mrs. Dolly Sumner Lunt Burge. She was a young widow with a nine-year-old daughter, and seemed to be an unusual person to run a one thousand-slave plantation. Originally from Maine and related to a noted abolitionist, Senator Charles Sumner of Massachusetts (who before the Civil War was caned senseless at his desk in Congress by South Carolina Representative Preston Brooks in an argument over slavery in Kansas), she came to teach in Covington and married Thomas Burge. On November 18 she slept lightly and in her clothes. Venturing outside several times, she saw buildings burning in the darkness.

Keeping watch by her front gate on November 19, Mrs. Burge saw streams of blue-suited soldiers marching toward her home. She prayed, "O

God, the time of trial has come. . . ." She requested and received a guard, but he proved powerless to protect her. "I cannot help you, Madam," the man told her, "it is the orders."

"But like Demons they rushed in!" Mrs. Burge remembered. "My yards are full. To my smoke-house, my Dairy, Pantry, Kitchen and Cellar, like famished wolves they come, breaking locks and whatever is in their way. The thousand pounds of meat in my smoke-house is gone in a twinkling, my flour, my meat, my lard, butter, eggs, pickles both in vinegar and brine, wine, jars, and jugs, are all gone. My eighteen fat turkeys, my hens, chickens and fowl, my young pigs are shot down in my yard and hunted as if they were the rebels themselves."

While the woman kept watch over her residence, soldiers stole her sheep and every horse and mule. They took a crippled, retired brood mare and a baby colt. When the stock was gone, they turned to her slaves. "My boys, my poor boys," she said, were forced to accompany the soldiers. Apparently she was a kind taskmaster, for her slaves tried to escape from the Federals by hiding under buildings, pretending to be sick in bed, and jumping out back windows. One slave begged protection from Mrs. Burge, but "a man followed in, cursing him and threatening to shoot him if he did not go."

The night passed in relative quiet as two Federal guards slept on her hearth. The last Federals passed by the next day. "Thus ended the passing of Sherman's army by my place," Mrs. Burge recorded, "leaving me poorer by thirty thousand dollars than I was yesterday morning. And a much stronger Rebel."

Her neighbors suffered that day. She saw that "the heavens from every point were lit up with flames from burning buildings." One neighbor, appropriately named Mrs. Glass, buried her crystal, but soldiers dug it up and smashed it to pieces. The silver of another family was stolen. Mrs. Burge

The Fateful Order

HEADQUARTERS MILITARY DIVISION OF THE MISSISSIPPI, IN THE FIELD, KINGSTON, GEORGIA, NOVEMBER 9, 1864

4. The army will forage liberally on the country during the march. To this end, each brigade commander will organize a good and sufficient foraging party, under the command of one or more discreet officers, who will gather, near the route traveled, corn or forage of any kind, meat of any kind, vegetables, corn-meal, or whatever is needed by the command, aiming at all times to keep in the wagons at least ten days' provisions for his command, and three days' forage. Soldiers must not enter the dwellings of the inhabitants, or commit any trespass; but, during a halt or camp, they may be permitted to gather turnips, potatoes, and other vegetables, and to drive in stock in sight of their camp. To regular foraging-parties must be intrusted the gathering of provisions and forage, at any distance from the road traveled.

5. To corps commanders alone is intrusted the power to destroy mills, houses, cotton-gins, etc.; and for them this general principle is laid down: In districts and neighborhoods where the army is unmolested, no destruction of such property should be permitted; but should guerillas or bushwhackers molest our march, or should the inhabitants burn bridges, obstruct roads, or otherwise manifest local hostility, then army commanders should order and enforce a devastation more or less relentless, according to the measure of such hostility.

6. As for horses, mules, wagons, etc., belonging to the inhabitants, the cavalry and artillery may appropriate freely and without limit; discriminating, however, between the rich, who are usually hostile, and the poor and industrious, usually neutral or friendly. Foraging-parties may also take mules or horses, to replace the jaded animals of their trains, or to serve as pack-mules for the regiments of brigades. In all foraging, of whatever kind, the parties engaged will refrain from abusive or threatening language, and may, where the officer in command thinks proper, give written certificates of the facts, but no receipts; and they will endeavor to leave with each family a reasonable portion for their maintenance.
—By order of Major-General W. T. Sherman

could foresee "nothing before me but starvation." It was an opinion shared by her neighbors.

As the Union columns neared Covington, an elderly farmer named Jones leveled his shotgun at four Federal horsemen in a vain attempt to defend his home. He blew one Yankee off his horse before the others killed him. Slocum ordered houses burned in retaliation, tallied up one dead soldier, and left old Jones in the street for some time. That may have been the first fatality of the March. Confederate resistance against this wing had been isolated. Two men had been shot in Decatur, six were captured near Stone Mountain, and two additional foragers were caught in nearby Oxford. They were rumored to have been hanged, but they had merely been imprisoned.

Sherman made only eight miles on November 18. He crossed the Yellow River and passed through Covington, "a place of some pretension, and on the whole . . . rather a pretty place," Connolly wrote. "The houses are very neat, built in modern Southern style, and painted white."

The roads and weather were exceptional. "This is the perfection of campaigning," Sherman remarked. The column was held up at the river while the cattle herd crossed; cows tended to crowd and rush across pontoon bridges in panic.

When the troops reached Covington, Sherman saw that "the soldiers closed up their ranks, the color-bearers unfurling their flags, and the bands striking up patriotic airs. The white people came out of their houses to behold the sight, in spite of their deep hatred of the invaders, and the Negroes were simply frantic with joy."

Here Sherman discovered that his march was perceived as "bringing the Jubilee" for Georgia's slaves. The situation was touching, but it would prove troublesome to the campaign. "Whenever they heard my name," Sherman continued, "they clustered about my horse, shouted and prayed in their peculiar style, which had a natural eloquence that would have moved a stone. I have witnessed hundreds, if not thousands, of such scenes; and can now see a poor girl, in the very ecstasy . . . hugging the banner of one of the regiments, and jumping up to the 'feet of Jesus.'"

"Glory be to the Lord," some cried. "The day of Jubilee has come!"

One Rebel woman rudely informed the passing soldiers that they were the first Yankees she had seen who were not prisoners. "Like a woman, that!" Hitchcock snorted. He received the parole of a young Confederate soldier who was recovering from a severe wound suffered at Spotsylvania, Virginia, that spring. Noticing the soldier was boarding at a home where an exceptionally pretty girl lived, Hitchcock remarked, "Parole probably welcome."

Covington, a fine town of beautiful homes and blooming gardens, was a trade center for a region famed for its large plantations. It had been visited during the siege of Atlanta by Union cavalry, who had burned a hospital center, depot, and bridges over nearby streams.

A young slave girl named Tabitha was outraged when soldiers went into her hut and removed her dresses and hat. Shaking her fist at one soldier, she declared, "Oh! If I had the power like I've got the will, I'd tear you to pieces."

When Sherman viewed the monolith of Stone Mountain, he never dreamed that it would become the South's largest monument to the vanquished Confederacy.

Tabitha's mistress, a young lady named Allie Travis, timed the passage of Sherman's army. She estimated the event lasted "from 9 o'clock in the morning to a late hour at night." A "moving mass of 'blue coats'—infantry, artillery and cavalry" marched past her home. "All during the day squads would leave the ranks, rush into the house and demand something to eat, seize what they could get, then go to the yard and garden to chase chickens and pull up turnips, and rush to the street again only to be succeeded by others."

Allie's mother slipped into the yard and cornered two fat turkeys, placing each in separate closets within the house. The woman's most serious worry was keeping Allie from expressing her strong Rebel sentiments to passing soldiers. During the brief Union occupation, Allie and her sister sat quietly within the house, knitting socks "from balls whose hearts were gold watches." From time to time Federal soldiers tried mightily to provoke her, but Allie controlled herself for several days. Finally, an officer entered and "attempted to reconstruct me by arguments to prove the sin of Secession and the certainty of our subjugation; my tongue was loosed and my heart was fired."

After a lengthy argument, the officer left, saying, "I see it is no use to argue with you."

"Nor I with you," she replied, thinking, *If you convince a man against his will, He's of the same opinion still.*

That afternoon Allie and a friend went onto her porch when a Union band played "Dixie." The young ladies smiled at the soldiers and remarked, "They must be at a loss for tunes, as they were playing one of ours." When "Dixie" ended and the band struck up "Yankee Doodle," Allie took her friend inside, saying, "We will not listen to that tune." Out of curiosity, a Federal officer asked someone to identify Allie. After the War ended, a cousin who had been imprisoned at Point Lookout, Maryland, brought a clipping from a northern newspaper reporting the following incident that had occurred in Covington: "They [the women] were very pretty and intelligent, but great Rebels. While the bands were playing 'Dixie' they were all smiles, but as soon as they commenced 'Yankee Doodle' they went in, shut the doors, and closed the blinds." Miss Allie was delighted by the notoriety.

Men who paused at one house for spring water and a rest grew suspicious when four women rocking on the porch kept glancing at a spot of freshly turned soil. Suspecting buried jewels or silver, the soldiers found shovels and dug energetically until they uncovered a small pine box. Prying off the lid, the men suddenly reeled in disgust. A decaying dog lay inside the box. After the soldiers quickly reburied the little coffin, one of the rockers called out, "It looks like pour [*sic.*] Curly will get no peace. That's the fourth time he's been dug up today."

Several miles away, at Chamblee's Mill, an old blind mule pulled six women and a coffin containing the body of a small boy to a cemetery. Federal cavalry took the decrepit mule, leaving the women to push the wagon three miles to the cemetery.

Sherman took a back street through Covington to avoid the congestion posed by his triumphant troops. He turned down an invitation to dine with the family of an old West Point classmate. Van Duzer and Hitchcock said two enterprising lieutenants from the Signal Corps, named Cole and Jones, heard that Sherman had avoided the mayor and other town dignitaries. Believing it a shame to waste such an opportunity, they "took it upon themselves to receive the delegation," Van Duzer wrote. The men enjoyed "all the honors attending such an occasion" and ate a fine meal that had been prepared for Sherman.

Sherman camped beside the Ulcofauhachee River on Judge Harris's plantation. In three days the army had covered forty miles with virtually no resistance. The general was very pleased with the progress.

Harris was a prosperous man who lived in town and kept sixty slaves on his plantation. A passing soldier, who had a ham perched on his bayonet, a jug of molasses tucked under one arm, and was munching on a big chunk of honeycomb, loudly greeted Sherman with his own order, "Forage liberally on the country." At this moment, Hitchcock noted, "General sober as a judge."

"On this occasion," Sherman wrote virtuously ten years later, "as on many others that fell under my personal observation, I reproved the man, explained that foraging must be limited to the regular parties properly detailed and that all provisions thus obtained must be delivered to the regular

Soldiers rip up a railroad, burn the ties, and wrap the heated rails around a tree.
[BATTLES AND LEADERS]

commissaries, to be fairly distributed to the men who kept their ranks." The mild reproof went unheeded by the entire army. Hitchcock heard constant firing in the neighborhood, each shot "the death knell of some luckless secesh pig or rebel foul."

Sherman asked an elderly slave on the plantation if he understood what the war was about. "Yes," the slave replied. He had been "looking for the 'angel of the Lord' ever since he was knee-high, and, though we professed to be fighting for the Union, he supposed that slavery was the cause and that our success was to be his freedom. I asked him if all the Negro slaves comprehended this fact, and he said they surely did." The slave added that without the War, "the right thing [abolition of slavery] wouldn't be done."

Sherman inquired why one slave had attached himself to the Union column. "Good trade or bad trade, I was bound to risk it," was the response. Overseers thought nothing of strapping slaves three hundred times, the man added. The owner and overseers of the plantation had taken the fit slaves to Macon, but he had escaped to join Sherman. "It is most striking and touching the faith in us these people show," Hitchcock wrote.

Sherman established good relationships with the blacks he encountered. Hitchcock noted the general had a "frank, pleasant, and unaffected [manner], without being familiar." The slaves returned his attention "with a mingled respect and confidence." The commanding general enjoyed these evening chats, and he told the slaves the war was a result of their masters' disobeying the law. While the conflict would result in their freedom, Sherman cautioned them, "*Freedom* means not being free to work or not as they please, but freedom to work for themselves—freedom from being bought and sold,—freedom to acquire and own property, bring up their children respectably and be secure in enjoyment of personal and family rights."

Sherman emphatically "discountenanced any violence toward their masters," but the reminder seemed unnecessary. "I have seen no vindictive feeling among them but universal hope and longing for freedom," Hitchcock observed. On another occasion, Sherman emphasized that the slaves should not "hurt your masters or their families—we don't want that."

The thousands of "contrabands" who flocked after the corps slowed the Federal advance, "a serious impediment," Hitchcock thought. Sherman explained to the slaves that he wanted them "to remain where they were and not to load us down with useless mouths, which would eat up the food needed for our fighting-men; that our success was their assured freedom." He would accept strong men as laborers, but he requested that the old and young, sick and women, remain on the plantation until the war was brought to a victorious conclusion. Sherman felt this message preceded his line of march and saved his columns much cumbersome human baggage.

The previous night Sherman had told a slave that he would pay for the labor of able-bodied blacks, but anyone with family responsibilities should remain.

Union soldiers captured a batch of Confederate mail during the day. Several of the letters expressed the belief that Sherman intended to advance through Augusta. The only other interesting letter was from Miss Izora M. Fair of nearby Oxford. She claimed to have stained her face black and frizzled her hair, then entered Atlanta disguised as a black to spy out Federal

The only known photo of slaves who flocked after Sherman's columns, believed to have been taken in Georgia. [LIBRARY OF CONGRESS]

defenses and plans. She had overheard a conversation at a headquarters tent and was fired on by pickets as she fled the city. Other letters from Fair's neighbors apparently criticized her unladylike attempts at espionage. When shown the letter, Sherman sent a team to bring her to him. He did not intend to harm Fair but wanted to "give her a scare." Fortunately for the young lady, she had wisely vacated the region.

During the day "some of our stragglers were shot by citizens or scouts," Hitchcock wrote. "Served 'em right." Sherman expressed the same opinion. Hitchcock was alarmed by the looting of homes and wrote, "Sorry enough am I for the women here and their anxiety and terror," but he continued, "I must say they show little *fear* of us."

Units of the 20th Corps entered Social Circle on November 18 and captured a Confederate surgeon and three thousand dollars in gold. They burned the railroad depot, a storehouse, and a large amount of cotton. One Federal described the community as "a dirty little village," made up of "shanties, superannuated negroes, wooly pickaninnies rolling in the dust, and squatting like huge monkeys on the fences, and half-naked, snuff-begrimed white women." Rice Bull resented the name of the town, because he could find no one around who would be sociable, but the Federals were happy over the joyous reception the slave population gave them. "I'm blessed if I thought there were so many of God's creatures in the world," one woman cried.

The invaders found the country "overflowing with sweet potatoes, corn, syrup and hogs." A commissary officer noticed his men spoiled more food than was eaten, an event that did not concern him in the least. "I think General Sherman didn't intend to leave anything for the Rebs," he said. The man did admit feeling guilty when "some women cried and begged so piteously for the soldiers to leave them a little food." On the whole, he agreed with Sherman's opinion that the South's people must be punished, even "exterminated," which was the word this man used. "They feel now the effects of their wickedness and who can sympathize very much with them?" he asked. The sergeant proceeded to describe bloated cattle that had been killed for their livers. The remainder of the carcasses were left to rot.

While Mrs. Burge's plantation was being overrun on November 19, Sherman crossed the Ulcofauhatchee River, known locally as the Alcovy. Connolly described it as "not very deep, rapid, without any well defined banks," and surrounded by swamps. The column had been crossing the Yellow River on two 120-foot-long bridges, but one was taken up and moved here to facilitate the advance. All the bridges in the region had been destroyed by Federal cavalry raids during the past summer.

Hitchcock awoke at 5:30 A.M. and for some time listened to rain falling against the tent. He found it difficult to roll out of bed. Sherman's staff covered fifteen miles on the 19th through a blowing rain and rode into Sandtown, also known as Newborn. It was "a little weather beaten village" of three hundred citizens, Connolly wrote. They came across an Augusta newspaper that criticized the legislature for discussing adjournment because of a "smallpox" outbreak. Earlier in the day Van Duzer and another officer had "skedaddled" when fired at by bushwhackers near the community.

The land was the poorest they had yet traversed. Connolly noticed ears of corn only six inches long. A farmer told him that the land "averaged six bushels of corn to the acre and some of it 'don't average anything.'" As a result, the region did not support the large plantations the Federals had become accustomed to encountering. The general and Hitchcock visited with the settlement's founder, John W. Pitts, a retired businessman.

While Sherman talked with Pitts about states' rights, secession, and the War, Union soldiers stripped Pitts of everything he owned and others despoiled the town with great energy. Hitchcock thought Pitts a curious character who agreed with Sherman's arguments and did not protest his property loss, because he agreed it was the "laws of war." Pitts showed them a pamphlet he had written in 1843 in which he advocated the removal of lawyers from public office.

Several of Sherman's officers had troubled consciences over the continual disregard of Special Orders No. 120. This incident, combined with the activity at Judge Harris' plantation the previous day, set them to questioning Sherman's intentions.

"The men are foraging and straggling, I am sorry to say, a good deal," Hitchcock recorded on November 19. "At and near every farmhouse we hear constant shooting of pigs and chickens." That day two foragers had been killed and three wounded by other foragers. There was also a growing number of soldiers participating in looting activities.

Earlier in the day, a woman had approached Sherman pleading for protection of her property, but the general refused her and promptly rode away. Around the campfire that night, he told Hitchcock the incident troubled him. "But how could I help her?" he asked, seemingly unable or unwilling to restrain his men. "I must harden my heart," Sherman concluded.

Hitchcock was very disturbed by this revelation. Two days earlier, after a house was criminally torched in Decatur, he had asked Colonel Charles Ewing, Sherman's brother-in-law, about the incident. To Hitchcock it seemed a gross violation of Sherman's orders. Ewing agreed, but what could be done? Officials in Washington, D.C., would not allow soldiers to be executed for this, Ewing said. "It is a great mistake," Hitchcock said of this policy. "Such 'mercy' damages us."

Hitchcock then approached Sherman's aide-de-camp, Captain Lewis M. Dayton, about the arson. Dayton said Federal soldiers must be allowed to take any course of action they thought appropriate, including scalping. A horrified Hitchcock called his attitude "typical."

Watching Marietta burn a week earlier, Hitchcock had asked Sherman if he had ordered such general destruction. Sherman had replied, "No," but claimed Jefferson Davis was responsible. Sherman explained that early in the war, he had personally beaten soldiers for trespassing on private property. "I don't think General would take same trouble now," Hitchcock confided, "indeed he admits as much. Evidently it is a material element in this campaign to produce among the People of Georgia a thorough conviction of the personal misery which attends war, and of the utter helplessness and inability of their 'rulers' to protect them." Sherman claimed that stopping stragglers was "hopeless," explaining that they "are harder to conquer than the enemy."

Another staff officer, Captain Pepper, described the usual routine when the army entered a town:

> A halt at noon beside a village, a besieging of houses by the troops, soldiers emerging from doorways and backyards, bearing quilts, plates, poultry and pigs, beehives attacked, honey in the hands and besmearing the faces of the boys, hundreds of soldiers, poking hundreds of bayonets in the corners of yards and gardens, after concealed treasure; here and there a shining prize, and shouting and scrambling, and a merry division of the spoils. In the background women with praying hands and beseeching lips unheeded.

One wing commander, Slocum, and two corps commanders, Williams and Davis, believed Sherman was in favor of wanton destruction of private property. As a result, they ignored Special Orders No. 120. None of them were reproved by Sherman for this course of action.

Hitchcock advocated roll calls for every company at each stop, but Rice Bull recorded that there were no such assemblies during the entire March. Hitchcock thought there should be "severe punishment" for stragglers and officers who ignored looting.

"I am bound to say I think Sherman lacking in enforcing discipline," Hitchcock concluded. "Brilliant and daring, fertile, rapid and terrible, he does not seem to me to carry out things in this respect."

Eventually Hitchcock partially shared Sherman's view of punishing the civilian population of the South. If the "terror and grief and want of these women and children" impair the fighting ability of the Confederate soldiers, then "it is mercy in the end." At least he had conscience enough to view the events with horror. *It is a terrible thing to consume and destroy the sustenance of thousands of people,* he thought.

The invaders not only hoped to end the rebellion by waging economic warfare on defenseless civilians, but many blamed the South's women for the conflict's continuation. One Ohio soldier lectured a woman:

> You urge young men to the battlefield where men are being killed by the thousands, while you stay home and sing "The Bonnie Blue Flag"; but you set up a howl when you see the Yankees down here getting your chickens. Many of your young men have told us that they are tired of war and would quit, but you women would shame them and drive them back.

The women fought this abuse with the only weapons they had—indomitable spirit and sharp words. In a quiet reply to abusive comments made by soldiers who stripped her farm, a woman said, "Our men will fight you as long as they live." Then she indicated her young children and continued, "and these boy'll fight you when they grow up."

Another woman, proud wife to a Confederate captain, defiantly said, "Take everything we have. I can live on pine straw the rest of my days. You can kill us, but you can't conquer us." A third, asked if her husband had been

The Murderous General ■ Jefferson C. Davis

Born in Kentucky in 1828, Davis volunteered to fight in Mexico at the age of eighteen. He became a lieutenant of artillery and remained in the service.

Davis was present in Fort Sumter when the Confederates bombarded it to start the Civil War, and legend states he fired the first return shot. After the friendly governor of Indiana made Davis a colonel, he fought at Pea Ridge, Arkansas, and Corinth, Mississippi.

On September 29, 1862, while in a hotel in Louisville, Kentucky, Davis deliberately provoked a confrontation with General William Nelson, who was his former commanding officer. Davis drew a pistol and killed Nelson, an act that Nelson's friends called premeditated murder.

Because of the influence of the friendly governor, Davis was not prosecuted. He fought well in the western campaigns and commanded the 14th Corps on the March. Davis remained a controversial figure, and many associates believed he was a copperhead who supported slavery.

Davis served in Alaska after the United States bought it from Russia in 1867, and he died in 1879. ■

[LIBRARY OF CONGRESS]

Bummers loot a plantation and set fire to a cotton press. [LESLIE'S ILLUSTRATED]

drafted into Confederate service, spat before she replied, "I wouldn't have a man if he had to be conscripted."

Sherman, so insensitive to the cruelties he visited upon the civilian population, became angry when women did not understand his actions. "I doubt if history affords a parallel to the deep and bitter enmity of the women of the South," Sherman wrote his wife. "No one who sees them and hears them but must feel the intensity of their hate." With one breath the women begged for food, and with the next they prayed "the Almighty or Joe Johnston will come and kill us."

The region east of Atlanta was extremely fertile and provided a wide variety of meat, fruits, and vegetables in great quantity. "We found abundance of corn, molasses, meal, bacon, and sweet potatoes," Sherman wrote. A plentiful supply of cattle, mules, and oxen was easily obtained. He found the country "quite rich, never before having been visited by a hostile army." A rich crop had just been gathered, seemingly for the exclusive use of the Union army.

Sherman had intended that foraging parties would consist of fifty men per brigade, led by two officers. They would leave before daylight on foot with local black guides, and the officers would know where to find their units in the evening. The party would locate food and fodder, load it on stolen wagons, and return to the column. Because of their isolation and the danger from Confederate cavalry and bushwhackers, the work was hazardous, but it was considered privileged duty and "seemed to have a charm about it that attracted the men."

When foragers located a plantation, they quickly searched for Confederates, then established guards for warning in case of attack. They secured provisions and a cook to see to their needs, then went about gathering food for their brigade. The foragers confiscated barrels of flour and cornmeal, cleared the smokehouse of cured hams and bacon, and gathered all the fruits and vegetables they could find. Honey, sweet potatoes, and molasses were in particular demand. Horses, mules, and cattle were tied to the back of wagons, grand coaches, buggies, or mules. Hogs, chickens, geese, and turkeys, often caught after amusing chases, were butchered on the spot and thrown across a horse or mule. Unwanted animals were shot and left to rot on the premises.

When their meal had been prepared, the foragers stopped their work and dined with hearty appetites. One man said he ate as "though I was hollow clear to my toes." If they had gathered enough food by noon, the men would sleep or sit around a warm fire and be entertained by the plantation slaves. Late in the day, they would return to camp and share their booty.

"The privates in the ranks have lived like princes every day," wrote one soldier of the bounty found on the March. A man from Ohio thought the army had contracted an "epidemic of good appetites." The "only remedy the surgeons have to prescribe," he continued, "is plenty of chickens, sweet potatoes, fresh pork, etc." A Connecticut infantryman was disturbed to see the richness of the South. He concluded, "It makes one sometimes laugh to think of the northern people's idea at the commencement of the war of starving out the southern army." A Minnesotan believed Georgia alone "could Subsist the Army of [Northern] Virginia Before the Raid was made for One Year with the crop that She had gathered But she cannot do it now."

"I have never seen a country better supplied than this," Van Duzer noted. "Turkeys, Chickens, Geese, beef Cattle, Sheep & swine in abundance. The story of starvation in the South is played out. Capt Cole returned from the

[LIBRARY OF CONGRESS]

Old Prayerbook ■ Oliver Otis Howard

Howard graduated from West Point in 1854 and rose rapidly in rank during the Civil War. He fought well at First Manassas, then served in the Army of the Potomac at Fair Oaks where a wound forced the amputation of an arm. He was the corps commander who was surprised and routed by Stonewall Jackson at Chancellorsville, and his performance at Gettysburg was criticized.

He was sent west late in 1863 and assigned to the Army of the Tennessee. When James McPherson was killed at Atlanta, Howard was given command of the army. He fought well at Ezra Church and Jonesboro, then led the army in the March to the Sea.

Howard was difficult for Sherman to accept on a personal basis, for he had no vices. The pious Howard did not smoke, drink, or swear, and he was a staunch New England abolitionist.

Howard did not just fight to end slavery. When the war was over, he became a vocal advocate of education for blacks. He helped establish a number of schools for former slaves, including Howard University in Washington, D.C.; and he also led the work of the Freedmen's Bureau in helping blacks adjust to life as free citizens. ■

days march in rather a dilapidated condition and how to account for it we did not know. We soon learned however that he had captured six quart bottles of blackberry wine and when he arrived in camp he had but two to show." Van Duzer found the region fertile, well-cultivated, and inhabited by an "intelligent class of people."

The first two days of marching had left many soldiers hungry because the foraging parties were inadequate and incompetent. With fifty foragers detailed per brigade, each man had to return with enough food to supply three meals for thirty men, and there was rarely enough for all. Competing parties fought over food, and Confederate cavalry frequently scattered the foragers. These problems were soon remedied, and larger parties, capable of defending themselves and gathering more food, were sent out as authorized foragers. A growing number of soldiers, sometimes entire regiments, left ranks without orders to forage on their own, and the rate of march was slowed to allow more time to gather food.

The countryside became bare as this growing legion of foragers, most unsupervised and all convinced that none would be punished, stole what could be carried and spoiled what could not. Tons of corn and sweet potatoes, unnumbered pig carcasses, and other food and fodder was discarded along the way. One disgusted soldier complained that the men "can't carry half the hogs and potatoes they find right along the road."

In attempting to save some food for their families, Georgians hung cured meat in the limbs of trees, and buried food, even live hogs, in the ground. The Federals took delight in searching out every morsel.

"They're all we've got left," cried a young mother after soldiers had rounded up her last chickens. "They've been coming by all day, stealing everything, but they said we could have those to keep my little ones alive!"

"Madam," replied a soldier smugly, "we're gonna suppress this rebellion if it takes every last chicken in the Confederacy."

Food was not the only thing taken. Soldiers ransacked homes, willfully smashed furniture, slashed bedding, and stole anything that caught their fancy for a moment. Men paraded in Revolutionary War uniforms, tricornered hats, wigs, gowns, ornate women's headgear, and ridiculously plumed militia hats.

A major from Indiana described an ancient carriage that was pulled by a donkey, a cow, and a goat. It trailed sheep and a calf and was burdened with "pumpkins, chickens, cabbages, guinea fowls, carrots, turkeys, onions, squashes, a shoat, sorghum, a looking-glass, an Italian harp, sweetmeats, a peacock, a rocking chair, a gourd, a bass viol, sweet potatoes, a cradle, dried peaches, honey, a baby carriage, peach brandy, and every other imaginable thing a lot of fool soldiers could take in their heads to bring along."

Sherman frequently saw these men alongside the March route and "was amused at their strange collections."

"This is probably the most gigantic pleasure expedition ever planned," said one man. "It beats everything I ever saw soldiering, and promises to prove much richer yet." He thought Sherman should burn the supply wagons because they were unnecessary and obstructed the roads.

"I wouldn't have missed it [the March] for fifty dollars," said another

Sherman's Evaluation of His Bummers

Although this foraging was attended with great danger and hard work, there seemed to be a charm about it that attracted the soldiers, and it was a privilege to be detailed on such a party. Daily they returned mounted on all sorts of beasts, which were at once taken from them and appropriated to the general use; but the next day they would start out again on foot, only to repeat the experience of the day before. No doubt, many acts of pillage, robbery, and violence were committed by these parties of foragers, usually called "bummers"; for I have since heard of jewelry taken from women and the plunder of articles that never reached the commissary. But I never heard of any cases of murder or rape; and no army could have carried along sufficient food and forage for a march of three hundred miles; so that foraging in some shape was necessary.
—W. T. Sherman

happy soldier. A comrade concurred, claiming the army was "eating the very foundations of the Confederacy." That activity was definitely preferable to fighting battles. One man felt it was his duty "to consume everything edible by man or beast."

The generals tended to be officially intolerant of unauthorized looting and plundering. They threatened to shoot looters but never carried out their threats. When one of O. O. Howard's men was sentenced to death, Howard commuted it to a prison term. Jefferson Davis forced several men to wear the dresses they had plundered; but when he considered executing men who had torched houses, an army chaplain loudly complained, "Just think of shooting American soldiers for the benefit of rebels. No man who really loves our cause could issue such an order. If an officer desires to shoot our men, let him join the rebel army at once."

Sherman was proud of the work done by his foragers. "The skill and success of the men in collecting forage was one of the features of this march," he wrote. Yet years later he felt a need to defend the behavior of his men in Georgia. "No doubt, many acts of pillage, robbery, and violence, were committed by these parties of foragers, usually called 'bummers,' for I have since heard of jewelry taken from women and the plunder of articles that never reached the commissary," he testified. "But I never heard of any cases of murder or rape; and no army could have carried along sufficient food and forage for a march of three hundred miles; so that foraging in some shape was necessary. . . . By it our men were well supplied with all the essentials of life and health."

Sherman's animals had been so well fed that on arrival in Savannah after a grueling three hundred-mile march, they were "pronounced by experts to be the finest in flesh and appearance ever seen with any army," Sherman boasted. ■

"It Looked Like the Whole World Was Coming"

O n November 19 the 20th Corps marched from Social Circle to Rutledge, where they destroyed the depot, warehouses, a water tank, and other railroad facilities. On November 20 they broke camp early and destroyed several miles of the railroad, then continued into Madison through a heavy rain. The railroad was easy for determined infantry to destroy; the rails were of easily bent soft, light iron.

Bridges and trestles were made of pine and burned quickly. Over seventy-five miles of track had been destroyed since the wing left Atlanta, and to the Confederates it certainly appeared as if Sherman would follow the road directly into Augusta. There was light resistance from Confederate cavalry, but foragers continued to do their work with vigor.

In 1845 Madison had been described as "the wealthiest and most aristocratic village" between Charleston and New Orleans. In the twenty years since, the town had become even lovelier. A Federal colonel called it "a wealthy place, mostly all rich planters." He considered it "the richest part of Georgia." Grand homes stood among extensive lawns dotted with ancient trees. Rufus Mead, a commissary sergeant from Connecticut, called Madison "the prettiest town I have seen in the state. One garden and yard I never saw exceeded." Mild weather had kept the grass green, and the soldiers were impressed by the profusion of roses and other flowers that bloomed in abundance here. The town's beauty did not prevent looting, however, which Conyngham said "went on with a vengeance."

Stores were ripped open, valuables and plate, all suddenly and mysteriously disappeared. I say mysteriously, for if you were to question the men about it, not one of them admitted having a hand in it. [When a fine shop was broken open, the rush of soldiers] was immense. Some of those inside being satisfied themselves, would fling bales of soft goods, hardware, harness, and other miscellaneous articles, through the windows. I have seen fellows carry off a richly gilt mirror, and when they got tired of it, dash it against the ground. A piano was a much prized article of capture. I have often witnessed the ludicrous sight of a lot of bearded, rough soldiers capering about the room in a rude waltz, while some fellow was thumping away unmercifully at the piano, with another cutting grotesque capers on the top-board. When they got tired of the saturnalia, the piano was consigned to the flames, and most likely the house with it. All the stores were gutted, and the contents scattered and broken around. Cellars of rich wine were discovered and prostrate men gave evidence of its strength, without any revenue test. A milliner's establishment was sacked, and gaudy ribbons and artificial flowers decorated the caps of the pretty fellows who had done it.

One cavalryman took a wire and wax clothes dummy from the milliner's and placed it on the saddle in front of him. Kissing and squeezing it, the man emitted high-pitched squeals in imitation of a woman who was being abused. He cried loudly, "Isn't there anyone in the crowd will protect a poor, lone female from such violence? Oh, oh! Is there any man at all?"

An officer, taken in by the play-acting, rode quickly up with leveled pistol and ordered, "Halt, you scoundrel, and let go that lady!"

The cavalryman handed over the lady amid peals of laughter from men lining the streets. The abashed officer dropped the dummy and quietly rode away.

This drunken, riotous revelry continued until General Slocum rode into town and posted guards. The 20th Corps had developed a taste for this behavior in the countryside. Private William Sharpe had seen a bummer "in an antique two-story stovepipe hat, a Revolutionary shadbelly coat, and black velvet knee-breeches, who pressed to his lips a six-foot stage-coach horn and blew it as if his name was Gabriel."

Two divisions and the corps wagons passed through Madison and camped just beyond. The courthouse, depot, a slave pen, and several houses were burned, and considerable food was stolen. The slaves cheered as the slave pen blazed. Soldiers were amazed when they were mistaken for black troops—they had not noticed how dirty and covered with soot they had become from campfires and less savory burning activities.

Rice Bull thought the town "quite a handsome place . . . something of a resort," and located in Georgia's most productive region. Although the town seemed to contain an inordinate number of beautiful women, their presense could only be glimpsed behind tightly drawn drapes. As in Covington, the women would peek out when a band played southern airs, but disappeared at northern selections. Bull found the men shouting themselves hoarse as they marched through town. It seemed they "wanted to impress on them [the citizens] some idea of the power and magnitude of the Army they so hated and despised."

Outside Madison, Slocum received an unusual emissary—Joshua Hill— who asked protection for the city. He was an anti-secessionist who had been the last southern senator to leave Washington, D.C., before the Civil War began. In May 1864, while fighting in the Confederate army, Hill's son, Legare, had been killed and buried at Cassville. After Union troops occupied Atlanta, Hill entered Union lines and asked to speak to Sherman. Hill introduced himself as a friend of Sherman's brother John and requested permission to recover his son's body for burial in Madison.

During the March to the Sea, most shooting done by Union troops was for killing pigs, cattle, and other animals for food. [LESLIE'S ILLUSTRATED]

Sherman asked Hill to eat with him at the officers' mess. Afterward, he ordered an escort and ambulance to accompany Hill on his mournful mission. Slocum assured Hill that he would protect private property to the best of his ability.

Slocum rode to Bonar Hall, where he met elderly Colonel John Walker. Walker proudly announced that his three sons were serving in the Confederate army, and he wished he were, too. Slocum laughed good-naturedly, and Walker invited the General in for a meal.

Slocum's men were overwhelmed by the welcome afforded them by the slave population. "Hundreds of slaves joined the Army," noted one officer, "some with a half a dozen children along with them . . . not a white man to be seen—all in the army or cleared out." The slaves had been told the Yankees would burn black men alive and drown the women and children. One slave, after realizing the invaders would cause him no harm, said his owner had convinced him that the Federals would have horns. The Yankees would force them to transport their wagons by cutting holes in their shoulders and attaching harnesses, the slaves had been assured.

Over four thousand men camped for the night at the home of Miss Emma High. Her mother, alarmed when some men raised a loud disturbance, ran into the house and returned to the porch with her husband's Masonic apron. Waving it over her head, she cried out, "I am a Mason's daughter and the wife of a Mason, give me protection." An officer responded to the plea and told the soldiers, "Leave this place and don't return." Turning to the woman, he said, "I will place a guard around your home, put out your light and go to sleep, and you will not be disturbed."

The High family spent a quiet night. Morning found a cook peacefully baking gingerbread cookies, and the delicious aroma attracted soldiers throughout the day. They entered politely, took a few cookies, and dropped coins into a pan in payment. The happy servant became excited as the collection of money grew, but finally one man placed every coin in his pocket and ran out the door. "Poor cook was in tears," Emma wrote, "and rushing to the door, she cried after him—'Our boys would not have done that way, for they has had some *raisin'* and has got *manners* too.'"

The army left Madison, Emma noticed, in a jolly mood. The rear guard halted at a house that boasted a particularly bountiful flower garden, stacking arms on the lawn and picking every flower. Soldiers wove roses into garlands and wore the flowers on their hats and draped over their muskets.

On November 19 General John Geary, who had served as the first mayor of San Francisco, was detached from the main column. His assignment was to burn the railroad and wagon bridges over the Oconee River, thirteen miles east of Madison, and make a feint on Augusta. He skirmished with

A Day's March

The order of march is issued by the army commanders the preceding night, from them to the corps commanders, and then passed along until every soldier, teamster, and camp-follower knows that an early start is to be made.

At three o'clock the watch-fires are burning dimly, and, but for the occasional neighing of horses, all is so silent that it is difficult to imagine that twenty thousand men are within a radius of a few miles. The wind sweeping gently through the tall pines overhead only serves to lull to deeper repose the slumbering soldier, who in his tent is dreaming of his far-off Northern home.

But in an instant all is changed. From some commanding elevation the clear-toned bugle sounds out the reveille, and another and another responds, until the startled echoes double and treble the clarion calls. Intermingled with this comes the beating of drums, often rattling and jarring

on unwilling ears. In a few moments the peaceful quiet is replaced by noise and tumult, arising from hill and dale, from field and forest. Camp-fires, hitherto extinct or smouldering in dull gray ashes, awaken to new life and brilliancy, and send forth their sparks high into the morning air. Although no gleam of sunrise blushes in the east, the harmless flames on every side light up the scene, so that there is no disorder or confusion.

The potatoes are frying nicely in the well-larded pan; the chicken is roasting delicately on the red-hot coals, and grateful fumes from steaming coffee-pots delight the nostrils. The animals are no less busy. An ample supply of corn and huge piles of fodder are greedily devoured by these faithful friends of the boys in blue, and any neglect is quickly made known by the pawing of neighing horses and the fearful braying of the mules.

Then the animals are hitched

into the traces, and the droves of cattle relieved from the night's confinement in the corral. Knapsacks are strapped, men seize their trusty weapons, and as again the bugles sound the note of command, the soldiers fall into line and file out upon the road, to make another stage of their journey.

A day's march varies according to the country to be traversed or the opposition encountered. If the map indicates a stream crossing the path, probably the strong party of mounted infantry or of cavalry which has been sent forward the day before has found the bridges burned, and then the pontoons are pushed on to the front. If a battle is anticipated, the trains are shifted to the rear or the centre. Under any circumstances, the divisions having the lead move unencumbered by wagons, and in close fighting trim. The ambulances following in the rear of the division are in such close proximity as to be available if needed. In

the rear of each regiment follow the pack-mules, laden with every kind of camp baggage, including blankets, pots, pans, kettles, and all the kitchen-ware needed for cooking.

The flankers are driving a squad of Rebel cavalry before them so fast that the march is not in the least impeded. The flankers spread out, on a line parallel to the leading troops for several hundred yards, more or less, as the occasion may require. They search through the swamps and forests, ready for any concealed foe, and anxiously looking out for any line of works which may have been thrown up by the enemy to check our progress. Here the General of the division, if a fighting man, is most likely to be found; his experienced eye noting that there is no serious opposition, he orders up a brigade or another regiment, who, in soldier's phraseology, send the Rebel rascals "kiting," and

(*continued on page 63*)

Confederate scouts at Buckhead, then burned the depot, water tower, five hundred bales of cotton, a considerable store of wood, ferry boats, and fifty thousand bushels of corn that had been destined for Confederate forces. The railroad was destroyed for five miles, and the railroad bridge, a four hundred-yard-long structure supported sixty feet above the water, was burned.

Geary camped for the night at Blue Springs (Swords) and marched on the following morning to Park's Ferry, where he destroyed boats and mills. His force then moved toward Eatonton to rejoin the 20th Corps.

Sherman camped the night of November 19 amid the ruins of Newborn. Before turning in, he sent up three signal rockets to indicate his location to Howard's distant wing.

Sherman left Newborn on the morning of November 20 and marched through a cold, foggy day. He passed through Shady Dale, a plantation of 7,600 acres and 250 slaves. They lived in fifty whitewashed cabins that belonged to Mr. Whitfield, a millionaire. Whitfield had left earlier with his able-bodied slaves and stock. The area had abundant crops that had been gathered recently, and no army had raided through the region previously. Food was plentiful, "till this army . . . passed," Hitchcock noted.

(from page 62)

the column moves on.

There is a halt in the column. The officer in charge of the pioneer corps, which follows the advance guard, has discovered an ugly place in the road, which must be "corduroyed" at once, before the wagons can pass. The pioneers quickly tear down the fence near by and bridge over the treacherous place, perhaps at the rate of a quarter of a mile in fifteen minutes. If rails are not near, pine saplings and split logs supply their place. Meanwhile the bugles have sounded, and the column has halted. The soldiers, during the temporary halt, drop out of line on the road-side, lying upon their backs, supported by their still unstrapped knapsacks.

These short halts are of great benefit to the soldier. He gains a breathing-spell, has a chance to wipe the perspiration from the brow and the dust out of his eyes, or pulls off his shoes and stockings to cool his swollen, heated feet. He munches his bit of hard bread, or pulls out a book from his pocket, or oftener a pipe. Here may be seen one group at a brookside, bathing their heads and drinking; and another, crowded round an old songbook, are making very fair music.

Sometimes a little creek crosses the path, and at once a foot-bridge is made upon one side of the way for those who wish to keep dry-shod; many, however, with a shout of derision, will dash through the water at a run, and then they all shout the more when some unsteady comrade misses his footing, and tumbles in at full length.

But the sun has long since passed the zenith, the droves of cattle which have been driven through the swamps and fields are lowing and wandering in search of a corral, the soldiers are beginning to lag a little, the teamsters are obliged to apply the whip oftener, ten or fifteen miles have been traversed, and the designated halting-place for the night is near. The column must now be got into camp.

Officers ride on in advance to select the ground for each brigade, giving the preference to slopes in the vicinity of wood and water. Soon the troops file out into the woods and fields, the leading division pitching tents first, those in the rear marching on yet farther, ready to take their turn in the advance the next day.

As soon as the arms are stacked, the boys attack the fences and rail-piles, and with incredible swiftness their little shelter-tents spring up all over the ground. The fires are kindled with equal celerity, and the luxurious repasts are prepared. After this is heard the music of dancing or singing, the pleasant buzz of conversation, and the measured sound of reading. The wagons are meanwhile parked and the animals fed. If there has been a fight during the day, the incidents of success or failure are recounted; the poor fellow who lies wounded is not forgotten, and the brave comrade who fell in the strife is remembered with words of loving praise.

Shortly after follows the peremptory command of "Taps." The soldiers gradually disappear from the camp-fire. Rolled snugly in his blanket, the soldier dreams again of home, or revisits in imagination the battlefields he has trod.

All is quiet. The army is asleep. Perhaps there is a brief interruption to the silence as some trooper goes clattering down the road on an errand, or some uneasy sleeper turns over to find an easier position. And around the slumbering host the picket-guards keep quiet watch, while constant, faithful hearts in Northern and Western homes pray that the angels of the Lord may encamp around the sleeping army.

—George Ward Nichols

Connolly had envisioned Shady Dale as "a nice, clean, aristocratic country town situated in a romantic, shaded valley." His idealized notion was destroyed, but he was amused to see a procession of slaves pour out of one house like mackerel from a barrel. The blacks were equally impressed by the number of soldiers who invaded their home. "It looked like the whole world was coming," one said.

The corps paused for dinner, and in an hour Whitfield lost an estimated fifty thousand dollars in property. While the soldiers ate, the slaves danced and sang. Connolly "laughed at their comicalities until tears rolled down my cheeks." When he asked an old man why the community was called Shady Dale, the slave grinned and replied, "Because there are so many of us here."

Connolly was told the slaves had received very little meat during the war. As a result, they had taken to "prowling about the country at night, foraging" for chickens and hogs and killing them in the swamps. Connolly decided that when the army left, Whitfield would not have "a sweet potato, a pig, chicken, turkey, horse, mule, cow, and scarcely a nigger left." Most of the slaves joined the column, and every private had a servant carrying his knapsack. "What soldier *wouldn't* be an abolitionist under such circumstances?" he wondered.

At midday Sherman's staff paused on the Farrar plantation, near Madison. Mr. Farrar was allegedly in Milledgeville helping prepare earthworks. "They're gonna fight you over there," warned a slave. "They been building forts and all for two years." Sherman discounted the possibility of resistance.

Mrs. Farrar, a beautiful but sharp woman, was home. She made no comment when subjected to Sherman's standard speech on the South's sins of rebellion. The commanding general became very angry when slaves told him that Farrar whipped them with saw blades and paddles with holes cut in them. The master would then rub salt in the wounds.

After a fifteen-mile march, Sherman stopped at 3:00 P.M. at Eatonton Factory, also known as Stanfordville on the Little River. Engineer Poe supervised the complete destruction of a textile factory located here, a large establishment that employed forty women and had five hundred spindles. The factory, outbuildings, one hundred bales of cotton, and cloth were burned. The women begged Sherman to spare their place of employment, but their pleas were ignored. Some Confederates attempted to burn a bridge that spanned the river, but the Federals captured it. To their dismay, Sherman ordered it burned. That road led to Eatonton and Milledgeville, Sherman explained, and Slocum had exclusive use of the route.

Sherman camped on a ridge that afforded the officers a beautiful view of campfires blazing on surrounding hills. Hitchcock learned the army had more supplies now than when they left Atlanta, and their animals were in good shape or had been "replaced by better."

The female proprietor of the property where they camped begged Sherman for food. Her provisions had been stolen by Union soldiers, she complained, and Sherman ordered supplies given to her. "It does seem terribly hard to treat people like this," Hitchcock observed. However, considering that this woman's husband was fighting in the Confederate army, he continued, "They and their families must pay the penalty—no help for it."

Hitchcock was still worried over the excesses that had so far attended foraging. He approved of a report that General Davis, after catching two men leaving a house with dresses, had them arrested and turned over to the Provost Marshal. As punishment, the soldiers were forced to don the dresses and, amid the jeers of their comrades, march down the road with *Stolen* signs hung around their necks. Still, Hitchcock was torn on the subject.

"Either we must acknowledge the 'C.S.A.' or we must conquer them: to conquer, we must make war, and it must *be* war, it must bring destruction and desolation, it must make the innocent suffer as well as the guilty, it must involve plundering, burning, killing. Else it is worse than a sham. Shall we then quit and acknowledge the C.S.A.? No, for that is simply to ensure the same thing hereafter, for separation means *ceaseless war.* God help us!"

Slocum and the 20th Corps camped that night at Eatonton, six miles to the east of the Little River and twenty miles north of Milledgeville. Bull called it "quite a good town."

Recent heavy rains protected Eatonton from the fiery destruction visited on other towns along the March route. Soldiers raided nearby Turnwold Plantation, where young Joel Chandler Harris was an apprentice printer. He watched the Yankees steal every horse on the property. When soldiers tried to torch the house, an officer swatted them with the flat of his sword and ran them off. As Harris sat on a roadside fence watching the excitement, a passing soldier commented, "If there was another one of 'em a'setting on the fence on t'other side, I'd say we was surrounded."

On November 21 the 14th Corps continued south. The weather had turned nasty and their advance was limited to eight miles. A driving rain that started during the night continued without letup until late in the evening. Then the weather turned cold, and a piercing wind started to blow. The roads turned to mud lanes that slowed the marching troops, and wagons sank hub deep into the slime. Cursing teamsters whipped their mules, and grunting infantrymen helped push the wagons out of deep holes. The men were cold, wet, and exhausted. Because of the direction of march, their exertions had brought them little closer to Milledgeville when they stopped for the night at Vann's plantation. The farm had an abundance of food, at least when the Federals arrived, but it was "a matter of severe doubt whether there will be much left" when they departed, commented one officer.

"The citizens say that the Yankees brought cold weather with them," a soldier remembered, "as it is much colder than they usually have." Late in the night there was an uncharacteristic snowstorm.

Road conditions delayed the March until 11:00 A.M. The men "floundered through heavy clay mud," which had the consistency of wax or molasses, Hitchcock wrote. "What would become of us if this weather should continue two weeks?" Connolly wondered. "We couldn't march; would be compelled to halt here in the midst of a hostile country, and thus let the enemy have time to recover from his surprise and concentrate against us."

At a lunch stop, Sherman's staff encountered a brave slave who had sheltered three escaped Union prisoners. Hers was a desperate situation. Her mistress was barren, and she had borne a child of her master. Predictably, the mistress treated her cruelly. She had heard of Union victories in the war, and when Sherman was pointed out to her, she exclaimed, "There's the man that rules the world!"

Mr. Vann claimed the county was predominantly Unionist in sentiment and expressed disappointment in the state legislature, which had just adjourned. He told Sherman he "did hope they would do something for peace."

Hitchcock was again disturbed by actions of Union stragglers. He could not "bear to see the soldiers swarm as they do through fields and yards." Still, he saw the necessity of their success. "Nothing can end this war but some demonstration of their helplessness, and the miserable inability of J. D. to protect them."

Connolly noticed the same situation. Every building they passed seemed to be burned, and food and fodder that could not be carried was also torched. "Citizens everywhere look paralyzed and as if stricken dumb as we pass them. Columns of smoke by day, and 'pillars of fire' by night, for miles and miles on our right and left indicate to us daily and nightly the route and location of the other columns of our army."

Advance elements of the 20th Corps entered Milledgeville on the evening of November 22. Most camped several miles north, at Meriwether Station and Butts Crossroads.

Freezing rain fell throughout the night, and road conditions again slowed the 14th Corps. They covered only twelve miles, and at 4:00 P.M. Sherman found the men halted in plowed fields on an exposed hill, miserable with "a high raw wind blowing."

Locating General Davis, Sherman urged him to send the men a little farther south. There they could find some relief in a valley. Sherman rode on ahead. Finding shelter behind a line of plum bushes, he dismounted and instructed his staff to set up camp. The general, taking a drink and a cigar from his saddlebags, entered a crude cabin to warm up beside a fire. There a slave woman told him that better accommodations could be found a short distance down the road. Sherman walked on a littler farther and found a hewn log cabin where some of his staff were already settling in for the night.

Standing in front of a fire, he noticed a small box with the name Howell Cobb stenciled on it. Cobb, as Sherman well knew, was one of the South's "leading Rebels," a man Hitchcock called a "head devil." Cobb had been Secretary of the Treasury, a U.S. representative, governor of Georgia, a Confederate general, and was currently commander of the Georgia Militia.

Cobb owned several plantations and five hundred slaves scattered across Georgia. He had removed the fifty fit slaves who worked this farm and had driven his mules, horses, and cows from the six thousand-acre enterprise. That left only fifty old men, women, and children who cowered near their fireplaces, fearful that the Yankees would kill them. "A more forlorn, neglected set of human beings I never saw," Nichols wrote. Hitchcock, who described the plantation's log buildings as shabby, said Nichols was unable to enter these "cold and hungry" cabins.

Sherman ordered Davis to "spare nothing" on the plantation. "That night huge bonfires consumed the fence rails and kept our soldiers warm," Sherman wrote. Many sacks of corn, beans, peanuts, and salt; five hundred gallons of syrup, four hundred pounds of sweet potatoes, and other food was consumed by Cobb's visitors. The slaves were given what remained. One soldier enjoyed a "queen's feast" that night. "Needless to add," he remembered, "our friend Mr. Cobb contributed quite a lot to our support and comfort."

The 20th Corps, camped nearby, had a "red letter day for our foragers," Bull wrote.

The leader of Sherman's personal cavalry escort was Lt. David R. Snelling. He had unerringly led Sherman across the Georgia countryside. In 1862 Snelling, a native of the Milledgeville area, had enlisted in the Confederate army. Unhappy with the cause and with slavery, he deserted in Bridgeport, Alabama, several months later and joined a Union cavalry regiment from northern Alabama. Nichols called him "a young man of good education, of high integrity, simple hearted, and brave."

That night Snelling recognized a slave from his family's farm. A staff officer gave the man a drink and asked if he knew what had become of Master David. Not recognizing the blue-clad lieutenant, the servant answered that the young man had gone off to war, "and he supposed him killed," said Sherman. "His attention was then drawn to Snelling's face, when he fell on his knees and thanked God that he had found his young master alive and along with the Yankees."

Snelling asked Sherman's permission to visit his uncle's nearby home. Sherman enjoyed the notion of Snelling's sudden appearance there, where the Georgian had been a poor relation, and agreed. The meeting was apparently as cold as one might imagine. "The uncle was not cordial, by any means," Sherman was told, "to find his nephew in the ranks of the host that was desolating the land, and Snelling came back, having exchanged his tired horse for a fresher one out of his uncle's stables, explaining that surely some of the 'bummers' would have got the horse had he not." When Snelling's men burned his uncle's gin and looted the home, Hitchcock quoted the frightened uncle as saying, "Sherman greatest general and meanest man in the world."

Snelling's decision of conscience cost him his heritage. Returning after the war for a visit, his life was threatened, and he fled in the night to establish a new home in Arkansas. His daughter later described him as a "tall, thin man with troubled brown eyes" who took long, lonely walks across his property.

Sherman was again quite amused by the number of slaves who crept into the hut for a glimpse of him. After eating his share of Cobb's fare, the General sat with his back to a roaring fire. An elderly black man quietly entered and asked an officer, "Is this Master Sherman?" Assured that it was, he crept closer and held a candle near Sherman's face. "I asked, 'What do you want old man?' He answered, 'They say you is Master Sherman.' I answered that such was the case, and inquired what he wanted. He only wanted to look at me and kept muttering, 'Dis Nigger can't sleep dis night.'"

Sherman asked why the old man trembled. The slave replied that once before he had joyfully welcomed soldiers in blue. They turned out to be Confederate cavalry, who beat the slaves unmercifully for their reaction. "This time he wanted to be certain before committing himself; so I told him to go out on the porch, from which he could see the whole horizon lit up with camp-fires, and he could then judge whether he had ever seen any thing like it before. The old man became convinced that the 'Yankees' had come at last, about whom he had been dreaming all his life."

Sherman gave the slaves food. According to Nichols, he "assured them that we were their friends, and they need not be afraid that we were foes." One old man wisely replied, "I suppose that's true, but master, you'll go away tomorrow, and another white man'll come."

According to Nichols, the slaves were told, "as soon as we got them into our clutches, they were put into the front of the battle, and were killed if they did not fight; that we threw the women and children into the Chattahoochee, and when the buildings were burned in Atlanta we filled them with negroes to be roasted and devoured by the flames." In spite of this propaganda, which Nichols called "terrorism," many understood that once the war was over, they would benefit. One reasoned, "Why do the Yankees want to hurt black men? Master hates the Yankees, and he's no friend of ours; so we are the Yankee's best friends."

"It is part of the rebel system to lie thus," Hitchcock had written at Judge Harris' plantation after hearing similar stories. When a servant was asked if they believed the tales, he replied, "No, Sir! We have faith in you!"

In every instance blacks were impressed by the might of the Federal army. One woman who watched the passage of a huge cattle herd was told that they came from Chicago, one thousand miles away. "Goodness," she replied, "what a population you Yankees are."

Nichols visited a slave hut near Milledgeville and talked for an hour with an elderly black couple. Abruptly the old woman stood up, pointed a bony finger at her husband, and scolded him, "Why do you sit there? Do you suppose I've been waiting sixty years for nothing? Don't you see the door open? I'm going to follow my child. I won't stay here. Tomorrow I'm going along with these people. Yes sir, I'll walk until I drop in my tracks."

Sherman's force marched away at 7:00 A.M., leaving the Cobb Plantation looking "as though it had been visited by a very healthy and vigorous cyclone." Not just rails, but buildings and all manner of property had disappeared in flames. Having enjoyed destroying the bounty of a chief secessionist, the soldiers now speculated on whether they would have to fight for the state's capital. ∎

CHAPTER
6

"Hurry Scurry, Run Here, Run There, Run Everywhere"

Sherman's rapid approach to the outskirts of Milledgeville caught the Georgia legislature completely by surprise. For several days wild rumors of the Federal advance had circulated throughout the state capital, and a curious collection of improvised "scouts" raced to and from the countryside bearing alleged sightings of the Union army.

Miss A. C. Cooper, who had fled Atlanta during the summer when Sherman arrived, described the familiar scene:

> The excitement increased; we could neither eat nor sleep. Scouts were sent out up this road, down that, across the country, everywhere the roads teemed with foam-flecked, hard-run horses bestrode by tired, excited men, and the greater part of these men were disabled soldiers, who had come home to rest and recover, if possible, from grievous wounds. These scouts would ride into the village almost exhausted and, not dismounting, take their food from the willing hands that would carry it out to them, then off again in the direction from which it was thought the raiding party would come.
>
> Reports varied; one would be that the enemy would be upon us ere long, as a few blue coats had been seen in the distance, and we women were advised to pack up and flee, but there was blank silence when we asked, "Where shall we flee?" . . . Hurry scurry, run here, run there, run everywhere. Women cried and prayed, babies yelled . . . dogs howled and yelped, mules brayed. Negro drivers swore while Negro girls giggled, more from excitement and fright than from any mirth-provoking cause."

By November 19 Milledgeville was Sherman's obvious target. This knowledge spurred the legislature into a frenzy of activity, and they passed a law that required every able-bodied Georgian to rise up and defend his state. The legislation exempted only themselves and judges from service. They then spent three thousand dollars of the taxpayers' money to rent a train that would carry them out of danger. The legislators claimed to be leaving for the "front" and said they would meet again at a time and place to be designated by the governor.

Governor Joseph Emerson Brown led the panicked exodus. His wife had already departed. One woman said Mrs. Brown had been "pale and terror stricken, flying hither and thither, not knowing where to turn—fearing that the house would be burned over her head before morning." Brown urged her "to leave the mansion and fly with the children, leaving the house to its fate."

The legislature and the governor acted no better. Leaving legislation on their desks in the State House, they abandoned the state archives and library. Most incredibly, in the midst of a prolonged war, they left the extensive contents of Georgia's arsenal and armory. Their special train, and many wagons and buggies ("a thousand dollars was cheap for a common buggy," Nichols noted) were loaded with furniture, clothing, and other personal effects. Brown stripped the governor's mansion of everything except very heavy items. Most of the furniture, bedding, curtains, carpets, a cow, and the contents of his pantry, down to the last cabbage, was loaded. Then the Governor left town.

Anna Marie Green, whose father, Dr. Thomas F. Green, operated the state asylum for the insane, recorded these events in her journal. On the morning of November 18 she and her father entered the capital to inquire after developments. She never forgot the pathetic sight she witnessed.

"The scene at the State House was truly ridiculous," she wrote. "The members were badly scared, such a body of representatives made my cheeks glow with shame. . . . They could [not] stand for the defense of their own capital."

After dark on November 19, her attention was drawn to fires on the western horizon. "My heart sank, and almost burst with grief as I beheld the horizon crimson and the desolation our hated foe was spreading. Great God! Deliver us!"

Hearing reports of fighting nearby, Miss Cooper rushed to the front porch to listen, but "we could not have heard a cannon, for from every house in the village came the sound of weeping and heart-rending cries." The reports were disturbing enough to lead her neighbors to bury not only food but other items, which Cooper found unusual. "Many of the white women were using the spade and hoe burying their treasures, not gold or silver, but pieces of homespun jeans and factory cloth, intended to be made up for the soldiers, also home-knit socks, pieces of bacon, etc. The scene would have been laughable had it not been so pathetic."

This situation prompted an unusual development in internal Georgia politics. General Ambrose R. Wright, President of the Georgia Senate, decided that Governor Brown could not effectively govern the eastern half of the state; so from Augusta he proclaimed himself leader of the state east of the Oconee River. Wright proceeded to issue an order similar to that recently passed by the legislature, urging all Georgians to fight the invaders. Georgia historian Charles Jones later said Brown was unable to govern at the time because of "territorial disability." Federal General Jacob Cox, in a history of the March, called this situation "a novel absurdity."

Although fortifications had been prepared for the defense of Milledgeville, most Confederate troops had been concentrated in Macon for an anticipated

A raucous mock session of the Georgia legislature was held in the State House when Sherman's forces occupied Milledgeville. [HARPER'S WEEKLY]

attack on that city. Since the summer, cadets from the Georgia Military Institute in Marietta, boys no older than seventeen, had guarded Milledgeville. They camped on the capital square and drilled, unaware that Sherman would burn their school before he started for the coast. There were two militia companies in town, a local organization known as the "Factory Guards" and one battery of artillery.

As the Yankees approached, Governor Brown moved to augment the city's defense. He went to the state penitentiary to address the prisoners, and after an appeal to their patriotism, Brown offered the inmates pardons in exchange for military service. Over one hundred accepted, leaving about twenty hard cases and murderers to be removed to South Georgia under guard. This "prison militia" helped load state property onto trains, then they were given arms and uniforms. Some deserted at the first opportunity, but others served honorably and were discharged when the campaign was over.

Henry Wayne, general of militia, loaded this sorry assortment of soldiers, about five hundred men and boys, onto a train late on November 19. They rode to Gordon on a spur that connected Milledgeville with the Central Railroad. One wonders what his father, James M. Wayne, would have thought of the situation from his seat on the United States Supreme Court in Washington, D.C.

With the government routed and the pitiful military force retreating, Milledgeville's civilians made preparations for occupation by a hostile army. On the road between the asylum and Milledgeville, Miss Green saw families on the move. They rode atop wagons loaded with furniture and "moving, they scarcely knew where. Some to plantations and some to the woods." Four wagons containing books from the state library were sent to the asylum for safekeeping. The Green family buried barrels of syrup, concealed their silver in the reservoir, and Anna placed a bag of jewelry beneath her clothing. "But we were despondent, our heads bowed and our hearts crushed—the Yankees in possession of Milledgeville. The Yankee flag waved from the Capitol—Our degradation was bitter."

That night Federal cavalry entered town to reconnoiter. They cut the telegraph wires, asked residents about the strength of Rebel troops, then rode back west to deliver their report to Sherman.

The Union advance was delayed by muddy roads and freezing temperatures, but late on the afternoon of November 22 a Federal skirmish line advanced cautiously into town past three empty redoubts. "Passed groves of pine cut down for works and abattis," Hitchcock noted, "not used: also very strong works partly built across road." They had expected resistance, but not even Confederate cavalry was present to contest their entrance into the city. One of the few white men still in residence was Mayor R. B. De-Graffenreid. He had remained to surrender his city and to ask protection for its people and property.

Divisions of the 20th Corps formed ranks, unfurled flags, and marched down Greene Street as bands played "Yankee Doodle" and "The Battle Hymn of the Republic." As they passed the capitol, the band derisively broke into "Dixie." Two regiments stopped to camp at the capitol square for provost duty, and they quickly raised a U.S. flag on top of the capitol dome.

Their arrival confirmed Miss Cooper's worst fears. "Then we learned the truth, the fearful truth! We were not threatened with a mere raiding party, it was Sherman. . . . Like a huge octopus, he stretched out his long arms and gathered everything in, leaving only ruin and desolation behind him. . . . There was not a place to which we could flee."

"Three of our scouts," Cooper continued, "their horses white with foam, flashed by shouting a 'goodbye'; bullets thick as hail whistled past and around us, burying themselves in the pillars and back of the veranda where we stood so paralyzed we could not move."

The remainder of Sherman's Left Wing entered Milledgeville in parade formation the next morning, November 23. It was "a bright, beautiful day; roads excellent and surrounding country magnificent," Connolly declared. Not a single white face greeted the conquerors, and the town seemed deserted by its residents.

The slave population thronged the sidewalks to welcome their liberators. "Bless the Lord," called one, "thanks be to Almighty God, the Yanks is come." An excited woman cried, "I can't stop laughing enough. I'm so glad to see you." A young girl rushed into the street and hugged several soldiers. "One of you's gotta marry me," she cried. Nichols found the welcome embarrassing. Some soldiers avoided marching near the sidewalks to escape frantic hugs from slaves in the crowd.

Milledgeville's blacks, decked out in their best clothes, and thousands more that had followed the wing from Atlanta, were in a festive mood. "Their ecstatic demonstrations were ludicrous in the extreme," observed a

Union sergeant. Officers were disturbed because their appearance in the city strained food resources to the breaking point. There was also some concern about the presence of so many unattached women among the soldiers.

Slocum quartered himself in the fine Milledgeville Hotel. Sherman, who entered later with the 14th Corps, made himself at home in the governor's mansion. A Union soldier described it as "beautifully finished off on the inside as any building I ever saw." Sherman complained good-naturedly about the former occupant's lack of hospitality.

The General was amused by the consternation his appearance had caused Georgia officials. While noticing that the people of the city remained at home, the government "had fled, in the utmost disorder and confusion; standing not on the order of their going, but going at once." Before leaving, they made "the most frantic appeals . . . for help from every quarter, and the people of the State had been called en masse to resist and destroy the invaders of their homes and firesides."

When W. C. Johnson heard that the legislature had fled at their approach, he wrote, "they adjourned for—; well, perhaps to attend Thanksgiving services at their respective homes."

Sherman's staff ate from an improvised table made of planks laid across chairs, and Sherman slept on the floor. Nichols believed Brown had fled "with extremely bad grace, . . . from his distinguished visitors."

Sherman read southern newspapers with great interest. He found "many charging that we were actually fleeing for our lives and seeking safety at the hands of our fleet on the sea-coast. All demanded that we should be assailed, 'front, flank, and rear'; that provisions should be destroyed in advance, so that we would starve; that bridges should be burned, roads obstructed, and no mercy shown us. Judging from the tone of the Southern press of that day, the outside world must have supposed us ruined and lost."

That proclamation had been issued by General P. G. T. Beauregard from headquarters at Corinth, Mississippi. "Arise for the defense of your native soil!" it thundered. "Rally around your patriotic Governor and gallant soldiers! Obstruct and destroy all the roads in Sherman's front, flank, and rear, and his army will soon starve in your midst. Be confident. Be resolute. Trust in an overruling Providence, and success will soon crown your efforts. I hasten to join you in the defense of your homes and firesides."

His emotional appeal was matched by this missive from Georgia's delegation to the Confederate Congress: "We have had a special conference with President Davis and the Secretary of War, and are able to assure that they have done and are still doing all that can be done to meet the emergency that presses upon you. Let every man fly to arms! Remove your negroes, horses, cattle, and provisions from Sherman's army, and burn what you cannot carry. Burn all bridges, and block up the roads in his route. Assail the invaders in front, flank, and rear, by night and by day. Let him have no rest."

One of Georgia's former U.S. Senators, Benjamin Hill, wrote from Richmond: "You have now the best opportunity ever yet presented to destroy the enemy. Put everything at the disposal of our generals; remove all provisions from the path of the invader, and put all obstructions in his path. Every citizen with his gun, and every negro with his spade and axe, can do the work of a soldier. You can destroy the enemy by retarding his march. Georgians, be firm! Act promptly, and fear not!" To this statement, the Confederate Secretary of War, James A. Seddon, added, "I most cordially approve the above."

Sherman and his men took these demands much more seriously than any Georgian. If the state did arise in such a manner, the March would be seriously delayed and Federal soldiers would grow extremely hungry. The army's progress might be slowed enough to enable Rebel reinforcements to reach Georgia and offer serious battle. To forestall such a possibility, on November 23 Sherman issued Special Field Orders No. 127 from the governor's mansion. If citizens obstructed the March, they were to be dealt with "harshly." When food or forage was destroyed, "houses, barns, and cotton gins must also be burned to keep them company." Furthermore, all subordinate officers must redouble their efforts at gathering food.

"First act of drama well played, General!" Hitchcock congratulated Sherman in his journal. He shared his commander's view that Milledgeville was the halfway mark of this military operation. The Major summoned Davis and Slocum to discuss straggling, looting, and arson. He was not encouraged by their response. "An army is a terrible machine to control," he concluded. He soon received a report from the Right Wing. Howard described similar incidents but expressed "regret" over them. "I do not see why this army cannot be kept in better trim as to stragglers," Hitchcock lamented. "I am much dissatisfied with this."

Colonel Ewing presented Hitchcock with a package of tobacco. After Hitchcock discovered it was contraband, the gift was returned.

According to Hitchcock, Kilpatrick met Sherman at the Oconee Bridge, "troops drawn up, grand reception, colors dipped, cheers, music." The officers were disturbed by reports that Federal prisoners were being ordered to take an oath of allegiance to the Confederacy and to help oppose Sherman's advance. If they refused, they were executed by Confederate cavalry. "If this proves true," he worried, "Sherman will retaliate, and *we must not be taken prisoner.* I confess I don't expect any mercy if captured." He feared his treatment would be worsened by the acts of their foragers.

Connolly was thrilled to occupy an enemy capital. "My boyish desire is gratified," he wrote. The Major was impressed with Milledgeville. "The dwellings are scattered and surrounded by large and tastefully decorated grounds," he continued. "As one rides along its sandy streets, even at this season of the year, the faint perfume from every variety of tree and shrub, bud, blossom, and flower fills the air with delicious fragrance. The exterior of the residences bespeak refinement within, and everything about the city serves to impress one with the idea that he is in an old, aristocratic city." The State House was "built of reddish looking sandstone and is a large square building, with rather a superabundance of fancy cornice outside. It has entrances on the north, south, east, and west, each having a broad flight of stone steps. The offices and State library are on the first floor, the legislative halls on the second floor, and also the committee rooms. Each chamber has life size oil paintings of the prominent old men of Georgia hung

Sherman established his quarters in the Governor's Mansion. Governor Brown stripped the magnificant structure of most of its furnishing when he fled the city.

around its walls in plain gilt frames."

Connolly thought the churches, which were clustered on the statehouse square, looked like public buildings. Although the streets and walks were unpaved, their sand construction seemed adequate. The homes were pleasant frame structures, with stores constructed of brick.

Riding to the soldiers' camp east of the Oconee River, he described the stream as being rapid but muddy, and about 350 yards wide. From the camp, the city had a "shabby, rickety appearance," for here were housed the slave quarters and homes of poor whites. Finished with his inspection, Connolly rode to headquarters and raised the flag he had so crudely obtained from Mr. Zachry. "Little did the old sinner think, when he first received this trophy from his rebel son, that Yankee hands would ever unfurl it in triumph over the capital of his State," Connolly wrote gleefully.

Sherman, Davis, and Slocum were immediately flooded with requests for guards and protection of property. Having met no opposition, Sherman was inclined to be generous. Guards were freely granted, including one to Miss Green's father at the asylum. This limited their loss during the occupation to two mules.

Two cotton warehouses, a textile factory, a flour mill, and a foundry were all spared destruction because they were owned by Yankees or foreigners.

Sherman accepted worthless bonds from merchants who swore their cotton would not be used by the Confederacy, although on every other occasion during the March, cotton was burned with particular vigor.

No more than four homes were torched in the Milledgeville area. One was owned by John Jones, the state treasurer, and a second by Judge Iverson Harris, who had urged Georgians to destroy anything useful in Sherman's path. Harris's advocacy of a scorched earth policy brought about Sherman's personal attention. The only fatality of the occupation was Patrick Kane, an overseer on the plantation of Dr. William A. Jarrett. He fired on approaching Federals, and the plantation was devastated. Although little harm was done to private homes in the city, one resident estimated damage to his house at twenty thousand dollars. Another man stated his loss at fifteen thousand dollars.

This lack of destruction can be attributed to the provost guards who vigorously patroled the city. It also helped to have the primary Federal camp located east of the city and across the Oconee River. There was still considerable vandalism, much of it resulting from the bitterly cold weather. Soldiers had discarded their warm clothing during the pleasant first days of marching, and tents were little shelter in the cold, wet wind. As a result, churches were occupied by soldiers who burned pews for fuel. They stabled their mounts in sanctuaries, and out of pure meanness, poured molasses down organ pipes to make the music "sweeter."

Tents sprang up in most yards, and every easily dismantled wooden structure was in peril for firewood. When the Federals left, Milledgeville was bereft of any picket fence or outhouse. Captain John Rizha spent the night of November 24 in a house that had been visited by unauthorized foragers. He slept hungry on the bare floor, for every stick of furniture and "everything edible" had been stolen "by our men."

The capitol building, seen as a seat of rebellion, was a particular target of vandals. The state library, housed in the basement, was destroyed. "In a very bad exhibition of a very lawless nature," as one Federal recorded, soldiers flung hundreds of books out windows to the wet ground. Soldiers, including one on horseback, stomped volumes of "choice literary and scientific works" into the mud, and men carted off armloads of books. The state museum was also rifled of valuable minerals and fossils. One man noted "that our limited means of transportation was about the only thing that prevented the entire State-house from being carried away." Fifty years' worth of valuable state papers became fuel for bonfires.

"It is a downright shame," complained Connolly of this destruction. "I am sure General Sherman will someday regret that he permitted this." That point is certainly debatable, but Connolly claimed to have rejected the opportunity to take a library worth one thousand dollars. "I should feel ashamed of myself every time I saw one of them in my book case at home. I don't object to stealing horses, mules, niggers and all such little things, but I will not engage in plundering and destroying public libraries." However, a week later Connolly was quoting from *White's Historical Collections of Georgia,* which he had apparently picked up here.

Fortunately, Georgia's most valuable papers had been saved by the foresight of a few public employees. Georgia's Secretary of State, N. C. Barnett, bravely remained in Milledgeville until the Federals arrived. Taking the great seal of the state and newly passed legislation, he stole to his home. His family buried the seal under the house, then wrapped the laws securely and secreted them in a pen with "four fine porkers."

Some of the state's archives had been salvaged by John Jones, the treasurer. One fourth of the archives were sent to southern Georgia and as far as South Carolina for safekeeping. After the Federal horde moved on, state documents were recovered from the streets and yards of the city. Many papers were found coated with wasted molasses, flour, and meal.

It was in January 1861, that Georgia had seceded from the Union in the State House. Now troops from Wisconsin and New York decided to hold a mock session of the legislature in those same chambers. Their assembly quickly degenerated into a drunken spectacle that was attended by thousands of soldiers and "boisterous Negroes who did not know what to do with themselves and their freedom," noted Conyngham. Officers of the legislature were appointed; their job, for the most part, was carrying out members of the "legislature" who had succumbed to the "bourbon fits, which disease was rather prevalent among the honorable members," an observer remembered. A major topic of debate was the merits of various brands of whiskey.

Cavalry General Kilpatrick, thoroughly inebriated, regaled the "legislature" with a story of a recent raid on a plantation wine cellar. "Though I am a very modest man that never blows his own horn," he began dishonestly, "I must honestly tell you that I am Old Harry on raids. My men, too, have strongly imbibed the spirit and are always full of it. I must confess that my fellows are very inquisitive. Having come so far to visit the good people of Georgia, who are famed for their hospitality, they live in the free and easy style among them. And if, perchance, they discover a deserted cellar, believing that it was kindly left for their use by the considerate owner, they take charge of it. It sometimes happens, too, that they look after the [silver] plate and other little matters."

"Mr. Speaker," interrupted a soldier, reeling to his feet, "I must raise a point of order! I believe it is always the custom to treat the speaker."

"Yes, I believe it's customary to treat the speaker," Kill-Cav replied. "I beg to inform this honorable body that I am going to treat the speaker." Kilpatrick brandished a bottle of brandy and drank deeply, to the accompaniment of thunderous cheers.

A committee that had been appointed to investigate the condition of the state of Georgia returned, singing "We Won't Go Home Until Morning" at the top of their lungs. The legislature then repealed the Ordinance of Secession, resolving:

"1. That the ordinance of secession was highly indiscreet and injudicious, and ought to be discouraged.

"2. That the aforesaid ordinance is a d—d farce, and always was, and is hereby repealed and abrogated.

"3. That Sherman's columns will pay the devil with the ordinance and the state itself.

Released inmates burn the Georgia Penitentiary as Union soldiers look on.

"4. As the Federal relations with the state are not very friendly, that a committee be appointed to kick Joe Brown and Jeff Davis, and also to whip back the state into the Union."

A committee, as recommended in Article 4, was appointed. It was composed of Sherman's army.

At this point men ran into the assembly hall shouting, "The Yankees are coming! The Yankees are coming!" The soldiers rushed out of the building in feigned panic, probably in a good imitation of the real legislature's departure several days earlier.

Other soldiers remained to smash chairs, desks, and windows, and to write obscene messages for Georgia's proper lawmakers, should they dare return. One man noted that the State House was knee deep in scattered papers.

Some troops found billions of dollars' worth of unsigned Georgia currency, which they used to light pipes. Poker games were held with million dollar stakes, and some of the money was given to female factory workers, who had not been paid for months. They were excited by their windfall until they discovered the value of the money. Slaves fought over the bills, and Conyngham overheard one say, "Bless the Lord—we're richer than poor massa now!"

Colonel William Hawley, commander of the Provost Guard, finally stepped in to stop further vandalism. He may have saved the capitol from destruction by establishing his headquarters in the building. A Savannah newspaper, quoting a report from Augusta, inaccurately reported, "The State House, Governor's mansion, and penitentiary were burned."

"I was not present at these frolics," Sherman wrote of the escapades at the capitol, "but heard of them at the time and enjoyed the joke." The dour Hitchcock frowned on the occasion, "I hear it was pretty flat and not very creditable—though no harm done."

While the festivities at the capitol were going on, soldiers worked to destroy Milledgeville's war material. The fireproof magazine, which was located on the west side of the capitol, was destroyed with explosives after six wagon loads of munitions were dumped into the Oconee River. Because most of Milledgeville's churches were grouped around the state square, several suffered structural damage from the blast. In the arsenal at the opposite side of the square, soldiers found an unusual assortment of ancient weapons—knives, muskets, Revolutionary War pistols, and shotguns, which were appropriated or destroyed.

The soldiers were amazed to find ten thousand unusual blades stored in barrels. One man described them as "a cross between a common corn-knife and a butcher's cleaver—a very crude, rough, ill-shaped implement." Early in the War, Governor Brown had discovered that the state was unable to arm its volunteers. To remedy the situation, he ordered these primitive weapons fashioned at factories across the state. The blades were to be fastened to long pikes, as three thousand of these were. Soldiers were encouraged to rush the enemy, impale one man on the pike, and chase down the remainder with knives. A military genius Joseph E. Brown was not. One incredulous Yankee, examining this curious hoard, observed, "It is one of old Joe Brown's ideas, and like him has vanished." Apparently none of the pikes was used during the War. Union infantry made off with many of the two-foot blades and pretended they were swords.

The Federals burned the pikes and 2,300 muskets. They pitched 10,000 cartridges, 170 boxes of artillery ammunition, and 200 kegs of powder into the Oconee River. A cache of 1,500 pounds of tobacco was distributed among the men.

The penitentiary was burned, although probably by the remaining inmates who escaped in the confusion, rather than by Union soldiers. One woman criminal, jailed for killing her husband, donned a blue uniform and briefly joined an Indiana regiment to ply "an ancient trade."

While the city was quiet, cavalry raided the surrounding countryside for food. Here occurred one of the best documented crimes of a type that the Federals steadfastly denied occurred. In her journal, Miss Green wrote, "The worst of their acts was committed to poor Mrs. Nichols—violence done, and atrocity committed that ought to make her husband an enemy unto death. Poor woman I fear she has been driven crazy."

Mrs. Kate Latimer Nichols had married James Hall Nichols in 1856. He was a captain in the Confederate army serving in Virginia, and Mrs. Nichols was sick in bed when two Union soldiers entered her room. They forced her black attendant to leave by threatening to shoot him, then raped her. She died later in a mental hospital.

Such a crime was rarely spoken of at the time, and afterward Miss Green attempted to erase the name from her diary. The number of such incidents during Sherman's March has been disputed. Certainly there were more than

Sherman claimed, and probably fewer than Georgians believed. An Augusta newspaper declared that the Federal "incarnate devils ravished some of the nicest ladies in the town."

After a brief rest in Milledgeville, the Union army started marching east across the Oconee River bridge, which Governor Brown had neglected to have destroyed. It was November 24, Thanksgiving Day, a holiday little observed by civilians in the city that year. At the river the Federals managed to leave many of the blacks who were following them, but they took a young slave, Allen Brantley, as a teamster. He won an army pension after the war and used the money to educate his family.

The Federal soldiers who remained in camp that night enjoyed a pleasant Thanksgiving, according to Conyngham. "Thanksgiving Day was very generally observed in the army," he wrote, "the troops scorning chickens in the plentitude of turkeys with which they have supplied themselves. Vegetables of all kinds and in unlimited quantities were at hand, and the soldiers gave thanks as soldiers may, and were merry as soldiers can be. In truth, as far as the gratification of the stomach goes, the troops are pursuing a continuous thanksgiving."

Bull had gone into camp across the river in a field which he estimated contained one thousand bushels of sweet potatoes. The men ate every one. He found the weather cold, with a rare snow blowing across the camp. Bull and ten friends pooled their food, which included hens, geese, pork, flour, and coffee, and hired a cook in the slave quarters of a neighboring plantation. The soldiers helped the woman cook over an open fireplace, then enjoyed a feast. Afterward, they nearly froze in their unheated tents.

The people who lived between Atlanta and Milledgeville thought the Federals had treated them badly, but an incident occurred in the capital city that would lead the invaders to greater acts of violence. As the soldiers rested in Milledgeville, escapees from the infamous prison at Andersonville, located one hundred miles to the south, stumbled into Union lines. They had dug out of the stockade, where over ten thousand men had died since spring, and made their way through hostile territory. Having eluded Rebel patrols and large, vicious hounds, some of the filthy, ragged, and emaciated men arrived as Thanksgiving feasts were being spread out in Sherman's camps. The escapees, near death from starvation and exhaustion, looked at the food with "wild animal stares," and wept at the sight of the American flag.

Colonel Charles D. Keen's men were "sickened and infuriated" to "think of them starving in the midst of plenty." Another officer shared that emotion, imagining "the thousands of their imprisoned comrades, slowly perishing with hunger in the midst of wealth untold, barns bursting with grain and food to feed a dozen armies." Many soldiers responded to this sight with hatred toward the civilians who were unlucky enough to live in their path.

Connolly commanded the rear guard in the city that night. He promised to "preserve 'Joe Brown's' capital from invasion by rebels until tomorrow morning anyhow."

W. C. Johnson thought their departure was greatly appreciated by the local inhabitants. "Our army presents a grand appearance, passing through

The old Georgia State house was rebuilt following a post-Civil War fire. The gates were constructed of bricks from the destroyed arsenal and magazine.

the capital of the Rebel State of Georgia. Female citizens in large numbers look upon the scene with wondering eyes—at the long files of Yankees continually passing—and doubtless breathe a sigh of relief as they witness our departure from their city, looking down upon us from their windows with an air of supremest contempt, and doubtless wishing, down deep in their hearts, that the atmosphere of their lovely city may never again be contaminated by the presence of such hordes of Yankee mudsills. This some of them manifest by their sneers, scoffs, etc., but we bid them a gentle farewell, and march out on the State road leading to Savannah."

A brigade remained in Milledgeville to round up stragglers, while a team prepared the magazine for destruction and warned citizens to stand clear. They applied a match at 9:00 A.M., and "in an instant the State magazine was blown into the air with a terrific explosion."

The soldiers completed their movement on November 25. Kindling, which had been gathered at the wooden toll bridge, was fired. The span burned in monumental fashion and collapsed into the river just ten minutes later. Now "the broad Oconee rolled between us and Milledgeville," Connolly wrote, "with no means of crossing it; but our men were all across and, of course, it's no business of ours whether anybody else gets across or not." He was amused by the toll taker, "a fat, dirty, lazy looking citizen. . . . He stood there looking at us with a woeful countenance as he beheld us fire the bridge. . . . He assured me he had 'allers bin for the Union, and wus yit.'"

Accompanying the exodus were Kilpatrick's five thousand troopers. They had guarded the flanks of the Right Wing past Macon and had arrived from Gordon on November 24 to protect the Left Wing as it approached Augusta. Sherman had invited Kilpatrick to a private conference in which he outlined a special mission for the troopers. The cavalry was to sweep northeast of the march route and feint on Augusta. If the movement fooled the Confederates, then gray reinforcements would concentrate there instead of at Savannah, his real goal. This would lessen opposition on Sherman's route and draw off the Confederate cavalry, which had begun to capture and, according to rumor, kill members of foraging parties. Kilpatrick was ordered to destroy the Augusta-Savannah Railroad between Millen and Waynesboro and, if possible, to effect a rescue of twenty thousand Union prisoners being held near Millen. Kilpatrick left two brigades to screen the infantry advance and to set out to search for additional glory.

Before leaving on this raid, Kilpatrick inspected his command and weeded out five hundred weak horses. After blankets were thrown over their heads, the horses were killed by axe blows and the carcasses left to rot on a farm. "My God," cried the owner when he realized what was happening, "I'll have to move!"

"Day never to be forgotten," Miss Anna Green wrote in her journal, "scene of tumult and joy unwitnessed before. This morning through the spy glass, we watched the burning of the bridge after the retreating enemy, and afterward stood and hailed the entrance of our beloved soldiers amid shouts and tears."

Dr. J. R. Bratton, Chief Surgeon at the state hospital, dispatched a report to his superiors immediately after Sherman's departure. "They left here in a hurry as if they were afraid the devil was behind them, or some other Evil spirit with a sharp Stick. . . . The people have been plundered and robbed of their provisions & clothings & many families today have nothing to eat. Many who were nursed in the lap of wealth and luxury before the enemy came have nothing now but a few sweet potatoes upon which the most fastidious ladies made their breakfast this morning with much gusto and smacked their lips with apparent satisfaction & thanked God that they have plenty of sweet potatoes still left them in the ground."

Bratton had sharp words for the Georgia government, which had "been fighting the [Davis] administration and not the Enemy for the last two years, and have thus been unprepared to meet the Enemy when he came."

Sherman would have been disconcerted to realize that his route of travel had already been discovered. Bratton disclosed that the enemy was "on their way to Savannah by Sandersville & Millen."

Kilpatrick's horsemen had barely disappeared before Wheeler's gray cavalry arrived to prevent the Federals from capturing Augusta. When Federal pressure eased on Macon, Wheeler had mounted his men and moved quickly to the Oconee River. They swam the stream near Dublin on November 24, and a brigade was left to help defend the Oconee against passage by the Right Wing. The rest picketed the two main roads from Milledgeville to Sandersville.

These men were seen as saviors by some, like Miss Green, who was moved to tears by the cry, "Our cavalry is coming," and sight of the ragged men. "The tears streamed from our eyes—strong men wept—God bless our soldiers our poor suffering soldiers," she wrote. Another witness called them a "plundering band of horse-stealing ruffians," who were dreaded as much as a visit by Sherman's foragers. The ragged horsemen constructed a crude raft, and men crossed the river on it, swimming their horses alongside. Green watched the "cheerful, determined and confident" men all day. "One man as he drew near said he was too dirty to come to talk to ladies, but how we honor their dirt and rags."

Green's servant, Harriet, gave one of the barefooted soldiers her new shoes. "If the Yankees knew of that little incident," she confided, "of one of our Negroes doing that kindness to a soldier and because he was a Confederate soldier they might feel a little less kindly to our servants than they present."

However bitter Miss Green's degradation, she was ready to fight again after the Yankees left. She walked around her house singing, "We live and die with Davis," and asking rhetorically, "How can they hope to subjugate the South. The people are firmer than ever before."

Firmer perhaps, but definitely hungrier. Mayor DeGraffenreid delivered an ugent request for relief from Macon, which had narrowly escaped the fate of Milledgeville. "Our citizens have been utterly despoiled by the Yankee army," he pleaded. "Send us bread and meat, or there will be great suffering among us. We have no mules or horses. What you send must be brought by wagon trains. . . . Send us relief at once." Although inflation had nearly ruined most of the citizens—coffee cost eighteen dollars a pound and cloth fifteen dollars a yard—the people had never lacked for food until now.

Howell Cobb, whose plantation had been so thoroughly plundered, arranged for the Confedcrate commissary in Macon to send five thousand rations of corn meal and eighteen head of beef to Milledgeville. Several weeks later a London businessman, Alexander Collie, donated five thousand dollars for relief of the city's citizens.

One resident, Peterson Thweatt, wrote Confederate Vice President Alexander Stephens to describe his loss. "All our provisions, crockery, silver, bed clothing, our own clothing, . . . were taken or destroyed. Our parlor furniture given away to negroes. . . . Our nurse was taken and has never been heard from since. My wife and children lived on Potatoes for several days."

A Milledgeville newspaper reporter wandered the town's quiet streets the Sunday after the Federals departed. He found papers strewn knee deep in the State House, plaster cracked, and windows shattered. "A full detail of all the enormities . . . would fill a volume, and some of them would be too bad to publish. In short, if an Army of demons just let loose from the bottomless pit were to invade the city, they could not be much worse than Sherman's army." Walls of the capitol and hotel were "black with tobacco spit." The capitol was "shockingly defaced, like everything in the town," one woman angrily wrote. It looked "as though struck by a cyclone."

Three weeks later Eliza Frances Andrews began a difficult journey from Washington, Georgia, to Albany. The trip took her through the swath of destruction left by Sherman's legions. While arranging transportation from Sparta to Milledgeville, she overheard someone say, "Milledgeville's like hell; you can get there easy enough, but getting out again would beat the Devil himself." Learning that she intended to continue on through Gordon, a man said she had better be a good walker. "Sherman's done licked that country clean," he said.

Three miles from Sparta, Andrews encountered the "Burnt Country." For the next forty miles she did not see a single fence rail standing. "The fields were trampled down and the road was lined with carcasses of horses, hogs, and cattle that the invaders, unable either to consume or to carry away with them, had wantonly shot down to starve out the people." Miss Andrews held a handkerchief, doused with perfume, to her nose to contain the stench. Every house seemed pillaged, and ruins of gins, mills, and a number of homes lined the route. "The infamous wretches!" she cursed the Union soldiers.

A number of Confederate soldiers could be seen tramping along the road, so many that it looked like "the streets of a populous town. . . . They were mostly on foot, and I saw numbers seated on the roadside greedily eating raw turnips, meat skins, parched corn—anything they could find, even picking up the loose grain that Sherman's horses had left."

After a lengthy wait, they crossed the Oconee on an improvised ferry and inspected the field where the troops had camped. The poor of Milledgeville wandered over the camp "picking up grains of corn that were scattered around where the Yankees had fed their horses." The invaders had left a great deal of plunder, gathered on the first half of their March, but now little remained except loose cotton, rotten grain, and animal carcasses. The land was being plowed in expectation of next year's harvest.

After attending services that day at St. Stephen's, which Union soldiers had thoroughly trashed, Miss Green thundered, "God will not permit desecration of his holy temple to go unpunished." ∎

CHAPTER 7

"I'm Going to Burn This Town"

Hitchcock left Milledgeville with Sherman on November 24, beginning what he called the "second Act of the drama." He marched thirteen miles before stopping for lunch near Gum Creek. It was a perfect day for campaigning; the weather was cool and the sky clear and blue. After negotiating steep hills near the Oconee River, the army had found sandy land, and the country was studded with large farms and extensive fields of corn, "not yet gathered, that is, *not this morning.*"

Hitchcock and Sherman were briefly excited when soldiers appeared to deploy into line of battle, but the men were merely preparing to stack their arms for a rest break.

At lunch they paused at a house occupied by a woman and her thirty-five-year-old, unmarried daughter, who was described as fat but pretty. The mother was concerned by the loss of her property, but when she discovered that one of the Federal officers was unmarried, she "began to praise daughter 'powerful fast knitter,—could keep a bachelor's ankles mighty warm.'"

Hitchcock, noting the complete absence of white men in Georgia, believed that the Governor's plea for Georgians to rise up en masse and destroy the enemy would be ineffectual. It appeared that every able-bodied male was already in the service. As Sherman had previously observed, "Pierce the shell of the C.S.A. and it's all hollow inside." Hitchcock concurred, observing that the March "shows the real hopelessness of their 'cause.'" That would be demonstrated first to the suffering people of the South, then to the entire world.

The Left Wing was buzzing with rumors of Kilpatrick's mission. The men were excited by the possibility of liberating an estimated twenty thousand men who were incarcerated at a prison near Millen. Connolly privately believed the Confederates had had time to move the prisoners to a more remote location, but he waited anxiously for word from Kilpatrick.

Hitchcock and Nichols camped in front of a house while Sherman slept within, beside a roaring fire. "Scene all round is striking," Hitchcock wrote. "Across the road directly front of house, and on both sides of house, is pine forest, dense shadows, sombre growth. Gen. Slocum's tents are pitched across the road: and one division camps all around us: camp fires light up the open sky in rear of house: horses picketed in yard: sentry pacing before fence—heard his sharp 'Halt! who goes there?' just now. Camp sounds all around—voices in conversation in other tents—braying of mule now and then, lowing of cattle, occasional shout of soldier in the woods."

On the following night, as a band serenaded Sherman in camp, Hitchcock observed, "This part of a campaign,—life in open air, riding daily, and tent life, is very jolly: don't wonder men like it."

Before leaving his bivouac, Sherman paid the elderly owner for her trouble. A young daughter complained that the Yankees "had no right to punish helpless women." Hitchcock asked where the men were. In the army, she replied. "Did you attempt to persuade them to remain at home?" Connolly continued. The answer was negative, and Hitchcock lectured her, "Then you have done all you could to help the war, and have not done what you could to prevent it."

The rate of march slowed considerably on November 25, to eight miles. Rebel cavalry felled trees across the roads and burned a series of nine bridges over swampy Buffalo Creek. The stream spread into a quarter-mile-long swamp that covered seventy acres in a low, densely wooded region. There were also disturbing reports of heavy skirmishing in the advance. Federal infantry was repeatedly forced to deploy and disperse small groups of pesky Confederate cavalry. The invaders were surprised to discover Wheeler had managed to cross their front from Macon.

Captain Poe tackled the task of repairing the bridges with great energy, but the difficult job consumed four hours. Each of the bridges had been thirty to one hundred feet long, and they were separated by earthen causeways. Poe spanned the main channel with pontoons, and the smaller structures were repaired with trees.

Sherman was so angered by the delay that he set about to discover who was responsible. He found a diverse selection of culprits. Residents and slaves variously blamed a local man, Rebel cavalry, and people from Sandersville for the destruction. Sherman wanted to burn the nearest houses in retaliation, but Hitchcock tried to stay his hand. "In war everything is right which prevents anything," Sherman argued. "If bridges are burned I have a right to burn all houses near it."

Hitchcock told Sherman that "indiscriminate punishing was not just." Sherman replied that it would dissuade those who were responsible. "Let him look to his own people, if they find that their burning bridges only destroys their own citizens' houses they'll stop it."

"From this on we shall be impeded and harassed and have skirmishing every day," Hitchcock wrote, "and also from this out there will be houses burned—I guess."

Sherman camped four miles short of Sandersville, on a large farm that was being stripped by soldiers. Hitchcock believed Sherman was disturbed by the woman of the house, who hoped "the Lord would reward us all according to our deeds—very hard for poor old woman to have all she had taken."

Sherman's men found plenty of fresh pork and sweet potatoes to eat, and countless pine rails warmed them through the clear, cool autumn nights. They complained about the "fearful swamps" and sandy roads that made marching difficult and slowed the advance. Most of the men, however, had taken a fancy to this excursion. They were essentially removed from contact with the outside world and normal military discipline. "There was something intensely exciting," Oakly wrote, "in this perfect isolation."

Connolly had covered fifteen miles on his first day out of Milledgeville, and he was impressed by the grandeur of the pine-covered land. "Grasshoppers couldn't live in these 'piney woods,'" he wrote. "The pine trees grow so thick in them that a man can scarcely walk through them. They grow tall, straight and without limbs for from 30 to 60 feet from the ground, and the ground is covered with a thick matting of the dead pine leaves that have fallen, so that when walking through these 'piney woods' your feet feel as if treading on a carpet well stuffed with straw underneath. Citizens say that strangers traveling through these woods will get lost as readily as on a prairie if they go far from the road, and I can readily believe it, for we passed over many miles today in which every tree and spot looked exactly like every other tree and spot. . . . We now and then passed a miserable looking little cabin today, about which we generally found two or three sickly, sallow women and from five to fifteen children all looking like persons I have read of called 'dirt eaters'. . . . I think they must live on it, for I don't see a place for anything except children to grow in these 'woods.'" Local people said the land would be unproductive until they reached the Ogeechee.

Despite the poor appearance of the soil, foragers returned to camp "pretty well loaded, and I can't imagine where they found so much stuff," Connolly continued. "Georgia is an excellent state for foraging. We are living finely, and the whole army would have no objection to marching around through the State for the next six months. Indeed, the whole trip thus far has been a holiday excursion, but a very expensive one to the Rebels."

Food gathered by foragers still did not reach all the soldiers. Rice Bull's unit was reduced to eating rations from supply wagons.

Connolly was surprised by the lack of resistance. "Where can all the rebels be?" he wondered. "Here we are riding rough shod over Georgia and nobody dares to fire a shot at us. We burn their houses, barns, fences, cotton, and everything else, but none of the Southern braves show themselves to punish us for our vandalism." Bull concurred, writing, "The Confederates seemed to have lost their old vigor." He noticed an increase in Rebel desertions.

When Connolly heard that bridges had been burned and there were skirmishes with Rebel cavalry, he fumed:

Let them do it if they dare. We'll burn every house, barn, church, and everything else we come to; we'll leave their families houseless and without food; their towns will all be destroyed, and nothing but the most complete desolation will be found in our track. This army will not be trifled with by citizens. If citizens raise their hands against us to retard our march or play the guerilla against us, neither youth nor age, nor sex will be respected. Everything must be destroyed. This is the feeling that has settled down over the army. We have gone so far now in our triumphal march that we will not be balked. It is a question of life or death with us, and all considerations of mercy and humanity must bow before the inexorable demands of self preservation. . . . We'll get through, though; they CAN'T stop us now, but I would like to be able to see about ten days into the future—the next ten days will be the crisis with us.

Wrecking the Railroads

A division of infantry would be extended along the railway line about the length of its proper front. The men, stacking arms, would cluster along one side of the track, and at the word of command, lifting together, would raise the line of rail with the ties as high as their shoulders; then at another command they would let the whole drop, stepping back out of the way as it fell. The heavy fall would shake loose many of the spikes and chairs, and seizing the loosened rails, the men, using them as levers, would quickly pry off the rest. The cross-ties would now be piled up like cobhouses, and with these and other fuel a brisk fire would be made; the rails were piled upon the fire, and in half an hour would be red hot in the middle. Seizing the rail now by the two ends, the soldiers would twist it about a tree.

—General Jacob Cox

Confederate resistance was just beginning to firm up. Without waiting for infantry support, Federal cavalry boldly rode into Sandersville late in the afternoon of November 25. They feared no resistance, since the Confederates had so far seemed reluctant to fight in their communities. Suddenly Wheeler's cavalry fanned out in the streets and charged, driving the Union horsemen out of town and capturing eleven men. The prisoners, except for one wounded man who was taken to Rev. James Anthony's house, were incarcerated in a store and guarded by some of Wheeler's men.

That night a band of vigilantes, probably Confederates incensed by the senseless destruction they had witnessed from Sherman's marauding bummers, stormed the improvised jail. Overpowering the guards, they dragged the prisoners to a field outside town and shot them.

Three of the few remaining men in town roused Ella Mitchell's disabled father from bed at 3:00 A.M. to help them bury the unfortunate troopers. The entire town anxiously awaited Sherman's appearance with extreme dread, expecting a horrible retribution.

Wheeler made a stand at daybreak. His dismounted men fought furiously, but a horde of Union infantry put them to flight. The Rebels fell back stubbornly through a thick fog, fighting in the streets and from the courthouse. In the confusing swirl of battle, Federal cavalry fought alongside Confederates before discovering their mistake, and Indians from a Wisconsin unit attempted to scalp some Confederate dead.

"Wheeler's men went dashing by, firing as they went," Ella Mitchell described the scene. "The road was a mass of blue men, the surrounding fields were full of them. In a few minutes our house was filled with the surging mass. In a little while there was not a piece of china, silver, or even the table cloth left, and the food disappeared in a second. Fences were torn down, hogs shot, cows butchered, women crying, children screaming, pandemonium reigned. Then the jail, the court house, peoples' barns and a large factory . . . were all ablaze."

The skirmish lasted only half an hour. While it seemed impressive to the participants and observers, it was hardly worth noticing to veterans of Shiloh, Vicksburg, and Chickamauga. Federal losses totaled about twenty.

After the town was secured, Sherman and his staff entered Sandersville and approached a brick home. Sherman sent Hitchcock into the house, where he found a frightened woman who "begged protection."

Sherman was in a foul mood. In the countryside he had witnessed food and fodder destroyed by retreating Confederates. Such incidents could ruin his March. He was outraged to learn of his men being murdered and angered by Confederate resistance in the streets of Sandersville. Adding to Sherman's, and the army's, foul mood were several emaciated Federal prisoners who had escaped from the Millen prison and greeted Sherman's columns in Sandersville. Sherman replied sharply to the woman, "I'll protect you, but I'll give you no guard and I'm going to burn this town." On this

Sherman's "neckties" graced the Georgia countryside for many years following the Civil War. [BATTLES AND LEADERS]

occasion Hitchcock concurred. "General would be justified by the laws of war in destroying whole town," he confided to his journal. John Van Duzer, the telegrapher, wrote, "The Rebels used every house in this town nearly . . . and I should not be a particle surprised if the town would be burned tomorrow."

Fortunately, Sherman and the woman were able to strike up a pleasant conversation, and both relaxed. Rev. Anthony arrived to plead for Sandersville's innocent civilians, claiming that the murderers were not Georgians, "much less inhabitants of Sandersville or Washington County," according to Miss Mitchell. Hitchcock considered the preacher a "loud talker, vulgar fool," whom Sherman tolerated more than necessary until the woman hustled the clergyman out of the room. Sherman, apparently moved by the earnestness of the lady, reconsidered his harsh reprisal. "I don't war on women and children," he declared. "Houses will not be burned, but the courthouse and stores will."

Sandersville's commercial establishments and the courthouse, an imposing structure built with stuccoed brick in the Greek Revival style, were torched. Civilian lives and homes were respected, but personal possessions were either stolen or vandalized. After Sherman's departure, one resident recorded, "The ground was strewn with food, carpets were drenched with syrup, and then covered with meal."

Connolly was quite impressed with Sandersville. He called it "rather a neat, quiet, thrifty looking county seat of about 500 population." He inspected with interest a white marble monument to Jared Irwin, a former governor and Revolutionary general. The monument had been damaged by gunfire during the skirmish, and at that moment columns of Union soldiers were passing Irwin's grave and former home to the south of town.

One local resident, Mrs. "L. F. J.," was only sixteen. Married at fifteen, a year later she was a war widow, her husband killed fighting in the 1st Georgia Infantry in Virginia, and a new mother. She was living with her mother-in-law in Sandersville when sounds of battle were heard in the distance. Wheeler's skirmish line ended at the young woman's home, and Confederate and Union troops were soon firing volleys at each other. A southern soldier ran into the house and was astonished to find women watching the battle from a window. "For God's sake, ladies," he exclaimed, "go into your cellar! Don't you know those bullets will kill you?"

Lacking a cellar, the women huddled in front of a brick fireplace as "bullets rattled like hailstones against the house," the young woman wrote. Soon a second soldier ran into the house and shouted, "Take care of yourselves, ladies, we'll have to run. . . . Lock your doors; keep inside. If the Yankees come to the doors, unlock them and stand in them. Be sure to ask for a guard. Be polite, and you will not be mistreated, I hope. Good-bye; God bless you ladies."

The troopers ran to their horses and leaped over fences to escape capture, waving their caps at the women in farewell. A short lull ended when half of Sherman's army entered the city—a procession of infantry, herds of animals, and "then the wagons—Oh! the wagons—in every direction— wagons! wagons!"

Soldiers were immediately at the door and in the yard, stealing all their meat, grain, sugar, syrup, then the potatoes, "our last hope for food." For the next two days the stench of garbage permeated Sandersville. Smoke from hundreds of fires obscured houses across the street.

The women were able to obtain a guard, but the family had nothing to eat. On his second day of duty, the young guard heard the baby's wails and kindly inquired, "Why does that baby cry so?"

"He is hungry," Mrs. L. F. J. responded. "I have had nothing which I could eat in two days now, and I cannot nurse him."

The plight of the child-mother and her baby brought tears to the soldier's eyes. "I will be relieved soon," he declared. "I draw my rations this evening, and I will bring them to you," he promised, and did, returning with flour and coffee. At the woman's request, the soldier obtained permission to eat biscuits and coffee with the family. Mrs. L. F. J. recorded, "so a 'Boy in Blue' supped with the widow of a 'Boy in Gray,' right in the midst of the enemy's land, surrounded by the Federal army!"

Sherman dispatched a division to destroy the railroad to Tennille. He had heard further disturbing rumors about the execution of soldiers who fell into enemy hands. Four prisoners had had their throats cut, one report claimed, but two of the slashings had been bungled. Rebels left the men for dead, and they successfully returned to friendly lines. There were additional stories of

"The March to the Sea" (December, 1864) ■ By Herman Melville

Not Kenesaw high-arching,
Nor Allatoona's glen—
Though there the graves lie parching—
Stayed Sherman's miles of men;
From charred Atlanta marching
They launched the sword again.
The columns streamed like rivers
Which in their course agree,
And they streamed until they flashing
Met the flashing of the sea:
It was glorious glad marching,
That marching to the sea.

They brushed the foe before them
(Shall gnats impede the bull?);
Their own good bridges bore them
Over swamps or torrents full,
And the grand pines waving o'er them
Bowed to axes keen and cool.
The columns grooved their channels,
Enforced their own decree,
And their power met nothing larger
Until it met the sea:
It was glorious glad marching,
A marching glad and free.

Kilpatrick's share of riders
In zigzags mazed the land,
Perplexed the pale Southsiders
With feints on every hand;
Vague menace awed the hiders
In forts beyond command.
To Sherman's shifting problem
No foeman knew the key;
But onward went the marching
Unpausing to the sea:
It was glorious glad marching,
The swinging step was free.

The flankers ranged like pigeons
In clouds through field or wood;
The flocks of all those regions,
The herds and horses good,
Poured in and swelled the legions,
For they caught the marching mood.
A volley ahead! They hear it;
And they hear the repartee:
Fighting was but frolic
In that marching to the sea:
It was glorious glad marching,
A marching bold and free.

All nature felt their coming,
The birds like couriers flew,
And the banners brightly blooming
The slaves by thousands drew,
And they marched beside the drumming,
And they joined the armies blue.
The cocks crowed from the cannon
(Pets named from Grant and Lee),
Plumed fighters and campaigners
In that marching to the sea:
It was glorious glad marching,
A marching bold and free.

The foragers through calm lands
Swept in tempest gay,
And they breathed the air of balm-lands—
As who should say them nay?
The regiments uproarious
Laughed in Plenty's glee;
And they marched till their broad laughter
Met the laughter of the sea:
It was glorious glad marching,
That marching to the sea.

The grain of endless acres
Was threshed (as in the East)
By the trampling of the Takers,
Strong march of man and beast;
The flails of those earth-shakers
Left a famine where they ceased.
The arsenals were yielded;
The sword (that was to be),
Arrested in the forging,
Rued that marching to the sea:
It was glorious glad marching,
But ah, the stern decree!

For behind they left a wailing,
A terror and a ban,
And blazing cinders sailing,
And houseless households wan,
Wide zones of counties paling
And towns where maniacs ran.
Was it Treason's retribution—
Necessity the plea?
They will long remember Sherman
And his streaming columns free—
They will long remember Sherman
Marching to the sea. ■

91

other men being killed. "Yet the wives etc., of the men who fight in this devilish way 'demand protection' and get it," Hitchcock wrote angrily.

On November 26 the 14th and 20th Corps, which had taken separate roads from Milledgeville, converged on Sandersville at the same time. Their appearance created a massive jam of infantry, wagons, and artillery, but a royal entrance was still managed with flags flying and bands playing.

In retaliation for the resistance, according to Rufus Mead, for six hours soldiers "completely ransacked the whole town, only left the citizens unmolested. It was done to retaliate for burning the bridge and resistance of the day before. That is Sherman's motto."

Connolly, ever the worrier, was concerned by this show of resistance, however slight. "It behooves us to move cautiously." Rumors this day had the Right Wing at the Ogeechee and encountering stiff opposition. The Confederates were "on the opposite bank, in force," which "may give the whole army considerable trouble to get across." The Ogeechee was expected to be the first Rebel line of defense, and that stream was "said to be a difficult river to cross." On the following day Connolly heard that Confederate General James Longstreet had arrived on the Ogeechee with considerable reinforcements from Virginia.

These beliefs were echoed by Van Duzer, who heard from blacks in Tennille that a place called Sebastopol, twenty miles east along the Ogeechee, was "well fortified." He expected stiff resistance there.

The prospect of action pleased many soldiers. General John Corse, hero of a savage battle at Allatoona a month earlier, told Van Duzer, the "men are not satisfied with going along peacefully through the country." All commanders reported their men fit and "spoiling for a fight." The action in Sandersville was a poor appetizer for these veteran campaigners.

In Tennille, Van Duzer saw several large warehouses, three water tanks, and a "very fine" depot burned. He was impressed by the work his comrades were doing to the rails. "The destruction of this road will be complete," he noted. Twelve miles of road, from the Oconee River to Tennille, were destroyed. Two miles of trestle through the river swamp, plus a long bridge across the river, were burned. Hitchcock believed the line would be useless for four months.

Van Duzer and other telegraph operators occupied their time by tapping lines to listen in on Confederate traffic. In Milledgeville they had contacted Macon, but the Rebel operator was suspicious and refused to communicate with them. At Tennille, Van Duzer learned the name of the local operator and established communications with Confederates in Augusta. Unfortunately, the line was immediately cut by Federal cavalry operating to the north.

The early morning sun on November 27 shone dimly through a thick fog, but the weather turned cloudy and warm. Hitchcock accompanied Sherman on a four-mile journey from Sandersville to Tennille, where they inspected the smoking ruins left from the previous day's activity. A slave had told Sherman that on the 26th cavalry, then infantry, had come to Tennille, burned the depot, torn up and burned the track, then "sot fire to the well!" Sherman wanted to see the well in question. He was amused to discover that it had been a pump shed for a water tank. Sherman learned that Hardee had been present in Tennille the day before.

The officers stopped at a large house beside the tracks, occupied by a number of women without a man in sight. They were "hearty rebels, but not insulting," Hitchcock wrote happily.

Hitchcock and company engaged in yet another verbal clash with the southern ladies. His secret weapon was politely quoting the speeches of Confederate Vice-President Alexander Stephens. That Georgian had opposed secession and was a continual opponent of many Confederate government policies. The husband of one lady was fighting in Virginia, leading Sherman to "comment with some asperity on her husband being there killing our men, while we were called on here to protect his house and family."

Union cavalry brought in recent newspapers that kindled Sherman's anger—this time against the northern press. Sherman had a longstanding feud with newspapers. Early in the war, the press had nearly driven him from the service with reports that he was insane. Sherman had regularly threatened to forbid reporters from accompanying his army. Now he learned that the Savannah and Augusta papers were accurately describing his movements, but the accounts they quoted had been taken from northern newspapers.

"It is abominable," wrote Hitchcock. "So the first definite news the rebs had about this movement was from the Chicago *Times* of November 9th, a week before it commenced." He believed their early success was prompted by the Confederates' being deceived by the Union direction of advance, but now there would be greater resistance. Sherman began to rave about resigning when the present campaign was over. "It's impossible to carry on war with a free press," Hitchcock quoted Sherman, but he dismissed the general's threat to quit as just angry talk.

Sherman's officers were amused by accounts in the latest papers. "The fact that Sherman has been baffled thus far in his attempt to penetrate Georgia has been well known in this city for several days," the Richmond *Enquirer* announced a week after Sherman's occupation of Milledgeville. "He is floundering about now between the rapidly concentrating maneuvers of the state troops and such portions of the regular army as were not otherwise more advantageously employed." They believed additional troops would not be necessary to stop the northern incursion.

The Augusta *Constitutionalist* continued to urge Georgians to resist and cut up the Federal columns. "The opportunity is ours. The hand of God is in it. The blow, if we can give it as it should be given, may end the war. Sherman has many weary miles to march. . . . It is absurdity to talk about his making a winter campaign with no communication with his Government. He is retreating—simply retreating."

The Savannah newspapers predicted Sherman's "utter annihilation" by "an insulted and outraged people," who were urged to wage guerilla warfare. Hundreds of Yankees were straggling, "searching for somebody to take them into custody." Those who refused to surrender should "be beautifully bushwhacked. Let all the old and young folks turn out and give the rascals a taste of Georgia State Sovereignty. This demoralization of our enemy is most providential for us, and ought to stiffen the backbone of the most timid among us." The people were being urged to murder any straggler.

"Favorable grounds exist for checking the advance of Sherman towards Savannah," the Columbus *Daily News* stated, "grounds soft and moist." Georgia's swamps would destroy Sherman as Russia's snow had destroyed Napoleon.

The general's staff ignored the southern rhetoric and ate lunch. They dined on oyster soup and hardtack, which Hitchcock wrote "is *hard*, especially on one's teeth." Veterans of three years' campaigning had yet to master chewing it, he noticed.

Hitchcock camped in a field near Tennille and ruminated on the pleasures of military life. Campaigning has a "fascination . . . for many men: certainly it is full of an independent and vigorous enjoyment." Then he remembered that it was Sunday, and he longed for home. "I think I could have listened with more than patience today to even a dull sermon; and how dear the memory of Sabbath rest and quiet at home!"

On the following day, Sherman and his entourage joined the Right Wing for the final push on Savannah. ■

CHAPTER 8

"You May Hang and Mutilate Man for Man"

While Sherman toured Tennille, a division of the 14th Corps was carrying out orders to protect Kilpatrick's flank by advancing to Fenn's Bridge on the Ogeechee, twelve miles above the railroad crossing.

Connolly accompanied General Absalom Baird's division on this maneuver, which began at daylight on November 27. Close to the Ogeechee River, Connolly found "the country growing better; more land cultivated, soil more productive, and plantations larger." The men gathered persimmons, which grew in great abundance beside the road, and ate their fill. He compared their taste to "excellent figs."

Connolly realized he had not seen a bit of hay in this region. Forage for animals consisted of corn silk, picked when green, cured in the sun, tied in bundles, and stored in the field or barns for winter feed. Cattle seemed to find it delicious, but the diet seemed poor in nutrition to a man from a region where hay was a vital crop.

There were recent signs of cavalry traffic all along the road. As the Federals neared the river, regiments were deployed in a strong skirmish line and crept forward cautiously. Connolly rode to the front, "watching every tree and stump, listening very intently, and moving as quietly as a cat in the sandy road, expecting every moment to hear the crack of a rifle from some concealed rebel; at such a moment the excitement is so intense that all thoughts of personal safety are forgotten, the sense of sight and hearing are extraordinarily acute, but they take no notice of anything passing, being intent alone on discovering the enemy before he discovers you." Even the Major's horse, named Frank, was caught up in the anxious excitement, "his ears erect as if he too were looking for the graybacks."

The soldiers rounded a bend in the road and were pleasantly surprised by the sight that greeted them. "'Fenn's Bridge,' a long frame structure . . . not a plank disturbed and not a rebel in sight. . . . we hesitate a moment to assure ourselves that we are not mistaken, then at once and with a shout put spurs to our horses, dash ahead of the line of skirmishers, cross the bridge the first ones, and send our orderly back on a gallop to the General to inform him that 'Fenn's Bridge' is all right and we are across the Ogeechee."

Connolly was pleased, but puzzled, to find this important bridge intact and the army on the eastern bank of the river without a shot being fired. The mystery was solved by a woman toll collector who lived beside the river. She told Connolly that a large force of Confederates had crossed the bridge from east to west. They turned south to destroy what they expected to be the main Federal target, the Ogeechee bridge between Sandersville and Louisville. They had intended to return at dark to burn this bridge, but the Federals arrived first. Connolly said they "saved them that trouble by . . . burning it ourselves."

Without the bridge, the Federals would have spent a day spanning the river; they had expected to do so. Connolly believed, "We could not have built one at all if there had been a regiment of rebels on the east bank to oppose us." Their unexpected success ensured "the passage of the whole army across the river, for we can just sweep down the east bank and clear the way for those who are trying to cross lower down." If any defense had been planned farther south on the Ogeechee, it had just been flanked.

Connolly's division burned a bridge to the north, over Rocky Comfort Creek, and camped six miles from Louisville on the Wilkinson plantation. The land became more productive, the "weather warm as summer in the North," and the reddish hue to the sandy roads reminded him of New Jersey. At one point he helped chase a Confederate horseman who escaped by bounding into the woods.

Connolly's journal omits a day, but presumably he passed through Louisville. The remainder of the 14th Corps, and the 20th, traveled eighteen miles through Washington County on November 27. They destroyed a factory and five hundred bales of cotton and thoroughly wrecked the railroad from Tennille to Davisboro, which they left in ruin. On the following day, the Left Wing advanced to within a mile of Louisville, but was delayed by the burning of eight bridges over the Ogeechee River and its tributaries. The destruction had probably been accomplished by the Confederate cavalry that had crossed at Fenn's Bridge earlier, but the Federals convinced themselves that the citizens of Louisville were responsible.

Spanning the river with pontoons and corduroy roads through the swamps beside the smaller bridges required several hours. As a result, Union cavalry and infantry skirmishers, minus most of their officers, entered Louisville ahead of the main column. Most became bummers and enjoyed half a day of freebootery. A Minnesota soldier admitted in a letter to his wife that many of his comrades had broken into homes and "got Silver Pitchers & Plate of considerable value."

The worst event for the townspeople was a fire that started in a home on Broad Street. The conflagration spread, consuming half the avenue before Federal officers arrived and ordered men to create a firewall by demolishing a warehouse. One officer vainly attempted to identify the perpetrators, swearing, "I am getting ashamed to see such outrage committed." He made up his mind "to shoot the first scoundrel whom I may catch."

Infantry file over a footbridge while wagons cross a pontoon span as the Left Wing breaches the Ogeechee River barrier.
[HARPER'S WEEKLY]

Isolating the reason—if any existed—for the wanton destruction was difficult. One source indicated that the Federals were angered by a Broad Street establishment that defiantly flew the Confederate flag. There also were rumors that local women had made clothing for President Davis and Vice-President Stephens. Some Federal soldiers reported that they were simply responding to Confederates who sniped at them from homes and businesses, but there was no evidence of Rebel resistance in Louisville.

Crossing the river on bridge timbers that still smouldered, W. C. Johnson and others camped near Louisville. He found it a tidy community of one thousand, "with quite a number of stores of different kinds, all fairly stocked with goods. The delay in laying the pontoons, and getting trains and troops over, gave our boys ample time to go through the town, which, unfortunately for the inhabitants, they did most completely; everything was appropriated that could be used, and many things that could not be used. The town was thoroughly and completely ransacked, and by some unaccountable means, late in the afternoon, the town caught fire and was completely destroyed."

On November 27 a portion of the 14th was dispatched southeast to Grange. They were to round up all the horses and mules they could find, choose the strongest for their own use, and shoot the remainder. Over eighty animals were destroyed.

Two divisions of the 20th Corps ruined the railroad from Davisboro to Bartow. On November 29 the divisions broke up the rails through Wadley to the Ogeechee, at Sebastopol, where Rebel resistance had been expected before the position was flanked. The rail and passenger bridges had been burned by Confederate cavalry.

At Bostick on November 29, the Federals found two sawmills and two million feet of cut lumber. The wood was for the Confederate army and would have been transported north for use in Hood's campaign in Tennessee. They also found thousands of pegs meant to fasten the timbers together. The wood made a most satisfying bonfire. The soldiers wrecked the mill dam and fired a bridge just as two groups of foragers appeared on the opposite side of the stream. After the mounted raiders dashed over the burning bridge to safety just before the span plunged into the water, the divisions turned north and rejoined the wing near Louisville.

While Confederate resistance against the Left Wing could not be called strong, it was becoming vindictive. Rebel forces had seen massive destruction in Sherman's wake, and they realized that the people of Georgia would know hunger in the coming winter. The Federals had burned dozens of houses, and rumors of raped and murdered citizens were circulating. Mounted Georgia Militia, squads of irregulars, deserters, and some of Wheeler's men decided to exact retribution upon any Yankee who wandered away from his unit.

Near Davisboro on November 28, Confederate cavalry dashed out of the woods and fired several rounds at a Union column. They captured four Federals, then rode quickly away. The four men were never heard from again. The Yankees formed a skirmish line and loaded their weapons for the first time since leaving Atlanta.

On the fog-bound night of November 29, three men of the 14th Corps were captured and immediately shot. There was no doubt they had been deliberately executed after surrender; their hair and clothes were singed from burning gunpowder.

Since leaving Sandersville, the 14th Corps had been pestered by small units of Rebel cavalry. The corps, which guarded the exposed northern flank of the wing, deployed three Illinois regiments to drive the enemy from their rear. The determined Rebels charged the advancing infantry, but retreated after heavy skirmishing to a two-hundred-yard-long barricade. The Union troops stormed over the works and drove the Confederates from the vicinity, losing two men killed in the action. They recovered the bodies of the dead men and rescued a small group of foragers, who would likely have met the same fate.

Kilpatrick had encountered similar atrocities on his recent raid. On November 30 he wrote Sherman for permission to keep as hostages several Rebel officers he had captured. He reported a number of his men had been killed after surrendering, their bodies mutilated and throats slashed. He wished to retaliate against further such occurrences and requested clearance to communicate his intentions to Wheeler.

Sherman replied on the following day. He informed Kilpatrick that he could retain the prisoners. Under a flag of truce, he was to inform Wheeler of the consequences of additional murders. Sherman warned Kilpatrick, "You must be very careful as to the correctness of any information you may receive about the enemy murdering or mutilating our men," but, "when our men are found, and you are full convinced the enemy have killed them after surrender in fair battle, or have mutilated their bodies . . . you may hang and mutilate man for man without regard for rank."

Mrs. Nora M. Canning and her husband had left their home in Macon after Atlanta had fallen, expecting to find safety in the isolation of their

Ogeechee swamp plantation near Louisville. For days they heard "of Kilpatrick's cavalry all around us, and seen the heavens illuminated at night with the glare of burning gin-houses and other buildings. We could hear of houses being pillaged and old men being beaten almost to death to be made to tell where their money and treasures were concealed."

As the couple waited anxiously for raiders to appear, they hid the stock and buried food. Several quiet days passed before the enemy arrived from every quarter. "One could not look in any direction without seeing them."

Believing a Confederate soldier was hidden on the premises, the Federals searched everything in the house, including bureau drawers and a clock. "Sir," Mrs. Canning ventured at this absurdity, "there is one place in the room you have not looked into." "Where is it?" the Yankee demanded, taking the bait. "I pointed to a small pill box on the mantel, and asked him if the Confederate soldier might not be hidden in that. He turned away with a curse upon all the Rebel women."

Outside, the ginhouse, two hundred bales of cotton, and several hundred bushels of wheat were destroyed. "Well, madam," said a raider, "how do you like the looks of our little fire? We have seen a great many such, within the last few weeks."

"I had grown desperate," Canning wrote, "and I told him I didn't care. I was thankful that not a lock of that cotton would ever feed a Yankee factory or clothe a Yankee soldier's back.

Streams in middle Georgia were once spanned by iron bridges like this one.

Soldiers wreck the imposing railroad bridge over the Ogeechee River.
[LESLIE'S ILLUSTRATED]

"He turned with an oath, and left me."

Several soldiers had taken Mrs. Canning's husband, an "old and feeble" man, into the swamp to point out the location of buried syrup. He returned several hours later perched on a mule, a soldier on either side holding him erect. When the soldiers brought him into the house, he begged his wife to give them his watch. "Why?" she asked. "They have no business with your watch."

"Give it to them," he gasped, "and let them go. I am almost dead."

Taking every valuable object in the house, the soldiers left. Mr. Canning was faint, which his wife initially thought was the result of fatigue. "Imagine my horror, therefore," she continued, "when he revived sufficiently to talk, to hear that the fiends had taken him to the swamp and hanged him."

Two miles into the swamp they had taken Canning off the mule and had demanded, "Now, old man, you have got to tell us where your gold is hidden."

Mr. Canning explained that he had no gold and that he and his wife had come for a short visit from Macon, where his valuables were stored in a bank. "They cursed him and told him that story would not do," Mrs. Canning wrote, "that his wife had gone up to Macon and brought it all down, for a Negro man had told them she had brought a trunkfull of gold and silver down there, and that he could scarcely lift the trunk, it was so heavy."

They asked again where the gold was hidden, and Canning denied he had any. "They then took him to a tree that bent over the path, tied a rope around his neck, threw it over a projecting limb, and drew him up until his feet were off the ground. He did not quite lose consciousness, when they let him down and said, 'Now where is your gold?'"

Canning repeated his account—the truth—and one Yankee cried, "We will make you tell another story before we are done with you. So pull him up again boys!" Then hanged the elderly man until he lost consciousness, then lowered him and viciously demanded, "Now tell us where that gold is or we will kill you, and your wife will never know what has become of you."

"I have told you the truth," Canning replied, "I have no gold. I am an old man and at your mercy. If you want to kill me you have the power to do it, but I cannot die with a lie on my lips. I have no gold. I have a gold watch at the house, but nothing else."

The leader of the Federal squad refused to believe him. "Swing the old Rebel up again!" the soldier demanded. He was lifted off his feet by the rope and allowed to fall back heavily to the ground. Canning lost consciousness and came to beside a stream, where a soldier was bathing him with water. He overheard one say, "We like to have carried that game too far."

Mrs. Canning gave the men the watch and some silver she had buried, explaining, "They threatened to kill me if I did not tell. They even threatened to burn the house down if I kept back anything.

"Oh! the horrors of that night! None but God will ever know what I suffered. There my husband lay with scorching fever, his tongue parched and swollen and his throat dry and sore. He begged for water and there was not a drop to be had. The Yankees had cut all the well ropes and stolen the buckets and there was no water nearer than half a mile."

In the morning a rough soldier from Iowa appeared and asked if he could help. He located a bucket, brought water, and left some coffee and sugar. When the house was swarmed by more soldiers, the Good Samaritan went to the fields and brought potatoes in for the family. For this deed he was subjected to the jeers of other soldiers who called him "Old Secesh."

The family's troubles were not yet ended. Several men were convinced that Mr. Canning was faking his illness to conceal treasure, and they threatened to pull him out of the bed. "Is there no one in this crowd of men who will protect this sick man and prevent his being killed!" Mrs. Canning cried. A young man from New York stepped forward and announced that "the first man that touched either my husband or myself would do it at the risk of his life."

At that moment a man arrived on horseback and announced that he would burn the house. Mrs. Canning's husband was a Mason, and she appealed for a brother Mason to protect them. "We have none of those animals with us!" thundered the would-be arsonist. The soldier from New York announced that his officer was a Mason, and he gave his gun to the Iowan with instructions to "knock down the first man that dared to touch" the couple.

A colonel soon appeared and cleared the house. He sent for coffee, sugar,

Union infantry skirmish with Wheeler's troops in Sandersville. Because of the resistance, Sherman ordered the courthouse and commercial buildings torched. [HARPER'S WEEKLY]

rice, beef, and flour, and apologized for the trouble. The bummers, he explained, "were not representives of the army." A number of officers visited over the next several days. One said the destruction in Georgia was nothing compared to what would occur in their next target.

"God pity the people of South Carolina when this army gets there," he said, "for we have orders to lay everything in ashes—not to leave a green thing in the State for man or beast. That State will be made to feel the fearful sin of Secession before our army gets through it. Here our soldiers were held in check, as much so as it is possible with such a large body of men, and when we get to South Carolina they will be turned loose to follow their own inclinations."

The Left Wing finally moved on, leaving the countryside in abject ruin. The local black population had been treated as poorly as the plantation owners. The Cannings had distributed a month's rations to their one hundred slaves, but that had been stolen. One servant approached Mrs. Canning and told a horrifying story. She had buried a child a week earlier. Seeing a fresh grave in the cemetery, the Yankees dug into it and found a tiny coffin. Disappointed by the lack of booty, they left the body on the ground, where the mother later found hogs rooting at it. ■

CHAPTER 9

"A Calvary Fight Is Just About as Much Fun as a Fox Hunt"

After withdrawing from Sandersville on November 16, Wheeler received word from his pickets that Kilpatrick's command, five thousand horsemen strong, had left the main Union column and was rapidly riding toward Augusta. Wheeler was fully aware of Augusta's importance to the Confederate effort—most southern gunpowder and weapons of every sort were manufactured there and transported directly by railroad to Lee in Virginia. Considering the loss of Atlanta's munitions-producing capacity, Augusta's destruction could prove fatal to the Rebels. The Confederate cavalry chief left small contingents of cavalry under General Alfred Iverson to observe Sherman's movements, and took two thousand troopers to intercept Kilpatrick.

Kilpatrick's men had maneuvered far to the north, briefly occupying Greensboro and Gibson on November 20. They destroyed mills and commercial establishments but did not molest several Confederate hospitals. The raiders continued to Ogeechee Shoals near Warrenton and burned several additional mills. Here Confederate pickets discovered them and relayed their direction of march to Wheeler.

Finding Kilpatrick encamped near Sylvan Grove early on the morning of November 27, Wheeler rudely interrupted his sleep and scattered the Federals. He captured prisoners, flags, and eight hundred horses. Kilpatrick, spending the night in a nearby house, apparently with female company, ran half dressed to his horse and executed a harrowing escape highlighted by leaping fences to distance himself from pursuing gray troopers. Wheeler claimed Kilpatrick "escaped bareheaded, leaving his hat in our hands."

By daylight Kilpatrick gathered his scattered command, but the nightmare continued. Wheeler's men swarmed against the Yanks, driving them from successive lines of hastily thrown-up barricades. Throughout the day Confederate and Federal cavalry galloped in charge and countercharge, swords clanging and pistols cracking. Kilpatrick stopped to torch every house, crib, gin, and barn along the way, and Wheeler reported that his command managed to extinguish half the blazes. Kilpatrick finally reached Waynesboro and hastily fired the town, but Wheeler drove him out and extinguished the flames. As the running battle wore down, Wheeler claimed to have inflicted two hundred casualties on the Federals.

Wheeler harassed the Yankees during the night, keeping their exhausted horses on the move and denying the men precious rest. At dawn Kilpatrick's command was surrounded by the untiring Rebels, and Wheeler personally led a charge against Kilpatrick's front. However, because of the dense fog, the Federals escaped.

Wheeler found the enemy drawn up in another defensive position three miles south. Barricades were thrown up in front of the Yankees, and open fields protected their flanks. The determined Confederate general summoned a dozen buglers to the front, ordering them to blow with Gabriel's breath. Charging Kilpatrick's barricades, the ragged Rebel cavalrymen endured the intense fire of Federal repeating rifles and sailed their horses over the barricades to rout the Yanks and inflict three hundred additional casualties.

Kilpatrick raced his disorganized command two miles farther south and crossed Buckhead Creek, destroying the bridge in their wake. Finding his rapid pursuit rudely halted by fire from yet another barricade, this one erected across the creek, Wheeler stopped to reorganize his winded men. Rough estimates give Wheeler 1,800 men at this point in the conflict, and Kilpatrick 3,700.

Wheeler crossed his men above and below the ruined bridge and flanked Kilpatrick out of his barricades, then repaired the bridge with pews from Buckhead Church. Resuming the chase, they located Kilpatrick barricaded at Reynolds farm, near one of Sherman's infantry camps. Kilpatrick felt safe for the first time in three days, but his security proved to be false. Wheeler studied the enemy camp, analyzing the situation for further action, and finally attacked from two directions across a mile-wide field, but without the bugle clamor of earlier charges. All twelve buglers had been lost: killed, wounded, or afoot when their mounts were shot from under them. Federal cavalry rapidly discharged their seven-shot rifles, and a Union battery added to the din. Wheeler was repulsed, but he soon returned and recklessly hurled his command against a weak point of the Federal defense. Kilpatrick reeled again, losing men, horses, mules, arms, and equipment; and his troopers stumbled into the Union infantry camp near Louisville, exhausted, demoralized, and completely whipped.

Kilpatrick mildly recorded, "I deemed it prudent to return within supporting distance of our infantry. . . . I fell back under the most difficult circumstances, but successfully and with slight loss." He informed Sherman that after a determined battle, he had beaten off Wheeler's cavalry and had inflicted six hundred casualties. Wheeler reported that he had stampeded Kilpatrick's entire force, and proudly wrote, "The rout was complete."

This is a rare instance in which Federal sources concur with Confederate claims. Major Connolly was with General Baird's infantry division when one of Kilpatrick's officers stumbled in, desperately seeking assistance for the cavalry. The officer was "very much excited," Connolly wrote. "He told me in broken sentences that they had been fighting day and night for the past three days; that Wheeler's cavalry was all around them with a vastly superior force; that they were out of ammunition, and men and horses were utterly worn out; that Kilpatrick didn't know where our infantry was but had started him off at midnight last night to try and make his way to some infantry column and beg for support or they would all be lost."

Connolly was suspicious of Kilpatrick's "stories of hard fighting," but he roused Baird, and a brigade was sent to bail out Kilpatrick. Starting before daybreak without breakfast, they marched five miles before they heard the sound of skirmishing. They formed a line of battle and soon, Connolly reported, "Kilpatrick's jaded cavalry hove in sight, skirmishing with Wheeler and retiring before him; but when they saw the line of blue coated infantry drawn up in line across the road, and extending off into the woods on either side, they knew that they were saved, and sent up such shouts as never before were heard in these 'Piney Woods' which our infantry responded to with right good will."

At the approach of strong infantry reinforcements, Wheeler, in Connolly's words, "taking the hint, prudently refrained from pursuing any farther, and quietly withdrew; while Kilpatrick moved in near our camp and went into camp," which, Wheeler claimed, "he did not again forsake during the campaign." Hurrying to reinforce Augusta, Bragg asked Wheeler to "thank your gallant old command in my name for their brilliant services."

In his report of the action, Wheeler lavished praise on his men. "Nothing could have exceeded the gallantry with which these troops responded to the bugle's call," he wrote, "and hurled themselves upon the enemy, driving his cavalry in confusion. . . . This so terrified the enemy as to cause him to flee in uncontrolled confusion."

The Union cavalry was subjected to intense verbal abuse from the foot soldiers. They resented the privileged status of this highly vaunted corps,

The War Child ■ Joseph Wheeler

[LIBRARY OF CONGRESS]

The short history of the Confederacy produced many able and flamboyant cavalry leaders, and Wheeler ranks with J.E.B. Stuart and Nathan Bedford Forrest. Wheeler, a self-professed "War Child," fought in an incredible 127 battles and skirmishes and suffered 3 wounds. Sixteen horses bearing him in combat were killed. The attrition rate among his staff officers was legendary; eight were killed and thirty-two wounded.

The diminutive warrior—he was only five feet, five inches in height and weighed 120 pounds—commanded the Army of Tennessee's cavalry in all its major campaigns, which made him the country's acknowledged expert in covering retreats. His most important role was harassing the Federal March to the Sea, which he accomplished with such vigor that Jefferson Davis praised him for constricting Sherman's area of destruction. At war's end Wheeler was arrested near Conyers and served a month in prison.

After the Civil War, Wheeler entered private business, then won eight terms to the United States House of Representatives. When the Spanish-American War broke out, Wheeler joined the United States Army and led a division of cavalry against the Spanish in Cuba. His service became the symbol of a reunited nation and fulfilled Sherman's belief that if America fought a foreign nation, "Joseph Wheeler is the man to command the cavalry of our army."

Wheeler retired as a brigadier general in the U.S. Army. He died in Brooklyn in 1906 and was buried with full military honors in Arlington Cemetery. ■

particularly when they had been called upon to save the troopers from their own folly. Connolly later wrote that the horse soldiers only got in the way of fighting men. "Confound the cavalry," he swore. "They're good for nothing but to run down horses and steal chickens." He added, "In case we meet with a large force and serious opposition our cavalry won't help us much, for they act as if they thought the infantry was along for the purpose of doing all the fighting."

Kilpatrick explained that he failed to reach the prison camp at Millen because the Georgia Militia chased him away. He did discover that the prisoners had been removed. He reported abundant forage near Waynesboro but warned that Wheeler would destroy it and fell timbers to obstruct the roads. Connolly liked the situation. "If they do this they will seriously annoy us, but as the enemy are still under the impression that Sherman first intends to take Augusta, before moving on Savannah, they may do most of their timber-chopping on the roads leading to Augusta, leaving the roads to Savannah comparatively clear."

That night runaway slaves who had camped near the division put on a dance that Connolly found "highly amusing. The dress, general appearance, action, laughter, music, and dancing of the genuine plantation negro is far more grotesque and mirth-provoking than the broadest caricatures of 'Christy's Minstrels.' They require neither fiddle nor banjo to make music . . . and the dancers need no prompter, but kick, caper, and shuffle in the complicated and grotesque manner their respective fancies can invent, while all who are not actually engaged as dancers stand in a ring around the dancers, clapping their hands, stamping their feet, swinging their bodies, and singing as loud and as fast and furious" as was humanly possible. When the

Kill Cavalry ■ Hugh Judson Kilpatrick

No matter how hard they tried, Union cavalry leaders simply could not match the dashing figures cut by their Confederate counterparts, but Kilpatrick certainly tried. Part of the West Point class of 1861, which graduated early because of Fort Sumter's bombardment, Kilpatrick saw immediate action and was wounded before the battle of First Manassas was fought.

Kilpatrick joined the cavalry and led a famous raid on Richmond in February 1864 that failed in its objective of piercing the city's defenses to liberate Union soldiers in Libby Prison.

Sent west to lead Sherman's cavalry to Atlanta, Kilpatrick was wounded at Resaca and went home to recuperate. He returned to lead a failed raid on southern railroads south of Atlanta, then successfully commanded Sherman's cavalry on the campaign to Savannah.

Kilpatrick became extremely unpopular with the Union infantry. He was obnoxious, boastful, and a womanizer. Fittingly, he loved to participate in amateur theater. He gained the nickname Kill-Cav for impetuous attacks against Confederate forces and for long marches that fatigued troopers and their mounts.

After the war, Kilpatrick was appointed U.S. Minister to Chile, where he died in 1881. ■

[HARPER'S WEEKLY]

evening was over, Connolly's head and sides were hurting from laughter. It was one of the more pleasant aspects of "soldier life," he added.

Several quiet days passed near Louisville, as Kilpatrick "remained in camp resting the men and horses for the first time during the march," he reported. On December 1 Sherman ordered Kilpatrick to resume his feint on Augusta. He was to occupy Wheeler and to burn several bridges north of Waynesboro, with Baird's division accompanying the cavalry as a much appreciated support. Kilpatrick welcomed the opportunity to salvage his reputation, and on December 2 they set out on the mission from camps at Birdsville and Buckhead Creek.

Connolly was unhappy about being in the army's vanguard. "Sherman don't know what is at Augusta," he worried. "A rebel army of 50,000 men may be on us before daylight tomorrow." He did not relish the thought of being captured but was resigned to the mission. He wrote, "It will probably all turn out right. The whole campaign is an experiment—nothing more."

Bragg, commanding the sparse Confederate forces in Augusta, sent urgent word for Wheeler to gather up his scattered command and drive "back upon their infantry the enemy's cavalry, now apparently pressing in this direction." This complemented orders he had received on November 29 from General Hardee, who reported that the roads to Savannah had been obstructed. Wheeler was to "operate on the flank and rear of the enemy" to hinder Sherman's advance, and Wheeler hurried to comply.

On the March, Connolly noted that "so many cavalry in line in an open plain make a beautiful sight. But it's all *show;* there's not much *fight* in them."

Heavy skirmishing developed near Rocky Creek as Wheeler claimed to have forced the Federals to alter course at Rock Springs Church. Connolly nervously felt the resistance was due to a "largely increased" Confederate presence, which troubled him. The infantry advanced behind and on both flanks of the cavalry, who were in high spirits. They "well knew they could easily whip all the rebel cavalry Wheeler ever commanded. . . . Still we knew there might be a strong force of infantry and artillery on the east side of this creek." They were afraid that Wheeler might be luring them into a trap.

The army hauled in several characters during the day. One, a slave named Jerry, "a lively, rollicking, fun loving fellow," found a horse and accompanied Connolly and General Baird. Abruptly, Jerry started laughing loudly. He turned to the General and said, "Golly, I wish old master could see me now, riding with the Generals." They also found a rarity, a young white man. He was being questioned when skirmishers opened fire. The man fell to the ground and started shouting, "Oh, take me away, take me away; I can't stand it!" much to the amusement of the Union veterans. A wounded Texan who was captured informed the Federals that everyone knew the Yankees were heading for Augusta, and the Confederates had no men with which to stop them.

Connolly, always an expert observer and commentator, had been a peanut aficionado as a child and had wondered where peanuts originated. He was fascinated by the opportunity to examine the soil that produced the delicacy.

For protection that night, Connolly ringed the camp with three hundred pickets. He found Baird in a very bad humor. "It arises, I think, from the possible difficulties and dangers of our isolated position." One Union soldier reported, "Johnnies were pretty thick around us."

The running skirmish continued on December 3. The infantry tore up two miles of track, piled the ties for a bonfire, and proceeded to heat and twist the rails into useless hunks of iron. They found the road heavily obstructed by felled timber.

In his official report for December 3, Baird made another indictment against Kilpatrick's men. "The cavalry will not move one inch toward the enemy in advance of my column, and I have to go with it in order to accomplish what is necessary to be done."

That night the Federals camped at Thomas Station, which consisted of "a water tank, and an overseer's house, surrounded by about 20 white washed negro houses," Connolly wrote. At midnight Wheeler insisted on disturbing their rest by firing two guns. One was wrestled to the top of the railroad embankment and discharged at the Federal fires. The camp was rousted and the men searched for the Confederates, but nothing was found and the soldiers returned to bed at 2:00 A.M. in "bad humor." Another Yank acknowledged that the Confederate night "music was not being conducive to sound slumber."

Baird and Kilpatrick received orders from Sherman to press on to Brier Creek, beyond Waynesboro. At daybreak on December 4, Kilpatrick formed his cavalry division into a line that stretched across open fields; two infantry brigades formed immediately behind them, for *moral support,* Connolly waggishly announced. "Our cavalry all the time knew that there was no chance of their being whipped," he added.

At 7:00 A.M. the Federals advanced, determinedly driving Wheeler's skirmishers from several lines of prepared barricades. Wheeler gathered his men behind a final barrier and poured a deadly fire into the advancing enemy. The Union cavalry leaped the logs and shot, slashed, and captured Rebels. After a stubborn resistance that lasted half an hour, Wheeler saw that his position was about to be overrun and ordered a general retreat. The Confederates hitched their artillery, mounted up, and hurried beyond Brier Creek, eight miles north, without offering further resistance. A Federal acknowledged their own loss had been "quite heavy," but he saw many dead and wounded Rebels lying about, and one hundred had been captured. Kilpatrick counted his losses at two hundred and believed he had inflicted five hundred casualties on Wheeler. The Rebels left twenty-three dead and forty-one wounded on the field.

Attempting to paint this climactic engagement as a noble battle, Wheeler described a small band of Confederates fighting valiantly against overwhelming odds and retreating in order when threatened with encirclement. When the five-hour skirmish climaxed, however, his men had unarguably fled, and Connolly claimed this departure was at an "ingloriously rapid rate."

Connolly emphasized that Kilpatrick "did all the fighting and whipped Wheeler soundly." Kilpatrick was "full of fun and frolic and he was in excellent spirits all day, for Wheeler and he were classmates at West Point, and he was elated at the idea of whipping his classmate. A cavalry fight is just

Sluggish Buckhead Creek, where Confederate and Union cavalry fought fiercely.

just about as much fun as a fox hunt; but, of course, in the midst of the fun somebody is getting hurt all the time. But it is by no means the serious work that infantry fighting is."

Kilpatrick claimed that Wheeler would never bother the Federals again, but that was an empty boast. In reality, the Confederate general harassed the Union column as it turned to rejoin the 14th Corps near Jacksonboro. The Confederates continued to clash with the Federal rearguard until it approached Savannah, and, according to Union accounts, on several occasions Kilpatrick again availed himself of infantry assistance.

During the battle, a wounded Federal captain was captured by the Rebels. Later that day Kilpatrick sent a letter through the lines asking his friend Wheeler to allow the courier to attend the officer. "Please show him such attention as is in your power and at some future day you shall have the thanks of your old friend," Kilpatrick wrote.

Although the officer later died, Wheeler assured Kilpatrick that the man was receiving the best possible care. The southern cavalry chief used the message as a bully pulpit, explaining that he had gone to extreme lengths to impart "principles of chivalry and true soldierly honor" to his men. He accused his old classmate of regularly committing brutal, barbarous atrocities against a helpless civilian population.

After three hours of destructive work, the Federals withdrew from Waynesboro on the afternoon of December 4, closing, Connolly noted, "all demonstrations against Augusta. We have kept up the delusion of an attack on that place as long as we can, and with the sunlight of tomorrow the true design of our campaign will break upon the bewildered minds of the rebels."

He was quite concerned that a gap of one hundred miles separated them from Sherman's southernmost columns. "Tomorrow morning we commence closing up as rapidly as possible," a prospect that pleased the entire division. Sherman had correctly discounted the notion that Bragg would leave Augusta to attack the isolated force.

The column marched to Alexander, a village of three houses, and camped on a direct road from Augusta to Savannah. They had covered twenty miles during the day.

The feint on Augusta had been an unqualified success. Bragg had assembled ten thousand men from Georgia and the Carolinas to meet the threat, preventing them from obstructing Sherman's true route. The Confederate general remained in the city until he was certain that Savannah was the real goal of the Union army, then his troops were entrained for Savannah via Charleston. The maneuver had also slowed production in Augusta's vital war industries. A Confederate newspaper reported that the "powder works, arsenal, armories, and machine shops" had been dismantled and moved to safety. ■

CHAPTER 10

"It Made My Heart Ache"

While the cavalry fought for domination, the remainder of the Left Wing continued to march a few miles to the south. The 20th Corps, accompanied by Slocum's headquarters, passed through Birdsville from Louisville on December 2 and camped at the church beside Buckhead Creek. The remainder of the 14th Corps marched north of and parallel to the 20th.

The bridge across Buckhead Creek had been destroyed by some Alabama cavalry who stayed to fire a few shots at the Union advance. When the Federals unleashed a heavy return fire, they dashed away to burn the bridges over Beaver Dam Creek and Ebenezer Creek, which would seriously impede the 14th Corps. To this point, Slocum's biggest concern had been the wastage of ammunition by foragers shooting livestock and poultry. He levied a fifty-cent fine for each unnecessary cartridge fired.

At Buckhead Slocum heard of a local planter named Bullard who had zealously recaptured escaped Union prisoners for the Confederates. Troops were dispatched to burn his cribs, gins, press, and a warehouse containing fifty thousand dollars worth of cotton. If he persisted in his evil ways, Bullard was warned, the Federals would return and torch his house.

On December 3 Slocum reached a long-awaited objective—the prisoner of war camp located five miles above Millen. Unfortunately, it was empty.

The camp had come into existence after Andersonville proved to be a deathtrap. By mid-summer 1864, it had become obvious that a better site was needed. General John D. Winder, in charge of Confederate prison camps, directed two captains, D. W. Vowles and W. S. Widner, to select a place as far as possible from military activity.

The site near Millen was soon chosen. Its location in eastern Georgia guaranteed a mild climate, and the great pine forests would supply wood for a stockade and other needs. The site was located on the railroad line, which made for easy transportation of prisoners. Few places in the South would seem to have less military importance, and, best of all, a massive spring nearby issued nine million gallons of pure water daily. Lack of clean water had been a primary reason for Andersonville's notorious death rate.

An enormous stockade—1,329 by 1,390 feet—was quickly constructed by a force of 300 prisoners and 500 slaves. They used twelve- to fifteen-foot

A fanciful depiction of the interior of Camp Lawton, near Millen. [HARPER'S WEEKLY]

Georgia pine timbers, sinking then into the earth with seven feet of timber protruding and fastening them with iron bands. Atop the wall at fifty-yard intervals were sentry boxes. The forty-two enclosed acres made Camp Lawton the largest prison in the world. Designed to contain forty thousand prisoners, it would provide each man with forty-four square feet of space. A hospital, barracks for 350 guards, and large ovens made of brick transported from Macon were built. On high ground surrounding the prison, three extensive earthen forts were excavated and armed with eleven cannon from Andersonville to prevent escapes. The cannon were manned by the Florida Light Artillery.

By late October, Lawton contained 10,229 prisoners, its largest complement. An estimated seven hundred died of disease, exposure, and malnutrition.

Lawton's commander, Captain Vowles, ran a more humane prison than had been possible at Andersonville. Few, if any, prisoners were shot for venturing past a dead line, which was marked by light rails thirty feet from the stockade wall. Vowles allowed the soldiers to hold a mock presidential election just weeks before the camp was abandoned. He had hoped they would choose George McClellan, a peace candidate, but Lincoln was favored in a landslide.

On November 22, just 113 days after construction began on the prison, it was evacuated at Sherman's advance. The Federal soldiers were sent by rail to Savannah, then the enlisted men were dispatched south on the Savannah and Gulf Railroad to improvised prisons at Blackshear and Thomasville, Georgia. The officers were removed to South Carolina. Most of the men were soon back at Andersonville.

Slocum's 20th Corps raced to enter the stockade, but his men were severely disappointed to find the prisoners—in many cases comrades and relatives—gone. Their disappointment turned to rage when they saw the conditions within the prison pen. There were few huts in the compound to shelter the prisoners, and most of the men apparently had lived in crude, filthy holes they grubbed out of the bare earth.

"It made my heart ache," wrote Chaplain Bradley, "miserable hovels barely fit for swine." In a shed he examined seven sets of punishment stocks, which "appeared to be well worn." He heard shaken men "muttering loud curses on Jeff Davis and his murderous crew." Previously, Bradley had dismissed accounts of brutality toward Union prisoners, but this seemed positive proof. General John Geary agreed, calling the "foul and fetid prison" evidence that "the worst suffering of our prisoners at Andersonville [and] at Millen, were by no means exaggerated." Worst of all the sights was a long, freshly filled pit with a board that read, "650 Buried Here." Three corpses found in the huts were lovingly buried.

"Everyone who visited this place," ventured one officer, "came away with a feeling of harshness toward the Southern Confederacy he had never felt before."

The stockade at Camp Lawton, with sentry boxes placed at fifty-yard intervals.
[HARPER'S WEEKLY]

Officers and enlisted men alike were fascinated by the destruction of Millen's fine depot. [HARPER'S WEEKLY]

John Patter searched for keepsakes in the prison, but found the compound "the barest spot I ever saw. The trees and stumps and roots to the smallest fiber had been dug out for fuel; not a rag or a button or even a chip could be found." The atmosphere within the prison seemed foul.

Rice Bull examined the repellent holes and found some "quite large where several men were together," but others were barely large enough for a single man to "crawl in and have protection from storm and cold." He shuddered to think of Union soldiers "herded like beasts" into the holes, which covered a large portion of the enclosure. Bull heard many men swear they would never be captured alive. Death would have been preferred to life in this captivity.

"I am afraid if the soldiers generally could visit this pen, there would be no quarter given beyond here," warned Captain John Storrs. A soldier, Alex Downing, agreed. The men started their vengeance with the stockade. "We burned everything here a match would ignite," he wrote, and for good measure, a great deal of the surrounding countryside.

Nichols said the sight "fevered the blood of our brave boys." He was angered to think of the men with no protection, "exposed to heavy dew, biting frosts, and pelting rains, without so much as a board or a tent to protect them after the Rebels had stolen their clothing." Of the dead, Nichols wondered "from what misery did death release them! God certainly will visit the authors of all this crime with a terrible judgment!"

The previous day Nichols had ridden past the Stubbs plantation, where the "house, cotton-gin, press, corn-ricks, stables, everything that could burn was in flames." In the yard were the bodies of several bloodhounds, shot to death because they had been used to track down escaped Union prisoners. The killing of dogs had begun before Milledgeville, when soldiers were told how the animals were used to track escaped slaves. Now the Union army was killing "every thing in the shape of a dog. . . . The soldiers and officers are determined that no more flying fugitives, white men or negroes, shall be followed by hounds that come within reach of their powder and ball."

One small poodle had been taken from the arms of its master, a woman who pleaded that the dog be spared—"She's all I've got," the lady exclaimed.

"Sorry madam," the soldier responded. "Our orders are to kill every bloodhound."

"But she's a poodle," the woman cried, "not a bloodhound."

"Madam," the soldier replied seriously, "there's no telling what it'll grow into if we leave it."

At the Farrar plantation near Madison, Henry Hitchcock was told of a famed tracking hound at a neighboring farm. To the delight of the slaves, Sherman sent soldiers to shoot it.

December 5 dawned clear and cold as Baird's division covered another twenty miles through swampy country in its journey from Waynesboro. They passed Sardis Church and Jacksonboro, where they joined the other two divisions of the 14th Corps who had marched directly from Lumpkin's Station. From this point they would follow the River Road, which closely paralleled the Savannah River. This would prevent the Confederates from getting between them and the river. There was some skirmishing before dawn, but the March was undisturbed, probably, Connolly thought, because Wheeler thought he was still obstructing the Federal front, which was now their rear. The country was poor, and the few women and children they encountered "look utterly ignorant and stupid," he observed.

Connolly's division left camp at sunrise on December 6. Making slow progress through a country that was "very poor and sandy, and abounding in swamps," they covered only twelve miles in as many hours. Soldiers spent a great deal of time corduroying the roads with timber and brush. They crossed Beaver Dam Creek and camped at Black Creek, although Kilpatrick's men had reported that the Confederates were on the South Carolina side of the river, guarding every ferry and ford to prevent a crossing. Now expecting an attack on Charleston, Bragg had ordered Wheeler, "Press well on enemy's left flank so that if he crosses Savannah River, you will know it immediately and advise me."

"They [Confederate cavalry] are perfectly safe so long as they stay there," wrote Connolly, "for we don't intend to cross the river now. South Carolina is reserved for a future day; Sherman intends to finish Georgia, before beginning on South Carolina."

Kilpatrick's report of the recent cavalry clash reached Sherman on December 5. On the following day the commander thanked the cavalry "for their gallant and valuable service." Kilpatrick reported that he had lost several hundred horses and requested they be taken from infantry columns and

Pets on the March

As we journey on from day to day, it is curious to observe the attentions bestowed by our soldiers upon camp pets. With a care which almost deserves the name of tenderness, the men gather helpless, dumb animals around them; sometimes an innocent kid whose mother has been served up as an extra ration, and again a racoon, a little donkey, or a cat. One regiment has adopted a fine New-foundland dog, which soon became so attached to its new home that it never strayed, but became a part of the body, recognizing the face of every man in it. These pets are watched, fed, protected, and carried along with a faithfulness and affection which constantly suggest the most interesting psychological queries.

The favorite pet of the camp, however, is the hero of the barnyard. There is not a regiment nor a company, not a teamster nor an orderly, but has a rooster of one kind or another. When the column is moving, these haughty game-cocks are seen mounted upon the breech of a cannon, tied to the pack-saddle of a mule, among pots and pans, or carried lovingly in the arms of a mounted orderly; crowing with all his might from the interior of a wagon, or making the woods re-echo with his triumphant notes as he rides perched upon the knapsack of a soldier. They must all fight, or be killed and eaten. Hardly has the army gone into camp before these feathery combats begin. The cocks use only the spurs with which Nature furnishes them, and so but little harm is done. The gamecocks which have come out of repeated conflicts victorious are honored with such names as "Bill Sherman," "Johnny Logan," etc; while the defeated and bepecked victim is saluted with derisive appellations, such as "Jeff Davis," "Beauregard," or "Bob Lee."

—George Ward Nichols

The Left Wing passed through Jacksonboro near Springfield. The Dell House is all that remains of the town today.

left along his line of march. Sherman approved the request, and on December 7 Davis dismounted his foragers.

The army found the country's food resources depleted, although Connolly felt that they could survive if conditions did not worsen. His most important concern was a distant cannonading that could be heard from the direction of the coast, perhaps Charleston. The situation made Connolly anxious. "This blind groping of our way through the swamps and forests of Georgia, knowing nothing, what our friends are doing to help us, what our enemies are doing to oppose us, is the greatest annoyance of this campaign, but thank fortune, we are not relying upon our friends for assistance, and as to our enemies we dared them to do their utmost when we severed our communication with the north and started from Atlanta, and we will not fear them now."

What was to be feared was a message from W. C. Johnson, who reported Rebels in the rear. That situation worsened after a miserable night of hard rain, which returned to dampen the afternoon of December 6. Soldiers passed the night in misery, trying to sleep in the few comparatively dry spots while pickets stood duty on small boats and rafts. The column broke camp at daylight and made fourteen difficult, hungry miles, with Kilpatrick bringing up the rear. Johnson noted that the country was "short of everything to eat." After failing to negotiate a difficult crossing of deep Mill Creek before dark, the division slept on the western bank. The cavalry cautiously barricaded the rear of the camp.

Contrary to Kilpatrick's published report, Wheeler was not finished harassing the Federal advance. At dark he struck Kilpatrick, driving the cavalry "pell-mell" into the infantry. "The sounds of musketry informed us that the rebels in *some* force were following our rear closely," Johnson wrote. The pursuit was so close that "our headquarters were taken down again, preparations for supper suspended, wagons reloaded, and the troops disposed in proper order to resist an attack; our lines were opened and Kilpatrick's frightened cavalry permitted to come through and take shelter behind us." Kilpatrick never mentioned this encounter in his reports.

The Federals stumbled across Mill Creek in the dark after anxiously investigating a frightening report that the Rebels had blocked their escape route to Savannah. They then marched another seven miles to Sister's Ferry. The exhausted, hungry Yanks made camp again at 4:00 A.M., hopefully safe from the maurauding Rebs after "the hardest night march I ever made," Johnson insisted. The lead division did encounter light resistance and found the roads obstructed with timber, and General Davis rode near the rear in case of attack by Wheeler. At one point he grew irritated by a delay at the front. Riding forward, Davis found the colonel in charge of the advance, along with his entire staff, asleep in the road. They had paused to let a train of wagons take the lead, "halted for a rest, and falling asleep, overslept," Johnson recorded.

After investigating that report of Rebels to the front, Connolly lay down on a pile of brush and slept for an hour until Baird arrived. Then he slept on his horse as they rode, "and at every halt I dismounted and laid down beside my horse to snatch a little sleep, being afraid, all the time, that by some unfortunate mischance, the column might move on and leave me." The recent savage retaliations by Confederate cavalry made that a horrifying thought.

Back with the foot soldiers, Johnson fell asleep not only on his feet, but on the march.

A fearfully hard march. I became so worn out and fatigued with the continuous march, that I went to sleep while marching and lost consciousness, and when aroused . . . was for the moment lost, and could not realize where I was—a very strange experience. Upon being fully aroused, found myself marching right along in my place. How long the spell lasted I was unable to tell, but evidently for some time, as the sleepy feeling experienced before, in which it seemed impossible to hold my eyes open, or go farther, had left, and I experienced no further difficulty in remaining wide awake until morning came.

Johnson never heard "one word of complaint" from the soldiers about the difficult march, because "all realize the stern necessity of it." There were definitely hostiles in their rear, and the Federals desperately wanted to clear the swamps before resistance formed before them.

Rain turned the roads into swamps incapable of supporting the weight of men or horses, much less that of wagons and artillery. The troops were dispersed along the road and assigned a certain number of wagons to push forward. At one time an officer counted twenty-four wagons sunk to their beds in mud. He witnessed several mules sink out of sight.

Connolly was interested when they passed the home of Dr. A. Long-street, a relative of the great Confederate general, James Longstreet. He also discovered Spanish moss, which for several days had draped nearly every tree they passed. "It gives the forest an exceedingly gloomy (funereal, best describes it) appearance," he noted. The troops camped at Two Sister's Ferry.

In the distance the disturbing cannonade was heard again throughout the day and night. Connolly thought it might be Federals from Port Royal attack-ing Savannah, reflecting that it would be a "bore" to have come so far to find the city conquered by others. "[They] won't do it though," Connolly con-cluded. "Those eastern fellows never do anything clever, and, as we used to say up in Tennessee over a year and a half ago, we'll have to go over there and do their work for them yet." The firing turned out to be an exchange of fire between Fort Sumter and Fort Morris in distant Charleston.

After one or two hours' sleep, the corps moved again at 7:00 A.M. Connolly, "tired, sleepy, and worn out" from the forced night march, slept beside a burning stump until 6:00 A.M. He swallowed a cup of coffee for breakfast and fed his horse, and half an hour later he was on the road. "I don't think I could stand *this* kind of soldiering *more* than a month or two without *some* rest," he observed. After marching three miles through what Johnson called "the most fearful swamps we have yet seen," his unit was forced to halt. Confederates had destroyed the bridge over Ebenezer Creek, a deep, wide stream.

Wheeler showed up at noon and drove Kilpatrick into the protection of the Federal infantry once more. Connolly drily reported that the Union cavalry chief reported "being pressed by a superior force of the enemy (as *they* said)." The infantry barricaded the rear and deployed a line of battle. The cavalry covered the flank to the river, and skirmishing continued throughout the afternoon. The gun play "was very annoying," Connolly wrote, "as we were all very sleepy." Confederate cavalry cannon sporadically shelled the Union lines. Adding to the confusion were Confederate gunboats that fired on the road.

At midnight word was passed down the line to advance in absolute si-lence. The men filed across Ebenezer Creek through a dark, dismal rain and camped east of the stream at 6:00 A.M. "This night's work was harder than that of last night, and I never was so utterly exhausted and worn out as I was when the sun rose the morning after crossing Ebenezer Creek," Connolly concluded. It had been a "delicate undertaking," for the route traversed a mile "of the most gloomy, dismal cypress swamp I ever saw, on a narrow causeway, just wide enough for a wagon to drive along." Had the Confeder-ates discovered their movement, one cannon could have raked the causeway and "killed or wounded three fourths of the men . . . and we should have been utterly helpless to defend against it." There had been no other way to reach Savannah. If the other corps had been forced to use this route, Con-nolly believed that five thousand Rebels could have stopped the advance of Sherman's entire army.

The 14th Corps commander, Jefferson C. Davis, had long been viewed

A train of contrabands follow the rear of a Federal column. [BATTLES AND LEADERS]

with suspicion by many of his officers and men. His name was an obvious obstacle, and critics were quick to point out that he had been born in Kentucky. Beyond these surface objections, his intolerance toward blacks was pronounced even in a Western army not noted for its tolerance. Davis made no secret of his concern that contrabands who had attached themselves to his column would impede his rate of travel and hinder the corps' ability to deploy and fight.

Connolly had been disturbed several days earlier when he heard that Davis had turned back blacks at Buckhead Creek. "I don't doubt it," he wrote, "for he is a copperhead." During the frightful crossing of Ebenezer Creek, Connolly rode forward and found a Major Lee, the corps provost marshal, turning blacks off the road to wait in the surrounding swamp, by order of Davis.

"I knew it was the intention that the bridge should be burned," Connolly continued, "and I inquired if the negroes were not to be permitted to cross; I was told that Genl. Davis had ordered that they should not. This I knew, and Genl. Davis knew, must result in all these negroes being recaptured or perhaps brutally shot down by the rebel cavalry to-morrow morning."

Over six hundred blacks watched anxiously as fourteen thousand men and their artillery and wagons rumbled across the pontoon spans. They were assured that the delay was for their safety; Rebels on the far shore would have to be driven off before they could pass. When the last infantry had crossed, however, the bridge was cut loose and drawn to the eastern shore, leaving the refugees stranded. Their hopes of freedom were cruelly dashed.

"There went up from the multitude a cry of agony," recalled Chaplain John Hight. The slaves looked apprehensively down the long, narrow causeway behind them, aware that Confederate cavalry had pressed the column closely for days.

"Rebels!" someone shouted. "Rebel cavalry coming!" At that alarm the blacks "made a wild rush" forward, said Hight. Some "plunged into the water and swam across. Others ran wildly up and down the bank, shaking with terror."

Women and children started to drown. Horrified soldiers on the opposite bank threw pieces of wood into the stream for people to cling to, while others quickly took axes and felled trees into the water. Several black men lashed logs together to form a crude raft, then tied blankets to form a rope and repeatedly pulled the raft across the one hundred-foot-wide stream to rescue those who were thrashing about in the water. They transported dozens to safety on the eastern bank.

"As soon as the character of the unthinking rush and panic was seen," said one soldier, "all was done that could be done to save them from the water; but the loss of life was still great enough to prove that there were

Conclusion of the Ebenezer Creek Episode

While occupying Savannah, Sherman received a missive marked "Private and Confidential" from General Henry Halleck, the Army Chief of Staff. Sherman was being tipped off about a controversy that was fermenting in Washington.

"I take the liberty of calling your attention, in this private and friendly way, to a matter which may possibly hereafter be of more importance to you than either of us may now anticipate," the letter began. While most people were "praising your great march through Georgia, and the capture of Savannah," some important officials believed Sherman had "manifested an almost criminal dislike to the negro." He was accused of preventing 50,000 slaves from accompanying the army to Savannah. The slaves would have denied the South

much labor, and perhaps future soldiers. Halleck alluded to the episode at Ebenezer Creek.

While recognizing that Sherman did not wish his March impeded and could not have fed the slaves, Halleck wondered whether the slaves could not be brought in now. Such an act "will do much to silence your opponents."

Sherman denied the charges in his reply to Halleck. As for Ebenezer Creek, General Davis did not wish to abandon the slaves; he merely needed his bridge, Sherman stated.

While Davis was obviously an extreme racist, Sherman merely exhibited an intolerance typical of Western soldiers. He consistently refused to enlist black soldiers, despite the urgings of Grant and Secretary of War Edwin Stanton. Sherman employed them only as la-

borers. He did not believe blacks would be ready for political rights for a number of years.

On January 11 Stanton abruptly arrived with an entourage of other government officials. The sickly Stanton claimed he made the trip to enjoy the beneficial salt air and to escape the pressures of Washington, but the true purpose was made clear several days later when Stanton asked about General Davis' racial views. Sherman defended his subordinate and brought in Davis to present his version of events. Davis stated that he had not intended to block the slaves but had needed his pontoons to span another creek.

Stanton next instructed Sherman to bring in the leaders of slave society in Savannah, primarily preachers, for an interview. Sherman assembled

twenty men, who were universally described as intelligent and dignified individuals, and Stanton questioned their understanding of slavery and the Emancipation Proclamation. Their replies were "shrewd, wise, comprehensive," wrote Nichols. Stanton believed the men understood those important principles "as well as any member of the Cabinet."

After an hour, Stanton told Sherman to leave the room. The Secretary then asked the preachers' opinions of the general. Sherman is our friend, they replied. We have confidence in him.

Sherman was incensed by this slight, but after Stanton departed, he wrote his wife to express relief that the Secretary had been "cured of that 'Negro nonsense.'" ■

many ignorant, simple souls to whom it was literally preferable to die free men rather than to live slaves."

Harrison Pendergast saw over a hundred people still waiting anxiously across the creek, "huddled as close to the edge of the water as they could get, some crying, some praying, and all fearful that the rebels would come before they could get over."

Older people, women with babies, children, and men who could not swim disappeared beneath the brown water. No one could estimate how many died in this tragedy.

Wheeler's scouts reached the western bank, where they fired a few shots, then raced back to report the situation. The 14th Corps resumed its march, forcing soldiers at the creek's edge to leave as the refugees continued their attempts to save themselves. One soldier remembered a giant black man standing in the shallows who tirelessly pulled the raft across the creek.

The advance continued, and most Federals, inured to tragedy, put the matter aside, as they did the cries of women and children they left hungry and homeless. A few men of conscience were furious.

"Davis is a military tyrant," raged the chaplain, "without one spark of humanity in his makeup. He was an ardent pro-slavery man before he entered the army, and has not changed his views since."

Pendergast questioned Davis's salvation. He hoped President Lincoln would remove him from command as a result of the incident.

Predictably, Connolly expressed the most outrage. "The idea of five or six hundred black women, children and old men being thus returned to slavery by such an infernal copperhead as Jeff. C. Davis was entirely too much for my Democracy; I suppose loss of sleep, and fatigue made me somewhat out of humor too, and I told his staff officers what I thought of such an inhuman, barbarous proceeding in language which may possibly result in a reprimand from his serene Highness, for I know his toadies will repeat it to him, but I don't care a fig; I am determined to expose this act of his publicly," even if it cost his rank.

Connolly wrote a letter to the Senate Military Commission and mailed it at the first opportunity. General Baird read the letter and promised to lend his support to an investigation.

Sherman had no knowledge of the situation, but the controversy would generate considerable heat in Washington. When the issue surfaced later in Savannah, he defended Davis and denied that any wrong had been done.

Wheeler regarded the action of the past several days as a triumph. On December 5 and 6 he "pressed closely the enemy's rear, capturing one hundred prisoners." The Federals blocked the road in desperation and burned bridges to delay his pursuit, frequently building "fortifications two or three miles in length." On December 7 his men charged the Federal rear near Sylvania, capturing additional prisoners, horses, and arms. Late in the day they struck the Union cavalry a heavy blow, driving it in "wild disorder" two miles into the infantry column. They captured another 100 prisoners and chased many of Kilpatrick's men into the surrounding swamp. So pressed were the enemy, Wheeler claimed, that they "fortified their camps at every halt."

Wheeler's greatest success came on December 8 when, finding the 14th Corps "huddled" against Ebenezer Creek, he moved up an artillery battery and shelled their camp. This forced the hurried crossing in which the Federals abandoned horses, arms, and, by Wheeler's count, two thousand slaves because "the enemy, in their panic, refused to delay the destruction of the bridge." The slaves were returned to their owners, and there is no evidence that the refugees were slaughtered, as northern papers soon claimed.

The destruction of the bridge across Ebenezer Creek prevented Wheeler from pursuing the 14th Corps. He skirmished on the Middle Ground Road with the 20th Corps on December 9, then broke off the engagement on the following day, only ten miles from Savannah. The Confederate cavalry crossed the Savannah River to the South Carolina shore and, pursuant to Hardee's orders, defended a vital road from Savannah to Hardeeville.

Connolly stumbled on, finding time in his exhausted state to consult his purloined history of Georgia. He considered it interesting that this area was settled in 1734 by religious refugees from Germany. They called the area Ebenezer, which means "Stone of help." Connolly expressed the opinion that Georgia's founder, James Oglethorpe, was a "shrewd old land speculator" for foisting this swampy location on them. "They must have been very easily satisfied, to be content with such a place as this; if I were compelled to live here, I should feel as if the Lord were punishing me for my iniquity."

For the second day in a row, the corps had made a forced march through the night. Most of the men snatched two or three hours' sleep. "I was almost sick for the want of it," Connolly complained. He marched through the afternoon and camped eighteen miles from Savannah. Johnson had been with the rear guard, collecting pontoons after crossing streams and felling trees behind the column. He was "much fatigued and worn out" and believed the Rebels had finally been left behind. Unfortunately, there was a new concern—a heavy cannonading that could be heard from the direction of Savannah and Charleston. The gunboats in the Savannah River also increased their shelling of the corps.

Resistance was intensifying. Connolly heard rumors that Hardee had seventeen thousand troops to defend the city. Reports claimed the Right Wing was four miles from the city, and another dispatch suggested that the Union attempt to sever the railroad between Charleston and Savannah had ended in disaster. No surprise, he believed: "all these Eastern fellows appear to fail in everything they undertake."

Connolly believed the Confederates had to have a short line of defense drawn close to the city. If "they fight stubbornly, the entire city will be destroyed by our artillery. I saw one city [Atlanta] destroyed, and that was enough for me. I want Savannah to fall, but not in ruins."

After fending off determined Confederate attacks against their rear for several days, the 14th Corps experienced a moment of panic on December 9 when they encountered substantial resistance to the front of their swamp-bound march. The advance had bridged two creeks and covered eight miles when they came under accurate Rebel artillery fire.

Scouts crept forward and reported a battery of cannon were emplaced in two heavy redoubts astride a ridge in the road. Abatis obstructed the road for fifty yards in front of the guns, and infantry trenches extended into the swamps on both sides. The position was held, they thought, by about five hundred men.

Skirmishers advanced cautiously to determine whether the Confederates intended to hold the position. They ventured to within one hundred yards of the barrier but encountered fierce fire and retired. Davis was alarmed to find the Rebels commanding his only route to safety. He directed his men to enter the swamps and work their way around the Rebel flank, but the extensive morass was impenetrable. The soldiers returned to the causeway for the night.

Davis fretted throughout the dark hours, but dawn found the Confederates gone. A few Rebels had briefly held up the March, but with three other corps rapidly closing on Savannah, the enemy had gathered up their guns and headed back to the city.

A previous Union column had taken all the food and forage in this region, and the men were forced to march on short rations. Connolly had only a cup of coffee and a piece of cornbread for sustenance. When Savannah was captured, Connolly swore his first action would be to sleep for forty-eight hours. The night marching "begins to make me *feel old*," he wrote. He complained that the army "is a perfect dog's life, and I am almost surprised at myself sometimes, for not quitting it; but that would never do; the young man, who in these eventful times is found at home, is but a drone in the hive."

Honoring the Dead

During the Civil War, thousands of Union soldiers were buried on a dozen battlefields and in numerous communities across Georgia; and when the war was over, an effort was made to re-inter the men in national cemeteries. Federal dead from the Atlanta Campaign were buried in Marietta. Those who fell south of Atlanta were taken to Andersonville, where ten thousand Union prisoners had died.

The dead from several other Confederate prisons, including the pen at Magnolia Springs near Millen, were brought to Andersonville. Then a search was begun for Federals who

died on the March to the Sea.

Bodies of Union dead were transferred to Andersonville from Covington, McDonough, Worthville, Eatonton, Milledgeville, Clinton, Griswold, Irwinton, Sandersville, Davisboro, Louisville, Spier's Turnout, and Swainsboro. Some men had been killed in the battles at Griswold and Sandersville, but many had fallen victim to Confederate skirmishers while in the advance or to sharpshooters firing from the underbrush. Others were murdered by bushwhackers or shot while foraging. Soldiers were killed accidentally, in falls from

horses and by the chance discharge of a comrade's gun. Men sickened and died.

The soldiers were hastily buried and their graves marked by simple wooden markers, if at all. Most came to Andersonville unidentified. Some men remain in community cemeteries along the March route, while others rest in undiscovered graves. The bodies of officers and men whose families were financially able were usually taken home, but the common soldier remains buried on Georgia soil, most in Section B at Andersonville National Cemetery near Americus. Northern soldiers

who died during the siege of Savannah, including the heroic assault against Fort McAllister, are buried in nearby Beaufort National Cemetery in South Carolina.

Confederates who died resisting Sherman's March had a better chance of being returned home. Those bodies that were never claimed rest in city cemeteries, where their graves are still honored. Southerners who died at Fort McAllister and in Savannah's trenches were laid to rest in a large Confederate section in Savannah's Laurel Grove Cemetery. ∎

The 14th Corps finally managed an uninterrupted night's sleep, and they did not leave camp on December 10 until 10:00 A.M. The weather had turned cold as they marched through six miles of swampy terrain and stopped in an area of low pine woods between the road and river. The corps was only twelve miles from what Connolly now believed was the "doomed city."

Connolly heard heavy fire from Savannah throughout the day. His division was ordered to cover the river and protect the Left Wing's wagons and rear. This was in response to a warning Sherman gave Slocum that a brigade of Rebel cavalry was reported advancing on his flank.

Savannah was nearly shut off, except for one good road from Savannah to Charleston. It would have to be occupied if the Rebel garrison was to be captured. Still, to fight, the soldiers must eat, and their food was located on a fleet of transports located off Savannah. Every entrance to the sea was commanded by heavy Confederate batteries.

December 10 proved to be the last of twenty-six days of marching for the 20th Corps. All things considered, Rice Bull felt the jaunt had been enjoyable. This expedition would help end the War, he believed, and he would be able to go home soon. He helped construct some light breastworks and made a bed on the damp ground with pine boughs and moss taken from live oak trees. His only complaint was the food—half a ration of hardtack, rice, and slaughtered army animals. He and his comrades would live on that diet for two weeks.

The 14th Corps had experienced the most difficult march of the campaign. On December 8 Sherman found Davis still lagging behind the other columns. On December 11, Davis reported, "My trains are stuck in the mud for the duration of the night." On the following day he announced that his animals were out of food, and the "men soon will be."

The 20th arrived near Jacksonboro on December 4. They continued south on the Middle Ground Road through Sylvania, but they were forced to slow their march to accommodate the 14th Corps, which was bogged down on the River Road. On December 8 Slocum reached Springfield, while the 14th struggled across Ebenezer Creek. The 20th arrived at Monteith on the following day. By dusk of December 11, the two corps were reunited in front of Savannah's fortifications. ■

A DRIVING TOUR
■ The Left Wing ■

A tour of the Left Wing begins at Stone Mountain Memorial Park. From Atlanta, take I-285 East to U.S. 78. Follow U.S. 78 east to Stone Mountain, then follow the signs to the park.

This is an appropriate spot to start the tour. Here Sherman and half his army marveled at the bald, 850-foot-high granite monolith on their first day's march from the ruins of Atlanta. Ironically, the mountain's face now contains the most spectacular monument to the vanquished Confederacy.

Enormous mounted figures of Confederate President Jefferson Davis, legendary General Robert E. Lee, and his invaluable lieutenant, Thomas "Stonewall" Jackson, have been carved onto the mountain. It is the largest sculpture in the world. Memorial Hall, where Confederate artifacts are displayed, faces the carving. On summer

Map 4: From Stone Mountain to Lithonia.

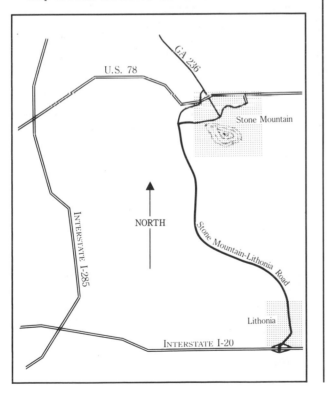

nights a dazzling laser show plays over the face of the mountain.

In Confederate Hall is a large relief map of Georgia illustrating Civil War activity that occurred in the state. Rivers, mountains, cities, armies, and trains are faithfully re-created, and a taped narrative describes the bombardment of Fort Pulaski, the Great Locomotive Chase, the Atlanta Campaign, and the March to the Sea, as lights trace the events on the map. Also on display are large figures of Confederate heroes created by Rich's Department Store for the Civil War Centennial.

At Stone Mountain park is a plantation consisting of authentic ante-bellum buildings.

Another interesting feature at Stone Mountain is the Antebellum Plantation, which consists of a dozen authentic pre-Civil War structures collected from across the state. They range from a grand manor house to necessary houses. The former Athens home of Thomas R. R. Cobb, who authored the Confederate Constitution, will soon be opened as a bed and breakfast inn.

Stone Mountain Park is a popular attraction that offers camping, an inn, lakes, riverboat and train rides, an auto museum, a skylift to the mountain's summit, golf, tennis, ice skating, wildlife trails, fishing, craft and food shops, and many other activities.

Sherman's March began in Decatur, west of Stone

Mountain. The DeKalb Historical Society operates an outstanding Civil War Museum in the old DeKalb County Courthouse. The Society also preserves four antebellum houses at their Historic Complex. Fighting during the battle of Atlanta swirled around the homes, but they escaped destruction then and later, when Union soldiers rampaged at the start of the March.

The DeKalb Convention and Visitor's Bureau and the DeKalb Historical Society have prepared an outstanding driving tour to towns, churches, homes, and other points of interest in the country.

Leave Stone Mountain by the west entrance, but do not follow the sign for U.S. 78 straight ahead. Instead, turn left onto East Mountain Street for .6 mile to the intersection in downtown Stone Mountain.

The historic village of Stone Mountain is filled with shops and restaurants. Up the street to the right is Stone Mountain Cemetery, where 150 soldiers are buried in a Confederate section. They died of wounds or disease during the War, and several were killed defending Stone Mountain against a Union cavalry raid in 1864.

Turn left onto Main Street, which becomes Stone Mountain-Lithonia Road. After 5 miles you will reach a stop sign. Turn left and drive 3.5 to a stop sign in Lithonia.

The name *Lithonia* is taken from a Greek word for stone. There are several granite mountains in DeKalb County that have been extensively mined for buildings, monuments, and highway construction. A number of local churches, homes, and businesses have been constructed with the beautiful stone.

Turn right onto Max Cleland Boulevard for .2, then right on GA 124 for .8 to the intersection with I-20. Enter I-20 East. This highway is also GA 402-U.S. 278. After traveling 5.8 miles, leave I-20 at Exit 41 in Conyers. At the end of the ramp, turn left onto West Avenue for .7. Just across the railroad, turn right for a short distance, then immediately left onto Peek Street for .2. Turn right onto Main Street for .1, then left on Milstead. After .1 the Old Jail Museum is on the right.

The Conyers jail, built in 1897, is used as a museum by the Rockdale County Historical Society. The bottom floor contains historical displays, while cells are preserved on the second floor. The Society has also re-

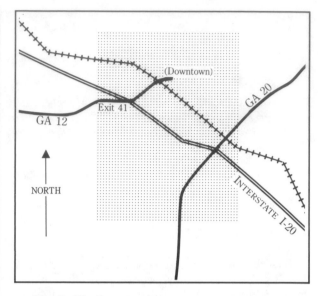

Map 5: The Conyers area.

stored the depot, which is used for local theatrical productions.

Although Rockdale County is Georgia's second smallest county in a state famed for small counties, it is interesting to explore. Eight miles southwest is the beautiful Monastery of the Holy Spirit. Visitors are welcomed, and Benedictine monks operate a museum and gift shop. Dial Mill, with its two-story high wheel, has been restored, and at the site of Costley's Mill is an old rock store and beautiful rapids. Four miles south of Conyers is the scenic Smyrna Camp Ground, and nearby is historic Salem Church. A drive around the county reveals a number of high ridges and rocky plateaus, part of the Stone Mountain formation.

Return to I-20 and continue east for 9.9 miles, then leave the interstate at Covington on Exit 45. Turn left onto GA 12 for .8, then left on GA 81 for 1.2. The old Georgia Railroad Depot you pass on the right was built in 1858. Turn left for .2 to enter the campus of Oxford College.

The highly respected Emory University, now located in Atlanta, was born here as Emory College in 1836. This campus is now a junior partner of Emory. There are thirty structures in this community that were built during the 1800s, including Orna Villa (1820), the Methodist-Episcopal Church (1841), and the Phi Gamma Society Debating Hall (1851). Oxford contains the home of Zora Fair, who spied on the Union army in Atlanta while dis-

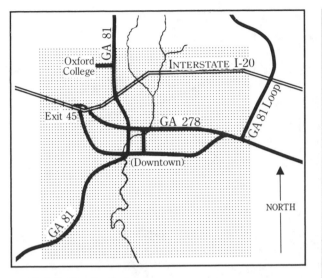

Map 6: The Covington area.

guised as a black. According to local legend, she hid in her attic to escape Sherman's search party, only to die tragically a few months later.

Like most educational institutions, Emory closed during the Civil War, and its buildings became a Confederate hospital. Behind the college gym is a quiet cemetery containing the graves of thirty-one soldiers who died here.

An impressive guide to Oxford is available from the Oxford Shrine Society, Inc.

Return on GA 81 to the intersection with GA 12-U.S. 278. Turn left and drive .2, then turn right onto Pace Street for .4. The courthouse will be on the right.

A driving tour prepared by the Newton County Chamber of Commerce, the Historical Society, and the Covington Garden Club directs visitors to many fine antebellum and Victorian homes in beautiful Covington, such as Swanscombe (1828) and the First United Methodist Church (1854), which was used as a Confederate hospital. In the city cemetery are the graves of seventy Confederates who died of wounds sustained in the battles for Atlanta. In July 1864, a Union cavalry raid destroyed thirty new hospital buildings in the city, four wagon and two rail bridges, two thousand bales of cotton, and railroad equipment. Along the Alcovy River, the explorer can find the three-story Henderson Mill, which has been restored as a home; an old iron bridge and scenic rapids at Newton Factory Shoals; and the Old Salem Tabernacle, established in 1854.

Return to GA 12-U.S. 278 and turn right. After 3.1 you will cross the Alcovy River. After .7 beyond it, GA 142 branches right to Shady Dale and Newborn, which is an alternate tour. Continue straight on GA 12-U.S. 278 for 2.8 to a four-way stop at the intersection with GA 11.

Social Circle, which boasts fifty beautiful antebellum and Victorian homes, is 4.7 miles north on GA 11. Hard Labor Creek State Park is about 16 miles northeast of this crossroads.

Continue straight on GA 12-U.S. 278. At .3 the Brick Store is on the left.

The store was constructed in 1822 and has been used as a courthouse, jail, school, store, and stagecoach inn. It has been restored by the Newton County Historical Society and contains local history displays.

Drive east for 8.2 and turn left to Rutledge. After .2 turn left for .1, then right, and you are in the lively downtown district. City Hall is located in the old depot.
Return to GA 12-U.S. 278, turn left, and drive for 8.6. You must stop at the intersection with GA 24-U.S. 441. Bear left into Madison. At .5 to your right is the Cultural Center.

Map 7: The Madison area.

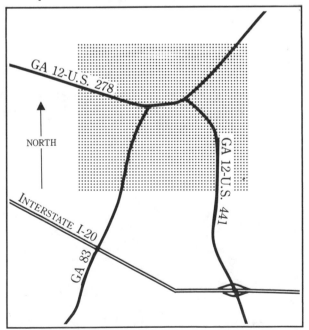

The Center is uniquely housed in a large brick Romanesque school built in 1895. It contains a history museum, which features Civil War artifacts and a reconstructed log cabin and other displays. One room has been furnished as a turn-of-the-century classroom. The Cultural Center also hosts lectures, workshops, and art exhibits, and theatrical productions in the old school auditorium. Here you may purchase a valuable guide to Morgan County's extensive history and architectural heritage. A brochure and taped audio guide to Madison is available from the Chamber of Commerce.

Be certain to see the beautiful Presbyterian Church, built in 1842. The church retains its original pews and has wonderful Tiffany stained glass windows. A communion service was stolen by Federal soldiers, but General Slocum ordered it returned.

Turn right from the parking lot, and after .2 the Historical Society is on the left. The Society occupies the Jones-Turnell-Manley House (1835) and offers a slide show displaying Madison's gems. Continue east for .2 and City Hall, and the Courthouse will be to the right.

In the city cemetery are the graves of fifty-two Confederate soldiers who died of wounds or disease in Madison hospitals. Also buried here is U.S. Senator Joshua Hill and the son he brought home from Cassville, Legare.

This beautiful town has only one drawback. It is heavily advertised as a town so beautiful that Sherman refused to burn it. Sherman was with the 14th Corps to the

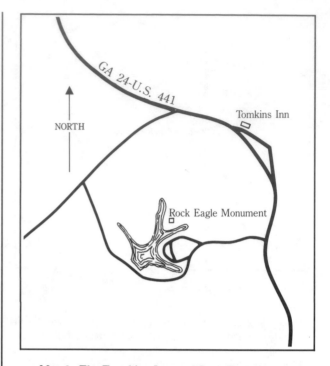

Map 8: The Tompkins Inn and Rock Eagle area.

south when the 20th Corps briefly occupied Madison. The town was lucky that its conquerors were relatively mild-mannered Easterners under the command of Slocum. They sacked the business district but left the residences alone, which was not uncommon in larger towns along the March route.

To the east, between Madison and the Oconee River, are several towns that were visited by one of Sherman's columns. At Apalachee are closed stores and several nice homes, including one huge house. Buckhead has a beautiful brick church, a fine wooden store, and other stores and warehouses—all, unfortunately, closed.

Return to the intersection with GA 24-U.S. 441 and follow it south, toward Eatonton, through Georgia's premier dairy country. The road skirts the Oconee National Forest. For information about hunting, fishing, camping, boating, and hiking, contact the National Forest Service. After 13.4 miles the Tomkins Inn is on the left. This structure was built in 1811 as an overnight stagecoach stop. It has been restored by the Eatonton-Putnam County Historical Society.

Continue south for 1.4 and turn right into the 4-H park. Follow this road for .7, then turn right for .1, and left to the Rock Eagle.

On the outskirts of Eatonton, Union troops passed this 3,000-year-old effigy constructed by Indians.

This fantastic artifact is a mound of stones that represents an eagle in flight. It is 102 feet in length and 120 feet across the spread wings. The body is 60 by 35 feet and rises 10 feet above the surface of the ground. This ceremonial figure was constructed between 1,500 and 3,000 years ago by American Indians. They also built two similar mounds in Putnam County. A wonderful view of the eagle is afforded from a stone tower that rises three stories above the effigy. The eagle is preserved on the grounds of the Rock Eagle 4-H Assembly, a popular retreat for church groups and other organizations.

Return to GA 24-U.S. 441, turn right, and after 6.7 the Putnam County Courthouse is on the right.

Prominent on the grounds is a colorfully dressed character known to the literary world as Br'er Rabbit. Joel Chandler Harris was born in Eatonton in 1848 and at age thirteen became a printer's devil for a plantation newspaper, *The Countryman,* at nearby Turnwold. There Harris learned to write, and at night he heard wonderful stories spun by slaves around cabin fires. While working for the Atlanta *Journal-Constitution,* Harris wrote a series of famous stories based on tales he had heard on the plantation.

Turnwold survived the war and is the center of a working farm east of Eatonton. Also in that direction is the crumbling remains of Rockville School, established in a community of the same name in 1889.

Eatonton has preserved a number of outstanding homes. A driving tour is guided by signs throughout the town.

Resume your journey south. At .4 the Uncle Remus Museum is to your right.

The log cabin museum was formed from two slave cabins. It represents the home of Uncle Remus, who is thought to have been based on "Uncle" George Terrell, a Putnam County slave who regaled local youth with his stories. The cabin is furnished with typical furniture and implements from the early 1800s. Skillfully carved wooden figures illustrate many of Harris' most beloved stories.

From the museum turn right. After 1.8, at the intersection with GA 44-U.S. 129 to Macon, bear left to Milledgeville. Beaver Dam Creek is crossed after 9.4, and after an additional 8.9 is a traffic signal. Turn left onto Montgomery for .2, then right onto Clarke Street. In the center of the second block to your left is the Old Governor's Mansion.

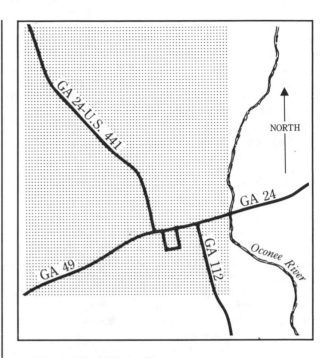

Map 9: The Milledgeville area.

Built in 1838, this structure was home to ten Georgia governors. The magnificent Greek Revival structure, plastered with pink stucco, cost fifty thousand dollars to build; it has a fifty-foot-high central rotunda. Sherman stayed here during his brief visit. Federal troops arrested Georgia Governor Joseph Brown at the Mansion in May 1865. This beautiful home now belongs to Georgia College. After two years of restoration, it was opened to the public in 1967. The Mansion is exquisitely furnished. Across the street is the Museum and Archives of Georgia Education.

A historical guide to Milledgeville is available from the Chamber of Commerce, which also sponsors a trolley tour. This city has forty-four buildings built before 1860, the earliest in 1812. Greek Revival, Plantation Plain, Victorian, and—rare for Georgia—a number of Federal period homes remain. The city was carved out of the wilderness in the early 1800's, a planned community with nineteen broad streets named for Revolutionary figures, and 4 large parks.

In Memory Gardens are buried state legislators, a governor, 3 veterans of the Revolution, a number of Confederates, including twenty-four unknown in one section, and 3 Union soldiers. Perhaps the most famous grave is that of noted author Flannery O'Connor.

At 220 South Wayne Street is St. Stephen's Episcopal Church, constructed in 1841. The church suffered considerable abuse during Sherman's occupation. While it was used to quarter Federal horses, soldiers poured molasses into the pipe organ to "sweeten" the sound. The original roof was damaged when the state magazine was exploded.

Continue straight on Clarke to the end of the block, and turn left onto Greene Street for .4. The Old State Capitol is to the right. The Gothic style building housed the General Assembly from 1803 until 1868, when the capital was moved to Atlanta.

This was Georgia's seat of government in January 1861, when a convention to consider leaving the United States was convened and eloquent arguments for secession and for remaining in the Union were presented to Georgia's most distinguished leaders. When the convention voted to secede on January 19, there was a torchlight parade through the city, and candles burned in most windows to indicate support for the act. Three and a half years later, Georgia's citizens had reason to regret that action.

The capitol building was reconstructed after a fire in 1941. Now part of Georgia Military College, it houses classrooms, administration offices, and a museum that contains Civil War material. The impressive gates at three entrances to the campus were constructed after the war with bricks from the destroyed arsenal.

From the capitol, drive straight down Jefferson Street for .1, and turn right onto GA 24. At .4 you cross the Oconee River.

Artifact hunters are excited over potential discoveries just downstream from here. Sherman's men dumped seventeen wagon loads of rifles, cannon, and shells from the arsenal into the river; so far little has been recovered. A short distance east of the Oconee is the site of a plantation where most Left Wing troops camped.

After 3.8 bear right at beautiful Montpelier Church on GA 24 as GA 22 branches to the left. After 16 miles on GA 24 cross Buffalo Creek.

Sherman's Left Wing was slowed here on November 21 by a series of burned bridges. The column camped the previous night at nearby Hebron. Gaping quarries and enormous refining facilities dot these rolling hills

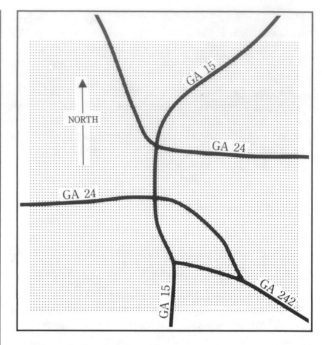

Map 10: The Sandersville area.

and give ample evidence that this region is the center of Georgia's important kaolin region.

After 9 miles the Sandersville cemetery is on your left. In it are buried several Confederates killed while defending the town. Local residents believe several Union soldiers, perhaps those murdered, rest in an unmarked, raised brick crypt.

Continue east on GA 24 for .2 to the traffic signal where GA 15 intersects. Turn left, and after .1, the Washington County Courthouse is to the left. Note the tiny police station at the corner of the square and beside it a monument commemorating the passage of Jefferson Davis.

Because of resistance in the streets of Sandersville and the murder of Union prisoners, the courthouse and surrounding business district were razed. The present courthouse is thought to be built on the foundation of the building burned in 1864. The central portion was erected in 1868, with later additions. The gazebo beside the courthouse houses the Chamber of Commerce. Behind it is a monument to Jared Irwin, a two-time governor of Georgia. The stone bears scars from bullets fired during the fighting in Sandersville.

Immediately behind the courthouse is the old jail, a Victorian structure erected in 1891. It has been re-

130

Just north of Sandersville at Warthen, is an old jail where Aaron Burr was held overnight while being taken north for his famous trial for treason in 1807.

stored and is home for the Washington County Historical Society. The grim cells remain in what doubled as home to the sheriff's family.

The Historical Society has compiled an impressive guide to Sandersville's historic treasures. The city has its share of antebellum and Victorian jewels. Still standing is the Brown House, where Sherman spent a night. The couch on which he slept is on display in the museum.

Ten miles north of Sandersville is Warthen. Here is preserved a jail of hewn logs that was constructed in 1784. Aaron Burr, a vice-president of the United States, was confined there overnight in 1804 while being taken from New Orleans to Richmond for trial on charges of treason.

Six months after Sherman passed through, Confederate President Jefferson Davis spent a night at Warthen on his flight from Richmond. He saw ruined Sandersville at noon on May 6, 1865, and camped that night at Ball's Ferry.

Eight miles north of Warthen is Hamburg State Park, which features fishing, camping, and picnicking, and also a working mill. Built in 1921, the mill has water turbines that turn three large grinding stones. A museum of agricultural implements is located in the mill.

Continue north on GA 24-GA 15. After .4 from the courthouse turn right to follow GA 24. The countryside becomes rolling farmland, punctured with pine tree farms and pecan orchards. After 12.9 turn right for .7 to downtown Davisboro, which was Station No. 12. At the railroad tracks are a number of old brick stores, only one open.

Return to GA 24, turn right, and drive 10.2 miles to cross the Ogeechee River. Two miles beyond in Louisville is a stop sign at the intersection with GA BUS 4-U.S. BUS 1. Turn right for .2 to the Old Slave Market, which is on the left in the center of the divided street.

This is apparently Georgia's only remaining slave market. It was a community trading center long before Louisville was established, where everything from vegetables to property was exchanged. The structure is made of hand-hewn oak timbers. Hanging in the cupola is a bell cast in France in 1772. It was meant for a New Orleans covent, but after being hijacked by pirates it appeared in Savannah. It was used as an alarm for fires and Indian attack.

Because Louisville was virtually destroyed by Union bummers before the main column arrived, little of the town's history remains, except for some fine Victorian homes. On the outskirts of town is a cemetery where four Revolutionary soldiers are buried. Between Louisville and Millen on GA 17 is Old Towne

Map 11: The Louisville area.

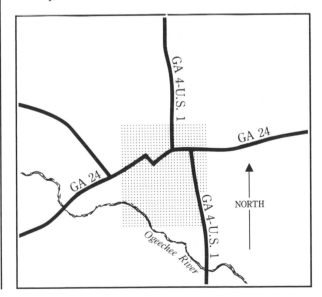

Plantation, which was established in 1767. It is believed to have inspired some of the Uncle Remus tales.

Continue straight for .1 to the Jefferson County Courthouse on the right.

The courthouse, which stands on the site of Georgia's capitol from 1796 to 1805, was constructed of materials from that building. A monument on the lawn describes the end of Georgia's worst political crisis, the Yazoo Fraud. In 1795 the Georgia legislature sold thirty-five million acres of land, which now constitutes the states of Alabama and Mississippi, for a penny and a half an acre. Some lawmakers had been bribed to approve the legislation, and after a wave of indignation swept the state, the Yazoo Act was rescinded in 1796 and the papers were burned on this spot.

Return to the slave market and turn right opposite it onto Mulberry Street. Off to the left is the Louisville cemetery, where a number of Confederate soldiers are buried.

After 1.3 Mulberry becomes GA 24, which you will follow for 9.9 to the stop sign in Vidette.

Enjoy the flat, sandy soil which for many decades produced more cotton than any other area in Georgia. The dirt roads off the highway are hardly distinguishable from the surrounding fields. Wheeler and Kilpatrick skirmished continuously across this land.

After 14.3 miles the Waynesboro Cemetery is to the left on Jones Street. A monument to Confederate soldiers is surrounded by the graves of unknown Rebel and Yankee soldiers, mostly cavalrymen who died in the battle for Waynesboro.

Continue in the same direction for .2, and the Burke County Courthouse is on the left. It was built in 1857, partially destroyed by Kilpatrick's troopers, and repaired. Two Civil War cannon guard the entrance. At this intersection turn right, and the Waynesboro Museum is immediately on the left.

This building, which also houses the Chamber of Commerce, was built in 1857. Across the street is the site of the Carter-Munnerlyn House, where President George Washington slept during a post-Revolutionary tour of Georgia. The museum houses a collection of Civil War artifacts, some of them retrieved locally, and other displays related to Burke County history and geology.

This is a large, historic county that contains many beautiful homes and churches, the site of a Revolutionary War skirmish, and an old mill. Northeast of Waynesboro, along the Savannah River, is a unique geological formation, Shell Bluff, an extensive bed of giant, fossilized oyster shells. The shells are up to two feet in diameter.

To the north are the crossings of Brier Creek, where Union soldiers burned important bridges in their feint on Augusta. South of Waynesboro, almost on the Jenkins County line, is Bellevue Plantation, which was a royal grant from King George III in 1767. The handsome house, constructed a year later, is a two-story clapboard structure made with heart of pine and cypress timbers. Cavalry skirmishes swirled around the home in 1864, as crowds of refugees from the Waynesboro fighting cowered in fear. Between Waynesboro and Millen are two communities visited by Sherman's forces: Munnerlyn, which consists of several crumbling buildings, and Thomas Station.

This is your closest approach to Augusta, located twenty-five miles north of Waynesboro. It is a city filled with history from Colonial times to the present. Of Civil War interest is the Confederate Powder Works Chimney, a 176-foot brick obelisk that marks the site of the Confederacy's largest gunpowder factory. The facility stretched for two miles along the Savannah River and produced three million pounds of gunpowder in its three-year existence. Augusta College occupies the site of an arsenal that manufactured

Map 12: The Waynesboro area.

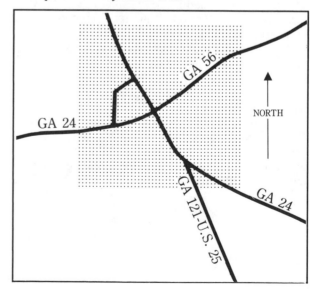

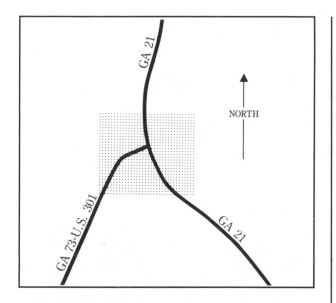

Map 13: The Sylvania area.

75,000 rifle cartridges daily. In the Augusta-Richmond County Museum is a collection of munitions that were made in Augusta, then dumped into the Savannah River when the Civil War ended. The museum building was used as a Confederate hospital during the War.

From the Waynesboro Museum drive south on GA 24-GA 121-U.S. 25 for .9, then follow GA 24 as it branches east to Sylvania. The route passes through Sardis, then intersects GA 73-U.S. 301. Continue south toward Sylvania. A Georgia Welcome Center is located a few miles east on U.S. 301 near the South Carolina border. After traveling 29.6, to the right is the Goodall-Dell House.

This structure, built in 1815, is all that remains of a vanished town called Jacksonboro. According to legend, the community was destroyed by a curse. In 1821 a traveling preacher, Lorenzo Dow, was harassed as he spoke in a local church. Rowdies threw rocks through the windows, and when Dow followed the men into a tavern and destroyed a barrel of whiskey, the ruffians began to beat him. Goodall, who built the house, rescued the preacher and cared for him. When Dow departed, he asked God to destroy all of Jacksonboro, sparing only Goodall's residence. The county seat was moved to Sylvania in 1847, and Jacksonboro, except for the Goodall House, disappeared. Jacksonboro's other claim to fame is the fact that

George Washington ate breakfast here on May 17, 1791.

Continue south. At .5 GA 24 turns left, to the southeast, but you will continue straight. After 3.9 leave the four-lane highway and turn left to downtown Sylvania. At 1.1 you are at a traffic signal and the main intersection in Sylvania.

Ten miles east of here, on Brier Creek, is a memorial and park at the site of a Revolutionary War battle. In February 1779, the British skillfully maneuvered an American force into a trap, and over two hundred Colonials were killed or drowned in the disastrous encounter.

Continue straight to follow GA 21 South. At 9.3 miles south of the intersection, turn right onto a narrow lane leading to Robbins Mill, which is operated on Saturdays.

The mill, placed amidst large pines and moss-draped oaks, presents a beautiful scene. A pond provides power for the milling stones. A mill was first located

Map 14: The Springfield, Jerusalem Church, and Rincon areas.

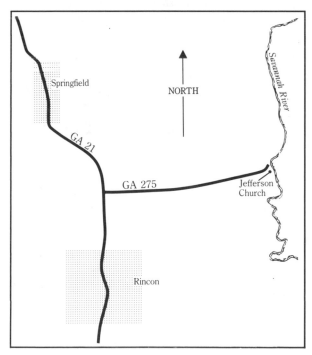

This re-created Salzberg house at New Ebenezer houses a museum.

here in 1807, but it was destroyed by Sherman's forces in December 1864.

> *From the mill turn right, and after 4.8 is the intersection with GA 24 in Newington. Continue south on GA 21. After 18.5, GA 119 will intersect. Bear right into Springfield, and after .2 the Effingham County Courthouse will be to your left a short distance down Raburn Street.*
>
> *Return to GA 21, turn left, and after 1.4 a Methodist campground is on the left.*

The Methodist Campground was founded in 1790, and the present meeting area was constructed in 1905. Like the other campgrounds we have encountered, it is surrounded by cabins.

While the 20th Corps marched easily through this portion of Effingham County on the Middle Ground Road in early December 1864, the 14th struggled through swamps and streams on the Old Savannah Road, near the river to the east. They probably did not appreciate the fact that George Washington traversed that route on a tour from Augusta to Savannah in 1791. That route can be partially traced today on GA 24.

> *After 3.2 turn left onto GA 275 for 5.3 to historic Jerusalem Church at New Ebenezer, which is on a bluff overlooking the Savannah River.*

New Ebenezer was settled by the Salzburgers, a Protestant sect subjected to persecution in Austria.

When they fled to Georgia, James Oglethorpe helped them establish this settlement in 1736. A town that sprang up around the church reached a population of two thousand, but in 1779 the community was captured by the British. The residents moved to the country and never returned. The 14th Corps passed this church, and General Davis ordered the contrabands abandoned at nearby Ebenezer Creek.

The magnificent church remains. It was built of locally manufactured brick between 1767 and 1769. Beside it is a museum, which illustrates the history and lifestyle of the Salzburgers. Constructed in 1971, it is a replica of Georgia's first orphanage. Beside it is an original Salzburger home, a wooden structure with a detached kitchen, built in 1774 and moved here for restoration. In the nearby cemetery are buried many of New Ebenezer's original settlers.

Between New Ebenezer and the town of Clyo, to the north, is Sister's Ferry, where half of Sherman's army crossed to invade South Carolina during the

Map 15: From I-95 to downtown Savannah.

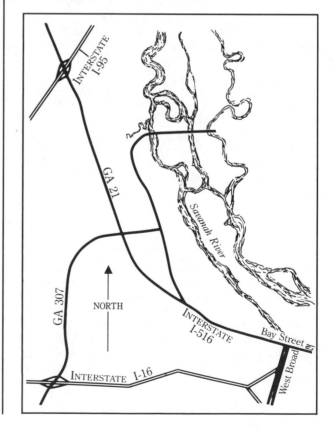

winter of 1865. It is very difficult to reach today. Clyo, and another community up that way, Stillwell, are pleasantly sleepy little towns.

Return to GA 21 and turn left. Drive through Rincon, and after 6.7 historic Goshen Church is on the left. The church was established by the Salzburgers in 1751, and the existing building was erected in

1820. *It has a beautiful walled cemetery.*

Continue south. After 4.5 pass under I-95. Monteith, which was Slocum's headquarters, is west of this point. Remain on GA 21 as it turns into four-lane I-516. After 8.4 exit onto 17-A/Bay Street, and turn right to follow Bay. After 2.0 turn right onto West Broad Street, and after .3 turn right into the Savannah Visitors Center. ■

■ Left Wing Tour B ■

Tracing the route followed by Sherman and the 14th Corps from Covington to Milledgeville makes an interesting side trip. It was during this portion of the March that Hitchcock and others began questioning the morality of waging war against innocent civilians.

Begin at the intersection of GA 12-U.S. 278 and GA 142, about 4 miles east of Covington. Follow GA 142 south for 4.3 miles to the intersection with GA 11. There are some very impressive homes along this highway. Continue straight on GA 142 for 3.7 miles to the center of Newborn.

Newborn has a gutted business district, as well as some pretty homes and a notable Methodist Church. The old depot was once a store and bears a name familiar to this area, J. W. Pitts.

Remain on GA 142 south for 5.7 and enter Farrar. The name of the community is emblazoned upon the side of an old store. The Baptist Church was established in 1807, and the existing building was constructed in 1907.

Driving south on GA 142, Kelly, also called Midway, is to the left after 1.6. Beside the railroad are the concrete foundation of a depot and the rusted remains of a baggage cart.

Drive south 3.6 to the intersection with GA 83, which is Shady Dale.

Shady Dale is the site of the plantation that so amused Connolly, and that today is famed for its eggs. To the left is a covered well and monument to a hotel that sheltered many travelers along the stage routes from Covington to Milledgeville, and from Augusta to Macon. According to local legend, Sherman spent a night here. The hotel burned in 1868. The community has a fine Baptist Church that was founded in 1810; the present structure was erected in 1902.

Continue south on GA 142 for 9.6 to the intersection with GA 16. Turn left onto GA 16 and cross Little River on this stretch.

In this area the 14th Corps destroyed a large textile factory located on the stream. Sherman and the 14th swung further south than this road and entered Milledgeville via Howell Cobb's plantation, which is honored with a crossroads community named Cobb in Baldwin County.

After 5.6 you will meet GA 24-U.S. 441 at the courthouse at Eatonton, and can resume the Left Wing tour. ■

The Right Wing

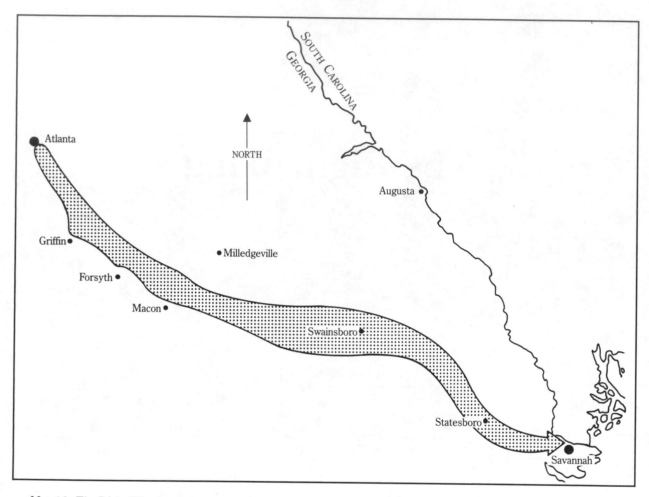

Map 16: The Right Wing headed south toward Macon, with feints toward Griffin and Forsyth, before heading toward its objective: Savannah.

CHAPTER 11

"It Was a Harvest of Death"

T he interior of Georgia lay virtually unprotected. The state had made an enormous contribution to the Confederate war effort, and her manpower was exhausted. Tens of thousands of Georgians served in the Army of Northern Virginia, the Army of Tennessee, and in every other major arena of the Civil War, but they would be unable to protect their own homes. Hood's Army of Tennessee, which had recently left the region, was hundreds of miles away at Florence, Alabama, preparing to invade Tennessee and unavailable to impede Sherman's advance. The militia that remained in Georgia were mainly "cradle and grave units," men younger than sixteen and older than sixty who were exempt from the draft. There was also a hodgepodge of factory workers, city guards, and railroad patrols. Governor Joseph Brown had exempted a number of men from Confederate service, but these "pets," as they were known, had little military training and virtually no combat experience. When Sherman started for the coast, most of the militia had recently returned to duty from their "harvest furlough."

The Georgia militia, commanded by General Gustavus W. Smith, was positioned south of Atlanta, at Lovejoy, to protect the most direct route to Macon. It consisted of 2,400 infantry, 300 cavalry, and 3 batteries of artillery.

The cadets from the Georgia Military Institute were an unlikely force of southern warriors. They had served briefly with the Confederate army during the Atlanta Campaign, then were sent to Milledgeville for guard duty in August. These soldier-boys drilled for three months and found themselves in harm's way when Sherman moved directly for their camp.

Another unusual group of Confederates set to resist Sherman's advance were the remnants of the famed Orphan Brigade. These Kentuckians, known for their unstinting valor, had been abandoned when their home state refused to secede from the Union, and their ranks had been decimated by the end of the Atlanta Campaign. Before he captured Atlanta, Sherman had launched a massive cavalry raid into central Georgia that ended disastrously. Hundreds of horses were captured, and in early September the Orphans were mounted on Union horses and mules, although most were forced to ride bareback. The nearly one thousand men were commanded by General

Alfred Iverson and had orders to picket roads leading south from Atlanta.

Confederate military authorities had decided that Hood would receive cavalry support from the incomparable "Wizard of the Saddle," Nathan Bedford Forrest. So Joseph Wheeler, who had scouted for the Army of Tennessee and covered its flanks on many campaigns, returned to Georgia to keep an eye on Sherman.

Many Georgians were less than happy at Wheeler's return. His 2,500 troopers, while ferocious in battle, were notoriously lacking in discipline. When Wheeler left Georgia for a fruitless raid behind Sherman's supply lines in August, Robert Toombs, former United States Senator and Confederate Secretary of State and general, believed the expedition was useless. "The enemy care nothing for Wheeler," he wrote in a letter to Confederate Vice-President Alexander Stephens. He accused Wheeler's men of avoiding any place guarded by "as much as armed sutlers."

There was a bright spot to the Tennessee raid, Toombs concluded. "I cannot say he has done no good for he has relieved the poor people of this part of the country temporarily from his plundering marauding bands of cowardly robbers. . . . I hope to God he will never get back to Georgia."

As Wheeler attempted to impede Sherman's path across Georgia, complaints about his men multiplied. His best officers had departed, and discipline deteriorated even further. "They are the meanest set of men that ever lived," one Georgian told a Federal soldier. Their thievery of food and valuables rivaled that of Sherman's men, and the arrival of Confederate cavalry was often dreaded as much as a visit by the Federal army. "The whole of Georgia is full of bitter complaints of Wheeler's cavalry," wrote General Daniel H. Hill as the March concluded. Citizens referred to the notorious Confederate cavalry as "Wheeler's horse thieves."

Wheeler arrived at Jonesboro on November 13. He was informed by an escaped prisoner that there was a great deal of activity on the Western and Atlantic Railroad, primarily men and material moving north from Atlanta. Fires were also observed in the conquered city. On the following day, when Union captives were brought in, they revealed that Sherman had returned to Atlanta. His troops were being readied for a move to Augusta and Savannah, and the railroad was being destroyed before they departed.

Early on November 15 came word of extensive destruction in Rome, Marietta, and Atlanta. Later in the day, Wheeler's scouts observed a massive exodus of infantry, cavalry, artillery, and wagons moving south on the McDonough Road. Half of Sherman's army was coming.

Judson Kilpatrick's Union cavalry division led the Right Wing from Atlanta to protect the flank from expected Confederate resistance near Macon. The cavalry left East Point on November 15 with five thousand men and six guns and followed the west bank of the Flint River. Their assignment was to feint on Forsyth and deceive the Confederates into believing that Macon was Sherman's first major objective.

Clashes between the two cavalry forces would provide most of the military action during the March to the Sea. It would be a slashing, vicious series of combats, with no quarter given on either side and considerable atrocities committed by all.

The two cavalry commanders were well acquainted with each other. They had been classmates at West Point. Wheeler graduated in 1860 and served briefly in the West fighting Indians; Kilpatrick's class graduated a month early, in May 1861, because of the bombardment of Fort Sumter. Kilpatrick had quite an edge on Wheeler in academics, and the two strove to be ideal cadets. In 1859 Wheeler earned only six demerits; Kilpatrick had none.

Twenty-one months after entering Confederate service as a lieutenant, Wheeler was commissioned a major general; at age twenty-eight he was the youngest in the Confederacy. Wheeler had been wounded six times, and sixteen horses were shot from under him in the 127 battles and skirmishes in which he participated. The native Georgian was a small man, only 5 feet, 5 inches tall, and weighed 120 pounds, but he fought with reckless abandon. Wheeler had a strong sense of chivalry, and when he felt an enemy had violated that code, the reaction was savage.

Kilpatrick shared Wheeler's recklessness, but many officers in the Federal army disliked his frequent womanizing and grossly exaggerated tales of battlefield success. Sherman recognized these traits, but before leaving for the coast in November, he said, "I know that Kilpatrick is a hell of a damned fool, but I want just that sort of man to command my cavalry in this expedition."

Wheeler's force was driven from Jonesboro by Kilpatrick's superior numbers at 7:00 A.M. on November 15. The Rebels retreated into the militia

Private Upson and other soldiers visited the Indians Springs Hotel and enjoyed mineral waters found nearby.

lines at Lovejoy, where they occupied earthworks thrown up by Hood after the evacuation of Atlanta in early September.

Kilpatrick was in hot pursuit. A Union battery unlimbered and fired into the southern position while Kilpatrick's cavalry dismounted and scrambled over the works. The Rebels were scattered, and the Federals captured thirty men, three caissons loaded with artillery ammunition, and two three-inch rifled guns. Ironically, the Confederates had captured the guns in July when a northern cavalry expedition had been surrounded and forced to surrender near Macon. A Federal reported finding five hundred muskets abandoned by fleeing militiamen.

"We were so completely run over that we were scattered in every direction," wrote one Georgian, "those of us who were not killed or captured."

The militia hastily withdrew to Hampton and barricaded the road with rails. At noon Kilpatrick arrived and overwhelmed the position, capturing twenty additional prisoners. The militia and Wheeler's men retreated to prepared works at Griffin, hoping to protect that supply and hospital center from capture.

On November 16 Wheeler identified four Federal corps and estimated Sherman's strength at sixty to seventy thousand men. The infantry was being skillfully shielded by Kilpatrick. Wheeler believed, and continued to report, that Sherman was marching directly to Macon.

From his headquarters in Griffin, on November 17 Wheeler ordered the roads leading to Macon, Columbus, and Augusta picketed. He then dispatched this urgent message to General P. G. T. Beauregard, who commanded the Military District of the West: "I have no orders regarding the holding of any city should enemy besiege or assault. Please give me instructions and intentions of Government," he pleaded, or send someone who knows what is happening. Unfortunately, no one in the Confederate high command had an inkling of the true situation.

Believing they had saved Griffin from destruction, the militia was sent south toward Forsyth. On November 18 they trickled into Macon, delayed by lack of transportation, arriving on two separate trains. Their fourteen pieces of artillery came later.

On November 17 Kilpatrick rode from Hampton to the Towaliga River to threaten Griffin and Forsyth. The feint was plausible enough to cause Wheeler to burn the Towaliga bridge to protect Forsyth, and a brief skirmish developed.

Wheeler soon received his instructions. The Confederate cavalry was to impede the enemy's advance in any possible manner and attack isolated Federal troops and foragers to keep destruction limited to a narrow track. His men would harass the Federal rear and burn supply wagons. Wheeler was to keep his superiors informed of Sherman's movements (he spent a great deal of time writing dispatches to half a dozen generals and Governor Brown) and to defend cities, supplies, railroads, depots, arsenals, and other public property. Furthermore, he was to give civilians living along Sherman's route a day's notice of the enemy's arrival, so that valuables could be hidden. Private property was not to be burned. When horses, mules, or cattle were removed by the Confederate cavalry, they were to leave receipts and return the animals as quickly as possible.

Men are more important than cities, Beauregard warned Wheeler. He was ordered to abandon cities before his men were trapped by a siege.

Howell Cobb, a former United States Secretary of Treasury and briefly an indifferent Confederate general, commanded the state troops in Macon. On November 17 he wired President Davis in Richmond, asking that the garrisons stationed at Charleston, Savannah, and Augusta, and reinforcements from Hood's army, be concentrated to defend Macon.

"Sherman's move upon this place is formidable," he wrote, "and the most dangerous of the war. His policy is universal destruction." By concentrating all available forces in the region, Cobb believed Sherman could be defeated, with "the greatest result of the war."

On the same day, Robert Toombs wired Governor Brown from Macon, "Things are very bad here." He urged Brown to inform the legislature that the state was in serious danger. "Let all of her sons come to her rescue," Toombs proclaimed.

On November 18 Davis replied to Cobb, directing him to obstruct the roads. Beauregard dispatched torpedo experts from the munitions facility in Augusta to bring mines and plant them in the enemy's path, but they could not reach Macon. He also sent General Richard Taylor, who was in Mobile, to assist in Macon's defense. Beauregard, in Mississippi on an inspection tour, gave General William Hardee temporary command of all Confederate troops in Georgia. "You should endeavor to get out every man who can render any service, even for a short period," Beauregard lectured the authorities congregating in Macon. "You have a difficult task but will realize the necessity for the greatest exertion."

On November 19 most of Wheeler's men had reached Macon. Hardee arrived from Savannah and assumed command of the troops; Beauregard would soon appear. To boost manpower, Governor Brown issued an edict that drafted every man in the region. Brown, refugeed from Milledgeville, joined the throng. With General Taylor's arrival, the city of Macon boasted nearly as many generals as it had infantry.

An appeal for the men of Macon to defend their city had been issued, and a number of state legislators, in ignoble flight from the state capital, were pressed into service by military authorities. Forced to prove they were members of the legislature, which had exempted themselves from duty, most continued their journeys to South Georgia.

Joseph Johnston, former commander of the Army of Tennessee and a resident of Macon since his dismissal in July, left town with his wife. Hundreds of frightened citizens joined them, crowding onto trains heading south to Albany.

As the civilians fled, the generals, Confederate and militia, and Georgia politicians held a strategy meeting in Macon. It was a classic session of intrigue. Cobb and Brown were deadly political enemies; and the fiery Toombs, who hated all professional soldiers, held Wheeler's renegade cavalry in the highest contempt. Fortunately for Macon, as these men met, Sherman skirted the city and continued toward the coast.

At dawn on November 20, Wheeler led his cavalry out of Macon to locate

The Prussian General ■ Peter J. Osterhaus

Osterhaus was born in Cobleny, Prussia, in 1823. After participating in the failed European revolutions of 1848, he fled to America and became a clerk in St. Louis.

Osterhaus saw action at Wilson's Creek, Missouri, and Pea Ridge, Arkansas. By 1863 he was a general and participated in the Vicksburg Campaign. Later he helped Joseph Hooker capture Missionary Ridge, then advanced to Atlanta. Sherman disliked Osterhaus for absences he attributed to political activities and unsuccessfully opposed his promotion to major general.

Osterhaus was one of the few Union generals who tried to prevent looting on the March; it violated his Prussian idea of order. At Savannah he was succeeded as commander of the 15th Corps by John "Blackjack" Logan.

Osterhaus returned to business after the war. Later, he served as a U.S. Consul in France and Germany. He died in Germany at the age of ninety-four in 1917, just before the United States entered World War I. ■

[LIBRARY OF CONGRESS]

During a cavalry raid in the summer of 1864, a cannonball bounced into this Macon home.

Sherman's legions. On the ride to Clinton, only ten miles northeast of the city, they were menaced by small parties of roving Union cavalry. Because of a dense fog, Wheeler did not see General Peter Osterhaus's 15th Corps until his men collided with the column in Clinton. Six Rebel troopers dashed to within twenty feet of the General's headquarters and captured his servant before Federal cavalry chased them out of town.

Confederate and Union cavalry clashed repeatedly as Wheeler was steadily driven back to Macon and passed through the militia lines—General Smith said he was forced through. Earlier in the day the militia had occupied Macon's defenses, a series of rifle pits, infantry trenches, and cannon placed in redoubts located east of the Ocmulgee River. The city's protection was left in the hands of the militia, cavalry, convalescents, and local men who had heeded the call to arms.

Union cavalry was hard on Wheeler's heels. At 3:30 P.M. they pushed Confederate skirmishers across Walnut Creek. Kilpatrick personally led a saber charge toward the Confederate line. The defenders, probably militia, the Federals later wrote disdainfully, left in a "stampeded and panic stricken" rout at their approach. The Yankees forced their way into the earthworks and briefly occupied a two-gun battery. Behind the works, a stiffer Confederate line deployed and advanced resolutely, and Kilpatrick was forced to retreat with seven wounded men. Captain J. H. Hafford, who had been the first man into the Confederate line, was trapped beneath his dead horse and captured.

Kilpatrick left twelve dead horses behind. According to one witness, "a Yankee had run off and left his foot and a leg in a boot" beside Walnut Creek.

The feint on Macon had been completely successful, and the Confederates had concentrated their forces there, far from Sherman's front. Smith and Wheeler, who would never believe the truth, accepted credit for having saved Griffin, Forsyth, and Macon.

While Kilpatrick threatened Macon, part of his cavalry was dispatched to destroy Griswoldville, a manufacturing center on the Central Railroad. The men charged through town, drove off Wheeler's pickets, then went to their destructive work under sniper fire. They destroyed thirteen rail cars, twenty tons of iron, twelve wagons, a water tank, factories that produced pistols, soap, and candles, four hundred boxes of soap, and the depot. Before leaving, they set fire to the town in retaliation for the continued resistance.

Kilpatrick's men returned to Griswoldville on November 21 to cover the flank of the Right Wing, which was slowed by bad weather. They destroyed some track, then burned the few structures that had managed to survive the earlier onslaught.

The previous night Wheeler had left Macon to harass the Federal advance. On November 21 he attacked the Union cavalry at Griswoldville and captured sixty prisoners. Union accounts claim Wheeler attacked a barricaded position and lost sixty-five men killed and wounded.

The Orphan Brigade mounted a fierce raid against Clinton and was driven off only when Union reinforcements arrived.

Fearing Wheeler's fierce troopers, the Federals transferred trains to the inside track being taken by the 17th Corps to the east. Union troops camped close together for support, but the swarming southern troopers persisted in interrupting their rest.

On November 22 the Federal columns, which were approaching Gordon, east of Griswoldville, were still vulnerable to attack by Wheeler's determined horsemen. Kilpatrick was dispatched with infantry support to guard the Union flank near Griswoldville and to protect the wagons. Wheeler promptly struck the Federal pickets a surprise blow and chased them into camp. A brigade of blue infantry came up to support the cavalry, and the Union force waded a creek and pitched into the Confederates with a cheer. It developed into "quite a little action," noted a Union participant, "charge and counter charge of cavalry." Wheeler claimed to have inflicted forty-five casualties and captured eighty horses, but he was forced to concede the engagement to superior forces and withdrew.

Having removed the cavalry threat, the Federals withdrew to a position just north of Griswoldville's smoking ruins. There was still considerable concern about the safety of their strung-out wagon trains. Since Kilpatrick occupied Clinton on November 19, three divisions of the 15th Corps had passed; but rain, boggy roads, and a difficult crossing at the Ocmulgee River had delayed a division under General John Corse. A dangerous six-mile gap had developed between him and the remainder of the column, and Jesse Dozier, a forager, was forbidden to leave the column on account of the danger. The men drew three days' rations and were required to march twenty miles in a single day to clear the tough Rebel cavalry operating about Macon.

For protection against the Confederates, General Frank Walcott's brigade, a force of 1,500 men and 2 cannon, was left to guard the flank. They occupied a slight ridge on an overgrown farmstead and erected light rail breastworks. Fires were kindled, and the troops began to prepare lunch.

By the evening of November 21, Hardee was convinced Sherman had bypassed Macon. He sent a brigade of militia and two small battalions of city defenders marching to aid the defense of Augusta, which was thought to be Sherman's next target. The remainder of the Georgia militia—three brigades—followed in the morning. Hardee hoped the Federal troops had swept east. If they had, the militia could advance unopposed directly to Augusta. If the enemy were encountered, the men were to avoid battle and return to Macon. While the militia marched away, Wheeler sent the bulk of his force quickly across the Right Wing's path to impede the Left Wing as it approached Augusta. Beauregard also left for Augusta to help Braxton Bragg gather Confederate strength from the Carolinas to protect that city.

While Gustavus Smith remained in Macon to organize supplies for the move, General P. J. Phillips was placed in command of the militia. Phillips had little military experience and, according to some sources, had been drinking.

At Griswoldville, Phillips found the fourth brigade waiting, and they reported skirmishing between Federals and Wheeler near the town. Discovering that his 3,700 men outnumbered the Union detachment, Phillips disregarded orders and deployed his men for battle in three long lines. The soldiers would leave the shelter of a wooded area and charge seven hundred yards across the old fields to a ravine one hundred yards from the Union position. There they would regroup and storm over the Federal works. Part of his command would threaten the Federal flanks, which were strongly protected by a swamp and the railroad embankment, and six pieces of artillery would support an assault on the Union center.

"We were getting dinner, not dreaming of a fight," wrote Union Colonel Charles Wills, "when lively musketry opened on the picket line, and in a minute our pickets came in flying."

Lunch was hastily dumped in the fires as the soldiers scrambled to unstack their arms and load the new seven-shot repeating rifles. The Confederate artillery opened and soon silenced Walcott's cannon—one caisson was immediately exploded by a shot.

The gray infantry fared worse. Some men stopped to rout Yankee skirmishers out of old farm buildings, and others advanced in the wrong direction. One Rebel brigade fired on their comrades. Despite all the difficulties experienced by the green troops, an attack endangered the Union right flank.

At 250 yards the Federals opened a blistering fire that littered the fields with shattered Rebels. Still the Confederates advanced, firing and shouting. A shell from the well-served Confederate artillery wounded Walcott, and the defense fell to Colonel K. J. Catterson. Catterson rushed reinforce-

In Macon's Riverside Cemetery are the remains of a Confederate artillery battery that helped defend the city.

ments to the right, where his men drove off seven separate assaults.

"It was awful the way we slaughtered those men," Colonel Wills remembered. As the attack continued, it was obvious to the Union veterans that they were facing brave but inexperienced militia. Real soldiers, they remarked, would have refused to make such a suicidal assault.

Confederate casualties mounted as fire from the Federal repeating rifles crashed into their ranks. Rebels who paused to return fire made a common error of new soldiers—they fired high and inflicted few casualties.

The Confederates advanced to within fifty yards of the Federal line, but they were slaughtered by deliberate shooting. After several hours of heroic but foolish fighting, the militia—boys and old men—broke and fled for the rear or found shelter in the ravine.

"With the ignorance of danger common to new troops, the Rebels rushed upon our veterans with the greatest fury," Nichols wrote of the affair, "but were bloodily repulsed."

"Once when we were so hard pressed that it seemed as though they were going to run over us by sheer force of numbers, our boys put on their bayonets [and] resolved to hold their ground at any cost," Private Theodore Upson wrote. "We had but slight works thrown up hastily with rails but we had one thing that helped us greatly and that was part of our men are armed with repeating rifles which enabled us to keep up a continuous fire."

By 4:30 P.M. Smith had received word of the action and ordered Phillips to withdraw. After the Confederates crept away at dusk, the Federals swarmed over their works to sweep the field of any remaining enemy. They found 47 wounded Rebels and 150 abandoned rifles.

Colonel Wills was aghast by the sight of "grey-haired and weakly looking men and little boys not over 15 years old, lying dead or writhing in pain." He had never been "so affected by the sight of dead and wounded. . . . I hope we will never have to shoot at such men again. They knew nothing at all about fighting, and I think their officers knew as little."

"We went down on the line where lay the dead of the Confederates," Upson remembered. "It was a terrible sight." Hearing groaning, the Federals shifted some bodies and found a fourteen-year-old boy with a broken arm and leg. Beside him, "cold in death, lay his Father, two Brothers, and an Uncle. It was a harvest of death."

Another boy, whose heart could be seen beating through his torn chest, begged for water. "We never wanted to fight," gasped one kid, but Wheeler's cavalry had scoured the countryside for males, regardless of age. They were given rifles and marched off to fight.

That night a sixteen-year-old Confederate who had managed to escape the carnage counted the bullet holes in his bedroll, which had lain across his shoulder during the battle. There were twenty-seven.

"There is no God in War," said a Union soldier who surveyed the battlefield. "It is merciless, cruel, vindictive, un-Christian, savage, relentless. It is all that devils could wish for."

Some Confederate casualties from the battle at Griswoldville are buried in Macon's historic Rose Hill Cemetery.

The Yankees gathered the wounded Southerners around their fires and cared for them through the night. They were left for their own people in the morning, and the dead were buried on the field.

The Confederates had lost 51 men killed and 472 wounded. The Federal toll was thirteen dead and seventy-nine wounded. Among the Federal dead was a beloved soldier known to his comrades as "Uncle Aaron" Wolford. On the previous night, Wolford had told Upson of a premonition. "He was greatly depressed, something unusual for him," Upson wrote. "To my inquiry as to his trouble, he said, 'I do not know, but I feel that I have not long to live and when I am gone I want you to promise me that you will take charge of my things. Send them to my wife and write to her all about me.'"

Upson tried to cheer his friend, but Wolford "felt sure his time was nearly out." During the thick of the fighting, Uncle Aaron was shot in the head. "I put my hand on him and spoke his name," Upson wrote, "but he was gone where I hope there are no wars, no sudden partings. That night after the Johnnys had gone we buried our dead. We had no coffins, but I could not bear to think of putting my old friend into his grave in that way. I remembered that at a house a short distance away I had seen a gum or hollow sycamore log of about the right length and size. We got it, split it in halves, put one in the grave dug in the sandy soil, put his lifeless body in it, covered it with the other half, filled up the grave and by the light of a fire we had built with the rails, marked with a piece of lumber pencil his name, Company, and Regiment."

True to his word, Upson wrote Mrs. Wolford when the army reached Savannah. He enclosed what little money Wolford had, his watch, and "a well worn Testament." For the memory of his eight children, Upson described "what a good man," and "how brave and faithful to duty he was." Upson began to cry as he wrote, and his tears blurred the ink on the letter. He left camp to gather his thoughts. "I hope they will realize what a grand soul he had," Upson prayed.

The decimated Confederate force arrived in Macon at 2:00 A.M. In an official message, Smith expressed his appreciation of Phillips in "driving before you the enemies of your country." Unofficially, Smith remained angry about the slaughter for the remainder of his life. The battle was "contrary to my instructions," he rumbled, and "will be remembered as an unfortunate accident whose occurrence might have been avoided by the exercise of proper caution and circumspection. It in no wise crippled the movements of the enemy and entailed upon the Confederates a loss, which under the circumstances could be ill sustained." ■

CHAPTER 12

"The Whole World Turned to Yankees"

hen the Right Wing began leaving Atlanta on November 15, the 15th and 17th Corps feinted on Jonesboro, but turned southeast and camped around Stockbridge for the night. They met minor resistance from the Orphan Brigade, who were quickly forced to retreat to Lovejoy.

The relentless advance continued on November 16 as the columns reached McDonough. When Confederates attempted to delay them by burning the bridge over the Cotton River, the mounted infantry making up the Federal advance guard drove them off and extinguished the fire. Only the planking needed repair, and the March was continued within an hour.

While the successful feint on Macon was carried out, the Right Wing proceeded on its journey with virtually no resistance. Leaving McDonough on November 17, Howard's Army of the Tennessee camped around Jackson and prepared to cross the first major river in its path, the Ocmulgee. Osterhaus sent cavalry ahead of the column to seize a crossing at Planters Ferry, also known as Seven Islands. The troopers were to cross the stream and guard the opposite bank until dawn, when the entire wing would follow.

At daybreak on the 18th the pontoon train began slowly passing through the column. At 11:00 A.M. it reached the river, and by 1:00 P.M. two bridges had been thrown across the Ocmulgee and troops began crossing. Infantry units were the first over the river. They scrambled up the high ground and established light works to protect the rest of the wing. The cavalry rode out to screen the army's flanks.

That night the 17th Corps crossed and marched through Monticello to Blountsville, Haddock, and Fortville. The 15th Corps was abreast to their right, moving south to Hillsboro and Clinton. Both corps would concentrate around Gordon, roughly halfway to Savannah. Bad weather would delay the crossing, and the last division would not pass through Clinton until November 22.

Thomas Osborne, an artillery officer in Howard's command, kept a full account of the March for his two preacher brothers. He camped at White Hall in south Atlanta for several nights before beginning the campaign. His unit found few provisions in Clayton and Henry counties, which had been stripped by both armies during the summer and fall. That unfortunate circumstance ended as the column neared Jackson, where plentiful provisions were secured and horses and mules were appropriated in abundance. The artillery animals with which he had left Atlanta were scrawny, half starved from lack of fodder on account of Hood's breaking the railroad. Now new mounts were impressed to make up that deficiency.

Osborne rode into camp at Jackson around noon on November 17. He found it a "beautiful little place and evidently occupied by the most prosperous people" of the region. Osborne noticed that most of Jackson's three hundred inhabitants had left their homes. This was a pattern that frequently occurred throughout the March. Fleeing citizens who abandoned their homes at the approach of one corps or wing would usually encounter another. Their animals would be impressed, and the people quartered in nearby houses until the army passed.

Osborne said Jackson was left "a little sadder if not a wiser community." Nothing remained but a few civilians and their houses.

Part of the column camped a few miles south at Indian Springs. Private Upson discovered it was "a summer resort and there is a low long building here called the Hotel. I think there must be some 250 rooms in it. No one lives in it." Soldiers found a chest with silver coins and ivory poker chips, which they divided among themselves as souvenirs.

Finding that Upson had fallen ill, his captain told the soldier to rest in a house until he felt better. The owner gave Upson a canteen of mineral water that seemed to help. "There are a great many mineral springs here, and all seem to be different kinds of water," he marveled.

As Osborne prepared to cross the Ocmulgee, a severe storm drenched the area, turning the roads into red clay quagmires. Once across the river, there was a steep slope that became nearly impassable. The 15th Corps required thirty-six hours to complete their crossing; over one thousand soldiers were stationed between the bridges and the crest of the hill to help wagons and artillery make it up the slope.

Officers were stationed at the bridge to seize horses and mules that had been collected by foragers. Enough animals were taken to mount an infantry regiment, and a thousand puny animals were weeded out and shot. Residents said the bones were visible for decades afterward.

A squad of men burned a large textile factory that lay on the banks of the river. The facility had seventy-five looms and made finished cloth from raw cotton. It employed 150 workers and had 1,500 spindles and 20 gins in operation. The facility had recently been sold for nearly half a million dollars. A company store, housing, and seven hundred bales of cotton were also destroyed. A number of slaves used at the factory promptly volunteered to join the Federal Pioneer Corps; they would lay pontoons, corduroy roads, and build earthworks.

On November 18 Osborne covered twenty miles of rolling countryside,

Portions of the Right Wing camped at Indian Springs near Jackson.

which he found well cultivated, and a considerable quantity of cotton was burned. Since the weather had cleared, it was possible to trace the progress of several corps by the smoke. Osborne counted twenty-five separate fires at one time. The local men were civil, he said, but "the women were not inclined to take our motivation so good naturedly."

After hearing that Sherman's army had left Atlanta, Miss Emma Manley decided to leave her Spaulding County home and travel to Macon for safety. She packed on November 16, and with her niece and several local militiamen, left early on the following morning. Before she could leave, Federal cavalry rode up and demanded to know where Wheeler's cavalry was. The soldiers called her a liar when she replied that she did not know. "Sir, I'll have you know I am a Southern lady!" Miss Manley responded angrily. As the Federals rode away, she heard "the rumbling of the great army at a distance coming."

This encounter convinced Manley and her party to depart immediately. Crossing the Ocmulgee River without incident, they paused for lunch. Looking behind them, they saw a "blue cloud of Yankee soldiers coming." The men were forced to take the horses and flee to avoid capture, and Union cavalry soon approached the women. When Manley nervously asked for a gentleman to protect her party, one man stepped forward and announced, "I have a mother and sister. I'll protect you at the risk of my life."

The ladies were delivered into the care of General George Spencer, who commanded the 1st Alabama Cavalry. He took them to a nearby house and told the occupants, "Take these in or I'll burn your house damn quick." Spencer surrounded the house with forty troopers and personally brought the women three meals each day.

Manley and her niece watched as their wagon was unloaded and their trunks broken open. One trooper wrapped his horse in fifteen yards of silk, while another covered his mount with a white crepe shawl.

"There we sat until Sherman's entire army passed, resting our heads in each others lap," Manley wrote. Spencer left food and a horse for the women and departed. After the War ended, Manley received several letters from the General. "My niece said he was smitten," she confided.

Protecting Manley and her niece was apparently the only decent thing Spencer did during his passage through central Georgia. He drew a reprimand from General Francis Blair, commander of the 17th Corps, on November 20. "The outrages committed by your command during the march are becoming so common, and are of such an aggravated nature, that they call for some severe and instant mode of correction," it read. "Unless the pillaging of houses and wanton destruction of property by your regiment ceases at once, I will place every officer in it under arrest, and recommend them to the department commander for dishonorable dismissal from the service."

It was frigid when Miss Manley returned to Spaulding County riding on an oxcart. She found the house ransacked, the outbuildings burned, and animal carcasses scattered across the property. While soldiers pillaged the place, Manley' sister had glanced out a window and commented on the snow. "No, misses," a servant replied, "those men are ripping up all your feather beds and pillows to see the feathers fly."

The sister had an adopted five-year-old daughter. The girl had but one keepsake from her mother—an exquisite ebony box. "A rude Yank jerked it from her little hands," Manley remembered indignantly. "He dashed it against a tree and broke it into splinters."

Osborne entered Monticello on November 19. He called it a "pretty little village . . . remarkable for the great number of young ladies." The only remaining men were old; the rest were in the army or hiding in the swamps to avoid conscription, which "these people appear to dread more than they do our army."

While resting in Monticello, Osborne participated in a "decidedly ludicrous" incident. A young woman reported that a cruel Confederate cavalry captain was armed and hiding in town. The man, who was a "notorious rough and boasted that he could whip any man in Georgia," was located and, being an officer, was paroled. At this point the Rebel whipped out a pistol and fired at the soldier who had granted the parole, but missed. The Yankee handed his rifle to a friend and lit into the cavalryman, knocking him down and bruising his face, and the Confederate was ordered to join enlisted prisoners who were marching with the column. He refused until a guard put an inch of bayonet in his rear. Osborne saw the man later, "and he was a sorry looking specimen." Osborne found it interesting that the officer's own people had turned him in. The women of Monticello seemed to enjoy the man's situation "intensely."

Erasmus H. Jordan was in the Georgia militia trying to slow the Union advance when the enemy reached his parents' home near Monticello on November 20. Alarmed by reports of Yankees in town, they had turned out their stock the previous night. Unfortunately, the cattle and horses wandered back as the Federals arrived. The Yankees stole the animals, then ransacked the house. The soldiers "played a chord or two on Mother's rosewood piano in the parlor," wrote Jordan's Aunt Rebecca, "and then poured molasses on it, cut a feather bed open and poured feathers over the molasses." The hogs were shot, and then the foragers loaded up all their loot on horses and "rode off down the road; each man barely visible on account of the plunder."

Osborne continued to Hillsboro on November 19, which he called "no town." He rode to Clinton on the following day through a countryside that "abounds in peaches." Another artillery unit covered thirty-two miles that day, losing ten horses to exhaustion. Federal cavalry had burned all but a few houses in Clinton because of an embarrassing defeat suffered at nearby Sunshine Church during the past summer.

Mrs. Louise Caroline Reese Cornwell anxiously awaited Sherman's approach at her home in Hillsboro. A cousin on furlough from the Confederate army rode out to scout the Union approach and was captured. A squad of thirty Confederate cavalry had stopped at the house for breakfast, but Mrs. Cornwell urged them to leave quickly. "We knew that the Yankees were near for we could see the black smoke as it passed from the burning gin houses, mills, and residences."

The Confederates mounted up and rode off with Union cavalry in pursuit. Volleys were exchanged, and the Federals returned leading two empty horses.

The enemy cavalry passed the house throughout the day. They drove off the stock, "indeed every living thing on the farm," and "took every bushel of corn and fodder, oats and wheat—every bee gum, burnt the gin house, screw, blacksmith shop, cotton, etc."

Cornwell's elderly mother failed under the excitement, and by nightfall she "could not rise from her chair." The woman never recovered from the experience.

When General Howard and his staff stopped for tea, Cornwell prepared the last food in the house to serve her "guests." She thought it strange that while Howard "sat at the table and asked God's blessing, the sky was red from flames of burning houses."

Howard's officers performed "many pretty pieces and sang several pretty songs" at Cornwell's piano. After they left, late at night, a soldier pounded on the door and asked if she was frightened by them. "I replied if they were gentlemen I was not."

For the next four days the infantry passed, marching four abreast with flags flying. The weather turned cold, but Mrs. Cornwell stood on her porch to prevent trespass. One man forced his way into the home, spoke coarsely to the women, and pocketed knives, combs, and other items that suited his fancy. He committed such "petty, low, mean acts" that Cornwell was led to question whether God had "created man in his own image."

The Cornwell family suffered from hunger and cold, for the Federals stole all their food and wood, even taking their axes. "What could not be carried off was destroyed by being made unfit to eat." Howard had left a guard, who saved them from greater loss. One night when several soldiers knocked at the door, Mrs. Cornwell informed them that she had a guard. The men returned and asked to see the soldier. The guard was asleep, and it was with difficulty that Reese roused the soldier, and he made the threatening men leave.

A number of homes, left vacant by women and children who congregated for safety at neighboring houses, were burned. Several times the Cornwells were ordered out of their home by soldiers who intended to burn it. "If you will burn our house you can burn us in it," she declared. "You have taken everything we possessed, now burn us up if you will, for we will not get out."

The family was frightened by the arrival of several drunken soldiers, stragglers from the column. A neighbor, identified as Mrs. "G," was forced to disrobe partially to prove she was not hiding valuables on her person. Many families lost property they had buried when it was found by soldiers or pointed out by slaves.

Between Hillsboro and Clinton was Sunshine Church, site of a decisive defeat of Union cavalry in July 1864. When Dr. D. C. Huntington of Sherman's medical corps passed through Hillsboro, he was given a list of Federal troopers who had been wounded there and taken to Hillsboro for care, but later died. "I am happy to state that I feel convinced that they were well and kindly treated," he wrote.

Mrs. Cornwell had helped care for those wounded Federals. A Dr. Bondo stopped by and "thanked us for our kindness to their wounded men, said he was sorry that we had suffered so severely. So while the majority were indeed enemies and frequently showed their baser feelings, there was among them one who had some feelings of humanity in his heart toward females."

After several "sleepless nights and fasting days," the Right Wing completed its journey through Jasper County. "Thus passed the great Union Army, composed of many nations and kinds of people, through our beloved country leaving desolation and ruin in its track," Mrs. Cornwell concluded. "Many who had always known comfort, even luxury, were made poor—some penniless and homeless."

From Clinton, Howard's columns made a sharp left turn away from Macon as Kilpatrick attacked the outskirts of the city. The 17th Corps found a brigade of Confederates at Gordon and reported driving them out with ease.

With the state militia concentrated in Macon and Wheeler now riding against the Left Wing, there was little Confederate strength to oppose the Right Wing. Henry Wayne, abandoning Milledgeville with his boy cadets and convict militia and their guards, a motley force of seven hundred, retreated to Gordon. When scouts reported the enemy approaching, Wayne arranged for a train to take his pitiful force to the Oconee River, where he could defend the vital railroad bridge. The telegraph to Macon had been severed, and Wayne anxiously asked Augusta for news. He also requested ammunition and artillery but was cut off from many of his guns in Macon.

Wayne was at his headquarters in the Solomon Hotel when an interesting character rode up. It was Rufus Kelly, a veteran of Lee's Army of Northern Virginia who had been discharged after losing a leg in battle. Kelly rode with a crutch and rifle slung across his pommel. Volunteering to scout in the direction of Griswoldville, Kelly saluted and galloped out of town when Wayne accepted the offer.

Kelly returned at noon, reporting the Yankees' approach. He then left to observe the enemy as Wayne entrained his force for the Oconee River. The train was building up steam when Kelly rode up with the Union advance guard close behind. "General," Kelly asked, "what does this mean? Don't we make a stand?"

From a train window, Wayne replied, "No, Mr. Kelly, it would be ridiculous to attempt to check Sherman's army of one hundred thousand or more men with a force of seven hundred. We go to Oconee, where I make a stand at the long bridge."

According to Wayne's adjutant, T. D. Tinsley, Kelly cursed the General "for a white-livered cur with not a drop of red blood in his veins. His vocabulary of profanity was equaled only by his reckless bravery. Finally he said: 'Well, you damned band of tuck-tails, if you have no manhood left in you, I will defend the woman and children of Gordon.'"

Howard's skirmishers entered Gordon about 4:00 P.M. and fired at the departing train. Tinsley watched Kelly and another man, John R. Bragg, unlimber their Winchesters and fire on the Union skirmishers. One Yankee was killed and the rest scattered, leaving the two men alone in the town for an hour. Soon, Kelly said, "the whole world turned to Yankees."

Amid a hail of bullets, the two foolishly brave men rode for safety. Bragg escaped, but Kelly's horse fell and he was captured. Kelly was treated as a guerilla and sentenced to death by firing squad, but he escaped into the swamps several nights later as the wagon in which he rode crossed the Ogeechee River. He returned to Gordon and lived to teach school for the next fifty years.

Howard established his headquarters in Gordon and reported the results of the first half of the March. His command had captured 115 Confederates, and Kilpatrick had 50 additional prisoners. Nearly two thousand bales of cotton had been destroyed.

Howard revealed troubling problems with foragers and bummers in his ranks. "I regret to say that quite a number of private dwellings which the inhabitants have left, have been destroyed by fire, but without official sanction; also many instances of the most inexcusable and wanton acts." The "inhabitants are generally terrified," he continued.

Howard issued orders regarding the problem, expressing a hope that they would be "effectual." The order read, "It having come to the knowledge of the major general commanding that the crimes of arson and robbery have

Henry C. Wayne and the U.S. Army Camel Corps

Born in 1815, Wayne graduated from West Point in 1838 and served as an artillery officer on the Canadian border during the boundary disputes. He taught at West Point for five years, where his speciality was sword combat. Wayne was brevetted major for bravery in Mexico, and in 1850 the government published his textbook on sword fighting.

In 1855 Secretary of War Jefferson Davis sent Wayne to Egypt and Turkey, where he bought a number of camels and brought them to the American southwest. Davis thought the animals could be made into "gunships of the desert," which would be ideal for fighting the Indians. Wayne felt they could be domesticated for use on southern plantations.

When the Civil War began, Wayne refused a Confederate commission because of conflicts with Davis; but he accepted duty with the Georgia militia. His wife and children remained in Washington, D.C., throughout the war, with his parents. His father was a Supreme Court justice.

After the Civil War, Wayne became a successful Savannah businessman. Declaring secession "folly" he embraced the Republican party. President U. S. Grant bestowed a government position on him, one of many given former Confederates. Wayne died in Savannah in 1883. ∎

become frequent throughout this army, it is hereby ordered: that hereafter any officer or man of this command discovered in pillaging a house or burning a building without proper authority will, upon sufficient proof thereof, be shot."

Howard's men immediately proved that his directive would not be "effectual": virtually the entire town of Gordon was burned. Residents commented on the number of animals slaughtered from which only the best cuts were taken; the remainder were left to rot. Jesse Dozier saw "several fine buildings burned." In nearby Irwinton on November 25, an officer wrote, "the boys had a good time last night. Wrecked town; recovered valuables." Hundreds of men were seen "prospecting," probing the earth with sharpened sticks, ramrods, and bayonets. After the men were lined up, they were read Order No. 26, prohibiting looting and arson, for "I guess the twentieth time," the officer concluded.

Fearing further attacks by Wheeler, Howard faced a number of units to the rear. They entrenched to protect the Right Wing's flank as the column was closed up.

Osborne reported that Howard had been ordered to reach Gordon in seven days. The mission had been accomplished, although bad roads had killed hundreds of mounts. On November 22 cavalry was sent to locate Sherman, who was rumored to be in Milledgeville. Sherman had not arrived, but the mayor showed up to surrender the city. The troopers rode to the mayor's home for wine, then burned the depot and a train and returned to Gordon.

On November 23 Osborne saw the Union casualties from Griswoldville. One man had both legs cut off; another had lost an arm and a leg; and a shell fragment had taken two ounces of flesh from General Walcott's leg. Osborne believed the healthy marching conditions and clean open air saved many of the wounded.

Eliza Frances Andrews continued her journey from Milledgeville and crossed the railroad between Milledgeville and Gordon at a ruined stationhouse. Nearby was a mill, destroyed, Andrews believed, "out of pure malice, to keep the poor people of the country from getting their corn ground."

Near Gordon she forded Commissioner's Creek, which had overflowed from recent rains. "The Yankees had thrown dead cattle in the ford," she wrote, "so that we had to drive about at random in the mud and water, to avoid these uncanny obstructions."

At Gordon, Andrews found "the desolation was more complete than anything we had yet seen. There was nothing left of the poor little village but ruins, charred and black as Yankee hearts. The pretty little depot presented only a shapeless pile of bricks capped by a crumpled mass of tin that had once covered the roof. The R.R. track was torn up and the iron twisted into every conceivable shape. Some of it was wrapped round the trunks of trees, as if the cruel invaders, not satisfied with doing all the injury they could to their fellowmen, must spend their malice on the innocent trees of the forest, whose only fault was that they grew on Southern soil." ■

"We Begged Them to Leave Us Something"

After wisely deciding to abandon Gordon and save his force for future operations, General Wayne fortified several positions west of the Oconee River along the railroad. He placed most of his men on the eastern river bank at Jackson's Ferry, near a railroad village called Oconee. There he was reinforced by Major A. L. Harbridge, who brought 1,200 men and 6 cannon. A smaller force was sent eight miles south to defend Ball's Ferry. Those were the only practical crossings of the swampy river south of the road from Milledgeville to Sandersville, where the Left Wing would cross.

Howard arrived with the 15th Corps at Gordon on November 22. His extended columns would trickle in for two days and enjoy a short rest. With Macon bypassed, the Right Wing expected little resistance on the remainder of its way to Savannah, and Kilpatrick was dispatched to join the Left Wing in Milledgeville. The cavalry would guard the northernmost Union column from Confederates defending Augusta.

The 17th Corps again took the inside track, moving from Gordon through McIntyre and Toombsboro to destroy the railroad to the Oconee. Federal cavalry discovered Confederates behind a barricade two miles from the river and drove them out. Infantry took the advance and found a stockade of logs and trestle timber on the west bank of the river. Supported by a cannon, they endured a hot fire and chased the Confederate skirmishers across the railroad bridge.

The 17th Corps had reached its objective, but Blair informed Howard, "There is no Jackson's Ferry." The swampy route had been abandoned years earlier. Blair could not reach the railroad bridge because of impenetrable swamps that bordered both sides of the river, and the bridge was protected by a Confederate fort on the eastern shore that commanded the approach with accurate cannon and rifle fire. An assault would be suicidal, and the swamps prevented a flanking movement north and south of the bridge. Blair did not believe the Rebel works were very formidable, but even if the bridge could be secured, the soil would never support masses of men or wagons. The general suggested that the 15th Corps move quickly to capture Ball's Ferry to the south before the Rebels were reinforced.

On November 24 the 17th Corps skirmished with the Confederates and burned two miles of trestle and destroyed three miles of track. During the day a train arrived at Oconee and was greeted by loud cheering; apparently southern reinforcements had arrived. Blair's men moved south through Toombsboro on November 25 to Ball's Ferry.

Federal cavalry reached Ball's Ferry on the previous day to seize and hold the west bank for the 15th Corps. Finding the opposite shore guarded, the cavalry deployed up and down the river, crossing the Oconee on several crudely constructed rafts. They emerged from the swamps behind the Confederates and routed the surprised defenders. Wayne hastily dispatched cavalry and infantry reinforcements, with cannon support, from Oconee. They arrived at 3:00 P.M. and drove off the Yankees, who retreated across the river with heavy losses.

Confederate Private Erasmus Jordan and his cavalry comrades opened fire on one of the fleeing Union rafts. "Almost every Yankee in the ferry was killed or wounded," he remembered. "The ferry broke loose from the cable and drifted down stream. The Yankees on the west bank immediately took cover and a steady cross fire commenced between us."

By morning the 15th Corps had arrived from Gordon and Irwinton. Howard found the narrow causeway that led to the ferry swept by a deadly fire and directed Osterhaus to "deploy your skirmishers more and more till there is no reply." Union artillery was unlimbered to make the Confederates keep their heads down, and a brigade from the 17th Corps crossed the river two miles north of Ball's Ferry. The wide Oconee had a swift current, so engineers attached ropes to several pontoon boats and swung the soldiers across. Working through the swamps, they found the Confederate works evacuated.

Private Jordan provided an amusing account of the Confederate withdrawal. Union artillery fire was increasing as darkness fell on the previous evening. "Cannon balls were hitting trees and knocking off limbs," he remembered. "What was the sense of remaining where we were and, as likely as not, being killed? I sought the advice of the man deployed on my right. He was not there. Neither was the man on my left. So, I too, abandoned the place and made my way back to the horses, where I found the rest of the company." While defending the Oconee, four of Wayne's boy cadets had been wounded; one would die.

Late on November 24 Hardee arrived at Oconee after an exhausting journey from Macon, Albany, Thomasville, Savannah, and Millen, to evaluate the situation. Finding the Left Wing crossing the Oconee River from Milledgeville, and Ball's Ferry hard pressed, he directed Wayne to evacuate his men from the east bank. They would withdraw through Tennille and prepare defensive positions along the next river barrier, the Ogeechee. Hardee left for Savannah at 1:00 A.M. on November 26.

Howard brought up his pontoon bridges, and by noon on November 26 his troops were crossing. He had a provost guard set up at the approaches to

Foragers leave camp early in the morning before most soldiers stir.
[HARPER'S WEEKLY]

the bridges, and officers seized horses from foragers, as they had at the Ocmulgee. Dozier and others attempted to escape the dragnet by swimming their horses across, but Dozier's was confiscated. He stole a new one the next day. The guards also "turned back a large number of Negros who have been following us," Upson wrote. "We cannot feed them and must look out for ourselves."

A large number of the paroled convicts were captured along the Oconee River. "The most of these desperadoes have been taken prisoners," wrote Nichols, "dressed in their state prison clothing. General Sherman has turned them loose, believing that Governor Brown has not got the full benefits of his liberality."

Across the Oconee, Osborne found an unusual type of quicksand. The ground was firm enough for several wagons to pass without difficulty, and it supported ordinary civilian traffic, but when a four-inch thick crust gave way, horses sank to their knees in muck. Nothing could move until five miles of this "peculiar soil" was corduroyed. Howard reported two hundred wounded men were being cruelly jolted on the corduroyed roads, most of them casualties from the Griswoldville battle.

Because both corps were using this site, pioneers cut two roads from the river to the first road fork to prevent the congestion that had delayed the wing at the Ocmulgee River. The 15th Corps marched to Irwin's Crossroads and on to Sandersville. The 17th Corps advanced to Oconee, where they burned the railroad bridge denied them on the western side. By noon on November 27, the pontoons had been taken up and the entire wing was on the move again. As the last Confederates withdrew from Tennille, the first Federals entered, troops from the Left Wing who had advanced from Milledgeville to Sandersville. They destroyed the rails to Davisboro, while soldiers from the 15th Corps destroyed the road from the Oconee to Tennille, where they burned the railroad facilities.

The Left Wing swung south from Sandersville. The 17th Corps, with Sherman in attendance, crossed the Ogeechee at Burton to follow the east bank of the river and the railroad to Savannah. The 15th ventured even further south on the outside track to guard the flank of the wing and clear the right bank of the Ogeechee. At any point along the river that Hardee attempted to defend, Howard, traveling with the 15th, would lay pontoons and cross to flank the Confederates. "This always started the enemy at once," Osborne wrote. "They did not wait to fight."

Howard made his camp at Irwin's Crossroads on November 26 and 27 to see the entire wing over the river. On November 28 Howard, with Osborne present, "struck out into the great pine forest of eastern and southern Georgia." Their maps showed lines that "purport to be roads," Osborne wrote, but which were mere trails at best; most looked like cross-country wandering to him. Dozier noted it was "not safe to straggle in this area."

The 15th Corps moved down into Johnson County to strip it of food and livestock. According to Osborne, the trek was a mistake. The 15th was directed to march to Johnson's, but the column traveled so far south that officers began to question their location. Locals had never heard of a town called Johnson's, but told the Yankees that was the name of the *county*. The county seat was Wrightsville, which was found to be a village of a dozen families.

Howard rode off north to locate the 17th Corps, leaving Osborne to lead the 15th Corps fifteen miles back to the proper track. Osborne was terrified. It was night, roads were nonexistent, and he was riding a half-broken colt. Out of desperation, Osborne decided to trust the horse's instincts, and the animal led them to an isolated cabin, where Osborne pretended to be part of Wheeler's cavalry to obtain directions. The exhausted column reached the 17th Corps near modern Kite at 10:30 P.M., after traveling twenty miles in four hours.

Except for this episode, Osborne enjoyed campaigning in the Georgia piney woods. The immense forests were pleasant, and the roads were solid, except for quicksand in the frequent creek bottoms. But supplies were scarce.

On December 1 Osborne found nothing of interest "except the vast extent of these pine forests." A few days later he crossed deep Sculls Creek and saw "southern characteristics": cypress, magnolias, and live oaks hung with moss. A new group of foragers had been appointed for Dozier's brigade, and he found himself afoot for the first time in three weeks. He did not like duty in the infantry; after a day's march Dozier wrote that he was "plaid out." Luckily, he remained in camp on December 3 and enjoyed the first opportunity to wash his clothes since leaving Atlanta. The 15th Corps had several days of rest waiting for the Left Wing to come abreast, then they passed through an extensive quiet pine woods while moving through Summerville to Cannochee.

The village of Summerville was in turmoil over rumors of Federals in the vicinity, but the stories seemed unfounded. On November 30 the enemy abruptly appeared at Rachel Samples' plantation, seven miles away. Rachel's sister-in-law, Sue Samples, suddenly found "a Yank was at each window with a cocked pistol in their hand, swearing all the time, and others were searching for 'Rebs.' . . . I was never so frightened in all my life," she stated.

The cavalry forced the Samples to prepare dinner for them. One Yankee ate and drank so much he became sick, and the trooper accused Rachel of poisoning him. He threatened to shoot her. Before the men left, they tore open the feather beds, chopped the bedsteads to pieces, and stole their books. "Rachel fell across the bed and wept," Sue wrote.

The infantry followed in the cavalry's wake and shot all their hogs. "We could hear nothing but guns all day and the squealing hogs," Samples continued. "We begged them to leave something, but no answer." The soldiers attacked the corn cribs, but Sue's pleas led them to leave enough for the family.

General Giles A. Smith arrived with his division as Sue surveyed the waste. "Our men are carryig on a great destruction," he bragged. Sue said it should be stopped, but Smith "made no reply."

Discovering that Sue was from South Carolina, the soldiers went out of their way to annoy her. The men threatened to leave no house standing in the Palmetto State. "I do not think any race of people can swear so much as the yankees," Sample declared after they left.

The army camped around the Sample plantation that night, their tents and fires stretching for a mile and the camp ringing "with music which made our hearts bleed." When they left, Rachel and Sue scavenged what they could from the enemy bivouac. "Persons were obliged to pick what they left, or perish." The women lived on parched corn for several days.

The 15th Corps moved into Bulloch County on December 4. They left a ten-mile-wide strip of desolation from Statesboro to the Ogeechee River. Two divisions passed through Statesboro, while the other two followed the Old Savannah Road near the Ogeechee through Mill Ray. Sherman was on the opposite side of the river.

Osterhaus expected trouble on his line of march. He received word that Bragg was bringing ten thousand men to fall upon his rear, and while camped near Statesboro, the 15th Corps established a strong defensive position. Osterhaus sent this message to his officers: "The expected approach of a large force of the enemy renders sudden attacks very probable." His divisions should camp with flanks resting on creeks and swamps. They were ordered to carefully picket their camps, a practice that recently had been neglected but would now be "enforced with the utmost strictness." The Confederate force never materialized.

Federal foragers rode into Statesboro on December 4 and were scattered by a determined attack by Confederate cavalry. Eight men were wounded, and twenty-seven were ridden down and captured before the fleeing Yankees reached the ranks of infantry, who promptly deployed into a skirmish line. The soldiers unleashed a volley and advanced behind fixed bayonets, causing the Rebels to abandon the town and ride for the Ogeechee River with ten casualties. Union records claimed there were six hundred enemy cavalrymen in town.

Seeing his home undefended, a local man named Charnock Fletcher rounded up thirty neighbors. Armed with antiquated weapons, his intrepid band rode to repel the invaders. The northern hordes were encountered, and a few ragged shots were exchanged before the makeshift militia fled for

The Great Piney Woods

All day long the army has been moving through magnificent pine-woods—the savannas of the South, as they are termed. I have never seen, and I can not conceive a more picturesque sight than the army winding along through these grand old woods. The pines, destitute of branches, rise to a height of eighty or ninety feet, their tops being crowned with tufts of pure green. They are widely apart, so that frequently two trains of wagons and troops in double column are marching abreast.

—George Ward Nichols

Mill Creek, leaving one of their own and two dead Yankees on the field.

Although established in 1803, Statesboro did not amount to much in 1864. It boasted only a courthouse, two boarding houses, a bar, and four residences. A confused Union officer, following his inaccurate maps and sketchy information from hostile locals, asked a bystander how he could reach Statesboro. "You are standing in the middle of it," the man replied, no doubt shaking his head at this simple abolitionist.

The following holiday season was bleak in Bulloch. "I remember the Christmas of 1864," one resident recalled. "The chief dishes were sweet potato pone and a sweetened corn cake. It was great. There was not a biscuit in our house for about four months."

At every community along the Central Railroad, the Confederates fled as Howard threatened them from the opposite river bank. The Right Wing commander was interested when residents informed him that they saw rockets rising into the sky from the coast every night. The Union fleet was searching for the "lost army."

Osterhaus's columns converged at Jenks Bridge late on December 5 to cross the Ogeechee, but they found the bridge burned. In the morning a brigade from Corse's division was advanced to the front, accompanied by two wagons filled with ammunition and four ambulances to remove the inevitable casualties. The troops paddled across the wide stream in pontoon boats and found a battalion of Confederates sheltered behind a half-mile-long line of rail barricades five hundred yards from the river bank. The Federals charged the works and routed the Confederates, capturing thirty and losing two of their own men killed and three wounded. They were soon joined by a brigade that had crossed at a ferry site three miles north. This force hurried forward to clear the road of timber obstructions, finding a carefully constructed line of works three miles closer to the city. The Rebels had abandoned the defenses and had boarded a train for Savannah.

Corse's two remaining brigades crossed the Ogeechee, and he marched the division south along the east bank. Giles A. Smith's division paralleled his route on the west bank, protecting Corse's flank and transporting the trains of both divisions. On December 8 Corse reached the Savannah and Ogeechee Canal where it joined the Ogeechee River near old Fort Argyle. Dillon's Bridge, which spanned the Ogeechee at that point, was in flames. The bridge was repaired after several hours of work, and Corse went into camp.

On the following morning, Corse learned that the Confederates were in force at the intersection of Dillon's Bridge Road and King's Bridge Road, between Dillon's Bridge and Savannah. Hardee had sent six hundred men with two cannon to build earthworks at the junction and slow the Federal advance, and Corse immediately set out to capture the position. He charged the works with a brigade, supported by a battery of artillery, and the outnumbered defenders were surprised by the audacious assault. They were forced to withdraw toward Savannah.

When Jenks Bridge was secured on December 6, Osterhaus accompanied the divisions of William B. Hazen and Charles B. Woods down the west bank of the Ogeechee. These divisions would cross the Cannochee River to seize

Foragers return from a successful day's work bearing plenty of loot. Soldiers to the left are enjoying a cock fight.
[HARPER'S WEEKLY]

King's Bridge, which would be a supply base. They would then continue south and destroy the Savannah and Gulf Railroad. This move would open an avenue of attack to Fort McAllister, situated near the Atlantic Ocean on the Ogeechee. It was a deadly obstacle to supply ships approaching King's Bridge.

On December 7 a brigade of Hazen's division started for the bridge over the Cannochee River, two miles southeast of Clyde, also known as Bryan Court House. Heavy skirmishing delayed them from Black Creek, twelve miles north of the bridge, to the river. They removed obstructions from the creek and pushed rapidly to Mill Creek, where they captured the bridge intact. They were motivated to move quickly by rumors that the Confederate skirmishers had twenty-three Federal prisoners who were being fed on sorghum stalks.

Reaching the Cannochee River at last, they found the bridge in flames. The situation did not look promising. The bridge spanned several lagoons, and the opposite bank was held by Confederate infantry and artillery commanded by Colonel John C. Fizer. The Confederates were emplaced in a strong position with their flanks protected by extensive swamps, so the Federals withdrew to Clyde to wait for the remainder of Hazen's division to arrive.

Osterhaus came up with Hazen early the next morning. Drawing support from Woods's division, which had marched to Dillon's Bridge, the officers found a narrow levee that led to a series of three now burned spans with a combined length of eight hundred feet. Every inch was swept by deadly Rebel fire. Hazen's men scouted twelve miles north and south of the bridge, but found the swamps inpenetrable.

Late in the evening, Hazen was told of an abandoned ferry landing nearby, and after dark the Federals scouted the site. A few men crossed the river and routed several Confederate pickets they found on the high ground beyond. The approach of an enemy in their rear caused great alarm in the Confederate camp. Hazen reported the Rebels "opened with infantry and artillery most vigorously, and to my astonishment" abandoned the river around 2:00 A.M. They retreated to Cross Roads (also known as Way's Station and modern Richmond Hill). Hazen believed he could not have stormed the ferry site if it had been strongly held.

In the morning, Hazen crossed men in pontoon boats to hold the eastern shore. The bridge was vigorously rebuilt, and two brigades filed over. One brigade moved to occupy King's Bridge, but when they found it burned, they immediately began rebuilding it, also constructing a long wharf. The second brigade destroyed the Savannah and Gulf Railroad at Cross Roads and Fleming, Stations 2 and 3. Eventually Union troops destroyed twenty miles of track on the road, and Corse captured a cannon, mules and wagons, and one cart loaded with hogs.

As Union cavalry neared the railroad, a train leaving Savannah approached with a load of important passengers who hoped to escape before the city was besieged. Seeing the bluecoats, the engineer reversed as the cavalry fired on the train. Thinking quickly, a Captain Duncan rode rapidly behind the train. He led a mule onto the tracks, then shot the animal. The rear car struck the mule and derailed, and the locomotive, eighteen cars, and forty prisoners were taken. On the train was R. R. Cuyler, President of the Central Railroad. Sherman was well acquainted with his son and a brother, George, who had been a surgeon in the pre-War army.

Woods's division returned north and crossed the Ogeechee at Dillon's Bridge. On December 10, he, Corse, and Smith advanced down the canal until they reached the main Confederate defensive line along Salt Creek. The soldiers deployed to face the Rebels and dug in, and when Hazen arrived, his division was held back as a reserve. ■

CHAPTER 14

"The Yankees Is the Most Destructionest People Ever I Saw"

O n November 27 Sherman and his staff joined the 17th Corps of the Right Wing in Tennille. The general was pleased to learn that on the Left Wing Davis had crossed the Ogeechee River and was nearing Louisville. If Hardee had planned a defense at any point along the Ogeechee, it had been outflanked.

The 17th marched south of the railroad and the Ogeechee River until they were opposite Burton, where they would cross. The 20th Corps was busy destroying the railroad to Sebastopol, where the rails crossed the Ogeechee three miles west of Burton. The 17th would destroy the rails from that point. Howard and the 15th Corps were moving to the south, guarding the flank from the opposite bank of the river. They would be ready to cross the Ogeechee behind any significant resistance. That threat alone was sufficient to keep the Rebels retreating closer to Savannah.

Confederate newspapers claimed Sherman was retreating for the coast because Hood had severed his supply lines. The reports stated he had 25,000 men and was marching only ten miles a day. Confederate reinforcements were rapidly concentrating to destroy his force.

"Sherman appears to be making no progress in his invasion of the State," wrote the Savannah *News*. "He is no nearer the coast than he was several days ago. He appears to be hesitating and acting altogether as though he were caught in a bad box and don't know how to get out. Afraid to go forward and cannot go back, his men tired and hungry, with our forces rapidly closing in around him. All these things excite the liveliest hopes of his early destruction."

The Richmond *Whig* presented a strange theory. Even if Sherman reached the coast, it stated, "the Confederate cause will be vastly the gainer, and the Yankee cause vastly the loser." The paper did not elaborate on the reasons behind this idea. Another Richmond paper said the campaign would cost Sherman "half his army." "Sherman and his robbers are marching to doom," an Augusta publication predicted.

On November 28 the 17th Corps traveled southeast across Washington County for fifteen miles through a sandy region rich with corn. The abundance of food made Hitchcock laugh at the thought of the Confederacy's being starved out.

Van Duzer found the area rough, sandy, and sparsely populated. He foraged for turkeys, writing that he was sick of chicken and pork. That was "well Enough for fifty or sixty meals," but no more. He shot three pigs and caught ten chickens for the mess.

There was no enemy in sight on November 29, but soldiers were reported "gobbled" in the rear. The weather was warm, and the roads led through extensive pine forests. Sherman camped in a grove, where Hitchcock found the ground so covered by pine needles that it was as soft as a mattress. He stretched out for a nap but was rudely awakened by a blaze that spread like wildfire through the matted covering.

Reports from the Left Wing indicated Kilpatrick had been in a fight. This information pleased Sherman, as it drew Confederate strength away from the army. Slocum had reached Sabastopol, and Davis was believed to be in Louisville.

Sherman stopped for a while at Tarver's Mill on Limestone Creek. The dam, mill, and pond presented a beautiful scene; surrounding swamps were decorated by moss that hung from live oaks and cypress trees. Because the staff was tiring of hardtack, Nichols appropriated some meal for cornbread. Hitchcock complained that his teeth had become sore from eating the government-issue biscuits.

When they visited Judge Tarver's fine home, the women there complained of wholesale thievery by Union soldiers. Sherman directed the ladies to put their meat in tubs and keep it in the house for protection. When a black servant hurried to Hitchcock and pleaded, "Please, Sir, soldiers are robbing me of all I got, clothes and everything," Hitchcock ran to the rear of the big house and chased the men away.

Beyond Tarver's Mill they began to skirt Williamson Creek Swamp. This region was a nearly treeless area dominated by wiregrass, which is long and slender.

Around midnight Hitchcock heard "someone poking round campfire." He arose to investigate and found Sherman, clad in slippers, red flannel drawers, wool shirt, an old dressing gown, and a blue cloak. He was the "most restless man in the army at night," Hitchcock wrote, "never sleeps a night through." Sherman ignored the constant requests from his officers to get out of the cold. They believed it brought on attacks of neuralgia that had bothered his right arm and shoulder for months. Before this campaign began, Howard had visited Sherman and "found his servant bathing and continually rubbing his arm," which had a muscular lameness.

Hitchcock joined Sherman around the fire. The general explained that he usually awoke around 3:00 A.M. and could not get back to sleep until after dawn. He found this the "best time to hear any movement at a distance," and he made up his sleep with naps during the day.

On November 30 the 17th Corps advanced along the east bank of the Ogeechee River to Burton, also known as Station 9½, and modern Midville. They forded a number of creeks in the warm weather and appropriated tons of corn and sweet potatoes from fertile farms. When they reached the Ogeechee, they found it was a swift, narrow, muddy river, about two hundred feet wide and bordered by dense forests on each bank. Sherman, threading his way between the single file of wagons, was often stopped on the narrow causeway that led to the main channel. Except for this lane of packed sand, the swamps were impassable and covered with quicksand. A short bridge took them to an island, where they saw their first palmetto plants.

"Our army is across the Ogeechee without fighting a battle," Nichols gloated. "This river is a line of great strength to the Rebels, who might have made its passage a costly effort for us, but they have been outwitted and outmaneuvered." The crossing would have been impossible, the staff believed, had Hardee defended it with a few cannon.

The infantry crossed on a charred, shaky foot bridge consisting of planks with no side rails that could accommodate two horses side by side. A pontoon bridge for wheeled vehicles was being laid twenty yards away; it took only ten boats and less than two hours to complete, but the crossing required eight hours.

After dark Hitchcock rode to the river to watch the infantry cross by torchlight. "The fires of pitch pine were flaring up into the mist and darkness," Nichols remembered, "figures of men and horses loomed out of the dense shadows in gigantic proportions; torch-lights were blinking and flashing away off in the forests."

The brick railroad depot stood two hundred yards from the river; other structures in town were constructed with logs. The corps found five thousand yellow pine ties that made fine bonfires to chase away the autumn chill. The railroad agent here was Johnny Wells, an old fellow who sat beside Sherman's fire and talked away the night, contributing many coarse jokes to the conversation. Wells despised the "lying editors and warlike preachers" for leading the South into the War. These few men were responsible for the conflict, he declared. "I told my wife these preachers said the God of battles was on our side and would be round playing the d—l, but you look for him [the preachers] tonight and he's out hid in the swamp."

Brother Wells also spoke with a reporter from New York. "They say you are retreating," he said, "but it is the strangest sort of retreat I ever saw." Southern authorities claimed the Confederate "army was always whipping the Feds, and we always fell back. I always told them it was a damned humbug," and Sherman's arrival was the proof.

Hitchcock had been amused earlier in the day by a slave who declared, "The Yankees is the most destructionest people ever I saw."

Sherman was interested to see an Augusta newspaper of November 26 that called on the people of Georgia to make the Oconee "Sherman's river of death." The Federals had crossed it seven days earlier and were now across the Ogeechee.

Van Duzer recorded that Sherman met a Union man he was "favorably impressed" with and shook his hand. They had met another Union man several days earlier, but that fact had not saved his chickens and pigs, Van Duzer observed.

The March was delayed for a few hours on the first morning of December while the infantry destroyed six miles of railroad and the foot and rail bridges across the Ogeechee. A lieutenant in Wheeler's command was brought in and reported there would be no opposition until the Yankees arrived at Savannah, where *Lee* was waiting. Sherman dismissed the report. Rebel cavalry had struck the Union rear guard, which had yet to cross the river, and the Yankees had scattered; but the threat was not serious.

Van Duzer arrived at Herndon and reflected on the fact that they had covered two hundred miles without opposition. At every place they were told the Rebels were fortifying about two days' travel up the road. He thought this country had a "greater capacity for protection than any I have yet seen," but no one had tried to stop them. He tapped into a Confederate telegraph, but the enemy was on to the trick. They sent a false message reporting that Lee, Longstreet, and Jubal Early were bringing reinforcements to Savannah from the Army of Northern Virginia.

Sherman camped at the plantation of Joseph B. Jones, a member of the Georgia legislature. Jones had reportedly left for Savannah, leaving his wife, who had lost twin infants four days earlier, sick in bed. She had nine children, including two sons in the Confederate army, and had lost two other children. Hitchcock did his arithmetic and expressed pity for Mrs. Jones. "Poor woman had 13 children," he noted, "about one each year."

Sherman visited Mrs. Jones and assured her the family would be treated well. Soon she and her children were talking with the soldiers as if they were old friends. The previous day Yankees had stripped the extensive farm of all its food, but Sherman provided the family with enough food to subsist them until "brave Jones" returned to care for them. Some sources indicate that foragers dug up the dead children while searching for valuables.

A servant named Louisa confided that the children had been "suckled by colored women." Before Sherman arrived, she said, Jones had bragged about killing enough Yankees to make the plantation run knee deep with blood. As the enemy approached, he fled.

Louisa wanted the fine house burned. She loved the children but hated Jones, whom she called a "bitter" Rebel. The master was fond of "whipping niggers most to death with paddle and strap," Hitchcock recorded. Louisa approached the Union servants and asked if she should accompany them to Savannah. She gave serious consideration to the idea but declined for the sake of the children. "The poor little things, they so scared and cry so, that I don't see how I can leave them." Hitchcock encouraged her to stay and wondered at the strange, but "beautiful 'patriarchal relationship'" that often developed between slaves and the families that owned them.

Sherman received a delegation of local slaves. He had heard a rumor that Jefferson Davis might arm the slaves. "Would you fight us?" Sherman asked

Scenic Tarver's Mill in Washington County caught the attention of Henry Hitchcock and artist Theodore Davis. [HARPER'S WEEKLY]

the men. "No sir," their spokesman replied, "the day they give us arms, that day the war ends." Sherman took great pleasure in the response.

The Jones plantation was one of the most luxurious in Georgia. According to Hitchcock, it was a "two story double frame house, wide porch three sides, fine large rooms, and wide hall on first floor, and cupola on top— finest house we have seen yet, and extensive out-buildings." Jones had owned the land for ten years, and he had another plantation near Waynesboro where one hundred fifty slaves cultivated cotton.

A man named Mallory came to see Sherman. He was a Confederate tax assessor and had been worth fifty thousand dollars the previous day, but today he was penniless. All he owned had been stolen by bummers. Hitchcock was angered by the conduct of the soldiers, but he was convinced it would continue until divisional commanders were punished for allowing the looting.

On December 2 the corps marched twelve miles under perfect weather conditions. Railroad trestles were burned, then the supporting timbers were sawed off at the ground, piled up, and fired. Around noon they crossed Buckhead Creek, a deep stream about one hundred feet wide. Men crossed on an old railroad bridge, and mules swam alongside. Hitchcock enjoyed the spectacle, for the animals were "obstinate, unwilling to go in." Wagons passed on a pontoon bridge.

Sherman was interested to read a captured letter from a Confederate cavalry captain to his wife. In it the woman was advised to sell their slaves and buy land with the money. "This people is whipped," the officer wrote, "and will make peace within a year on the basis of liberating their negroes."

The Confederates were growing alarmed by Sherman's relentless advance. Hardee told General LaFayette McLaws, a former divisional commander under Longstreet who had arrived in Savannah to assist in its defense, to expect 3,500 men from Augusta over the next several days. At the same time, President Davis sent a message to Bragg in Augusta. "I trust you will pardon my presumption in writing you on military subjects," he said, then proceeded to offer military advice. He suggested that Savannah be surrendered rather than Charleston, but he encouraged Bragg to destroy tobacco and cotton that were stored in the city and remove railroad stock before it was too late to take action.

Confederate General H. H. McKay responded to orders from McLaws to fortify the Ogeechee River near King's Bridge and the Altamaha River at Doctor Town and to picket both streams. He had only 360 men for the job. A telegraph operator reported that Federal scouts briefly occupied Millen and could be expected in force on the following day.

The pace of advance slowed on December 3 to eight miles, but the Federals occupied Millen, or Station 7, an important rail center. Here the Central Railroad intersected a road that extended north to Augusta through Waynesboro.

Engineer Poe complained to Sherman that the infantry had been doing a poor job of destroying the railroad, and he asked for more diligent men. The idea was rejected, leading Hitchcock to comment on Sherman's most prominent fault. "General don't persist in having orders carried out," he complained. He found Sherman "impatient of detail." After giving orders, he turned his energy and attention to other matters. Sherman was "far-sighted, sagacious, clear, rapid as lightning, personally indefatigable," but too impatient to attend to details like straggling or the destruction of railroads, Hitchcock decided.

The column paused to carry out Sherman's orders to thoroughly wreck the railroad. "The general-in-chief . . . wishes you to make the most complete and perfect possible break of the railroad about Millen," the directive read. "Let it be more devilish than can be dreamed of." Instructions issued by 17th Corps headquarters stated, "Nothing must be left but the old iron and the roadbed."

Millen boasted "a really fine frame depot" two hundred feet long, Hitchcock wrote. It had a magnificent roof supported by arches that sprang from wooden columns. A large, two-story frame hotel, with many rooms and a large dining hall, stood one hundred feet away. Among the outbuildings was a machine for making the gas that lit the hotel. The grounds were decorated by handsome trees and bushes, and nearby were three large frame storehouses, each fifty by one hundred feet, that had contained supplies for the Confederacy and recently had housed Union captives.

The Federals were told that a crazy white woman had taken up residence in the hotel and was fed by the charity of the owners. Around 10:00 A.M. stragglers, including a recently released prisoner, invaded the hotel. The rear of the building was soon consumed by a "roaring big fire," and officers were told the woman was still inside. Hitchcock and others rushed in and found one soldier systematically knocking a row of hat hooks off the wall.

The hotel was empty, but the woman, a "poor wretch," was found in the garden on her knees, stroking a goose. "Pitiful sight," Hitchcock observed. She looked to be fifty years old and had a gray, wrinkled, sad face. Before leaving, Hitchcock gave a slave money to look after the lady.

Moved by the inspiring hotel fire, soldiers soon eradicated the town of Millen. The men found a cache of one hundred bales of cotton that had been concealed in a vault located fifteen inches beneath a dirt floor in a slave cabin. It was set afire, and the depot and storehouses soon followed. Sherman and his staff retired to a hill to watch the spectacle, and soldiers marching through town were awed by the depot's destruction.

"The depot made a superb fire," Hitchcock thought, "even at noonday. Densest black smoke in immense volumes—then broad sheets of flame licking the shingle roof and pillars and *sucked* in under the eaves like a sheet of blazing fluid." He called Millen the "late town" and found no excuse for its total ruin. He was pleased that Howard had arrested several men for looting and arson. If convicted, he ruminated, they could be shot for their crimes. They were not.

"The extensive depot at Millen was a wooden structure of exceedingly graceful proportions," wrote Nichols. "It was ignited in three places simultaneously, and its destruction was a brilliant spectacle; the building burning slowly, although there was sufficient wind to lift the vast volume of smoke and exhibit the exquisite architecture traced in lines of fire. This scene was so striking that even the rank and file observed and made comments upon it among themselves—a circumstance which may be counted as unusual, for the taste for conflagrations has been so cultivated of late in the army that any small affair of that kind attracts very little attention."

He had overheard an Irish soldier, engaged in twisting rails, comment several days earlier, "When the war is over General Sherman will buy a coalmine in Pennsylvania, and occupy his spare time with smoking cigars and destroying and rebuilding railroads."

From Millen the Right Wing executed a sharp change of direction to the southeast. The feint on Augusta was over, and it was time to charge quickly on Savannah before the Confederates had an opportunity to strongly fortify it. Sherman continued with the 15th Corps as it followed the eastern bank of the Ogeechee River, and Howard accompanied the 17th Corps on the western bank, to the south of Sherman. To mark his route for Howard and for Slocum's Left Wing to the north, Sherman directed General Blair to "burn the buildings and culverts, and also enough cotton gins and barns to mark the progress" of his corps. With these signals the other columns could keep pace.

Sherman's staff left Millen and camped for the night at Paramore Hill. As they rode, Hitchcock saw a group of men digging a grave beside the road.

At Scarboro a telegrapher named Lonergan exchanged messages with Savannah. He sent General Howard's compliments and said the army would be there in a few days. An official report was sent to Sherman, who was very displeased. "The Genl don't wish our track known in this manner," Van Duzer wrote.

Nichols found the men ready to reach the coast for culinary reasons. They had tired of chicken and sweet potatoes and looked forward to "oysters in abundance, and without price. In short, the soldiers don't wish to be delayed." He noted extensive corn fields, from one hundred to one thousand acres in size. Most planters had grown cotton before the War, but they now followed the suggestion of their government to raise food. The army had found no extensive stores of cotton, and Nichols believed Southerners had wisely scattered it.

On December 4 Sherman covered sixteen miles and camped at Paris Academy, near Cameron at Station 5½. The weather was clear and the roads fine. These conditions brought to Hitchcock's mind a statement Johnny Wells had made: "The Lord must be on the side of the Yankees, he sends them such weather."

Sherman was growing excited about the possibility of finally encountering resistance on the March. He expected a fight near Ogeechee Church, which occupied a neck of land between the Ogeechee and Little Ogeechee rivers, about fifty miles from Savannah. Blair reported heavy skirmishing and expected to find two to five hundred of the enemy on the other side of the Little Ogeechee, entrenched with artillery support.

Sherman's staff had several accidents this day. For some reason Ewing, the general's brother-in-law, carried a scalpel in his coat pocket. As he mounted his horse, it penetrated his inside thigh to the bone. Hitchcock's mount was frightened by a bloody ham that hung from a wagon, and the horse ran out of control for a distance and was stopped when horse and rider became entangled in a net of vines. Hitchcock had little complaint with the horse. It had covered two hundred miles and was getting thin in the flanks, and although the horse shied at the sound of shots, it liked to lead the staff column.

Sherman stopped for lunch beside a rice field, the first they had seen. There the conversation grew so vile that Hitchcock wrote, "I would give a great deal if I knew how to stop the profanity I have to hear all the time."

Sherman sent soldiers to scout the Confederate defenses in their front, and they returned, having rescued eighty foragers who were nearly compelled to surrender. Three men had been killed in the skirmishing. Sherman learned that the enemy, about five thousand in strength, was ten miles ahead, busily felling trees and digging earthworks. "General will not butt this army against breastworks," but would outflank the Rebels, Hitchcock believed.

At Halayondale the Confederates struck and captured a few slaves and horses, Van Duzer noted. He found plantations in the region situated close together, the land better cultivated, and the people more intelligent and refined. He insulted the South's non-gentry, writing, "Deliver me from spending any great length of time" with poor whites.

Van Duzer considered the Georgia telegraph system adequate. There were thirty poles per mile, and the poles were heart of pine twelve inches in diameter, supporting two wires, one for railroad use and the other commercial. The telegraph offices he inspected were well built and appointed. Nichols was impressed by the railroad station houses, which were generally made of brick and positioned at fifteen-mile intervals. Many soldiers believed the Central Railroad was the best they had destroyed in the South.

During the advance on December 5, the Federals passed a nice house that had been burned. Hitchcock felt "very indignant and grieved," but then learned it had belonged to a Mr. Stubbs, who kept six bloodhounds used to track escaped Union prisoners and slaves through the swamps. Accompanying the column was a colonel who had escaped Rebel captivity. He swore "that no dog shall be left alive on the road he marches on. The troops sympathize with this man and his feelings, and I have repeatedly seen dead dogs [just shot] lying in the roadside and yards." The six dogs and a number of pups were killed, despite the appeals of a young woman.

Sherman stopped at the Stubbs house for two hours while his troops stripped for action. Wagons were halted, skirmishers sent forward, and artillery deployed. A division was readied for combat as Sherman sat on the porch and studied his map. The railroad crossed the Little Ogeechee at a point called Halcyondale, and across the stream lay Ogeechee Church, or Station 4½. There it seemed the Rebels "had determined to stand," Hitchcock stated. The enemy had destroyed the railroad bridge and had removed

"Marching Through Georgia" ■ By Henry Clay Work

Hurrah! Hurrah! We bring the Jubilee!
Hurrah! Hurrah! The flag that makes you free!
So we sang the chorus from Atlanta to the Sea,
While we were marching through Georgia.

Bring the good old bugle, boys! we'll sing another song—
Sing it with a spirit that will start the world along—
Sing it as we used to sing it, fifty thousand strong,
While we were marching through Georgia.

How the darkeys shouted when they heard the joyful sound!
How the turkeys gobbled which our commissary found!
How the sweet potatoes even started from the ground,
While we were marching through Georgia.

Yes, and there were Union men who wept with joyful tears,
When they saw the honor'd flag they had not seen for years;
Hardly could they be restrained from breaking forth in cheers,
While we were marching through Georgia.

"Sherman's dashing Yankee boys will never reach the coast!"
So the saucy rebels said, and 'twas a handsome boast.
Had they not forgot, alas! to reckon with the host,
While we were marching through Georgia?

So we made a thorough fare for Freedom and her train,
Sixty miles in latitude—three hundred to the main;
Treason fled before us, for resistance was in vain,
While we were marching through Georgia.

Hurrah! Hurrah! we bring the Jubilee!
Hurrah! Hurrah! the flag that makes you free!
So we sang the chorus from Atlanta to the sea,
While we were marching through Georgia. ■

the planks from a wagon bridge. They were entrenched half a mile from the fifty-yard-wide stream.

While Sherman made his preparations, skirmishers—some say stragglers—splashed across the deep creek at about 2:00 P.M. and occupied the abandoned Confederate works without resistance. The fortifications were found, "but the birds had flown," Hitchock wrote. "It seems our skirmishers came down to the creek and pitched in with a cheer . . . three shots fired in return and the rebs all left, whereupon our fellows walked in and took possession, 'nobody hurt.'"

"This is better than having to fight those fellows in these bushes, ain't it?" Sherman asked cheerfully. "Flanking is good—very," Hitchcock concurred.

A double row of half-mile-long works crossed the main road. These works were made of earth and rails piled to a height of four feet, with a ditch in the rear. Trees had been cut to obstruct the road. Hitchcock called the abandoned works "hate's labor lost." Sherman thought the works had been erected by about two thousand inexperienced soldiers. The Rebels "could have poured on artillery fire right on the road and bridge," Hitchcock observed.

Henry Wayne and his small force had fallen back through Millen and had entrenched at Ogeechee Church. They were under the command of McLaws, who arrived from Savannah with two brigades of reinforcements on December 3. Two additional brigades arrived the following day. Wayne and McLaws prepared to fight their four thousand men here against the 17th Corps, which skirmished with their force late on December 4. Wayne expressed confidence of holding the position until he learned that the 15th Corps was preparing to cross the Ogeechee from Mill Ray to his left. He was also informed that the 20th Corps was a short distance to his right. During the night, the Confederates retreated to obstruct the roads with felled timber and prepare works closer to Savannah.

Sherman counted this as the fifth time the Confederates had failed to stand and fight. Finding themselves outflanked, "They *had* to leave," Hitchcock noted. "Now you understand what a flank movement means," Sherman told him with a smile, leading Hitchcock to observe, "No man in the army is bolder or more rapid and daring than Sherman . . . but no man is more unwilling to throw away his men." Sherman believed an army was too valuable to damage. As a result of this policy, the men had great confidence in their commander.

Sherman's staff camped for the night at a beautiful house that was approached by a three-hundred-foot-long avenue lined with oak trees. "The General's aides show most excellent taste in the selection of camping grounds," Van Duzer wrote. The plantation had extensive outbuildings, lots of rice, and rice hulling machines. In the garden Nichols poked around with a sword and found buried barrels of sugar, molasses, lard, butter, and preserves. "Surely the people of the south must have some Yankee blood in them to do this," Van Duzer believed. During the night, the owner of the plantation, Matthew Luthurrow, and fifty of his slaves trickled in from a nearby swamp.

Sherman decided to destroy the railroad to this point, but afterwards the troops would march as quickly as possible to gain Savannah before its defenses were improved. He instructed his scattered commands to fill their wagons with food and fodder because the country in their front would be bare.

Earlier in the day, Nichols had come upon a beautiful mansion that "was a scene of shocking confusion: articles of furniture, soiled and broken, were strewn about the floors; household utensils lay in ill-assorted heaps; crockery, shattered into pieces. . . . This was the work, not of our soldiers, but of Wheeler's Rebel cavalry, who had been on picket duty at this place on the previous night."

At the plantation he overheard a slave couple discussing whether they should accompany the Union army. The man, believing his master's stories that the Yankees would kill them, did not wish to go; but his wife hissed at him vehemently, "Shame on you, black man. Stay here! Be whipped like the dog." She joined the column.

On December 6 the corps remained near Ogeechee Church, which was a large, plain frame structure nestled in a grove of beautiful live oaks. Sherman was waiting for the other columns to come abreast before they encountered the powerful works that undoubtedly protected Savannah. While there, he received information about Kilpatrick's action at Waynesboro. The cavalry commander reported a loss of two hundred men. He had burned a number of bridges on the Augusta railroad, including one over Brier Creek that was five hundred feet long.

Sherman was pleased by the appearance of photographer George Barnard, who had taken a number of pictures of the Atlanta Campaign battlefields and forts surrounding the city. He brought the negatives with him and would develop prints at the first opportunity. Barnard had just inspected the Millen prison, where he saw six unburied bodies. Darkness had prevented his taking any photographs of the pen. "I used to be very much troubled about the burning of houses," Barnard told Sherman, "but after what I have seen I shall not be much troubled about it."

Looting

As rumors of the approach of our army reached the frightened inhabitants, frantic efforts were made to conceal not only their valuable personal effects, plate, jewelry, and other rich goods, but also articles of food, such as hams, sugar, flour, etc. A large part of these supplies were carried to the neighboring swamps; but the favorite method of concealment was the burial of the treasures in the pathways and gardens adjoining the dwelling-houses. Sometimes the graveyards were selected as the best place of security from the "vandal hands of the invaders." Unfortunately for these people, the negros betrayed them, and in the early part of the march the soldiers learned the secret. It is possible that supplies thus hidden may have escaped the search of our men; but, if so, it was not for want of diligent exploration. With untiring zeal the soldiers hunted for concealed treasures. Wherever the army halted, almost every inch of ground in the vicinity of the dwellings was poked by ramrods, pierced with sabres, or upturned with spades. The universal digging was good for the garden land, but its results were distressing to the Rebel owners of exhumed property, who saw it rapidly and irretrievably "confiscated." It was comical to see a group of these redbearded, barefooted, ragged veterans punching the unoffending earth in an apparently idiotic, but certainly most energetic way. If they "struck a vein" a spade was instantly put in requisition, and the coveted wealth was speedily unearthed. Nothing escaped the observation of these sharpwitted soldiers. A woman standing upon the porch of a house, apparently watching their proceedings, instantly became an object of suspicion, and she was watched until some movement betrayed a place of concealment. The fresh earth recently thrown up, a bed of flowers just set out, the slightest indication of a change in appearance or position, all attracted the gaze of these military agriculturists. It was all fair spoil of war, and the search made one of the excitements of the march.

—George Ward Nichols

The March was proceeding to Sherman's liking. "The weather was fine, the roads good, and every thing seemed to favor us," he wrote. "Never do I recall a more agreeable sensation than the sight of our camps by night, lit up by the fires of fragrant pine-knots. The trains were all in good order, and the men seemed to march their fifteen miles a day as though it were nothing. No enemy opposed us." However, Rebels picked up by his skirmishers "insisted that we would meet with strong opposition at Savannah."

Unaware of Sherman's location, other segments of the Union war effort were preparing for his appearance. Quartermasters were told that Sherman would soon arrive at the Atlantic coast. They were to send him 30,000 coats and pants, 100,000 pairs of shoes and socks, 60,000 shirts and undershorts, 20,000 forage caps, 10,000 greatcoats, 20,000 blankets, 10,000 tents and knapsacks, and thousands of other articles.

Grant penned an order that would anger Sherman. Reporting his lack of progress against Lee, Grant wanted Sherman to establish a base on the coast, leave his artillery and cavalry to garrison it, and join him in Petersburg's trenches "with all dispatch" by sea. Sherman would receive the communication on December 15.

On December 7 Sherman rode fourteen miles to Station 3. The roads were barricaded at three different points, and a heavy, night-long rain created mud that slowed the column. The sandy roads were bordered by creeks and treacherous swamps, and after several vehicles had passed, the heavy crust would collapse, and men, animals, and wagons would sink deep in nasty mud. A number of spots had to be corduroyed.

Sherman stopped for lunch near Egypt, or Station 4, at the home of Mrs. Elkins. She was a queer sort, Hitchcock thought, who took snuff and buried her clothes in the smokehouse to prevent their theft. Asked if Stubbs hunted men with his hounds, she replied, yes, but "they don't worry 'em much."

Along the road Hitchcock saw another soldier being buried by his comrades. "Perhaps by some once happy fireside his place is now empty forever," he wrote, "and loving eyes will look vainly for his return. Only one more of how many!"

Sherman learned that Slocum had reached Springfield, and Howard was on the west side of the Ogeechee River, opposite him. The 15th Corps was laying pontoons and would soon cross. The Confederates were reportedly fortifying a position in their front.

On the following day, Sherman covered twelve miles and crossed three creeks before camping near a church at Eden. When a burned bridge delayed the March, Sherman claimed to have identified the culprit, whose home was burned. Informed that Slocum was camped a mile away, Sherman invited him over for a conference. They had not seen each other since leaving Sandersville.

Southern newspapers brought into camp angered Sherman. They contained his Special Order No. 120 and Slocum's general order on the same subject. The documents had certainly been obtained from a northern source. "General very much provoked, and quite bitter on newspaper men everywhere," Hitchcock remembered. The Commander was also inflamed by southern embellishments of his activities. They claimed he gave a grand ball for black women in Milledgeville and alleged that rape had been common along his route.

Sherman had heard cannon fire the previous day, marking a failed southern attempt to prevent Howard from crossing the Ogeechee. This day he received a report from Corse that the Savannah Canal had been reached. Osterhaus had a fight on the west side of the Ogeechee River, and Howard sent Hazen's division across the Canoochee River to sever the Gulf Railroad. There was a rumor that Union prisoners had been sent down the Gulf road to Doctor Town. "Possibly we may rescue them yet!" Hitchcock hoped. "So far all goes admirably well," he continued. "Rebs seem puzzled and act strangely."

Sherman camped the night of December 9 near the railroad tracks at Pooler, Station 1, only nine miles from Savannah on the main road leading into that now embattled city. He had ridden ten miles through a raw wind and had passed several abandoned Confederate fortfications.

Approaching Pooler, Sherman was puzzled to find a column marching through a field on the side of the road. His inquiries revealed that an officer [Lt. Tupper of the 1st Alabama Cavalry] had trod on an eight-inch shell buried in the road. A friction trigger had detonated the torpedo and mangled the man's foot. The blast had torn off his foot at the ankle, and he lay on the ground, pale and covered with a blanket. Tupper was described as a good officer whose enlistment had just expired. Sherman saw him later in a house, waiting for his "horribly torn and mutilated" leg to be amputated by a doctor. A piece of shell had run inside the leg bone and exited near the knee, shattering the bone.

"This was not war, but murder, and it made me very angry," Sherman wrote, livid at the memory. He equipped a group of Confederate prisoners with picks and shovels and marched them along the road, "so as to explode their own torpedos or to discover and dig them up." The Rebels were "greatly alarmed," Hitchcock wrote, "and no wonder." They begged Sherman to let them off, but he angrily refused. "He told them their people had put these things there to assassinate our men instead of fighting them fair. . . . If they got blown up he didn't care," Hitchcock remembered. The general nearly laughed as the prisoners stepped gingerly down the road, but reported no more buried torpedos. Other sources indicate the prisoners found up to ten "of these treacherous, death-dealing instruments."

The shells had been laid in a single line across the road. Hitchcock said that half were twelve-pound shells with a nipple sticking out of the fuse hole. The others were large copper cylinders, thirteen inches long and seven inches in diameter. These contained five pounds of explosive and were detonated when the rounded ends were depressed. As the cavalry crossed, one exploded and killed a horse and wounded a man. Tupper had uncovered a second mine, but a man working behind him backed onto one and it exploded. "Perhaps when we take Savannah the 1st Alabama Cavalry won't make somebody suffer for this," Hitchcock thundered, seemingly more outraged than Sherman. "Rebs are certainly insane," he stated. "They can not stop the Union advance, and these puny attempts just exasperate their enemy."

Sherman "did exactly right," in his approach to this incident, Hitchcock continued. "These cowardly villains call us 'barbarous Yankees'—and they adopt instruments of murder in cold blood where they dare not stand and fight like men." Torpedos defending a fort might be permissible, he thought, but to leave them in roads with no warning and then run away was unsportsmanlike. "These murderous instruments of assassination—contrary to every rule of civilized war," he concluded.

What Sherman seemed to forget was that while his troops were destroying the railroads at Jonesboro in late August before Atlanta fell, he directed his soldiers to leave live shells in railroad cuts, which were then filled with brush. Repair crews would be blown to pieces.

While the Federals detoured around the torpedos, Confederate cannon in the distance began to fire. The unseen Rebels cheered as each shot bounced down a straight, forty-foot-wide causeway. Sherman rode into a pine forest, dismounted, and walked toward the enemy battery, which was about half a mile ahead. The Confederates had two cannon behind a strong stockade and earthwork, and infantry hidden in a twin line of trenches that extended into the extensive Monteith Swamp for thirty yards on either side of the road. A twelve-pound shot almost killed General Blair; it bounced two feet over his head and killed a captain riding behind him. Hitchcock saw Federal soldiers stack their arms and start erecting protective works without orders. They threw up three layers of logs and topped that with earth until the breastworks were four feet high.

Blair deployed a strong skirmish line into the swamp on both sides of the road, and Union soldiers began "to cheer and push ahead in prospect of a fight," Hitchcock saw. The men advanced as two Federal guns unlimbered and replied to the Rebel fire. As the Yankees struggled through the muck and tangled undergrowth, the Confederates fled their position amid a "brisk" exchange of fire. The advancing Federals captured twelve prisoners and one cannon, an English ten-pound Blakley Rifle. Incredibly, the first shot from the Union artillery had hit the muzzle and knocked the cannon off its carriage. Osborne inspected it later and found that it had apparently just been unloaded from a blockade runner, probably in Wilmington, North Carolina, and transported south. White painted shipping marks were still visible.

It had been the 17th Corps' roughest day. Casualties had been inflicted by torpedoes and by cannon and rifle fire. A piece of heavy artillery mounted on a railroad car gave the column a good bit of trouble. On that day it fired thirty-one shells, killing six men and wounding ten.

In the evening Sherman heard that Howard was south of the Savannah Canal. After 15th Corps men cut the Gulf Railroad, Union cavalry rode up and fired on the soldiers, supposing that any troops that far advanced must be Rebels.

Van Duzer estimated that the army would reach Savannah in two more days. There would be "no doubt as to the results." The weather was good, and many prisoners were being captured. Houses gave the appearance of having been quickly vacated, and roads had been hastily barricaded.

In the morning, Sherman was on the road when he heard cannon fire. The

General stopped at a house and warmed himself beside a fire as wounded skirmishers were brought in. His curiosity aroused, Sherman walked down a road near where the Federals had halted and entered a thick forest to examine the Confederate works. Sherman clambered down into a deep railroad cut and found that the rails extended eight hundred yards in a straight line to an entrenched Rebel fort.

"I could see the cannoneers preparing to fire and cautioned the officers near me to scatter, as we would likely attract a shot," Sherman wrote. "Very soon I saw the white puff of smoke and, watching close, caught sight of the ball as it rose in its flight, and, finding it coming pretty straight, I stepped a short distance to one side."

Hitchcock had just caught up with Sherman when the cannon fired. He heard a "loud rushing and whispering in air . . . very like the noise of a rocket" and threw himself to the ground as the ball hit the ground and bounced. A Union soldier was fascinated by the sight of the thirty-two-pound cannon ball as it grew in size from a tincup to a plate and finally a barrel that approached with a roar. The officers dove for cover, but a slave crossing the railroad never realized his danger as the cannonball "struck the ground, and rose in its first ricochet, caught the Negro under the right jaw, and literally carried away his head, scattering blood and brains about," Sherman wrote.

A soldier covered the body with a coat as Sherman wisely decided to withdraw out of range. "This place is not safe, they are firing down the road, we had better go back," he told the men. Hitchcock saw the shot roll back to the house they had just left. The staff settled into the woods for lunch, with an occasional Confederate shell exploding nearby.

Hitchcock believed the army was stymied. "How long will it take us to get over the *last* mile of our march?" he wondered. His commander issued Special Field Order No. 130, which organized the investment of Savannah. The 20th Corps would hold the Federal left; Howard would open communications with the fleet on the right; and Poe would chart the enemy fortifications in preparation for an assault.

Hitchcock thanked God for his health and the safety of the army, considering the March "a great and important success," even without Savannah's capture. The army had advanced "with impunity through the heart of the richest rebel state" and had subdued it. They had hardly touched their provisions and had better teams and more cattle than when they left Atlanta. Victory, he decided, "implies and requires . . . suffering . . . war now so terrible and successful that none can dream of rebellion," after this devastating experience.

There were rumors that Beauregard, Longstreet, and Hardee were defending the city, but Sherman did not take them seriously. He was convinced of one fact: there would be no more reinforcements. Savannah was under siege. ■

A DRIVING TOUR
■ The Right Wing ■

To begin this tour, drive south from Atlanta on I-75. Leave the interstate at the Southlake Mall Exit, and turn right onto GA 54. After 3.6 miles turn left to cross the railroad, and immediately turn left onto McDonough Road. Follow it for .4 to the Confederate Cemetery at the corner of Johnson Street.

A tour of the Right Wing's march begins at the Patrick Cleburne Confederacy Cemetery in Jonesboro. Here the Atlanta Campaign ended in early September 1864, and in November Kilpatrick's cavalry drove out Rebel horsemen to clear the way to the coast for the 15th and 17th Corps.

This cemetery contains the graves of hundreds of Confederates who died at the battle of Jonesboro. The men had been left on the field by retreating Rebel forces and were buried by the victorious Federals in two mass graves. Individual stones, marked Unknown, have been erected.

Jonesboro was visited repeatedly by Union troops during 1864. In July Federal cavalry burned the courthouse and depot, and a large part of the town was destroyed during the two-day battle on August 31 and September 1. Union foragers scoured the countryside during Atlanta's occupation, and by the time the Right Wing swept through, the citizens were destitute.

It is surprising that so much of Clayton County's heritage remains. The Chamber of Commerce has prepared a superior driving tour of Jonesboro and the county. Mansions and plantation homes abound in this region, including one that is thought to be the inspiration for Twelve Oaks, from Margaret Mitchell's novel *Gone with the Wind*. There are also beautiful churches and scenic mills in the area.

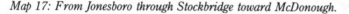

Map 17: From Jonesboro through Stockbridge toward McDonough.

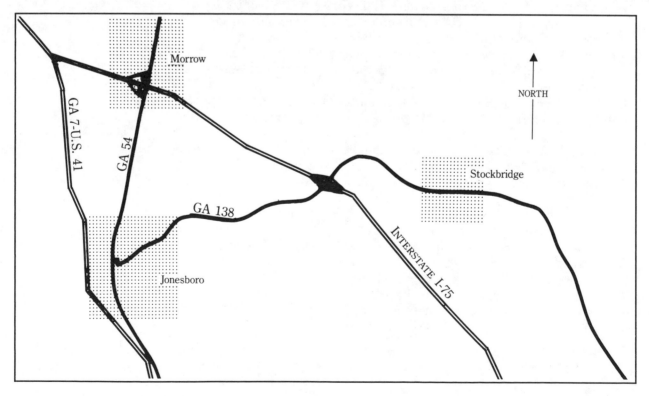

Week-long services are held every summer at Shingle Roof Camp Ground near McDonough.

From the cemetery drive south on McDonough Road. Continue straight after the stop sign at .3, and after .1 turn left onto GA 138. Pass under I-75 after 5 miles, and at 1.3 stop at the intersection with GA 42-U.S. 23. Turn right, and at 1.7 you are in Stockbridge. The highway crosses Stockbridge on an overpass, but a turn-off to the town is on the left just before the bridge.

Continue east on GA 42-U.S. 23. After 1.6 mile follow that highway south as GA 138 branches straight. After 7.3 miles the Henry County Courthouse (1897) in McDonough is on the left. The courthouse faces a beautifully tree-shaded square.

The old county jail, also built in 1897, is located behind the courthouse and is being restored. On Jonesboro Street is the Old Globe Hotel, constructed in 1833.

The people of Henry County recorded that Sherman's men burned two churches during their passage and slaughtered animals in the sanctuary of another. At Peachtree Shoals they destroyed mills that residents depended on to grind their corn and wheat.

North of McDonough is Shingle Roof Campground, a place of religious instruction and socialization during the summer months. It has a huge roofed auditorium that is open on all four sides. Cabins, dorms, and dining facilities surround it. Panola Mountain State Park is located 14 miles north of McDonough. It is a rocky peak similar to Stone Mountain, and visitors may hike several trails up the rugged slopes. To the east, at Snapping Shoals, are an old stone store, an old iron bridge across South River, and some scenic rapids.

Drive straight past the courthouse in the direction you have been traveling, on GA 42-U.S. 23. Along the route is Cotton River, where Union soldiers brushed aside resistance by the Orphan Brigade. After 7 miles the Locust Grove Institute in on the right.

This large, two-story brick building once housed a well known educational institution. It is now the town's municipal center. About half of the business district is open, and the Baptist Church has nice columns and stained glass.

Map 18: From McDonough to Locust Grove.

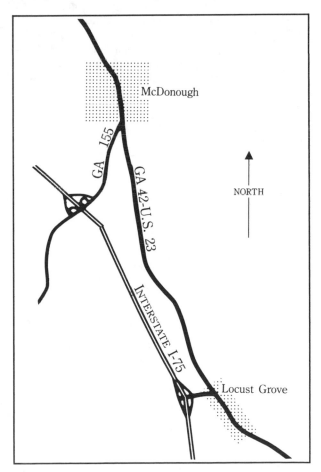

Continue south on GA 42-U.S. 23. After 5.4 Jenkinsburg will be on the left.

According to local lore, the women of this community were so hungry that they held up a Union wagon train for food. There is a well at city hall, and the beautifully shaded Methodist and Baptist churches both have stained glass windows.

Continue in the same direction. After 4.9 is a stop sign at the intersection with GA 16 in Jackson. Turn left for .5, and the Butts County Courthouse is on the left. After Sherman departed, only the Masonic Hall remained on the courthouse square. An estimated one million dollars' worth of damage was done to the county.

Continue straight past the courthouse for .7, and bear right to follow GA 42-U.S. 23 south toward Macon. After 3.5 bear right on GA 42.

On the right you will pass a Holiness campground that was established in 1890. This quiet, shady community has a number of year-round residents, but the population swells during summer when people travel from across Georgia to attend the yearly religious services. The open-sided assembly area is topped with a metal

Map 19: The Jackson area.

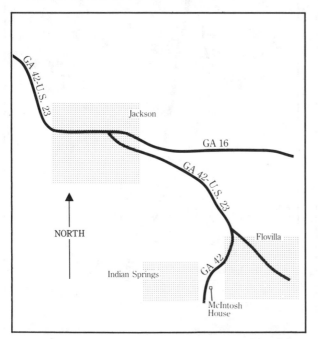

roof, and many numbered houses, bearing the names of family owners, surround it.

The entrance to Indian Springs State Park is to the right at 1.5.

This has been a gathering spot since long before Europeans arrived in Georgia. For centuries Indians came here for the spring water, which was thought to be medicinal. Large resort hotels sprang up around Indian Springs, but all have burned except the McIntosh House. People once traveled here from across Georgia to spend their vacation playing cards, bowling, and dancing. An amusement park operated until 1968. The main spring is still quite an attraction, as people daily bring jugs to fill with the water. Wading among the rocky shoals is a popular pastime, and the park has camping facilities, cottages, nature trails, swimming, and fishing. A museum explains the history of Indian Springs from prehistoric times to the present. The stone buildings mark this park as a Depression-era project.

The McIntosh House is located a short distance south on GA 42, opposite the second entrance to the park.

The two-story, Federal style structure was built in 1823 by Chief William McIntosh for use as a hotel and tavern. Two years later he signed a treaty that ceded the last Creek Indian lands in Georgia to the state. He was soon killed by other Creeks, who felt the act was treasonous. The house was recently restored by the Butts County Historical Society.

Nearby Flovilla, where Union troops camped, has some nice old homes along the railroad tracks, and closed buildings downtown. The Baptist and Methodist churches have beautiful stained glass windows.

While the Right Wing proceeded unmolested along this route, Confederate cavalry and Georgia militia kept pace to the west, guarding several hospital centers. In Griffin's Stonewall Cemetery are buried several hundred Rebels and one Yankee who died of wounds following the battle of Jonesboro. It contains one of the first monuments erected to honor the war dead, a stone angel with the inscribed command, "Rest! Soldiers! Rest!" In Barnesville's Greenwood Cemetery are the graves of 155 Confederates and two Federal soldiers who died in five local hospitals. The buildings of Forsyth's Tift College were used as hospitals, and the city cemetery contains the graves of three hundred southern soldiers. Historic driving tours of Barnesville and Forsyth are available from their chambers of commerce.

Just south of Indian Springs is High Falls State Park. It was a prosperous industrial town that supported a grist mill, shoe factory, and cotton gin, until Wheeler burned the facilities as he retreated toward Forsyth. Although the town was rebuilt, High Falls was soon deserted after the railroad bypassed the community in the 1800s.

The park is located along a long section of beautiful falls on the Towaliga River. Several mill stones can be found beside an old bridge that spans the river, and nature trails line both sides of the rapids. One leads visitors to a concrete shell that housed a hydroelectric power house, built in 1903. The park offers camping, fishing, and the usual activities.

Return north on GA 42 to the intersection with U.S. 23. Retrace your path to the intersection with GA 16. Turn right onto GA 16 for 7.3 and cross the Ocmulgee River.

Along the way you pass Iron Springs, where Union troops camped overnight. Just before the river is a road to the left that leads to Lloyd Shoals Dam and recreational facilities at Jackson Lake.

The Right Wing crossed farther south than this route, at Planters Ferry, also known as Seven Islands, where they destroyed a substantial textile mill. The shoals there, where water power was harnessed for the factory, are still accessible down rough dirt roads that can best be traced on a county map. The bones of hundreds of horses and mules, weaker mounts killed by the Yankees, were visible on an island in the river for decades.

The Jasper County Courthouse in Monticello is to the left after 9.5 miles from the river.

A guide to historic Monticello is available from the Chamber of Commerce. It directs visitors to many of the town's fine homes, including the Hitchcock-Roberts House (1817) and Reese Hall (1820). The old high school, constructed in 1921, is on the National Register of Historic Places. Notice the Bank of Monticello, which was built in 1966 as a replica of Thomas Jefferson's famous home Monticello.

From the courthouse, continue south to follow GA 11 toward Gray and Macon. After 9.8 an old school in Hillsboro is on the right.

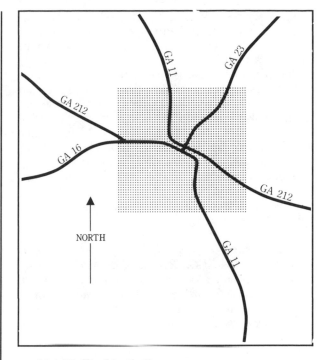

Map 20: The Monticello area.

This community is one of the oldest in central Georgia, dating to 1790. A marker on a stone here indicates that this was the home of noted Georgia politician Benjamin Hill. The community has several pretty churches, a closed two-story wooden store, and a nice brick store. Half of the Right Wing marched directly from Planter's Ferry to Hillsboro on roads that no longer exist. One Union soldier who died during the March is buried in the Baptist Cemetery.

Drive south. After 5.9 Sunshine Church II is sharply to the right, almost hidden in the trees.

This is Round Oak, where in July 1864 a Federal cavalry raid was destroyed. Acting out of revenge, the Right Wing burned the church, where Union soldiers had received medical care following the battle. After this neat church was built in 1880, B. F. Morris, a Union cavalryman wounded in the July battle, returned to preach in 1890.

Proceed south from Round Oak for 3.6. Turn right onto SR 779 (Green Settlement Road) as GA 11 continues to Gray.

Much of the surrounding countryside is part of the

Piedmont National Wildlife Refuge, a 35,000-acre preserve that was established to protect 182 species of birds and other creatures. Hunting, fishing, and nature trails are attractions.

Not far to the west is the Jarrell Plantation. This state site is a seven-acre farm that operated between 1840 and 1940. It was not a Greek Revival, moonlight and magnolias operation, but a self-sufficient working farm. One house on the spread dates to 1840, another to 1895. There are also a barn, arbor, chicken house, well, implement shed, facilities for processing every type of food grown on the premises, and machinery for working wood, leather, and iron. The farm was stripped of all its provisions by Union troops on their way to the sea.

After 5.3 you are in Clinton. Just before reaching four-laned GA 11-GA 22-U.S. 129, turn sharply left onto the county road. After .3 Clinton is to the left. Also on the left is a large sign with a map of Clinton and a monument that commemorates the visit of LaFayette, the French hero of the American Revolution.

Clinton is considered the best-preserved example of a southern county seat from the 1830s era, a community frozen in time. It was a rough pioneer town in the 1820s, when prosperous people built homes in the Plantation Plain style. A college for women, the seed of renowned Wesleyan University in Macon, was established, and Samuel Griswold arrived from Connecticut to build a factory for manufacturing cotton gins.

Then a downward spiral started. Macon was settled and stole Clinton's economic thunder. Griswold moved his business south to the railroad, and Sherman soon showed up to burn one third of the town. After the Civil War, residents decided they did not want dirty locomotives passing through their quiet community. As a result, the rails were established just north, in Gray, which became the county seat. Thus Clinton was left a pre-Greek Revival town. The McCarthey-Pope House dates to 1809, and the Methodist Church was built in 1821. Eleven other houses were constructed before 1830. The Clinton Historical Society has prepared a guide to Clinton's architectual treasures.

This is your closest approach to Macon, which has a number of historic attractions and accommodations for travelers. Literature about the city, and a wonderful driving tour, is available from the Visitors Bureau.

Macon served as an important quartermaster center for the Confederacy. From the city supplies, ordinance and munitions were distributed to armies in the field. Cannon, smaller weapons, and ammunition were also manufactured here. After fighting approached Atlanta in 1864, Macon became a haven for military hospitals and refugees.

In Confederate Square of scenic Rose Hill Cemetery are the graves of 600 Confederate soldiers, including some killed at the tragic Griswoldville battle. In nearby Riverside Cemetery is a remarkably preserved artillery battery, part of the line that helped repulse Kilpatrick's attack in November 1864 and a Union cavalry raid four months earlier.

Macon's destruction during the War was limited to a single cannonball that struck the sidewalk in front of Judge Asa Holt's home. The ball pierced a column and bounced into his parlor. Known today as the Cannonball House, this elegant 1853 structure is open to the public. Behind the house, in the old servants' quarters, is a Confederate museum. The prize artifact is Mrs. Robert E. Lee's rolling pin.

Drive straight for .1, then turn right for .1 to GA 11-GA 22-U.S. 129. Carefully cross the highway to SR 799, also called Lite-N-Tie Road (sic.). To the left of the road is an enormous kaolin mine. Such pits crater much of middle Georgia and constitute an important part of the local economy. After 6.6 turn right at the sharp bend, and after .8 stop at the intersection with GA 49.

Remain on SR 799 and drive straight across GA 49. Along the way note the group of weathered farm buildings on the left. After 3.4 cross a set of rails, which is about all that remains of Griswoldville, now called Griswold.

Samuel Griswold bought four thousand acres here after the railroad was built between Savannah and Macon, and he constructed an enormous factory that produced nine hundred gins a year. He also had a saw mill, grist mill, and factories that produced bricks, soap, and candles. Griswold built a twenty-room, three-story mansion for himself and sixty cottages for his workers. All was destroyed by a Union cavalry raid in July 1864, and repeated visits by blue troopers in November. The battle in which inexperienced Georgia militiamen were slaughtered occurred north of the railroad.

Drive 1.4 miles beyond the rails to the intersection with GA 57. Turn left, and after 8.4 turn left onto GA 18. After 1.2 turn right onto GA 18 SPUR for .5 to downtown Gordon.

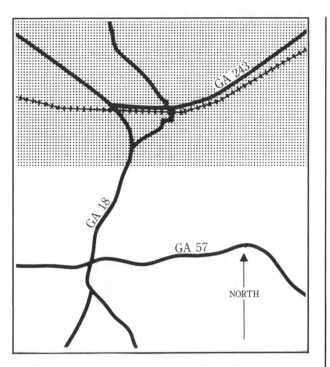

Map 21: The Gordon area.

Notice the old water tower to the left, which houses a barber shop. Beside the depot is a monument to the suicidal bravery of Rufus Kelly. Downtown Gordon is mostly deserted, but note the old theater and hotel, a jail dating from 1917, and several pretty churches. There is a great deal of train traffic, as kaolin is shipped to and from the huge Englehart operation.

A Federal cavalry raid on Gordon in July 1864 destroyed 11 locomotives and 140 cars loaded with supplies for Confederate armies. Rail facilities here and at McIntyre and Toombsboro were also ruined. What survived, including many residences, was destroyed by Sherman's men in November.

Return to GA 57 and turn left.

On your right is historic Ramah Church. Here a military unit called the Ramah Guards was raised and left for the battlefields of Virginia in 1861.

This is a region of wooded hills. Notice the view to the right where the forests have been clear cut.

After 11.7 miles, the Wilkinson County Courthouse in Irwinton is on the right. On the grounds is an old

well house, which was once the community water source and gathering place. Off the highway, Irwinton is one of those quiet walk-in-the-road places.

Union soldiers burned the courthouse in Irwinton, but fortunately the records had been hidden in a swamp. That type of story is frequently repeated along the route of the March to the Sea. On a hill just east of the courthouse is Union Church, which was built in 1856. The name comes from the fact that Methodist, Baptist, and Presbyterian congregations shared the church. This impressive structure has been meticulously restored and is always open, so please stop in.

Continue east on GA 57 for 6.1, then turn left onto GA 112 for .3 to Toombsboro, where residents have been attempting to restore their old community.

This old water tower in Gordon houses a barber shop.

Prominent downtown is the Swampland Theater, formerly a two-story store, which on weekends seats up to seven hundred people who enjoy live gospel and bluegrass music. Old buildings from the surrounding area have been transported to a spot near the tracks and depot and await restoration.

Return to GA 57 and turn left. After 7.8 a picnic area, which contains a monument to the battle at Ball's Ferry, is on the left.

A very rutted trail leads to fishing spots beneath the high bridge that spans the Oconee River. A dirt road leads northeast from the little park to the actual site of the ferry. There the entire Right Wing crossed on two pontoon bridges. A boat ramp and picnic area have been prepared in this very scenic setting. The site of Jackson's Ferry, where the 15th Corps was blocked, is inaccessible because of swamps.

Continue east on GA 57 to cross the Oconee River. After 2.2 turn left onto GA 68. At this intersection the 17th Corps marched for Tennille and Riddleville; the 15th Corps diverged far to the south into Johnson County. After 2.2 remain on GA 68 as GA 272 turns left to Oconee, which is six miles to the north.

General Hardee visited Oconee and authorized abandoning the river line when it was threatened by Union troops crossing from Milledgeville and Ball's Ferry. The quiet town, Station No. 14, consists of residences and some tumble-down buildings.

A historical marker on this route describes the career of Governor Irwin, whose home stood nearby. His grave is not far from GA 68 on SR 273.

After traveling 11.4 miles on GA 68, stop at the intersection where GA 15 enters from the south. Turn left for .4, then left to follow GA 68 for .1. Turn right across the railroad tracks to the mostly open old stores in downtown Tennille, which was Station No. 13. The old depot is located here, and some interesting structures associated with the railroad are south along the tracks.

Continue in the same direction you were traveling, and after .2 is a Stop sign.

To the left is the Tennille Police Station and beside it a Confederate monument guarded by two small cannon. Behind that is a pleasant park maintained by a civic club.

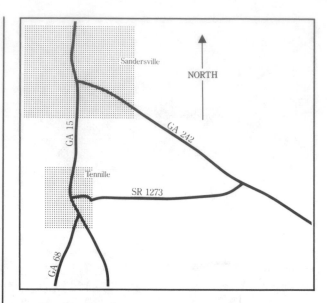

Map 22: The Tennille area.

Turn left to join GA 15 and drive 2.4 miles. Turn right onto GA 242 to Riddleville, which is reached after 9.6.

There are several closed stores, and opposite the two-story one is Riddleville's oldest home, an academy that was organized in Riddleville during the 1830s and operated until 1891. Between Riddleville and Davisboro to the north is the site of Tarver's Mill, a pastoral scene that impressed Hitchcock and other Federals.

Drive east on GA 242 for 12.2 miles to the intersection with U.S. 221. Turn left, cross Williamson Swamp Creek, and drive .3 to Bartow, which is to the left.

Bartow was known as Spier's Turnout during the Civil War but was renamed for General Francis Bartow of Savannah, who died at First Manassas. Bartow has a large warehouse, a colorful feed and seed store, a nice six-columned home, moss-draped trees, a beautiful white frame Methodist Church (1890), and a beautiful brick Baptist Church (1925) beside it. The city cemetery, surrounded by a rock wall, is across the street from the churches; two sons of William Spiers, both killed in the Civil War, are buried in it. Downtown are two rows of largely closed stores, but signs promise they are open as flea markets on Saturdays. Between the buildings are the grassy expanse of Heritage Park and an old depot. On the park lawn are a gazebo and a monument.

From Bartow drive east on U.S. 319 for 4.3 miles to Wadley. Stop at the sign, then turn right onto U.S. 1 (Bus.) for 1.9 to the intersection with U.S. 1.

On the outskirts of town you passed a Church of God campground. In Wadley the Baptist and Methodist churches are found on the same corner, but in this case the Baptists have the white frame building, the Methodists brick. The railroad depot is now a feed and seed. Wadley was originally called Shakerag, allegedly because local residents would wave a cloth to flag down trains on the Central of Georgia Railroad.

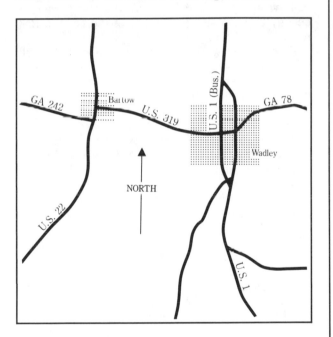

Map 23: The Bartow and Wadley areas.

Continue south on U.S. 1 for 2 miles, then left onto SR 622, which is the Old Savannah Road followed to Millen by Sherman and the 17th Corps. Signs show the way to Coleman Lake. After 3.5, bear left onto SR 457 for 4.8, then turn left onto SR 76 for 1 mile to Coleman Lake, on the Ogeechee River.

This is a family retreat from another, regretfully disappearing, age. Large oaks, dripping moss, shade the

campgrounds; and there are a skating rink, a concert area, a large covered picnic pavilion, and many other attractions for a summer vacation. Fishing is a big draw.

To the south are several communities visited by Howard and the 15th Corps: Wrightsville, Kite, Summertown, and Canoochee.

Return to SR 457 and turn left for 2.1 to GA 56. Turn left, and immediately cross the Ogeechee River. One can imagine the 17th Corps crossing the stream by torchlight. Pass through downtown Midville, which consists of warehouses and two columns of closed brick stores. After 1 mile the highway intersects GA 17. This town has several structures that date before the Civil War, including the Jones House, which is held together with wooden pegs.

Turn right onto GA 17 and drive east through farm land and piney woods for 9.5 miles. Turn left onto SR 195 for 3.5 miles, and right onto the rough dirt of SR 89 at Birdsville.

To the left is one of Georgia's premier plantations. The land was given to Welshman Francis Jones by King George III and originally included 66,000 acres. Only 1,400 acres remain part of the plantation today. The house was begun in 1782 as a two-story Colonial structure constructed with hewn pine timbers, but additions were frequent. The Greek Revival front entrance dates from 1847, and there are Victorian side porches. The interior of the house is exquisitely furnished, and extensive outbuildings remain from the plantation and the community that sprang up around it. To the right is an old stagecoach inn that resembles a school, and several log buildings are on the left. Long avenues of oak trees stretch in every direction.

After 2.4 miles on SR 89, turn right onto SR 79 for 1.4, then left on SR 81 for 1.2 to Buckhead Church.

Wheeler and Kilpatrick fought near this magnificent wooden structure, which has four simple square columns in front, that was built around 1800. Mercer University, now located in Macon, was planned here. Across the road is a path that leads through dense woods to an old cemetery.

Continue east on SR 81 for 3.5 miles to the Stop sign. Straight ahead is Perkins, site of a Civil War skirmish. Turn right onto GA 121-U.S. 25 for 2.2, then turn left to the Millen National Fish Hatchery.

Over two million fish grown annually in twenty-five deep ponds here are used to stock lakes, streams, and ponds in forty-three Georgia counties. Tours are available, and there is an impressive aquarium that displays seventy different species of fish. Water for the ponds comes from Magnolia Springs, which issue nine million gallons of water daily.

Return to GA 121-U.S. 25 and turn left. After .5 turn left into Magnolia Springs State Park.

The prison was destroyed by Sherman's men, but the earthworks, where artillery was placed to prevent escapes, are on a hill to the right just inside the gate. The park offers the usual activities, but signs warn against swimming in the lakes, which contain alligators.

Return to the highway and turn left for 4.9 miles to the intersection with GA 17 in Millen. Turn left onto GA 17 (Winthrope Street) for .6, and the Jenkins County Courthouse is on the left.

A boulder on the lawn honors a Wayside Home, which cared for traveling soldiers during the Civil War. The

Map 24: The Millen area.

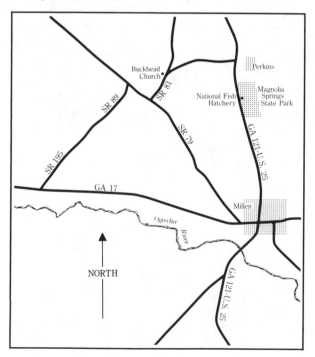

town has a red brick Baptist Church (1895), and the Methodist Church features columns and a metallic cupola.

Turn right opposite the southwest corner of the courthouse onto North Daniel Street for .1, and the depot is in front of you on Cotton Avenue.

This depot, built in 1915, is a good imitation of the original wooden structure. It is situated on the site of the depot destroyed by fire.

The depot houses the Chamber of Commerce. Inside is a large picture of the prison, assorted displays, and a thorough pictorial tour to historic homes found throughout the county. Before leaving, notice the coal shute behind the depot, built in 1925, and the water tank, which dates to 1910. Similar structures can frequently be seen along the route of the Central Railroad.

From Millen we will follow the route of the 17th Corps as it passed through Statesboro to Savannah. The path taken by Sherman and the 15th Corps is traced on an alternate tour.

Drive west down Cotton Street and turn right onto the first street, which is North Gray Street, to return to Winthrope Street. Turn left and return to the intersection of GA 121-U.S. 25 and GA 17. Turn left to follow GA 121-U.S. 25 south toward Statesboro. At .7 a marker to the left marks the burial site of several soldiers who died at the Wayside Home. The Ogeechee River is crossed just outside town. Dirt lanes lead to the stream, where people pursue an age-old pastime in the Ogeechee region, fishing.

Drive 21.6 miles south to the intersection with U.S. 80. Bear left to follow U.S. 25 to the intersection with GA 73-U.S. 301, which appears after another 6.4 miles. Turn right to follow GA 73-U.S. 25. The Bulloch County Courthouse appears on the left after .4. Continue south and turn left onto the Georgia Southern College campus after 1.3; this road becomes Sweetheart Circle. Follow it around to the Herty Museum, which is located in the Rosenwald Building, and park in the lot behind it. The museum has an outstanding permanent collection of fossil remains, and there are changing exhibits.

The Statesboro Bicycling Club has prepared a handy guide to historic attractions in the city. Homes, commercial buildings, monuments, and other landmarks are noted. It can be obtained from the Chamber of Commerce.

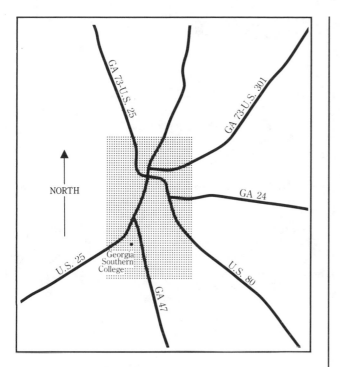

Map 25: The Statesboro area.

Three miles west of Statesboro on U.S. 301 is a complex of buildings maintained by the Historical Society. A museum is housed in a warehouse-like structure. The log Mill Creek Primitive Church, built in 1826, and a one-room schoolhouse, also obtained from the old Mill creek community, have been restored here.

Follow the circle back to GA 73-U.S. 25, and return to the intersection with U.S. 301 and U.S. 80. Turn right on GA 26-U.S. 80 toward Savannah.

This is pleasant farm country. The soil is black and sandy, and the area is dotted by decaying barns and outbuildings, old sharecroppers' shacks, and cattle dips and pens. Swampy land is encountered with increasing frequency. The traffic is predominantly commercial trucks, as tourists tend to take the path of least resistance on nearby I-16.

Pass through Brooklet after 9.1, and drive another 22.1 to reach the Ogeechee River at Jenks Bridge, where the 15th Corps forced a crossing.

Residences line both sides of the river. While driving through Eden, a small community that sprawls on both sides of the highway, notice the East of Eden Paint and Body Shop. Large oaks overhang the highway, which takes on the look of a causeway. When Sherman's forces advanced along this route, Confederates barricaded the road with timbers and periodically emplaced cannon to shell the marching Federals.

Pooler, where Confederates seeded the road with torpedos, is reached after 9.9. Another 2.1 brings you to I-95.

When U.S. 80 turns right after 7.3 beyond I-95, continue on what becomes North U.S. 17-A, following the sign for Fort Pulaski. To the left is a high bridge that spans the Savannah River into South Carolina, and straight ahead rises the gold dome of City Hall. After 2.0 turn right onto West Broad Street to follow the Visitors Center sign. After .4 turn right into the Visitors Center. ■

Map 26: Savannah.

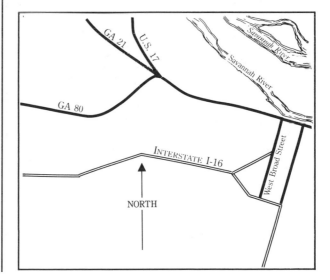

■ Right Wing Tour B ■

This side tour allows the traveler to trace the route taken by Sherman from Millen to the outskirts of Savannah. Sherman, with the 17th Corps, followed an old road along the eastern bank of the Ogeechee River, which also paralleled the railroad. On the opposite bank was the 15th Corps. At the first sign of resistance the 15th would threaten to cross behind the Confederates, forcing the enemy to withdraw. As additional support, the 20th traveled not far north of Sherman, on the Middle Ground Road; and the 14th scoured the western bank of the Savannah River.

From the depot in Millen, travel east on Cotton Avenue for .1 to GA 17, and turn right. After 4.3 Paramore is to the left on SR 62, but nothing remains except the railroad.

Continue south for 3.3; Scarboro is on the right. The white frame Baptist Church was built in 1854, and several closed wooden stores line the dirt road that leads to the Ogeechee River.

Drive another 4.5 miles south, and Rocky Ford is to the right, situated .5 down the road. There are some nice old homes and churches, and several brick stores, a few open, others not. In 1765 this community was the county seat.

Continue south on GA 17. After 5.1 turn right onto SR 242 to Ogeechee, which is at .5. The river, which is a mile beyond Ogeechee, is spanned by a new bridge; but the scenic wooden skeleton of an older bridge still stands.

Return to GA 17 and turn right. After 3.9 you are in Cooperville, with the business district to your left. Cooperville, established in 1790, once boasted important religious and educational institutions. You may want to turn right for 1.4, then take another right to Dover, which is a pleasant place with some older homes. The road loops back to GA 17 at Cooperville.

Continue south on GA 17 for 2.9, and SR 224 will be to the right. Large trees overhang a rough dirt road that leads to the railroad after 1.2 at what was Cam-

eron. This would have been a typical road during Sherman's March. Nothing remains of Cameron, and the road is blocked beyond the railroad.

Resume the journey south on GA 17; after 8.4 miles is the village of Oliver.

The Baptist Church just to the right on GA 24 occupies the site of Ogeechee Church, where Sherman expected resistance. The church was established in 1809, and the cemetery behind it is pre-Civil War. By traveling west on GA 24 for 5.9 from this point, you will cross the Ogeechee and reach Mill Ray, where Howard's flanking column forced the Confederates to evacuate their entrenched position at Oliver.

Continue southeast on GA 17 along one of the straightest roads in the South.

Swamps line both sides of the road for considerable stretches. On this poor route Sherman's men first became hungry and miserable while struggling through the low country.

Pass through Egypt, and after 15.8 is the Guyton business district.

Guyton was established in 1838 and became a summer haven for Savannah's wealthy, who sought to escape yellow fever. The town has a number of Victorian treasures and a few antebellum homes. Behind the high school on Cemetery Road is the city cemetery, where a section contains Confederate soldiers who died of wounds or disease in a hospital established in Guyton.

Pineora is 3.2 miles south of Guyton on GA 17. After 5.7 miles, Zion Church, where Sherman spent a night, is to the left.

GA 17 intersects GA 26-U.S. 80 after 4.4. Turn left to join the Right Wing tour to Pooler and Savannah. I-95 is 6.4 miles east. ■

Savannah

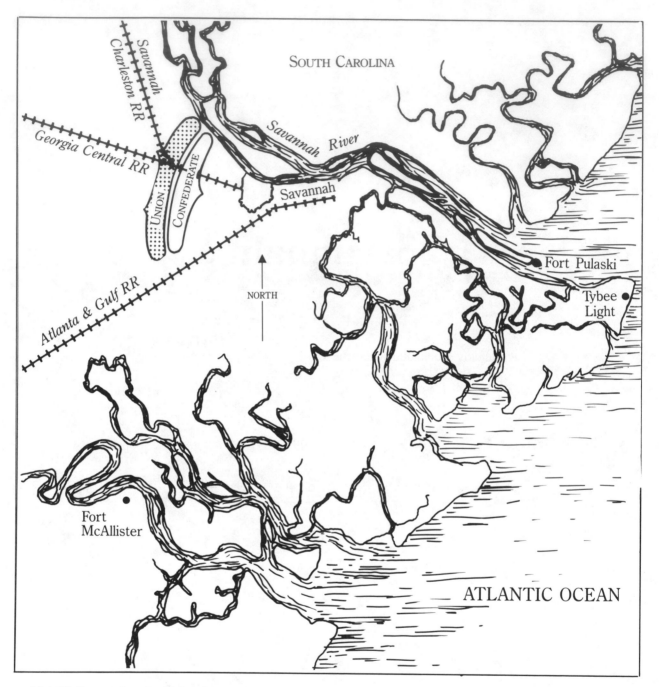

Map 27: *Savannah under Union siege.*

CHAPTER 15

"The Old Ones Can Fight in the Trenches as Well as the Youngest"

T he people of Savannah were used to crisis. Living in a vulnerable port city, they lived amid constant alarms of Federal invasion. The city had been quickly blockaded when the Civil War started, and a Union amphibious flotilla captured nearby Port Royal, South Carolina, in November 1861. Then Fort Pulaski, Savannah's primary defense, was bombarded into submission in 1862, and numerous attempts were made to capture Fort McAllister, which guarded the Ogeechee River to the south, during 1863.

To prevent a naval attack on the city, the Savannah River was obstructed by a double row of cribs placed in the water at the northern edge of Elba Island. The cribs consisted of twenty-inch-thick timbers, securely bound together and filled with bricks and cobblestones from city streets. The cribs had a height of thirty-five feet and extended across both channels of the river.

Confederate authorities built a number of batteries and mounted dozens of heavy cannon to protect the rivers that led to the city. After several outlying works were abandoned early in the war, the Federals commanded Ossabaw and Wassaw sounds, which gave them control of the approaches to the Savannah, Vernon, and Wilmington rivers.

Savannah was considered sufficiently important for Robert E. Lee, Jefferson Davis, and P.G.T. Beauregard to inspect the fortifications and offer suggestions for improvements. They agreed that Savannah had a formidable coastal defense; the powerful guns gave the garrison an impressive firepower, which the Federals respected.

After Sherman left Atlanta, William J. Hardee assumed what amounted to an independent command in Savannah. His immediate superior was P.G.T. Beauregard, who traveled from Macon to Augusta when the latter was threatened and finally settled in Charleston.

After the Federals had bypassed Augusta, Savannah seemed the most likely target. Braxton Bragg promised Hardee the ten thousand troops he had concentrated in Augusta, but only about three thousand arrived. On November 29 Hardee reported having a force of ten thousand men, but he expected Gustavus Smith to arrive shortly with three thousand militia.

On November 28 Savannah's mayor, R. D. Arnold, issued a call to arms:

Fellow Citizens—The time has come when every male who can shoulder a musket can make himself useful in defending our hearths and homes. Our city is well fortified, and the old ones can fight in the trenches as well as the young, and a determined and brave force can, behind entrenchment, successfully repel the assaults of treble their number.

Kilpatrick so effectively screened Sherman's advance that Hardee could obtain little accurate information about Union movements. In late November, after returning from Tennille, Hardee shifted heavy guns from the river approaches to the western edge of the city, then put every man in Savannah to work preparing fortifications. Hardee did not care whether his new militiamen were furloughed soldiers, convalescents, civilians, or foreigners among captured Federals being held in the city. All were organized into military units under General LaFayette McLaws, who retreated to the city after his position at Ogeechee Church had been outflanked.

While Sherman marched inexorably on, the Georgia militia took a strange voyage. After the massacre at Griswoldville, Smith's men were sent to Savannah in a roundabout manner. They left Macon on the morning of November 25 for a one-hundred-mile ride to Albany, where the rails terminated on the Southwestern line. The men marched to Thomasville, covering the sixty miles in fifty-four hours, and arrived at noon on November 28. At Thomasville, Smith was angered to find only two of the five trains he had requested. Because of the condition of Georgia's rolling stock, those two trains, containing only one brigade, did not arrive at Savannah until 2:00 A.M. on November 30. The officers and men were "broken down by fatigue and want of rest," Smith wrote.

In Savannah, Smith was confronted by an outrageous request. The Georgia troops were needed just across the Savannah River in South Carolina. Federal General John Foster had been trying to sever a vital railroad that linked Savannah and Charleston. Foster's pathetic attempts had led Federal and Confederate officers alike to ridicule his military abilities; Sherman's advance, however, had inspired him, and he marched a division from Hilton Head to break the railroad. If successful, the action would have trapped the Confederates in Savannah.

Smith found Hardee in bed and announced: "You know that the militia of this State cannot be legally ordered beyond its limits without a special act of the Legislature. But if you can satisfy me that it is absolutely necessary that my command go into South Carolina, 'I will endeavor to carry out your orders. If you do not satisfy me, and persist in your orders, I will be under the disagreeable necessity of withdrawing the State forces from your control."

It has been suggested that the Confederacy died of states' rights, and this incident is a classic example. Fortunately, Hardee, General Richard Taylor, and Robert Toombs convinced Smith that Savannah's defense required him to leave Georgia. Although a number of Smith's enlisted men complained of the mission, his officers were supportive. So before the trains actually reached Savannah, they were switched onto the Charleston line, and Smith's exhausted men awoke in South Carolina. General Taylor quipped that they were "unconscious patriots."

The Federal division, led by General John P. Hatch, failed to reach the railroad on November 29. He blamed inaccurate maps and worthless guides, but his own competence seemed in question. Early on the morning of November 30 the Georgia militia deployed east of the railroad near Honey Hill, South Carolina. They received excellent support from a battery of South Carolina artillery, which swept a narrow causeway over which the Federals had to advance. When Hatch attempted a flanking maneuver, the Georgians set fire to a dry field of broom sedge. According to Federal General Jacob Cox, "this prairie fire sweeping down before the wind upon our troops forced them to seek cover" in a ravine.

The Federals regrouped and forced the Confederates back to a ridge where a fort, mounting seven cannon, guarded all approaches. The Yankees charged this position repeatedly throughout the afternoon, but Smith's men, firing rapidly from their rifle pits, and the Confederate artillery soundly repulsed every attack.

Hatch disengaged at dark and retreated, leaving the railroad firmly in Confederate hands. Smith had lost eight men killed and forty-two wounded, while Union casualties totaled seven hundred.

Smith returned to Savannah that night, secure in the knowledge that his

Old Reliable ■ William J. Hardee

[LIBRARY OF CONGRESS]

Hardee was a native Georgian who spent the entire year of 1864 desperately defending his homeland, in vain. Born in Camden County, he attended West Point and fought the Indians and Mexicans before the Civil War erupted.

In 1856 he authored *Rifle and Light Infantry Tactics,* popularly known as *Hardee's Tactics,* which was adopted for use in the classrooms of West Point. With the outbreak of the war, many officers in blue and gray used the manual to train hundreds of thousands of civilian soldiers.

Hardee earned the sobriquet "Old Reliable" for his steady leadership in every battle fought by the Army of Tennessee: Shiloh, Perryville, Stone's River, Chickamauga, and Chattanooga. With the departure of Braxton Bragg, Hardee refused command of the army, preferring to serve under Johnston.

Following Johnston's departure, Hood blamed Hardee for the series of disastrous defeats suffered by the Confederates; and after Atlanta's surrender, Hardee demanded a transfer. When Hood marched away to Tennessee, Hardee was assigned to protect Georgia against Sherman's legions. He assembled a scratch force of ten thousand men in Savannah, but was unable to impede the Federal advance. When Sherman's sixty thousand hardened veterans invested the city at Christmas 1864, Hardee slipped across the Savannah River in an au- dacious move that caught Sherman completely by surprise.

Hardee ended the Civil War in the same capacity as he started the Atlanta Campaign. When Johnston was brought back to command the pitiful remains of the Army of Tennessee, he rushed to oppose Sherman in North Carolina, where Hardee once again came under his command.

Tragedy struck Hardee in one of the war's final battles. Succumbing to the pleas of his fourteen-year-old son, Hardee allowed the boy to join the Confederate cavalry at Bentonville. Hours after the father had kissed his son goodbye, Willie Hardee was killed in his first combat. ■

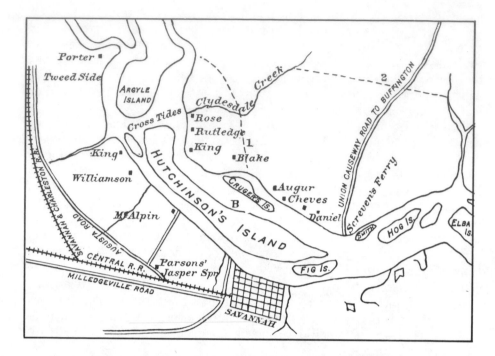

A map of Savannah prepared by Sherman's Chief Engineer, Orlando Poe.
[OFFICIAL RECORDS OF THE CIVIL WAR]

men had redeemed themselves for the debacle at Griswoldville. He proudly wrote, "A small number of men for so long a time successfully resisted the determined and oft-repeated efforts of largely superior attacking forces."

To Sherman's men, this setback merely confirmed a belief that they would have to accomplish the Easterners' work for them.

Hardee's reinforcements arrived from Augusta via rail, after first traveling to Charleston. Other soldiers were transported from Wilmington, North Carolina. Before the Charleston and Savannah road was cut on December 10, Hardee sent a considerable amount of railroad material to Madison, Georgia, which had recently been sacked by Sherman's Left Wing. It was transferred to Charleston, Augusta, and on to Madison by the Georgia Railroad.

On December 2 the Confederate quartermaster in Richmond urged President R. R. Cuyler of the Central of Georgia to move his rolling stock and other equipment north to Columbia via Charleston. Cuyler felt it more prudent to evacuate south on the Savannah and Gulf; he was captured on one of the last trains out of the city.

Roads leading to Savannah were barricaded with timbers, and bridges and ferry boats were burned to prevent Sherman from crossing into South Carolina. Torpedo experts were dispatched from Charleston to help obstruct the roads, and navy gunboats began patrolling the Savannah River.

Beauregard had earlier expected Sherman to march directly to Port Royal and to continue north to reinforce Grant, but on December 5 he wired Hardee, "Everything now appears to be moving toward Savannah."

On December 8 an alarmed Beauregard asked Hardee to come to Charleston for a conference. Believing the situation in Savannah was too desperate for him to leave, Hardee invited Beauregard to visit him.

As Beauregard left Charleston, he sent Hardee a telegraph, advising him that there was "no army of relief to look for." Hardee's soldiers were all the Confederacy had to defend Georgia and South Carolina, and "whenever you shall have to select between their safety and that of Savannah, sacrifice the latter."

On the same day Wheeler informed Hardee that Sherman would soon reach Savannah. Hardee sent men out to fortify a few positions in a rough circle several miles from the city: Monteith Swamp, the intersection of Dillon's Bridge and King's Bridge roads, and the Canoochee River. At dawn on December 9 the enemy was only six miles from these flimsy barriers, and the positions were brushed aside during the day. Throughout December 10 Sherman's four corps came into contact with Hardee's primary defenses.

Beauregard met with Hardee on December 9 as Sherman enveloped the city. Hardee explained his plans to evacuate the city by boat, if it became necessary, but Beauregard correctly believed that would be insufficient. He ordered Hardee to build a pontoon bridge across the Savannah River and reminded him again not to let his men be trapped.

The Confederate defenses extended across a thirteen-mile-wide peninsula that lay between the Savannah River and the Little Ogeechee River. The line formed a semicircle no more than two miles from Savannah. An interior line constructed on the outskirts of the city was thrown up between Fort Jackson and Laurel Grove Cemetery.

Gustavus Smith and the Georgia militia held the position from the Savannah River at Williamson's Plantation to the Central Railroad. His two thousand men had twenty cannon to cover a two and one-half-mile front. LaFayette McLaws commanded the next three and three-quarter miles to Telfair Swamp and Shaw's Dam, holding the vital center with Hardee's four thousand most experienced soldiers and twenty-nine pieces of artillery. Ambrose Wright, a Confederate general and president of the Georgia Senate, had 2,700 men and 32 guns to protect the remaining 7 miles of the line. His flank rested on the Little Ogeechee River where the Savannah and Gulf Railroad crossed. Wright's shaky force consisted of militia, local volunteers, clerks, and a few veterans.

The cannon were huge twenty-four- to thirty-two-pound siege guns removed from the coastal batteries. In addition, Hardee had eleven batteries of forty-eight field artillery pieces that he could place at any threatened point. That was fortunate, for he certainly had no reserve troops available to plug Union breakthroughs. The Confederates were outnumbered sixty thousand to ten thousand, but at least they were not outgunned by their opponents.

The Confederates took skillful advantage of a network of creeks that fed the rivers, situating their works behind the impenetrable swampy streams. Hardee then flooded the entire country to a depth of three to six feet by

The Confederate General Who Loved New York City ■ Gustavus W. Smith

Born in Kentucky in 1821, Smith graduated from West Point in 1842. During the Mexican War, he was promoted three times for bravery, and afterward he taught engineering at West Point and supervised construction of coastal fortifications. Smith left the military in 1854 to practice civil engineering, and the outbreak of the Civil War found him the street commissioner of New York City.

During the war's early months, Smith occupied high positions in the Confederate military, but he resigned following quarrels with his superiors. Governor Brown appointed him major general of the Georgia militia, which he directed through the Atlanta Campaign and the March to the Sea. His men performed admirably at Honey Hill, South Carolina, and in Savannah's trenches.

After the Civil War, Smith returned to private business for a while, then became insurance commissioner in Kentucky. He died in New York City, where he had returned to spend the last twenty years of his life. ■

cutting rice dikes and canals and opening sluices. A complex of large forts equipped with the heavy guns blocked five narrow causeways that led over the swamps, canals, and flooded rice fields into the historic city. Those causeways brought the Central Railroad, Gulf Railroad, and roads leading to Augusta, Louisville, and south to the Ogeechee River, into the city. They were the only practical means of access. Some of these formidable forts were advanced, giving the Confederate gunners a devastating enfilading fire against any Federal attack. Where permitted by the swampy terrain, the forts were connected by infantry trenches and rifle pits, and lines of sharpened logs occupied every inch of firm ground behind the water barriers.

As the northern soldiers approached Savannah, the weather turned frigid. Soldiers trooped through cold rains and struggled through bone-chilling, shoulder-deep water barriers. After wading through a swamp, one soldier wrote, "Our bones were fairly frozen and the marrow within them congealed." It was certainly a change from their operations around Atlanta during the summer, when heat prostration was often a more serious threat than Rebel bullets.

Union infantrymen scooped out shallow pits in the chilly black mud near the Rebel forts. Some managed to gather enough dry wood to kindle fires; but that was not a wise move, for Confederate gunners opened fire on the flames. Amid whizzing cannonballs and bullets, the Yankees hastily stamped out the embers. As the cold nights wore on, men danced vigorously in order to stay warm. They could never find enough dry land to camp on.

Rebel fire was not the only problem facing the Yankees in front of Savannah. They were getting hungry. "The question of our supplies begins to look 'threatened,'" Hitchcock noted. Many units had no provisions left, and hardtack was being sold for one dollar a biscuit. Confederate pickets taunted their counterparts about the situation, yelling, "Hello, Yank, don't you want some hard bread? Come over here and get something to eat."

The army had arrived just in time to capture an entire rice crop, and the men subsisted on it for two weeks. "Our men are now living almost entirely on rice," Connolly wrote, and there was no meat, crackers, coffee, or sugar. On December 15 Johnson described his menu as "boiled rice for breakfast, boiled rice for dinner, boiled rice for supper." On December 16 he had "rice on toast without the toast, for breakfast rice, dinner rice, for supper rice." He called it the "rice diet," and on December 20 he noted, "No change in 'bill of fare.'" He believed the diet was healthy, just not palatable.

The men often went hungry before they learned how to prepare the rice. It was hulled with rifle butts, then placed on a blanket and thrown into the air to separate the chaff. By the time a meal was prepared and consumed, it was time to start over. One officer advised his men to "draw in your belts one more hole each day."

R. P. Findley had deplored the wastage of food along the March route. Every morning soldiers left large quantities of provisions in camp, assured of finding more during the day. "Oh sufficient unto the meal was the evil," he quipped.

If the army was so poorly supplied, Connolly wondered how the estimated twelve thousand contrabands were surviving. Their camps ringed most headquarters tents, except General Davis's, he noticed. They seemed "cheerful and happy," despite the conditions. Connolly completed his letter concerning Davis's behavior at Ebenezer Creek and wondered to what authority it should be addressed.

"Mine eyes have beheld the spires of the city!" Connolly gloated on December 12. He and a friend had ridden along the river to examine the sights and were excited to view the "sacred soil of South Carolina." They glimpsed church steeples in Savannah, a sight that fired Connolly's imagination.

Union soldiers formed a line around the Confederate works in the shape of an irregular cresent. The 14th and 20th Corps of Slocum's Left Wing confronted the Confederates from the Savannah River to the Ogeechee Canal; the 17th and 15th of Howard's Right Wing faced the Rebels from that point to the Little Ogeechee River. The Federals were so close to Savannah that they could hear church bells ringing and wagons clattering through the streets.

These veterans of Atlanta dreaded the prospect of another drawn-out siege of a southern city, and they would have welcomed an assault that had a chance of success. However, the caliber of the Confederate guns denied

Poe's map of Confederate and Federal lines on the Left Wing. Note the Confederate water barriers and artillery batteries. [OFFICIAL RECORDS OF THE CIVIL WAR]

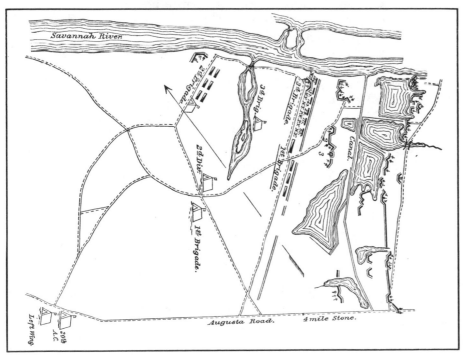

them the opportunity. As Engineer Poe wrote, the Rebel defenses "forbade all frontal attack." Osborne agreed, noting, "The city is substantially a fortress."

On December 11 a Federal unit on the Left Wing dug in 250 yards from a Rebel fort equipped with seven heavy guns. In front of the Confederates were flooded rice fields and a canal twenty-five feet deep. Three other forts also were within range of the Federals, and they all kept up a steady fire.

On the following day, the Yankees attempted to entrench their field artillery, but snipers kept up a deadly fire from a house near the Rebel line. Union sharpshooters responded as best they could.

Every day at high tide Confederate gunboats took station in the Savannah River and started a brisk bombardment. The vessels were able to lay down a deadly enfilading fire that caused the Federals to build earthen traverses during the night for protection. Between the forts, gunboats, and snipers, the Federals were unable to accomplish any work during the day.

Sherman slowly probed the Confederate line for weak points. Occasionally, limited attacks were launched to keep the Rebels on edge and make them uncertain of where a major assault might fall. The opposing defenses were mapped, likely avenues of successful advance plotted, and batteries of heavy guns transported across the boggy terrain. Sherman was in no hurry. He bided his time while trying to surround the city before he made a decisive move.

Late on December 15, men on the left were told to prepare for an attack at midnight. Brigades marched and milled about in confusion. "It was a very cold night, and the stamping of the men upon the frozen ground and rekindling of the subdued fire was sufficient to alarm the enemy, who gave palpable evidence of being ready to receive us," wrote an officer. The Confederate bombardment caused the assault to be canceled at 4:15 A.M.

On another occasion, a Federal battery fired on the distant forts. That action "caused the Rebels to open at once with six guns with great vehemence. . . . It was not considered prudent on our side to continue the fire." The Federals erected several batteries on their front, including one with four three-inch rifles, but that seemed puny compared to the Confederate firepower.

Theodore Upson had just bedded down for the night when an officer from a neighboring artillery battery advised him to keep his head down. "He was going to wake up the Johnnys," Upson wrote. "He fired both of his guns at a Battery perhaps half a mile away. He woke them up all right. They replied, knocked the muzzle off the gun next to us, the wheel of the other, blew up the caisson standing in the rear of the guns, and threw one shell into the muck in front of us which exploded and covered us with about 20 tons of black mud. We were not hurt but are quite sure the Johnnys were not asleep at all."

The Confederates daily fired "an immense amount of ammunition," a Federal report stated. Along one section of the line on December 16, Confederate gunners expended three hundred rounds on the besiegers.

The 14th and 20th Corps commanders reconnoitered the Confederate

Historic Midway Church was occupied by Kilpatrick's cavalry during the siege of Savannah.

defenses at night. On December 20 one officer reported an "almost impenetrable slashing 100 yards in width," before his sector. Between that barrier and the Confederate skirmishers was a one-hundred-yard-wide pond. He could see three floodgates within the Rebel line that had been opened to inundate the area.

Another regiment found felled, untrimmed pine trees in its front as far as the eye could see. The little dry ground was uneven, and a pond, twelve feet wide and five feet deep, was flanked by treacherous swamps. They could see Confederate camp fires and hear conversations, but they doubted whether they could ever reach the Rebel works.

On December 18 New Yorker Frederick Price wrote his wife: "We have been here a week today under dreadful fire from the enemy. We are so close to them that our men can talk with them." The Confederate camps stretched behind their works, where the Rebels gathered "with banners defiantly unfurled," another Union soldier reported.

Soon after the Union army arrived, Sherman's men set about reducing the water level. Breaks in canals were repaired, and flood gates were rebuilt so the Federals could shut off the water flow. By December 17 General Cox reported the water slowly subsiding. An "assault could hardly be thought of," along the causeways and dikes, and anyone wounded charging across the fields would drown, which would be an "unjustifiable waste of human life."

When Van Duzer heard heavy firing along Osterhaus' front on December 17, he rode in that direction and was treated to an "interesting artillery duel." The shooting on both sides seemed fairly accurate, but the Confederates were using explosive shells, which made it easy to see one hundred burst directly over the Union fort. The Federals fired solid shot, and occasionally timbers in the Rebel works would be sent flying. One southern gun was silenced. As the duel continued, an ambulance entered the Union lines, loaded up some casualites, and left for the rear. When the Confederates threw a solid shot bouncing down the road after it, the Yanks scampered and the Rebs cheered.

Slocum had several large earthworks built to accommodate six thirty-pound Parrott rifles that were being sent from Hilton Head, South Carolina. He believed an assault could be successfully supported when they arrived. Two guns arrived on December 20, and the others would soon be mounted. Slocum put his men to work corduroying roads within and behind his lines to facilitate quick movement through the quagmires.

On the Union right, Howard established two batteries, masked by bushes, near the railroad where Confederate artillery had fired at Sherman. He scouted along the Little Ogeechee River and found at least five southern batteries protected behind vast swamps. Because of the terrain facing the Right Wing, Sherman doubted that any of Howard's men could execute a successful assault.

The men busied themselves building hundreds of large fascines from rice straw and bamboo. These would be used to fill in the water barriers; light footbridges, planks, and a few pontoon boats would help the soldiers cross the canals.

Fortunately for the men's safety, many Federal positions lay within wooded areas, so that soldiers could move about concealed from prying Confederate eyes. Cox discovered that if a camp was located a half mile into a pine forest, the heaviest Confederate shot would not penetrate to it.

On December 18 Slocum told Davis and Williams that a major assault might occur in two days. He felt his men could penetrate the Confederate defenses at four or more points along the 20th Corps' line, and General M. D. Leggett said their success depended on the willingness of the Confederates to defend their positions. His troops would have to capture three forts simultaneously after they crossed a canal. If any one fort of the three was not taken, the men would be shot to pieces. Some Federals thought the assault would be successful; others saw failure and a slaughter.

Poe thought attacks could be mounted at Shaw's Bridge over the Ogeechee Canal and on the Ogeechee Road where it crossed Salt Creek. To distract the Confederates, Sherman directed the navy to bombard Confederate forts Rosedew and Beaulieu to the south. To further mislead the Rebels, several points of planned attacks were avoided by Federal scouts. It was hoped that attention would not be drawn to those places. The Confederates were heavy in artillery but weak in infantry support. If the Rebels could be convinced to draw men away to support other areas that would not be struck, the attack could succeed.

Federal infantry crept as close to the Confederate line as possible. Then they quietly cut through abatis, and advanced rifle pits to the edge of the water barriers, about 150 yards away from the Rebel works. When the heavy Federal artillery opened up and the infantry rushed forward, these sharpshooters would make the Confederate gun crews keep their heads down.

Sherman's veterans were ready for a battle. Since early September, the only combat they had seen were fights with blazing pine cones in Georgia's vast forests.

Of the proposed attack, Upson wrote, "It will be hard work. . . . But if we make a start we are going through and I think the Johnnys know it for they do not talk as saucy as they did at Vicksburg." ■

"When Sherman Marched Down to the Sea" ■ By Samuel Byers, 5th Iowa

Our camp fires shown bright on the mountains,
That frowned on the river below;
While we stood by our guns in the morning,
And eagerly watched for the foe;
When a rider came out of the darkness,
That hung over mountain and tree;
And shouted, "Boys up and be ready,
For Sherman will march to the Sea."

Then cheer upon cheer for bold Sherman,
When up from each valley and glen;
And the bugles reechoed the music,
That came from the lips of the men;
For we knew that the stars in our banner,
More bright in their splendor would be;
And that blessings from north-land would greet us,
When Sherman marched down to the Sea. ■

"God Bless You and the Army Under Your Command"

O ne outstanding aspect of Sherman's career was the avoidance of battle when maneuver could produce satisfactory results. Sherman was confident that his men could overwhelm Savannah's defenders, but the Rebel gunners were good, and the butcher's bill would be high. Sherman refused to waste his men in grinding combat if there was an alternative.

To seize Savannah without an assault required him to accomplish two goals. The first was to establish communications with the Union blockading fleet and open a supply base. A stationary army in a siege situation quickly runs out of supplies and consumes all the food available locally.

The Ogeechee River was Sherman's only viable supply route. He had seized King's Bridge as a delivery point, but the river was obstructed seven miles from the Atlantic Ocean by Fort McAllister. The fortification had withstood a number of fierce naval attacks in the past; but it must be taken quickly, or his men would starve. This mission fell to the Right Wing.

The second goal was to completely surround the city. The blockade had effectively isolated Savannah from the east three years earlier, and Sherman's forces sealed the city from the south and west. Hardee would have abandoned the city before Sherman's arrival if it had not been for the Union Causeway. That road lay on the Carolina side of the Savannah River, opposite Sherman's army and the city. If Hardee could transport his force across the river, he could march to Hardeeville, South Carolina, and entrain for Charleston. If Union forces occupied the causeway or the railroad, Hardee would be trapped, and Sherman's future course through the Carolinas would be virtually unopposed. Preventing Hardee's escape would be the job of the Left Wing and Foster's incompetent force at Hilton Head.

On December 12 Kilpatrick rode around the army from the Left Wing and crossed the Ogeechee and Canoochee rivers. Moving through Cross Roads and down Bryan Neck toward Fort McAllister, he camped for the night at the home of Colonel Joseph L. McAllister of the Georgia cavalry.

At dawn Kilpatrick led two regiments and drove Confederate skirmishers into Fort McAllister, then mapped the approaches to the fort for the infantry who would storm it. Afterwards he rode to Kilkenny Bluff, where he contacted the USS *Fernandian*. Kilpatrick sent dispatches that announced Sherman's arrival on the coast to the flagship of the blockading fleet.

For the assault, Sherman chose his old Vicksburg division, now led by General Hazen. At dawn on December 13 the men crossed the Ogeechee at King's Bridge and marched by Cross Roads to reach Fort McAllister at noon. McAllister's commander, Major George W. Anderson, saw the woods behind the fort crawling with blue troops, and at 2:00 P.M. the fort opened a sporadic fire on the soldiers, who were slow in deploying because of the difficult terrain.

McAllister's two-hundred-man garrison realized they were isolated. They had rations for a month and enough ammunition to hold out for a considerable time, but they had no illusion about their ability to withstand an infantry assault from the rear.

Since the last naval attack in 1863 (see Appendix C), Major Anderson had worked hard at improving Fort McAllister's defenses. The area facing the rear had been enclosed with a high earthen wall, and outside this work was a fifteen-foot-deep, seven-foot-wide ditch with steep sides. In the center of the ditch was a thick line of sharply pointed logs, six feet in height and projecting outward. Surrounding the fort was abatis, made of the tangled branches of oak trees, that would ensnare attacking troops. Marshes and streams protected the fort's flanks and, unknown to the Federals, Anderson

Plan of the assault of Fort McAllister. [OFFICIAL RECORDS OF THE WAR OF THE REBELLION]

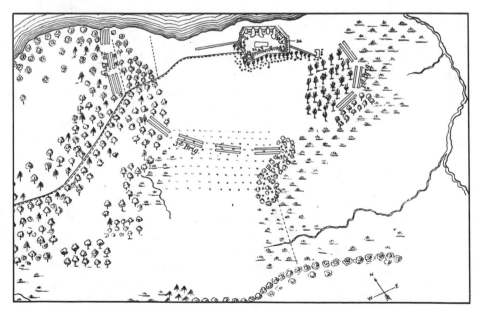

A remarkably accurate account of the furious attack on Fort McAllister.
[HARPER'S WEEKLY]

had torpedos thickly sown on the outer slopes of McAllister. Fields surrounding the fort had been burned to deny cover to the attackers.

Those were formidable obstacles for infantry to overcome, but McAllister was a small fort manned by a skeleton garrison. Her eleven big guns, including a massive forty-six-pounder, faced the river and were useless against infantry. The rear was guarded by twelve field cannon that sat in the open on the ramparts, unprotected by earthworks.

On December 13 Sherman left his headquarters for a long journey south to observe the assault. Because he had to detour around Confederate batteries, it was a twenty-mile journey. As Hazen's troops prepared for the attack, Sherman climbed atop Cheeve's rice mill on the opposite side of the river and impatiently awaited the combat. Late in the afternoon Sherman's attention was caught by a tiny cloud on the horizon. The object grew larger until a staff officer exclaimed excitedly, "It must be one of our steam ships from the blockading squadrons." Sherman said the United States flag flying on the ship was "a thrilling, joyful sight." It was the *Dandelion,* a tender of the gunboat *Flag,* anchored in Ossabaw Sound.

"Who are you?" the ship signaled. "General Sherman," was the reply. "Is Fort McAllister taken?" the signalman asked, fully aware of the fort's lethal reputation. "Not yet," Sherman answered, "but it will be in a minute."

As daylight waned, the irritated General commanded Nichols, "Signal General Hazen that he must carry the fort by assault, tonight if possible." Flags wagged and Hazen replied, "I am ready, and will assault at once."

By 4:30 P.M. Hazen had deployed three lines of men, to the rear and both flanks of the fort. Sherman saw a line of smoke erupt from the woods as Hazen's men opened fire. Seconds later the Federals marched confidently from the woods, "the lines dressed as on parade, with colors flying," Sherman noted with pride. McAllister roared to life, "its big guns belching forth dense clouds of smoke, which soon enveloped our assaulting lines. Then the fort seemed alive with flame; quick, thick jets of fire shooting out from all its sides."

The Confederate cannon fire seemed devastating, but it was largely ineffective as gunners fired over the advancing columns. Union snipers crouched behind large logs and opened a deadly fire against the artillery crews, slowing their rate of fire and impairing their accuracy. Anderson reported that one eight-man crew had three killed and three wounded. Confederate sharpshooters returned the fire, but there were too many Federals charging across the fields.

Union General William B. Hazen successfully stormed Fort McAllister to open a supply line for Sherman's army outside Savannah. [HARPER'S WEEKLY]

Hazen's men scrambled through the abatis and approached the ditch with steady, measured step. Rebel guns fired crashing salvos that tore gaps in the Union line, and smoke hid the advancing soldiers from view. Sherman turned away from the scene as if unable to bear the suspense, and his officers impulsively clutched one another's arms while they peered intently at the distant, darkening battlefield. "They have been repulsed," cried one officer.

Hundreds of soldiers tumbled into the ditch and tore paths through the palisade, braving a galling fire from Rebels on the parapet above. Federals streamed through the gaps and clawed up the opposite slope, rifles in hand. Soldiers screamed as they stepped on torpedos and were flung high into the air by the terrible explosions, but their comrades reached the top and fell on the enemy. Rebels fired their cannon until the Yankees were among them, then swung ramrods until they were shot, bayonetted, or clubbed to the ground. One Confederate captain was subdued only after sustaining two bullet wounds, three saber slashes, and six bayonet thrusts.

Other Confederates fell back into the fort's interior and fought with rifles and pistols. The men were finally forced into the bombproofs, where they were rooted out one by one. The "fort was never surrendered," Anderson proudly declared. "It was captured by overwhelming numbers." The assault lasted only fifteen minutes.

When a breeze dissipated the smoke, the Union officers packed atop the rice mill saw McAllister's ramparts blue with soldiers. "Crowds of men were visible on the parapets, fiercely fighting," Nichols wrote, "but our flag was planted there. There were a few scattering musket shots, and then the sounds of battle ceased. Then the bomb-proofs and parapets were alive with crowding swarms of our gallant men, who fired their pieces in the air. . . . Victory! The fort was won!"

"Around the general," Hitchcock wrote, "officers and orderlies joined in a yell of triumph, the General as much excited as any of them, and exclaiming, 'I don't sleep any dis night, sure!'" Sherman considered it "the handsomest thing I have seen in this war."

Van Duzer hurried to McAllister when he discovered Sherman's absence,

Fort McAllister's Union garrison drill in the use of heavy cannon, which had helped repulse several attacks by Federal ironclads. [LIBRARY OF CONGRESS]

reaching the mill barely in time to witness the assault. "Genl was beginning to get excited," he wrote. "Genl beside himself." After watching the brave defense, he thought the Confederates were "among the best men the south could boast."

As Civil War battles went, the assault of Fort McAllister was hardly a skirmish, but rarely was the gallantry of soldiers, blue and gray, more apparent. Union casualties were 24 killed and 110 wounded; the Confederates lost 17 killed and 31 wounded, or one-fifth of the garrison; there were 195 Rebel prisoners.

The Federals captured twenty-four guns and one mortar, sixty tons of ammunition, a large amount of food, and assorted arms and supplies. The victors were particularly joyous over a cache of wine valued at ten thousand dollars. Over the next few days work parties of Confederate prisoners were forced to explore any disturbed patch of ground for torpedos, which were then carefully removed. Sherman garrisoned the fort with three hundred men, and when he started for the Carolinas, the guns were dismantled and carried north as trophies of war.

The Ogeechee was open, and an incredible three-hundred-mile journey had ended. Men of all ranks and in both armies appreciated the significance of McAllister's fall. According to Connolly, when a report of the victory was read to the army, the men received the news by "cheering and yelling like

Indians all day. Everybody feeling jolly—bands all playing, batteries all firing, flags all flying, and everybody voting everybody else in the army a hero. The enemy rather quiet."

As the word spread that night from 8:00 to 9:00 P.M., a wall of cheers ran down the thirteen-mile Union line from right to left.

The subdued Confederates were truly invested now. One Rebel, who had not heard the news, shouted, "Hey Yank, what's all that yelling about?"

"Fort McAllister is taken," replied a Union soldier, "the Cracker line is open, that's what's the matter—how are you, Johnny?"

The unspoken answer was, not very well. The Confederates compensated for this setback by opening a savage shelling to spite the Yankees.

McAllister, "so long the bugbear of the navy," was taken, gloated Hitchcock, and "Savannah is doomed." The siege might take days or weeks, "but this army *will take it.*"

Connolly was excited to think of the North's receiving word of Sherman's arrival at the sea. With the coming of "daylight in the morning the news of our success will be on its way with all the speed of steam to electrify the millions of the north who are awaiting news from us with breathless interest. We all breathe freer to-night than we have for three months past."

Sherman wanted to talk with the commander of the blockading fleet that night, so he commandeered a small skiff found near the mill, and two of his staff volunteered to row him and Howard to Fort McAllister. The men pulled the boat up six miles of winding, torpedo-infested river, past the charred remains of a would-be Confederate raider, the CSS *Nashville.*

Sherman found Hazen at the McAllister plantation, where he was invited to supper with the recently captured Major Anderson. "I congratulated Hazen most heartily on his brilliant success and praised its execution highly," Sherman wrote. Anderson later said Sherman praised McAllister's defenders as well.

Sherman inspected the fort and found "the dead as they had fallen, and they could hardly be distinguished from their living comrades, sleeping soundly side by side in the pale moonlight." As he explored the fortifications, a torpedo exploded outside the walls, killing a Union soldier who was searching for a dead friend.

The early winter darkness had fallen over the country, but Sherman intended to board the steamer he had seen, "whatever risk or cost, as I wanted some news of what was going on in the outer world."

After supper Sherman walked the mile back to Fort McAllister and found a yawl tied to a stake. A strong crew of oarsmen was recruited, and Sherman and Howard started for the ship. Sherman was concerned when the ship was not encountered after a mile, but he directed the men to keep rowing. After navigating six miles of sharp curves, guided by a full moon, the *Dandelion* was spotted.

Captain Jesse Merrill of the Signal Corps had left Hilton Head the previous morning to search for Sherman. He obtained signal rockets at Fort Pulaski and explored Wassaw Sound. By dark he was in Ossabaw Sound and fired three rockets. A faint response was seen on the distant Ogeechee, and Merrill fired other rockets, which were answered, probably from Cheeve's

Union work crews remove Fort McAllister's artillery ammunition.
[LIBRARY OF CONGRESS]

rice mill, where rockets had been fired since December 10 to attract the navy's attention.

Merrill had rowed a small boat dangerously near McAllister on the following morning, and when he had heard skirmishing in the woods, he returned to the *Dandelion*. After the occupation, Howard signaled the boat, "Fort McAllister is ours. Look for a boat. General Sherman will come down tonight." Merrill returned to the *Flag* to file his reports and found Sherman and Howard being rowed down the river when he returned. The generals were greeted aboard by three cheers twice repeated. Sherman said he was "received with great warmth and enthusiasm."

Sherman was told that Admiral John Dahlgren, commander of the South Atlantic Blockading Squadron, and General Foster were aboard ships nearby. Vessels loaded with stores for Sherman's army were anchored near Tybee Island and in Port Royal. Sherman learned that Grant had made no progress against Lee at Petersburg. "All thoughts seemed to have been turned to us in Georgia," Sherman wrote, "cut off from all communications with our friends, and the rebel papers had recorded us to be harassed, defeated, starving, and fleeing for safety to the coast."

Sherman dashed off quick notes to Grant, Stanton, and Halleck, announcing his arrival and describing McAllister's conquest. "The army is in splendid order, and equal to anything," Sherman informed Stanton. "The weather has been fine, and supplies were abundant. Our march . . . not at all molested by guerillas." He had gathered a large number of slaves, mules, and horses, "and our teams are in far better condition than when we started." Sherman said he had not lost a single wagon. "We have utterly destroyed over 200 miles of rails, and consumed stores and provisions that were essential to Lee's and Hood's armies."

Sherman correctly estimated Hardee's force in Savannah at fifteen thousand and the city's population at twenty-five thousand. "If General Foster will prevent the escape of the garrison of Savannah and its people by land across South Carolina, we will capture all," he told General Halleck.

Around midnight Sherman asked the *Dandelion*'s captain to tow him back to Fort McAllister, but the captain refused to approach closer than a mile because of torpedos, "of which the navy-officers had a wholesome dread." Sherman returned to McAllister in the yawl and hiked the mile back to the McAllister house. Hazen was asleep on the floor when Sherman and Howard joined him.

When the *Dandelion* returned to the mouth of the Ogeechee, Foster was waiting on his ship, the *W. W. Coit*. Merrill went aboard Foster's ship and they steamed to the obstructions near the fort and signaled for Sherman. The General had hardly fallen asleep when someone called his name. Foster was "most anxious to see me on important business," Sherman related. A wound suffered during the war with Mexico prevented his coming to Sherman, so the commanding general hoofed it to the fort again, despite being exhausted from several days of almost constant activity.

Sherman met Foster three miles downstream from Fort McAllister. Foster described in the best possible light his efforts to sever the Charleston and Savannah road. He had failed to reach it, but his guns and a division of troops prevented the road's use south of the Broad River.

When Foster mentioned the food and clothing awaiting Sherman at Port Royal, Sherman suggested they locate Admiral Dahlgren and arrange for the navy to open a supply route.

The generals steamed down the Ogeechee into Ossabaw Sound, then followed an inland passage to Wassaw Sound, finding the Admiral aboard his ship, the *Harvest Moon*. Dahlgren's sailors "manned the yardarms and cheered, the highest honors at sea," Sherman wrote. Sherman and Dahlgren had never met, but Sherman found the admiral "so exceeding kind and courteous that I was at once attracted to him. There was nothing in his power, he said, which he would not do to assist us, to make our campaign absolutely successful."

Dahlgren immediately set about locating light draft ships to transport supplies from McAllister upriver to King's Bridge. He also volunteered to supervise the removal of torpedos in the Ogeechee.

Foster returned to Port Royal and arranged to send Sherman 600,000 rations "and all the rifled guns of heavy calibre" that could reach Savannah. On the next day Foster wrote Grant, "General Sherman is perfectly sure of capturing Savannah."

Sherman spent December 14 with Dahlgren, working out details of the navy's operations, and returned to Cheeve's Mill on December 15. He then moved his headquarters to a central location at Anderson's plantation, eight miles from Savannah, and told Slocum and Howard to prepare positions for siege guns "and to prepare for the general assault."

A one-thousand-foot wharf and a depot were built at King's Bridge, and roads leading to it were double corduroyed, "should the winter rains set in." Sherman worried about the low, marshy terrain, but "we have been so favored with weather" that the roads had been adequate.

Small boats were collected from plantations and placed in use on the Ogeechee Canal to ferry supplies to the widely scattered Union camps. Ships loaded with supplies for Sherman's sixty thousand hungry men soon steamed up the river. The first vessel reached King's Bridge on December 16. Aboard one was a welcome cargo, "the mails for the army," Sherman wrote, "which had accumulated since our departure from Atlanta. These mails were most welcome to all the officers and soldiers of the army, which had been cut off from friends and the world for two months, and this prompt receipt of letters from home had an excellent effect, making us feel that home was near."

"Such cheering I never heard," a soldier wrote when the mail arrived. What "a frantic sight, men snatching letters, whooping at this first touch with home." Men were seen "reading their letters held in one hand while devouring hard-tack with the other." Another exclaimed, "I can live a month now without eating. I have got five letters from my wife."

"With communication with friends at home, we shall be happy," Johnson wrote. "What a scene our camp presents as the boys are scattered here and there, perusing the letters just received from loved ones a thousand miles or more away, and talking over with each other the news from home. How glad we are to get their letters and know and feel that they do miss us and think of us at home."

Some men received sad news, the death of a loved one or a rejection from the girl left behind. Private Upson learned that his father's illness had forced the family to sell the farm, and a second letter informed him that his fiancée was sick and probably would not live through the winter.

Connolly wrote, "we are all more hungry for letters now than for anything else." Being on the extreme left of the line, they were the last to receive mail. On December 16 a large train was sent to King's Bridge to pick up provisions for the 20th Corps.

With the mail came Colonel A. H. Markland, who approached Sherman with a personal message from President Lincoln. "I was directed to take you by the hand wherever I met you and to say to you for him, 'God bless you and the army under your command. Since cutting loose from Atlanta, my prayers and those of the nation have been for your success.'"

Colonel Orville Babcock, a Grant aide, arrived the next day with the letter ordering Sherman to take his army to Virginia. "The contents of this letter caused me great uneasiness," Sherman wrote after the War, "for I had set my heart on the capture of Savannah, which I believed to be practical, and to be near." Sherman, expecting a fleet of one hundred ships to arrive shortly and transport his force north, prepared Fort McAllister for a staging area.

Sherman wrote Grant, hoping to change the orders. He explained his plans to capture Savannah. Poe was scouting the terrain, and the troops pressed closer to the city, "making attacks, feints, wherever we have fair ground to stand on." After heavy guns were emplaced, he planned to issue a surrender demand.

"If General Hardee is alarmed, or fears starvation, he may surrender, otherwise I will bombard the city but not risk the lives of our men by assaulting across the narrow causeway, by which alone I can now reach it. If I had time, Savannah . . . would surely fall into our possession."

Sherman believed Hardee could not feed the garrison and citizens for longer than a few days. The only passage from the city available to Hardee, Sherman declared, "was a disused wagon road. I could easily get possession of this," but he felt it was not worth isolating a force across the Savannah River.

Sherman was willing to transport his force to Virginia but "had expected, after reducing Savannah, instantly to march to Columbia, South Carolina; thence to Raleigh, and thence to report to you." Sherman estimated he could reach Grant in six weeks.

Sherman then sat down to write his wife, Ellen. After briefly describing the March, he said, "I never saw a more confident army." Since his destruction of Georgia, he felt, "Jeff Davis will now have to feed the people of Georgia instead of collecting provisions of them to feed his armies."

On December 18 Grant replied to Sherman's initial message: "I congratulate you and the brave officers and men under you on the successful termination of your most brilliant campaign." Lincoln had expressed fears for Sherman's safety, he continued, but Grant had assured the President that this army, under Sherman, could go wherever it wanted. Grant would not have entrusted the mission to "any other living commander." The campaign, he concluded, is one "the like of which is not read of in past history."

Halleck added his thanks. "I congratulate you on your splendid success." He gave his blessing to an ominous undertaking: "Should you capture Charleston, I hope that by some accident the place may be destroyed, and if a little salt should be sown upon its site it may prevent the growth of future crops of . . . secession."

On December 14 Kilpatrick sent parties south throughout Liberty County to picket roads and prevent Confederate reinforcements from threatening the Union flank. They were also to collect provisions. On December 12 Kilpatrick had reported to Sherman, "I find over here many rice plantations, and can subsist my command for months." He immediately set about proving the point.

Kilpatrick stripped the country of livestock and food. With wagons groaning from loads of loot, and with herds of cattle, mules, and horses, the cavalry returned to camp at Cross Roads. They had pillaged every community in Liberty County—Dorchester, Midway, Walthourville, and Sunbury. At Sunbury, situated on the coast, Union troopers burned a historic church as a signal to Sherman and to alert the fleet in Ossabaw Sound.

General Foster greets Sherman aboard his ship, the Nemaha, *after Fort McAllister was captured and the Ogeechee River opened to the ocean.* [LESLIE'S ILLUSTRATED]

Private Upson and his unit were sent to Liberty County on December 19 with 150 wagons to gather food for the Right Wing. "We got the greatest lot of corn and stuff," he wrote, "but I guess we shall need it all. It takes such a lot to feed an army." An incident occurred in a village that "I felt bad about," he added. The men saw a man ride "out of a side street ahead of us on a run whipping his mule." Colonel R. M. Johnson called for him to halt, but the man kept riding away. "Shoot him!" Johnson called. Several men fired and the man toppled off the mule, which fell a few feet away. "When we got to them, it was an old man, eighty years old. . . . We gave some of his folks some money to bury him with. It was all we could do. That was one of the accidents of war."

On December 1 units of Georgia militia commanded by General G. H. McKay were dispatched to protect the Savannah and Gulf Railroad bridge over the Altamaha River, which led to Doctor Town. The Confederates threw up two redoubts on the river bank and placed two thirty-two-pound rifled cannon to cover the approaches. A third gun was mounted on a railroad car. Two companies of infantry were emplaced at Morgan Lake to support the artillery.

On December 16 Hazen's division was sent to destroy the railroad to McIntosh, while Mower's division would tear up the rails from there to Doctor Town. When Mower was recalled to Savannah to rejoin the 17th Corps on December 19, the tracks had been destroyed to Morgan Lake. He left a cavalry brigade, which had screened infantry working parties, to complete the demolition work to Doctor Town. The cavalry was unable to fight through the Confederate infantry and to silence the deadly batteries at the bridge. Eventually they had to withdraw to rejoin Kilpatrick.

These activities, designed to protect Sherman's southern flank, gave some of his men the opportunity to engage in their beloved looting activities. One of their first victims was Mrs. Charles Colcock Jones. Her husband had been pastor of the venerable Midway Church, and after his death she managed three plantations. Her son, Charles, was a graduate of Princeton and Harvard Law School. A former mayor of Savannah, he now was a colonel in Confederate service. A daughter, Mary Jones Mallard, had come to Midway to escape the siege of Atlanta, never imagining the war would follow her here. On December 14 Mary's husband, part of the Home Guard, was captured in Walthourville.

At 10:00 A.M. on December 15 the Federals appeared. In searching for weapons, they demanded every key in the house and inspected each room and the tiniest boxes. Small parties showed up throughout the day to search the house.

On December 16 fifty men arrived at one time and took a number of chickens and ducks that Mrs. Jones had prepared for her family. "These the men seized whole, tearing them to pieces with their teeth, like ravenous beasts," Mrs. Jones wrote. They seized all the food and "said they meant to starve us to death," she continued. "It was vain to utter a word for we were completely paralyzed by the fury of these ruffians."
When the women asked an officer to discipline the looters, the men "instantly commenced cursing him and we thought they would fight one another."

After the ordeal had ended, Mrs. Jones wrote:

> It is impossible to imagine the horrible uproar and stamping through the house, every room of which was occupied by them, all yelling, cursing, quarrelling, and running from one room to another in wild confusion. Such was their blasphemous language, their horrible countenances and appearance, that we realized what must be the association of the lost in the world of eternal woe. Their throats were open sepulchres. Their mouths filled with cunning and bitterness and lies. . . . We look back upon their conduct in the house as a horrible nightmare, too terrible to be true.

At Dorchester on December 13, Union cavalry drove Colonel Arthur Hood's Confederates out of town, leaving Mrs. Cornelia E. Screven, a widow with young children, behind Federal lines. In preparation for the enemy's arrival, she drove her hogs into the woods and secreted fifty-four pieces of silver in a couch.

At dusk two polite officers rode up and asked for a glass of water while they rested on her steps. They were the "most wearied and exhausted-looking beings I ever beheld—ragged, filthy, and covered with dust from head to foot."

The Screven family slept little that night. In the morning men filled the house, cutting up her dresses and trampling them on the floor. One man was transfixed by a mirror. "I shall never forget that picture," Mrs. Screven wrote. "He wore a fine silk hat, stolen of course, a ragged coat made of three different patterns of carpeting, pants with the knees out and shoes with the toes out completed the picture which so fascinated him."

The two officers returned that night and apologized for the loss suffered by the family. The men were invited inside for tea, but when they sat on the sofa, it jingled. "Both looked around suspiciously." Mrs. Screven, explaining that the springs were bad, placed chairs for the men. When they stood up, the couch jingled again. The officers seemed amused.

On the following day the house became a thoroughfare for men. "Chewing, smoking, singing indecent songs and using profane language was the order of the day. We could not escape it."

On December 16 Mrs. Screven prepared food three times, and three times it was stolen. Her children were hungry, so she remonstrated with the soldiers. "Please don't take that meal, my children are very hungry, and we have nothing else to eat."

"D—n you, I don't care, if you all starve," the soldier said savagely. He pushed past the woman, almost knocking her to the floor.

A friend, Miss Maxwell, rushed forward and cried, "Oh you intolerable brutes! If I was a man I'd blow out every particle of your brains; if I had a pistol I'd do it anyhow, woman as I am."

A soldier stepped on the porch and announced, "Ladies, I am at your service; if I can do anything for you let me know it now."

"Come into the house and keep those brutes out," Miss Maxwell said. "Don't let one of them place a foot in this house to-day, or I shall have a thousand spasms."

The self-appointed guard produced a pistol and walked the hall, preventing the predators from entering. Despite his help, on December 17 "starvation seemed near at hand."

Mrs. Screven's thoughts turned to her sixteen-year-old son on duty with the Confederate artillery in Savannah. "I was wild with apprehension. . . . I pictured him wounded, bleeding, dying."

After several quiet days, four men showed up on Christmas Day and asked her daughter to play the piano. Mrs. Screven refused to allow it. "They were extremely boisterous, used very profane language, and were disposed to be very familiar with the young ladies. One of my daughters made an attempt to leave the room and was prevented by one of these rough creatures immediately getting between her and the door. I became exceedingly alarmed, but made every effort to conceal it. We were in the power of fiends incarnate."

Mrs. Screven was relieved by the appearance of a Union soldier from Kentucky, who had earlier done a favor for her. "For Heaven's sake, get these men out of my house," she whispered to him. He did so skillfully and left a pistol for their protection, with instructions to "hide it until you have occasion to use it." Mrs. Screven placed it in the piano.

The soldier, whose name was James Pope, also left a pocketbook that contained money and jewelry for the destitute family. In it was a love letter in which a young lady admonished Pope not to "let them rebble injuns kill you."

Sherman's Surrender Demand to Hardee

HEADQUARTERS MILITARY DIVISION OF THE MISSISSIPPI, IN THE FIELD, SAVANNAH, GEORGIA, DECEMBER 17, 1864.

General William J. Hardee, commanding Confederate forces in Savannah.

GENERAL: You have doubtless observed, from your station at Rosedew, that seagoing vessels now come through Ossabaw Sound and up the Ogeechee to the rear of my army, giving me abundant supplies of all kinds, and more especially heavy ordnance necessary for the reduction of Savannah. I had already received guns that can cast heavy and destructive shot as far as the heart of your city; also, I have for some days held and controlled every avenue by which the people and garrison of Savannah can be supplied, and I am therefore justified in demanding the surrender of the city of Savannah, and its dependent forts, and shall wait a reasonable time for your answer, before opening with heavy ordinance. Should you entertain the proposition, I am prepared to grant liberal terms to the inhabitants and garrison; but should I be forced to resort to assault, or the slower and surer process of starvation, I shall then feel justified in resorting to the harshest measures, and shall make little effort to restrain my army-burning to avenge the national wrong which they attach to Savannah and other large cities which have been so prominent in dragging our country into civil war.

I have the honor to be your obedient servant,

—W. T Sherman, Major-General

The mounted Orphan Brigade had been sent to patrol the Altamaha River and prevent Union cavalry raids. On one occasion, a Yankee persisted in sniping at an Orphan. Tiring of the exchange, the Rebel challenged his opponent to step out in the open for a square duel. The Federal did so, and after several shots the Yankee was killed. On his body was found fifteen thousand dollars worth of diamonds stolen from a nearby plantation.

People of the region became very protective of the Orphan Brigade. After the brigade had passed through one town, a stranger in blue entered and asked if any Confederates had been seen recently. "Yes, sir, they have just been after marching through, and there was twinty thousand 'o them if there was a single man!" an elderly resident replied. As the spy rode away, the old man yelled after him, "Yis, sir, that's every word the truth, it is. And they were domned big min at that!"

On the Left Wing, events were progressing to Sherman's satisfaction. The 20th Corps struck the Charleston and Savannah Railroad at Monteith Station, ten miles from Savannah. On December 11 Baird's division of the 14th Corps attempted to destroy the bridge that spanned the Savannah River. Leading to the bridge they found a long trestle, which was supported fifteen feet above the swamp on piles. Their mission was foiled by a Confederate battery and a large gun mounted on a rail car that swept the bridge with deadly fire from the South Carolina shore. The Federals burned the trestle and destroyed a mile of track on the Georgia shore.

Sherman was concerned that the Confederates could escape from Savannah via a road that lay across the Savannah River. It led to Hardeeville, South Carolina, and from there the Rebels could board trains for Charleston. To prevent this, General Williams ordered a regiment crossed to Argyle Island, which was described as "one grand rice swamp . . . thickly traversed by ditches, dikes, and canals." Flat boats, used to transport rice, were collected along the river bank, and two companies crossed on the evening of December 11. Six additional companies passed over the next morning, and two companies and an artillery battery remained to protect the Georgia bank. On the island the Federals camped beside a rice mill, where they found two thousand bushels of threshed rice. It would be their food supply for the next two weeks.

In the early afternoon sentries spotted the smoke of three steamers rapidly approaching their position from upstream. The battery was quickly readied to prevent the Confederates from reaching Savannah. At 2,500 yards the Yankees opened fire on the side wheel gunboats *Macon* and *Sampson* and their unarmed tender, the *Resolute*. The gunboats, in line behind the tender, returned fire with heavy guns, but the rapidly firing Federals struck the *Resolute* several times at half-mile range. As the ships entered a bend, which exposed them to a raking fire from the Union battery, the gunboats got up stream and turned back. In the confusion they rammed the *Resolute,* which drifted helplessly aground on Argyle Island.

Her crew had lowered small boats and were about to escape when Federal infantry appeared and fired a volley, wounding one man. The *Resolute,* with a complement of seven officers and twenty-two men, plus considerable munitions and provisions, was captured and taken to the Georgia shore.

The battery fired on another ship that crossed the river near Savannah and threw several shots into the city. Other cannon were emplaced to prevent ships from reaching Savannah from Augusta, and Sherman considered placing a boom across the river.

On December 15, five companies crossed from Argyle to the South Carolina shore, but they returned as night fell. An entire brigade crossed on December 19 and drove the Confederates from an important position around a rice mill on the Izard plantation. They found advance almost impossible because Wheeler's cavalry had been dispatched to the Carolina shore; his troops and South Carolina artillery were defending Hardee's escape route tenaciously. The area was a rice plantation that the Confederates had flooded to a depth of eighteen inches. Bridges across the canals had been burned, and artillery commanded the only approaches across narrow dikes.

Hard skirmishing continued throughout December 20 and 21, and, despite reinforcements, Wheeler was slowly driven back. Georgia historian Charles C. Jones described the fighting as "obstinate and bloody."

Several attacks were launched against the Confederate left. There also was a rebellion among Hardee's "galvanized Yankee" recruits, seven of whom were immediately executed and the rest deported to South Carolina. The Confederate situation was becoming desperate.

Sherman was impatient to trap Hardee in the city. On December 17 he rode to Slocum's headquarters on the Macon Road. Under a flag of truce, he dispatched his brother-in-law through the Confederate lines to deliver a surrender demand. Sherman declared that he controlled every means of access to the city and was adequately supplied for a siege. Furthermore, he had received guns that could destroy Savannah.

> I am therefore justified in demanding the surrender of the city of Savannah, and its dependent forts, and shall wait a reasonable time for your answer, before opening with heavy ordnance. Should you entertain the proposition, I am prepared to grant liberal terms to the inhabitants and garrison; but should I be forced to resort to assault, or the slower and surer process of starvation, I shall then feel justified in resorting to the harshest measures, and shall make little effort to restrain my army—burning to revenge the national wrong which they attach to Savannah and other large cities which have been so prominent in dragging our country into civil war.

Hardee replied immediately, disputing Sherman's superior position. "Your demand for the surrender of Savannah . . . is refused. With respect to the threats conveyed in the closing paragraphs of your letter, I have to say that I have hitherto conducted the military operations intrusted to my direction in strict accordance with the rules of civilized warfare, and I should deeply regret the adoption of any course by you that may force me to deviate from them in future."

Of this crude exchange, Osborne wrote, "They were both only talking, and both knew it."

Sherman reported this exchange to Grant. While continuing preparations

Hardee's Reply to Sherman

HEADQUARTERS DEPARTMENT SOUTH CAROLINA, GEORGIA, AND FLORIDA, Savannah, Georgia, December 17, 1864.

Major-General W. T. Sherman, commanding Federal Forces near Savannah, Georgia.

GENERAL: I have to acknowledge the receipt of a communication from you of this date. . . . The position of your forces [a half-mile beyond the outer line for the land-defenses of Savannah] is, at the nearest point, at least four miles from the heart of the city. That and the interior line are both intact.

Your statement that you have, for some days, held and controlled every avenue by which the people and garrison can be supplied, is incorrect. I am in free and constant communication with my department.

Your demand for the surrender of Savannah and its dependent forts is refused.

With respect to the threats conveyed in the closing paragraphs of your letter [of what may be expected in case your demand is not complied with], I have to say that I have hitherto conducted the military operations intrusted to my direction in strict accordance with the rules of civilized warfare, and I should deeply regret the adoption of any course by you that may force me to deviate from them in future. I have the honor to be, very respectfully, your obedient servant,

—W. J. Hardee, Lieutenant-General.

for a sea journey to Virginia, he hoped for time to subdue Savannah. "With Savannah in our possession, at some future time if not now, we can punish South Carolina as she deserves," Sherman wrote, "and as thousands of the people in Georgia hoped we would do. I do sincerely believe that the whole United States, North and South, would rejoice to have this army turned loose on South Carolina, to devastate that State in the manner we have done in Georgia, and it would have a direct and immediate bearing on your campaign in Virginia."

With Hardee's rejection of his ultimatum, "nothing remained but to assault," Sherman believed. However, the "ground was difficult, and, as all former assault had proved so bloody, I concluded to make one more effort to completely surround Savannah on all sides so as . . . to capture the whole of his army."

Sherman rode to King's Bridge and boarded a steamer to confer with Foster. Before leaving, he ordered Slocum and Howard to "make all possible preparations" for an attack during the two or three days he would be absent.

Dahlgren escorted Sherman on the *Harvest Moon* to Hilton Head, where Sherman told Foster to use Hatch's division to block the Union Causeway near Bluffton, South Carolina. Foster "promptly agreed to give his personal attention to it."

On the night of December 20 Sherman started his return trip, but a strong wind slowed the ship. Dahlgren ordered the captain to slip into the inland passages, but the ship was "caught by a low tide and stuck in the mud." After much effort to free the steamer, Dahlgren loaned Sherman his barge and sailors rowed him through an "intricate and shallow channel." As they struggled toward Fort McAllister on the evening of December 21, a tugboat appeared with messages from Savannah. Hardee had got out the previous evening. Savannah was captured. ∎

A DRIVING TOUR
■ The Siege of Savannah ■

This tour will take travelers through the heart of the Confederate defenses of Savannah and south to Fort McAllister. It will also examine sites associated with Sherman's efforts to tighten a noose around the city.

From I-95 drive east on GA 26-U.S. 80 to GA 307-Dean Forrest Road, or west from Savannah on the same highway. Turn south onto GA 307-Dean Forrest Road, which passes through the heart of the Confederate lines. You will cross the Ogeechee Canal, behind which the Rebels erected wicked timber obstacles and formidable artillery positions. The countryside had been extensively flooded in front of the canal.

After 4.1 miles GA 307-Dean Forrest Road dead ends at GA 25-U.S. 17. Turn right to follow GA 25-U.S. 17 and enjoy the beautiful marsh land that appears. You immediately cross the Little Ogeechee River, near the point where the Confederate defenses terminated. After 6.7 is the Ogeechee River crossing at Kings Bridge.

The site has been extensively developed to accommodate pleasure fishing. There are boat ramps, tables and grills, and other facilities; an old bridge beside the modern span has been left as a fishing platform. Sherman had a long wharf built here to receive supplies from naval vessels that had waited offshore for the arrival of his army.

Continue south for 2.4 to the intersection with GA 144 in Richmond Hill.

The Gulf Railroad was broken here, when the community was Way's Station, and Union soldiers trooped through to conquer Fort McAllister. A number of fine plantation homes survive in Bryan County. During the Depression, this area had the patronage of Henry Ford. Mrs. Ford hated Florida, so they stayed in Richmond Hill each winter. Ford, who had timber interests here, built a number of facilities for his employees.

Turn left onto GA 144. After 5.4 turn left onto GA 144 SPUR, and after 4.2 is Fort McAllister.

Fort McAllister marked a new age in fortifications.

The fall of Fort Pulaski proved that brick forts were obsolete, and McAllister's performance (see Appendix B) demonstrated the superiority of dirt works. McAllister consisted of strong earthen walls that

Map 28: From I-95 to Fort McAllister.

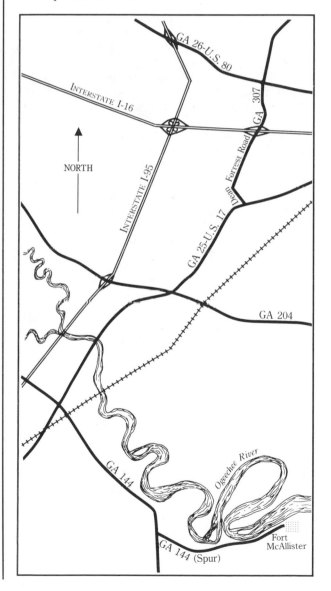

mounted heavy guns and a mortar. Large bombproofs, timber-supported shelters covered with dirt, housed magazines and supply rooms. The fort withstood seven attacks by Union ironclads and gunboats, but fell to an infantry attack from the rear. Sherman watched the assault from across the river, at Cheves rice mill. With McAllister's fall, the Ogeechee River was open, Sherman's army could be supplied, and the complete investment of Savannah was only a matter of time. McAllister's loss forced the Confederates to evacuate Savannah.

McAllister was stripped of her armament by Sherman, and the fort decayed after the War. When Henry Ford built a home nearby in the 1930s, he had the fort restored. Georgia acquired the site in 1958 to establish a state park. The earthworks have been impressively preserved, bombproofs have been reconstructed to wartime condition and outfitted as powder magazines and barracks, and guns have been mounted. Detached from the fort is the mortar battery, connected by a long earthen wall to facilitate safe movement during attack. In the museum are exhibits illustrating the history of Fort McAllister, particularly of the naval bombardments; an impressive diorama depicts the storming of the fort. Beside the parking area are large pieces of machinery salvaged from the wreck of the *Nashville,* which was sunk by a monitor just upstream from the fort. Legal arguments still rage between the state of Georgia and private divers who want to salvage additional material from the ship.

Richmond Hill State Park, beside Fort McAllister, offers camping and the usual amenities, with an emphasis on fishing. A few miles downstream the Ogeechee River comes to the end of its 250-mile journey through the heart of Georgia.

The guided tour of the March to the Sea officially ends at Fort McAllister, but there are many interesting historical attractions south of here. In Liberty County, 13 miles south on GA 25-U.S. 17, is Midway Church, a magnificent structure that looks as if it belonged in New England. A church built in 1754 was burned by British invaders during the Revolution, then rebuilt in 1792, then was threatened with the same fate by Kilpatrick's men, who lived in the church and the surrounding area for several weeks.

Midway Church is open to the public. Beside it is Midway Museum, situated in a replica of an 18th-century coastal cottage. Midway produced many of Georgia's early leaders, including three signers of the Declaration. A number of important figures in Georgia history are buried in the impressive cemetery across the highway.

East of Midway, off SR 631 on SR 18, is Dorchester Church, built in 1854. It is all that remains of an old community. Farther east, off SR 631 on SR 15, is Sunbury Historic Site. Sunbury was a busy port that rivaled Savannah in importance for a number of years. During the Revolution the Colonials established Fort Morris here, but it fell after a British bombardment. The earthworks of Fort Defiance, built to protect the town during the War of 1812, are well preserved. During the Civil War Kilpatrick entered Sunbury and burned a historic church as a signal to the Union fleet in Ossabaw Sound and to Sherman. The burning of the church is represented by a mural in the Visitors Center. A museum explains the history of Sunbury, which ceased to exist many years ago.

West of Midway, on GA 38-U.S. 82, is Flemington, which boasts a beautiful church, built in 1852. There are local history exhibits in Hinesville's Old Jail Museum, and on the courthouse square is a cannon excavated from Fort Morris. A few Civil War artifacts are displayed at nearby Fort Stewart Museum. Some of the units that make up the 24th Infantry Division stationed here fought in the Civil War for the Union armies, but a Georgia National Guard contingent traces its history to the Confederate military. South of Hinesville is Walthourville, which has a pretty church built in 1844.

In Long County, on GA 57-GA 23-U.S. 301, is Jones Creek Church, dating from 1856; and south of that highway on SR 1890 is Beards Bluff, an important site along the Altamaha River during the Revolution. In Ludowici is the Old Well Pavilion, which is covered with red brick tiles. The famous tiles were manufactured from local clay early in this century. Eighteen other buildings in town have these distinctive roofs. Foraging Union cavalry terrorized this region during Savannah's siege.

Just before the Altamaha River is reached on GA 23-GA 38-U.S. 25-U.S. 82-U.S. 301 [Note: All these roads designate one highway] is Morgan Lake, behind which Confederates erected an artillery battery. Across the river is Doctor Town, where other Rebels helped prevent Yankee infantry and cavalry from burning an important bridge on the Gulf Railroad. When the Civil War ended, an artillery piece here was loaded with a dangerous charge and spiked. Years later some brave soul disarmed the cannon, which is displayed in a park in Waycross, gateway to the Okefenokee Swamp. ∎

CHAPTER 17

"I Beg to Present You as a Christmas Gift, the City of Savannah"

S herman's capture of Fort McAllister and the encroachment of Federal troops near the Union Causeway convinced Hardee that he must soon leave Savannah or be trapped. Sherman was up to his old tricks, effecting a siege of the city in a slow, methodical manner. Hardee had come to respect that maneuver at Atlanta.

While Hardee's scratch force vigorously protected his birthplace, secret plans were being carried out to allow the beleaguered garrison to escape. Since Beauregard's visit on December 9, work had progressed on a pontoon bridge that would span the mile-wide Savannah River. To the Confederate high command, Savannah was expendable, but ten thousand troops were invaluable at this stage of the War.

Hardee's chief engineer, John G. Clark, had no ordinary pontoon material to work with. Ingeniously, he called for every skiff, barge, and rice flat along the Savannah River to be collected. Hundreds of men worked feverishly to lash the boats together with rope and chain. The boats were pushed into place in the river and anchored with rail car wheels, and the city wharves and several nearby buildings were dismantled and the wood used as flooring. A thick layer of rice straw coated the bridge to dampen the sound of tramping feet and rumbling wagons.

The bridge, surely the strangest construction in Civil War history, was built in three sections. The first extended from Broad Street across the 1,000-yard channel to Hutchinson Island. Hundreds of wagonloads of straw, brush, and wood were required to build a causeway across the marshy island that would accept the weight of cannon and supply wagons.

The cold, rainy weather increased Beauregard's wrath when he returned to Savannah on December 16 and found the bridge only one-third completed. Part of the delay was blamed on Wheeler, who found stacks of rice flats beside the river and burned them, assuming the boats were part of Sherman's preparations to storm the city. Beauregard unleashed a savage tongue-lashing to everyone associated with the project, then left for Charleston.

The chat produced spectacular results. In three days the remaining spans—from Hutchinson Island to Pennyworth Island and a final bridge to the South Carolina shore—were completed late in the evening of December 19. Thirty eighty-foot-long rice flats went into the construction.

More Federal troops had crossed to Izard's, and Foster was moving on the Charleston and Savannah Railroad near Pocataligo, South Carolina. These developments convinced Hardee that the evacuation could wait no longer; it would begin at dusk the following day. He had ten thousand men, valuable artillery, and supply wagons to save; five thousand additional men were holding open the escape route on the South Carolina shore.

During the day of December 20, civilians who did not desire to remain in an occupied city were allowed to cross the bridge. A Federal on the South Carolina shore near Izard's saw a "great number vehicles of all descriptions." There were "wagons, family carriages, men and women on foot," added another, all heading toward Hardeeville.

To prevent Federal interference with the retreat, the Confederate iron-clad *Savannah* appeared and lobbed shells into the Union positions near the

Savannah's citizens send off troops to Virginia in 1861. [LESLIE'S ILLUSTRATED]

Confederate troops evacuate Savannah on the night of December 20, 1864. [HARPER'S WEEKLY]

river. At 4:00 P.M. Wheeler was reinforced by three regiments of infantry to discourage a Federal assault.

As the sun sank below the horizon on December 20, the huge Confederate guns facing Sherman opened a massive bombardment of Union lines. The racket drowned out noises made at the bridge, and the exploding shells, bouncing solid shot, and dangerous grapeshot kept the Federals from attacking, scouting, or even sleeping. When the fire ceased two hours later, trees and underbrush between the lines had been shredded.

Since the big guns could not be evacuated across the improvised bridge, every possible projectile was expended, and then the cannon were spiked. Gunpowder was thrown into the canals and swamps, and artillery ammunition cast into the river. As the forts were abandoned, men chopped the spokes on the carriages and even destroyed their rammers and sponges.

The light artillery and caissons crossed the bridge before the infantry arrived. The garrisons of the coastal forts were picked up by steamers and taken to Screven's Ferry, on the Carolina side, at 9:00 P.M. Wright's men, stationed the greatest distance from the city on the Little Ogeechee River, left their works first, at 8:00 P.M., marching to Savannah and over the bridge. The center of the line, McLaw's force, evacuated their position at 10:00 P.M., and Smith and the Georgia militia withdrew at 11:00 P.M., beginning their crossing of the bridge at 1:00 A.M. Hardee took a steamer across the river at 9:00 P.M.

A strong skirmish line remained until 1:00 A.M. to keep camp fires burning and maintain the illusion of a strong defense. When rockets signaled the completion of the crossing, a provost guard, which had prevented wanton destruction by Rebel stragglers, rounded up the last skirmishers and hurried across the bridge.

Throughout the night of December 20, beyond the spires of Savannah, a long column of cannon, men, and wagons waited on Broad Street for their turn to cross the bridge. Fog rolled in, making the journey across the creaking, swaying spans seem like a terrifying nightmare; infantry stomped, wagons creaked, teamsters cursed, and mules brayed in fear. Erasmus H. Jordan witnessed "a cannon pulled by a team of mules roll off the planking and sink, pulling the mules down with it." Several wagons were similarly lost.

Early in the morning the extensive navy yard, a number of vessels under construction, and two steamboats, the *Isandiga* and *Firefly,* were burned. The last men to cross the bridge were silhouetted by the flames.

"The constant thread of the troops and the rumbling of the artillery as they poured over those long floating bridges was a sad sound," wrote one soldier, "and by the glare of the light from fires at the east of the bridge it seemed like an immense funeral procession stealing out of the city in the dead of night."

The Rebel rear guard soon scampered toward the waterfront. They presented a pitiful sight, those ragged soldiers and barefooted militia.

By dawn nine thousand soldiers, forty-eight cannon, and innumerable supply wagons had rumbled across to safety. Ironically, it was the fourth anniversary of South Carolina's secession. The first bridge was cut loose and ridden by engineers downstream to the Carolina shore at 5:40 A.M. One engineer, Captain Robert Stiles, saw Yankees running to the river's edge and yelling. Nichols said, "The forms of retreating enemy could be seen flying into the gray mist across the marshes on the other side of the river."

Hardee's men stalked through a freezing dawn to Hardeeville, where the conscripts and Georgia militia were dismissed to make their way to Augusta. Hardee had accomplished a thankless task; his inexperienced troops had kept Sherman's massive army at bay, then had executed the War's most difficult retreat. "Though compelled to evacuate the city, there is no part of my military life to which I look back with so much satisfaction," he wrote in later years.

During the last days of the siege, men of the 20th Corps lay in their damp trenches and listened to a noise from the city that sounded "much like the laying of a pontoon bridge," one report stated. As the evacuation was underway, the noise of the crossing carried to enemy lines, where Federal sharpshooters remained alert. They reported that the "noise of the retreating enemy could plainly be heard as they crossed the bridges from Savannah to the South Carolina shore," from 7:00 P.M. to 3:00 A.M. When officers were informed, they replied that there were orders not to interfere. The Rebels would be cut off at the railroad by Foster.

A Union officer said the Rebels "kept up an unusually severe fire," but at 11:00 P.M. "totally ceased his fire." The Federals, exhausted from hugging the bottom of their slimy works, fell asleep when calm returned. In the early morning, Yankees all along the line realized that something was wrong; it was too quiet across no man's land. There were no boisterous conversations, and no shadows were cast by men passing camp fires. By 3:00 A.M. several Yankees had slithered through the abatis and scuttled into the

Sherman's triumphant soldiers parade through Savannah. [HARPER'S WEEKLY]

empty Rebel trenches. Men from a dozen different units claimed to have been the first to enter the enemy works.

Before first light, General Geary led a New York division from the 20th Corps into the city. They found Savannah in turmoil. Some retreating Confederates had plundered stores and warehouses, and a crowd of poor whites and slaves were fighting over supplies of rice as the Federals approached, and several buildings were torched. The Yankees contributed to the looting until Geary posted guards and assigned a brigade to patrol the city. A force of four hundred men was sent to occupy Fort Jackson, and other squads secured the river forts.

In a replay of an event that had occurred three hundred miles to the east four months earlier, Savannah Mayor Dr. Richard Arnold and the city's aldermen rode out under a flag of truce to surrender their city. Confederate stragglers stole their horses, so they were on foot when Geary encountered them near the intersection of the Charleston railroad and the Augusta road. It was 4:00 A.M. on December 21. Sherman missed the climactic moment, as he had at Atlanta in September.

The Mayor's formal request read:

> *Sir:* The city of Savannah was last night evacuated by the Confederate military and is now entirely defenseless. As chief magistrate of the city I respectfully request your protection of the lives and private property of the citizens and of our women and children.

Union troops parade through Savannah after the occupation. The American flag flies over the U.S. Customs House. [LESLIE'S ILLUSTRATED]

The lead brigade, led by Colonel Henry Barnum, marched down West Broad Street to Bay Street "with lusty cheers at every step," he noted, and stopped at City Hall. In the "early dawn, and before the sun first gilded the morning clouds, our National colors, side by side with those of my own division, were unfurled from the dome of the Exchange and over the U.S. Customs house," Geary wrote. When two brigades arrived at Fort Jackson and "flung the Stars and Stripes to the breeze from the walls," the *Savannah* fired on the fort. A Union battery at the lower end of Bay Street opened on the ship at 10:00 A.M. and struck it, but with no effect.

The morning issue of the Savannah *Republican,* the last published under Confederate authority, printed a mournful message on its front page:

> To *the citizens of Savannah:*
> By the fortunes of war we pass today under the authority of the Federal military forces. The evacuation of Savannah by the Confederate army, which took place last night, left the gates to the city open, and General Sherman, with his army will, no doubt, to-day take possession.

The citizens were counseled to "obedience and all proper respect." They were told to stay in their homes until a provost guard was established and that "property and persons will be respected by our military ruler."

Boarding the tug that informed him of Savannah's evacuation, Sherman travelled to King's Bridge, then rode into Savannah and climbed atop the Customs House to view his prize on the morning of December 22. "The navy-yard and the wreck of the iron-clad *Savannah* were still smouldering," he noted, "but all else looked quiet enough."

Sherman entered the Pulaski House, where he had stayed during peacetime, and established his headquarters. The proprietor, a Vermont Yankee, "was very anxious to have us for boarders, but I soon explained to him that . . . we were not in the habit of paying board."

While making arrangements at the hotel, a rich English merchant, Charles Green, invited Sherman to use his fine home. Green explained that some other general would impose on his residence if Sherman did not, and he chose to be Sherman's host rather than subject a Southerner to the indignity. The general accepted the generous offer.

Sherman had hardly entered Green's residence when A. G. Browne, a Treasury agent, appeared to claim all captured material in the city for the Treasury Department. "Having use for these articles ourselves and having fairly earned them," Sherman thundered, "I did not feel inclined to surrender possession and explained to him that the quartermaster and commissary could manage them more to my liking than he."

Browne, described by the General as "a shrewd, clever Yankee," sought to ease Sherman's temper by suggesting that he present Savannah to Lincoln as a Christmas present. Realizing that the President "enjoyed such pleasantry," Sherman immediately sat down and wrote these few words to Lincoln:

> I beg to present you as a Christmas-gift the city of Savannah, with one hundred and fifty heavy guns and plenty of ammunition, also about twenty-five thousand bales of cotton.

The telegraph, which reached Lincoln on Christmas Eve, "was extensively published in the newspapers," Sherman wrote, "and made many a household unusually happy on that festive day."

"Many, many thanks for your Christmas gift, the capture of Savannah," Lincoln responded. Then, displaying his typical aggressiveness, he queried, "But what next?"

Grant and Stanton soon expressed their disappointment with Hardee's escape. Added to Hood's unopposed evacuation of Atlanta, this seemed to be a regrettable habit of Sherman's. Maneuver and territorial gains were fine, but a defeated or captured Rebel army would have been even better.

Van Huzen had received his discharge and boarded a ship for home on December 20. At sea he saw huge fires burning in Savannah, and around midnight there were a terrific explosion. He was disappointed that the Confederates had escaped, both for the Union cause and "for the good name of our commanding General." He and many others could see no reason for allowing the Rebels to get away.

Even the rank and file seemed disappointed. "The Johnnys got out last night," Upson wrote on December 21. "I think our officers knew they were going and did not try to stop them for we could hear them all night moving about and most of us think if we had pushed the fighting on our right front a little harder we might have cut them off and captured the whole of them."

Sherman's Telegraph to President Lincoln

SAVANNAH GEORGIA, DECEMBER 22, 1864

To His Excellency President LINCOLN, Washington, D.C.:

I beg to present you as a Christmas-gift the city of Savannah, with one hundred and fifty heavy guns and plenty of ammunition, also about twenty-five thousand bales of cotton.
—W. T. Sherman, Major-General

But, in one way, Upson was satisfied with the results. "I am awfully glad we did not have to charge their works for we would have lost a good many lives, that's sure."

Sherman had his defenders. General Cox blamed Hardee's escape on Grant's decision to bring the army north by sea. It had distracted Sherman from the job of besieging Savannah and had forced him to divide his attention and resources, Cox argued.

To completely encircle Savannah, Sherman wrote in his own defense, "would have involved the risk of isolating the troops across a deep river too wide for my pontoon train, and upon which the rebels had two gun-boats (one ironclad) at the city wharf, with boats to throw their whole force across against them. . . . Two days more and the garrison would have been hemmed in completely; as it is, the campaign ends with the capture of this important city." He believed Hardee's troops would be largely lost to the Confederacy. The Georgia militia would march to Augusta, and the other troops were already scattered among various cities in the Carolinas.

"I was disappointed that Hardee had escaped with his army," Sherman concluded, "but on the whole we had reason to be content with the substantial fruits of victory."

In Savannah the soldiers learned that the country had been following their progress with fascination. "We got some Northern papers today," Upson wrote. "It seems that the good people up there were terribly worried about us. They called us the *lost army*. And some thought we never would show up again. I don't think they know what kind of an Army this is that Uncle Billy has. Why, if Grant can keep Lee and his troops busy we can tramp all over this Confederacy; and by the time we were through with that, there would be nothing left but the ground."

During the March, Grant had said, "Sherman's army is now somewhat in the condition of a ground mole when he disappears under a lawn. You can here and there trace his track, but you are not quite certain where he will come out until you see his head."

The torpedos were barely removed from Savannah's rivers when swarms of men arrived to buy cotton for speculation. Others hired blacks as substitutes for northern men drafted into the army; hundreds of former slaves were locked up against their will and held until shipment north could be arranged. Sherman hated businessmen, a feeling that perhaps remained from his failed civilian enterprises. He released the blacks and ordered the businessmen arrested if they did not vacate Savannah immediately. Stanton took care of the cotton, declaring that it belonged to the U.S. Government.

Sherman believed that Savannah's population "had participated more or less in the war, and had no special claims to our favor, but I regarded the war as rapidly drawing to a close," and that belief led him to treat the citizens leniently.

On December 26 Special Field Orders No. 143 announced, "During war the military is superior to civil authority." However, Sherman encouraged "well-disposed and peaceful inhabitants to resume their usual pursuits; families should be disturbed as little as possible in their residences, and trades-

Savannah after Federal occupation, looking downstream toward the Atlantic Ocean.

men allowed the free use of their shops, tools, &c; churches, schools, and all places of amusement and recreations should be encouraged, and streets and roads made perfectly safe to persons in their pursuits." Citizens were not to be arrested except on orders from headquarters or the Provost Marshal. Fire protection and gas and water systems were to continue operating.

Employment would be given black and white civilians for needed public work. Provisions would be distributed to the poor, and refugees quartered in vacant houses. The mayor and the city council would remain in office and execute their duties. They would announce Sherman's dictate that the people must decide whether to remain in Savannah and accept Union occupation or be evacuated. Only two hundred people volunteered to leave Union lines.

Two newspapers would be allowed to publish in the city, but they would "be held to the strictest accountability, and will be punished severely in person and property for any libelous publications, mischievous matter, premature news, exaggerated statements, or any comments whatever upon the acts of the constituted authorities."

Sherman soon received the families of several prominent Confederate officers, who asked for protection. The wives of Gustavus Smith, LaFayette McLaws, and General A. P. Stewart of the Army of Tennessee, and Hardee's brother were assured that "no harm was designed to any of the people of Savannah."

Sherman also entertained delegations of local blacks, who crowded the Green mansion to see him. To his wife, Ellen, Sherman wrote, "It would amuse you to see the Negroes. They flock to me, old and young; they pray and shout and mix up my name with that of Moses and Simon and other scriptural ones as well as 'Abham Linkum,' the Great Messiah of 'Dis Jubilee.'"

Engineer Poe immediately started the task of reworking Savannah's defenses. By December 27 he had designed a much shorter line than the one held by the Rebels. It would be a series of detached lunettes, each capable of operating independently of the others. They would be armed with sixty guns, half large cannon captured from the Confederates and the other half field pieces; and a force of five thousand soldiers would garrison the city. Portions of the Confederate works were destroyed, but most were left for use as a first line of defense. Hardee's line was well constructed but too extensive. The Confederate earthworks facing road junctions were particularly valued, and Poe recommended opening the sluice gates and flooding the countryside if an enemy approached, as Hardee had done. Two forts were built across the Savannah River to protect causeways leading into South Carolina.

The Union line was so close to the city that some buildings had to be razed. The entire city would be within range of an attacker's guns, but Poe noted, "the presence of the women and children of the enemy . . . render such a fire improbable." Poe prepared for an attack that few, Federal or Confederate, thought would materialize.

Cannon from Fort McAllister, the river forts, and the city's fortifications that were not needed for Savannah's defense were dismounted and shipped to Fort Pulaski and Hilton Head.

On December 24 Sherman ordered torpedos in the Savannah River removed, and on New Year's Eve he sent crews to dismantle the crib obstructions. Islands of mud that had formed around the cribs had to be dredged before the stout cribs and their brick and cobblestone fillings could be removed. Only then was it possible to supply the army fully.

Christmas in Georgia

The Federal army enjoyed a pleasant Christmas in the captured city of Savannah. Sherman and Henry Hitchcock attended services at St. John's Episcopal Church, across the street from their quarters, then returned to the Green house for a delicious dinner. Nichols had secured several fine turkeys, which were served on Green's handsome china. Mr. Green, Slocum, Corse, and other staff members and officers attended the festival meal. With fine wines they drank to Sherman's health.

For thousands of Georgia families who lived between Atlanta and Savannah, Christmas Day 1864 was gloomy, cold, and hungry. Near Covington, Dolly Burge's daughter, Sadai, leaped from bed to check her stocking. "She could not believe but that there would be something in it," Burge wrote. "Finding nothing, she crept back into bed."

"I was hungry, very hungry," wrote Mary Gay in devastated Decatur. "There was nothing left in the city to eat. Yea, a crow flying over it would have failed to discover a morsel with which to appease its hunger."

Several weeks before Christmas, Gay learned that a Confederate commissary that had opened in Atlanta was exchanging food for lead. Gay took a pail to the place where Hood had destroyed his ordinance train in September, and with a dull knife she pried bullets out of the icy ground until her hands bled and her feet were frozen. "It was so cold!" she recorded. "I cried like a baby, long and loud." The people of Atlanta fed themselves throughout the winter by working the "lead mines."

It remains a tradition in the South to eat hog jowls and black-eyed peas on New Year's Day to ensure good luck for the coming year. On January 1, 1865, it was a lucky Georgia family that had been left a hog's head by the Yankees, and some seed peas the invaders thought worthless. ■

A toast is proposed at Sherman's merry dinner party at the home of Savannah merchant Charles Green on Christmas Day 1864. [HARPER'S WEEKLY]

Sherman allowed Geary and his men to keep order in the city. Geary, a former mayor of San Francisco, had administrative abilities, and the troops were orderly Easterners.

"He [Geary] very soon established a good police, maintained admirable order, and I doubt if Savannah, either before or since, has had a better government than during our stay," Sherman bragged. "The parades became the daily resorts of ladies, to hear the music of our excellent bands; schools were opened, and the churches every Sunday were filled with most devout and respectful congregations; stores were reopened, and markets for provisions, meat, wood, etc., were established, so that each family, regardless of race, color, or opinion, could procure all the necessities and even luxuries of life." Many poor families "were issued stores from our stock of supplies."

"A foreigner visiting the city would not suppose that it was so lately a prize of battle," Nichols wrote in support of Sherman's claim. "Ladies walk the streets with perfect confidence and security, and the public squares are filled with children at play; the stores and theatres are open; soldiers are lounging on the doorsteps of the houses in cheerful conversation with fair damsels."

Nichols expressed distaste for a class of inhabitants who "owned the human beings whose labor was the source of their wealth." These people "came to despise any man who gained his daily bread by the sweat of his own brow." He encountered one "highly cultivated lady" who had lost her money, slaves, and land, who told him, "I shall have to starve or work."

"Well, madam," Nichols replied, "I really wouldn't advise you to starve. Supposing you do work?"

"But I never did such a thing in all my life! I really fear, sir, that I shall have to submit to the disgrace of giving lessons in music."

"Madam," Nichols replied with disgust, "I hope so!"

The ladies of Savannah complained about petty theft by Sherman's men and minor harassment, but they could not understand that the Yankees were putting on their best behavior. Hundreds of families in eastern Georgia would not have recognized these soldiers as the vandals who had destroyed their every possession and gleefully stole the last morsels from their homes.

Miss Frances Thomas Howard told of two women who went to see Mr. Green on business during Sherman's stay in his house. Green politely asked if the women would like to be introduced to Sherman. One of them exclaimed, "Not for the world!" Howard's sister Nelly passed Sherman's "beautifully furnished rooms," and Green asked, "Don't you want him to rest comfortably?"

"No, indeed, I do not!" Nelly cried. "I wish a thousand papers of pins were stuck in that bed and that he was strapped down on them."

On Christmas Day a Union chaplain was on hand to help with services at St. John's. Miss Howard saw many people leave without "partaking of the sacrament. This has been a sorrowful Christmas day."

On New Year's another chaplain offered to assist Dr. Axson at the Independent Presbyterian Church. The pastor declined, saying, "Sir, my people need comfort, and that you cannot give."

Soldiers told a story that when Sherman was asked by a local minister if he could pray for the Confederate president, the General replied, "Hell, yes! Jeff Davis and the devil can both use all the prayer they can get."

Sherman visited the daughter of an old friend, Colonel John H. Kinzie of Chicago. His daughter was Eleanor Kinzie Gordon, whose husband was a captain in Wheeler's cavalry. Gordon's father had built the Central Railroad, which Sherman had recently destroyed. The Gordons' daughter was "Daisy," later Juliette Low, founder of the Girl Scouts of America.

Sherman missed his own family very much, and set Daisy and her sister on his knees. The General "kept them in shouts of laughter till long past their bedtime," Mrs. Gordon wrote.

Sherman enjoyed the homey atmosphere so much that he described the visit to General Howard. Thinking of his five daughters at home, Howard requested permission to visit the family. Mrs. Gordon consented, and Howard called one afternoon.

While sitting in Howard's lap, Daisy exclaimed, "Oh, you have only got one arm!"

"Yes, little girl," Howard said. "Are you not sorry for me?"

"Yes, indeed," Daisy said. "What happened to your arm?"

"It was shot off in battle," Howard replied.

Old Fort Jackson, flanked by earthworks, after the occupation. A Union monitor patrols the Savannah River.
[HARPER'S WEEKLY]

"Oh, did the Yankees shoot it off?"

"No, my dear, the Rebels shot it off."

"Did they," Daisy exclaimed. "Well, I shouldn't wonder if my Papa did it. He has shot lots of Yankees."

When the people of New York, Boston, and Philadelphia sent food to the residents of Savannah, Elizabeth Mackay Stiles wrote, "Then they think they are so liberal, giving us food, and they stole more from one plantation than the whole of New York subscribed."

Miss Fanny Cohen had to entertain several Union officers who called at her home. On December 23 Engineer Poe visited, "and I was obliged to receive him and never was so embarrassed in my life," she wrote in her diary. "My hatred for the Army in which he was an officer and my desire to be polite made me almost speechless—the contending feelings were more than I could control."

On the following day Sherman's quartermaster, Captain Gilbert Dunbar, arrived to speak with Cohen's father. "I was obliged to receive him but did so standing up so that he could have no excuse for remaining longer than his business required him to do." He left, "like a well bred dog," she stated.

On December 25 Cohen wrote, "This is the saddest Christmas that I have ever spent and my only pleasure during the day has been in looking forward to spending my next Christmas in the Confederacy." She gathered a group of friends for a "rebel *meeting*. . . . We abused the yankees to our hearts' content."

A trip through her beloved city saddened Cohen on December 27. "All our squares built up with wooden houses so that I scarcely recognized the streets," she said. Her spirits fell even further on New Year's. "How sad this beginning of the year to us surrounded by our enemies."

Miss Howard shared Cohen's view of the occupation. "Our cemetery is desecrated with their fortifications. The Yankees have broken open the doors and vaults, and in one instance that I know of, the coffin of a lady was opened and a cross and chain stolen from her body. Surely such men are not human."

John M. Glidden was stationed aboard a ship in the Savannah River in January 1865 and found the city in worse shape than that described by Sherman. "I don't know what the condition and appearance of Savannah was before the rebellion; but at present it is in the most dilapidated and miserable condition," he wrote: "The effects and ravages of war are noticeable everywhere, business is almost entirely suspended, and nearly every store is closed, the houses are also carefully closed, and very few civilians and ladies are to be seen, fences are broken down, sidewalks and wharves are going to ruin, and Sherman's dead horses are laying about the streets by the dozen."

On the night of January 27, "a terrible conflagration swept over a large portion of the city." Glidden was asleep when a shipmate roused him to view the sight. They decided to enter the city and were standing beside a large burning building when a black man ran by shouting, "'Look out for the magazine!' Before we had time to retreat the shells, in the very building we were standing by began to burst, throwing bricks, mortar, and iron in every direction." Finding their retreat blocked by a row of houses, the men banged frantically at a door, hoping to escape to the next street. "The explosions followed each other in quick succession, and the house shook to its foundation at every report." Glidden and his friend finally broke down the door and ran through the house, which was soon destroyed. They ran for the waterfront as shrapnel fell all around them.

Seven people were killed in the eighteen-hour fire, and two hundred houses were burned. The blaze almost detonated an arsenal filled with sixty tons of gunpowder. "The scene next morning was heart-rending," Glidden continued, "hundreds of families turned out of house and home, and carrying off what little they had saved from their burning houses.

"I saw one poor creature laying on the sidewalk, with the top of his head blown off exposing his brains to view."

Glidden believed that real sympathy for the Union in Savannah was small. Many residents took an oath of allegiance because the Confederacy seemed beaten, "but they still retain their Southern sympathies and have no love for the Union."

Glidden attended services at St. John's Church on January 29 and noticed that the pastor avoided praying for Lincoln. The tone of the sermon seemed "calculated to inspire the people with the hope that . . . rebellion will finally succeed."

"This is a most miserable hole," Glidden concluded, "and the sooner I get out of it the happier I shall be."

After Christmas, Sherman received a newspaper that reported the death of a son, Charles, whom he had never seen. Earlier in the War, Sherman and Ellen had lost an older boy, Willie. "I should like to have seen the baby of which all spoke so well," Sherman wrote his wife, "but I seem doomed to pass my life away so that even my children will be strangers."

On January 8 Sherman authorized units to add the word *Savannah* to their flags. He signed a resolution officially thanking the army and gave high praise to everyone associated with the March.

General Howard and Slocum are gentlemen of singular capacity and intelligence, thorough soldiers and patriots, working day and night, not for themselves, but for their country and their men. General Kilpatrick, who commanded the cavalry of this army, has handled it with spirit and dash to my entire satisfaction, and kept a superior force of the enemy's cavalry from even approaching our infantry columns or wagon trains. All the division and brigade commanders merit my personal and official thanks.

As for the infantry, "they seem so full of confidence in themselves that I doubt if they want a compliment from me; but I must do them justice to say that whether called on to fight, to march, to wade streams, to make roads, clear out obstructions, build bridges, make corduroy, or tear up railroads, they have done it with alacrity and a degree of cheerfulness unsurpassed. A little loose in foraging, they 'did some things they ought not to have done!'" but that could be forgiven such fearless warriors.

After occupying Savannah, Sherman received word that he would not be required to proceed by ship to Virginia. "Your confidence in being able to march up and join this army pleases me," Grant wrote Sherman, "and I believe it can be done. The effect of such a campaign will be to disorganize the South, and prevent the organization of new armies from their broken fragments. . . . Without waiting further directions, then, you may make your preparations to start on your northern expedition without delay. Break up the railroads in South and North Carolina, and join the armies operating against Richmond as soon as you can."

Sherman thanked Grant for his confidence in the army. He hoped to start for Columbia and Raleigh in ten days. The army would feint on, but bypass, Augusta and Wilmington. Charleston, while recognized as politically important, was not a military imperative and would also be ignored. In preparation for the campaign, on December 30 Sherman ordered sixty days' forage for 35,000 animals.

"I think the time has come now when we should attempt the boldest moves," Sherman wrote Halleck, "and my experience is that they are easier of execution than more timid ones, because the enemy is disconcerted by them.

"The truth is the whole army is burning with an insatiable desire to wreak vengeance upon South Carolina," Sherman continued. "I almost tremble at her fate, but feel that she deserves all that seems in store for her. Many and many a person in Georgia asked me why we did not go to South Carolina, and when I answered that I was en route for that State the invariable reply was, 'Well, if you will make those people feel the severities of war, we will pardon you for your desolation of Georgia.'"

On December 28 a Richmond newspaper reported that Sherman would soon leave for the Carolinas from Port Royal, "stealing and murdering as much as he can by the way. All very fine, but if Sherman proposes, Lee disposes."

Sherman scheduled a review of his troops for December 24. While the men quickly rehearsed their steps, officers practiced saluting reviewing officers. Despite their disdain for such frivolities, most soldiers managed to present a soldierly appearance. Dozier reported that he "marched clear around the city." There was a dress parade on December 27, and other drills and reviews were held to keep the soldiers out of trouble.

The Federals camped in Savannah and all around the outskirts of the city. For protection from the freezing winter wind, the men built shanties of appropriated lumber in Savannah's famous squares and any empty piece of ground. For entertainment, they gambled, raced horses, attended dances put on by blacks, and frequented houses of prostitution.

Sherman made sure his troops created no disturbances in Savannah. Soldiers were required to remain with their units, and officers were forbidden to seek billeting in the city; they were required to remain with their men. Only soldiers with passes could enter Savannah, and men had to be in camp at 9:00 P.M.

"This is a beautiful city, and very old," Upson recorded. He and his buddy Possum set up their pup tent in Savannah. "We dug a hole in the sandy ground 6½ feet long, 3½ wide, 4 ft deep, and lined it with boards we got out of an old house, put our tent over it, got a lot of hanging moss off a tree, put it in the bottom and have a very comfortable place to sleep. We do not have much duty to do and can go around a good deal."

Dozier enjoyed a tour of Savannah's forts, monuments, and historic cemetery on December 21. Men were fascinated to find earthworks remaining from the Revolutionary War, and they marveled at statues of familiar heroes like Nathaniel Greene and Casimir Pulaski. "The residences are more like those of New York" than traditional southern dwellings, Dozier commented. He and his buddies obtained a horse and wagon and gathered materials to build a shanty. On January 10 he helped construct a fort, and on the following day he marched to Thunderbolt and boarded a ship for Beaufort in preparation for operations in the Carolinas. The men had expected a period of rest, but "hopes blighted," he noted.

Osborne's artillery unit was rapidly refitted for future operations. He believed "next spring will finish this war."

Sherman had been declared a hero following the capture of Atlanta, and America was now ready to deify the temperamental genius after his triumphal arrival in Savannah. With Grant still stalemated at Petersburg and the Union war effort generally at a standstill throughout the fall of 1864, all attention had devolved upon Sherman. With his name again bandied about as a future presidential candidate, Sherman wrote, "Some fool seems to have used my name. If forced to choose between the penitentiary and the White House . . . I would say the penitentiary, thank you."

"None but an unusually bold man would have undertaken this campaign," Major Connolly wrote, "and none but a man of genius could have succeeded as he has. . . . I am no hero-worshiper, but what I have seen convinces me that General Sherman is a leader, of genius equal to that of Napoleon in the field."

Praise for Sherman and his stunning military accomplishments poured in from all quarters. "John [Sherman's senator brother] writes that I am in everybody's mouth and that even he is known as my brother," Sherman wrote his wife, "and that all the Shermans are now feted as relatives of me."

Sherman told Ellen he enjoyed "the singular friendship of General Grant, who is almost childlike in his love for me. . . . All sort of people send me presents, and I hope they don't slight you or the girls.

"Grant, the President, the army, and even the world," he continued, "now looks to me to strike hard and decisive blows. . . . I have again cut [the Confederacy] in twain and have planned and executed a campaign which judges pronounce will be famous among the grand deeds of the world. I can hardly realize it for really it was easy, but like one who has walked a narrow plank, I look back and wonder if I really did it; but here I am in the proud city of Savannah, with an elegant mansion at my command, surrounded by a confident, brave, and victorious army that looks to me as its head. Negroes and whites flock to me and gaze at me as some wonderful being, and letters from great men pour in with words of flattery and praise."

Sherman could easily have ridden his exploits into the White House or to considerable success in private business, but his attitude toward this acclaim was reflected in the letter. "I do more than ever crave for peace and quiet, and would gladly drop all these [accolades] and gather you and my little ones in some quiet place where I could be at ease."

Writing his account of the March after the War, Sherman negated its importance. Having completed his work in Atlanta, he had merely shifted base to the ocean, where his army could be employed to better use. "I considered this march as a means to an end, and not as an essential act of war. Still, then, as now, the march to the sea was generally regarded as something extraordinary, something anomalous, something out of the ordinary." To measure its relative importance, Sherman rated the March to Savannah a one and subsequent operations in the Carolinas a ten.

What Sherman seemed to underestimate was the severe shock Georgia received from his massive invasion. People in the North and South wondered at the audacious undertaking and the incredible destruction it caused.

Meanwhile, Back in Virginia

By the time Sherman left the ruins of Atlanta to march on Savannah, Robert E. Lee and U. S. Grant had been locked in mortal combat for six months. Since early May, the Army of Northern Virginia and the Army of the Potomac had fought desperate battles. They had suffered staggering casualties, at the Wilderness, Spotsylvania, and Cold Harbor, and in a savage siege at Petersburg since July.

The trenches extended from Richmond to a point south of Petersburg, forty miles in length. Lee's strength was daily stretched to the breaking point, and the Confederates starved, died of disease in the muck of their pits, and froze for lack of clothing. Many crept from their works at night to make their way home, while Grant patiently extended his lines.

Sherman's army was flowing through the Carolinas as spring approached, and Lee realized his only hope for survival was to break away from Petersburg to join Johnston in North Carolina. Perhaps together they could cripple Sherman, then turn on Grant.

The breakout depended on a successful attack against Fort Stedman. The assault on March 21, 1865, caught the Federals by surprise, but blue reinforcements smothered the Rebel offensive.

Grant knew the end had come. On March 31 he destroyed a southern force at Five Forks, and over five thousand irreplaceable Confederates were captured. On April 2 Grant launched a crushing blow against Lee's works at Petersburg. A Homeric stand by a few hundred Confederates slowed the Union juggernaut, allowing Lee to evacuate Petersburg that night.

A running battle ended a week later at Appomattox, where Lee and 25,000 exhausted, hungry Confederates found themselves surrounded by a vastly superior army. On April 9, 1865, Lee surrendered. As the stubborn soldiers of the Army of Northern Virginia began their long journeys home to work their farms, Grant's men prepared for a victory parade through Washington, D.C. ∎

After the army settled into Savannah, Sherman received reports from his officers. He learned that the troops had reached Savannah in remarkably good health. Only two percent of the men were reported sick or wounded. Out of 60,000 men, only 103 had been killed in combat or died of accident or illness during the March. There were 428 wounded men and 500 captured or missing. Of the latter, an estimated sixty men were killed by Rebel cavalry or irregulars after surrender. Many others were forced to join, at least temporarily, Confederate service.

Howard reported capturing 547 prisoners on the March; Slocum, 439. An additional 1,200 Rebels, mostly sick and wounded who could not be transported, were taken in Savannah. Some captive Confederates were deserters, but others were "galvanized Yankees," Union soldiers captured and then threatened with death if they did not join the southern army. In one night twenty-seven of these men deserted to Slocum near Savannah. Howard reported freeing 3,500 slaves, which seems a conservative estimate. Perhaps those were the ones who persevered to Savannah. Slocum claimed fourteen thousand slaves followed after the Army of Georgia. The best estimates are that twenty-five thousand slaves joined the column at some point, and six thousand remained at Savannah.

In Georgia, Sherman's men stole 6,900 horses and mules and over 20,000 head of cattle. They appropriated over ten million pounds of corn and an equal amount of fodder. The number of consumed or merely slaughtered hogs, chickens, and turkeys, and amounts of corn, sweet potatoes, and other vegetables and fruits consumed, is incalculable. One soldier estimated that 100,000 hogs were killed on the March. Howard's medical director found the men's health "peculiarly gratifying." He contributed it to an "abundance of nutritious food, and particularly of vegetables."

Slocum destroyed 7,000 bales of cotton; Howard, 3,500. An additional 35,000 bales were captured in Savannah. The city also yielded 209 cannon, most of them heavy siege guns, 2,300 rifles, and 6,500 bladed weapons. Among the cannon was a brass six-pounder bearing the state of Georgia coat of arms and engraved with the words *Georgia Military Institute*. Poe suggested sending it to West Point. The Confederates abandoned 27,000 rounds of artillery ammunition, and 51,000 infantry rounds. Left in the city were 13 locomotives, 190 rail cars, and 3 steam boats. Sherman was delighted to report the capture of Savannah, "a perfect string of forts," and a population of twenty-two thousand people returned to the Union.

Savannah's cotton yield, worth a fortune in the hungry factories of the world, had been distributed among cellars and warehouses throughout the city. When President Davis and the Confederate Congress demanded to know why it had not been destroyed or removed, Hardee explained that the railroads had been needed for military purposes and men were not available to gather it for burning. Such an act, he continued, might have destroyed the city and would certainly have tipped his hand. The Federal government sold the cotton for thirty million dollars.

Sherman's men had fired 1,250,000 small arms rounds, and 3,576 artillery rounds during the March, the vast majority during Savannah's siege.

The damage to Georgia's railroads had been spectacular. The West Point

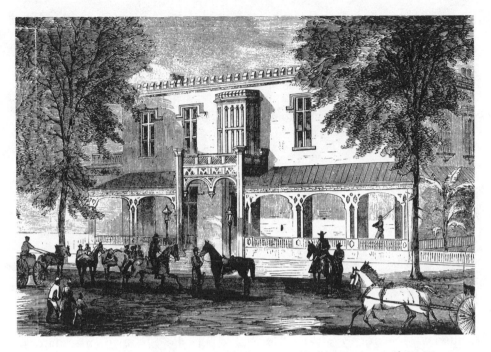

Sherman's quarters in Savannah were in the home of British cotton merchant Charles Green.

road had been completely destroyed to Fairburn, and eighty-four miles of the Western and Atlantic track was ruined. Railroad bridges were burned, and rolling stock not evacuated to Chattanooga was generally blown up.

The Georgia Railroad to Augusta was destroyed from Atlanta to the Oconee River, east of Madison. Six miles of track between Milledgeville and Eatonton were ruined, and two large bridges were burned. Ten miles of the Augusta-Savannah road, three station houses, a locomotive, and several cars were destroyed. The Gulf Railroad was torn up from Savannah to the Altamaha River, and the vital Central Railroad, between Macon and Savannah, was destroyed to Ogeechee Church, a distance of 140 miles.

Sherman informed Grant that the total amount of railroad wrecked was 265 miles. This massive destruction of the South's transportation system, "not Appomattox," wrote Robert C. Black III in *Railroads of the Confederacy,* "was the Confederacy's Gotterdammerung."

The army had accomplished an incredible feat by foot. The 15th Corps reported that in the 46 days since October 4, they had marched 684 miles, built 32 miles of bridge, laid 2,000 yards of bridge, constructed 770 yards of footbridge, corduroyed 7,000 yards of boggy road with timber, and destroyed 60 miles of railroad. For the year of 1864, one division in the 17th Corps marched 1,561 miles: 290 in November and 115 in December.

The pontooniers and pioneers were lavished with special praise. Slocum had 775 men to lay pontoons. They were equipped with 51 canvas pontoon boats that could make a bridge 850 feet long. The boats and attendant equipment, which included two thousand pounds of rope, were transported on seventy-four wagons. The Right Wing had a similar train. Together, the army laid fifteen bridges longer than four hundred feet. The pontoons were frequently used; and despite the fact that some had been carried from Nashville, not one had failed, and all arrived at Savannah in perfect shape.

The pioneers cut untold thousands of trees to bridge smaller streams and corduroy miles of roads. They built roads and defensive works and frequently cleared obstructions from the army's path. The pioneers with the Left Wing brought 1,500 axes and 1,500 shovels to Savannah for their work. Each brigade had 350 axes and a similar number of shovels to assist the pioneers.

Sherman estimated that his soldiers had inflicted one billion dollars' worth of damage on Georgia. Twenty million dollars' worth had benefited the army; the rest was pure waste.

"This may seem a hard species of warfare," Sherman wrote, "but it brings the sad realities of war home to those who have been directly or indirectly instrumental in involving us in its attendant calamities."

Most Federal troops had seen no opposition on the March. General Blair called enemy action "comparatively nothing." A Union soldier added, "They [Confederates] don't trouble our march a particle." Georgia's Governor Brown bitterly concurred. After the March concluded, he complained to the Confederate Secretary of War, "During the period of Sherman's march from Atlanta to Milledgeville, there were not one thousand men, of all the veteran infantry regiments and battalions of Georgians, now in Confederate service, upon the soil of this State. Nor did troops from other States fill their places."

Contemplating the army's activities since leaving Atlanta, one Union soldier wrote: "The destruction could hardly have been worse if Atlanta had been a volcano in eruption and the molten lava had flowed in a stream 60 miles wide and five times as long." The volcano had been inactive for a month, but it was about to erupt again, with even greater fury. ∎

Sherman's in Savannah ∎ Author Unknown

Like the tribes of Israel,
Fed on quails and manna,
Sherman and his glorious band
Journeyed through the rebel land,
Fed from Heaven's all bounteous hand,
Marching on Savannah.

As the moving pillar shone
Streamed the starry banner,
All the day in rosy light,
Beaming glory all the night,
Till it swooped in eagle flight
Down on doomed Savannah.

Glory be to God on high!
Shout the loud hosanna!
Treason's wilderness is past,
Canaan's shore is won at last;
Peal a nation's trumpet-blast,—
Sherman's in Savannah! ∎

A DRIVING TOUR
■ Civil War Savannah ■

Savannah is one of America's great cities. It contains a large concentration of restored historic homes, museums, and first-rate restaurants. There are 1,200 homes of historic significance, built in every imaginable style, and twenty squares filled with impressive monuments, where Sherman's men camped. Brochures available in the Visitors Center describe dozens of sites that can be enjoyed. For an orientation to the city, take any of half a dozen different tours, all of which leave the Visitors Center. Then take a walking or biking tour to become better acquainted with the character of the community. Several days are necessary to enjoy all that Savannah has to offer.

In the Visitors Center is the Great Savannah Exposition, housed in the old Central of Georgia Railroad Station, built in 1860. Savannah's history, from James Oglethorpe to the present, is wonderfully presented; included are a number of exciting Civil War exhibits. One feature is an animated figure of Sherman writing his famous letter to Abraham Lincoln, in which he presented Savannah as a Christmas gift. There are exhibit cases with figures dressed in local militia uniforms, material relating to the bombardment of

Fort Pulaski, the capture of Savannah, and other artifacts. On the walls are period photographs and artwork portraying Civil War Savannah.

On Madison Square is the Green-Medrim House, which was Sherman's headquarters. Now the Parish House of St. John's Church, it is open to the public.

Earthworks from Savannah's defenses are preserved in two state parks found just south of Savannah. At Wormsloe is Fort Wimberly, built by the Confederates in 1861–62 to protect an inland approach to the city. The works were rarely garrisoned and never used in combat. Fort Wimberly and another portion of earthworks may be seen on a walking tour. At Skidaway Island State Park are other works that are visible on a nature trail.

From the Visitors Center, exit from the rear past the Georgia Coastal Center. Drive straight across the first street, Turner, then turn right onto Oglethorpe to West Broad Street. Turn left for .2 to Bay Street, then turn right to follow the signs for Fort Pulaski and Fort Jackson. After .3 the Customs House is on the right.

Map 29: From downtown Savannah to Fort Jackson.

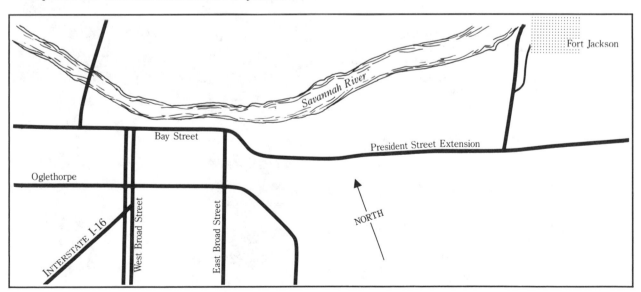

The remains of Wormsloe date from Oglethorpe's time. Confederate earthworks remain nearby on the Isle of Hope.

Within the thick brick walls are galleries that served as powder magazines, storerooms, cells, and offices. They house a number of historic exhibits about Savannah's Civil War history, particularly that of the iron-clads (see Appendix C). The *Savannah* and the *Milledgeville* were blown up before Sherman occupied the city, but the *Georgia* was merely scuttled. It remains the only relatively intact Confederate ironclad in existence. Divers have brought up artifacts from the hulk, including eight cannon. Some of the material is displayed in the fort. Also exhibited are munitions that were dumped into the moat as the garrison evacuated to South Carolina.

The reduction of nearby Fort Pulaski, a far stronger structure than Fort Jackson, alerted Confederate of-

The Silence Monument in Savannah's Laurel Grove Cemetery honors Confederate dead.

Sherman climbed to the top of this building to view his prize after Hardee evacuated Savannah. To the left is Factors Walk, where cotton merchants thrived in the 1800s. Below is the restored river front, where shops and restaurants thrive. Boat tours of the river are available.

Continue on Bay Street. After .8 bear left onto President Street Extension. After 1.9 turn left at the sign for Fort Jackson. After .5 turn right at a sign for the fort, and a parking area is reached after .8.

Fort Jackson was built in the early 1800s on the main ship channel of the Savannah River, just three miles above the city. It is surrounded by a nine-foot-deep tidal moat, which is crossed by a single drawbridge. The entrance was protected by two small cannon that could sweep the portal with a deadly crossfire of grapeshot if an enemy attempted to storm the fort.

The gun platform on top of the twenty-foot-high walls held eleven cannon. They were served by men of the 22nd Battalion of Heavy Artillery. The fort, headquarters for the defense of Savannah, was inspected by Robert E. Lee, Jefferson Davis, and P.G.T. Beauregard.

In the large courtyard is the brick foundation of an officers' barracks. A mess and boathouse have been re-created. A thirty-two-pounder cannon is mounted on the parapet, and a water battery has been built beside the river.

The interior of Fort Jackson. The Coastal Heritage Foundation is restoring the structure.

ficials to the limitations of brick forts. Six earthen batteries, containing thirty-six cannon, were constructed on both banks of the river near Fort Jackson. Fort Bartow, located eight hundred yards from Fort Jackson, was the largest earthwork in the Confederacy. It consisted of miles of heavy earthen walls, ditches, and magazines. Although the area is currently being developed, some of the fort may be preserved.

Map 30: The Fort Pulaski area.

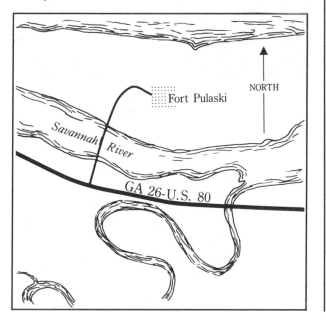

Savannah's imposing Confederate monument. Surrounding it are busts of Confederate generals from the city.

Return to President Street Extension and turn left. This highway becomes Islands Expressway. Cross the Wilmington River, and after 3.2 GA 26-U.S. 80 intersects. Bear left onto GA 26-U.S. 80 as it continues toward Tybee Island. Drive another 7.1 miles, crossing Turner Creek and Bull River, then turn left to Fort Pulaski, which is a mile down the access road.

Five-sided Fort Pulaski faces the sea and is surrounded by a seven-foot-deep moat that is crossed by a drawbridge. The brick walls are thirty-two feet high and eleven feet thick. Inside were officers' quarters, ammunition magazines, and a variety of arched, bombproof chambers that housed cannon. Heavier guns were positioned on top of the walls. Large cisterns gathered 200,000 gallons of rain for a water supply. The fort, which cost a million dollars to build, contains 25 million bricks.

After Pulaski was surrendered in 1862 (see Appendix A), the Federals mounted 60 guns and maintained a 1,100-man garrison in the fort until the war ended. Pulaski was abandoned in 1880, but the Federal government began restoring it as a national park in 1933.

A World War II tank guards Tybee Light near Fort Pulaski, south of Savannah.

It is an excellently preserved example of a brick coastal fort. The Visitors Center houses a series of exhibits that explain how Pulaski was built and how it was subdued. Cannon have been remounted around the fort, and rooms have been restored as quarters and messes. The magazine, cisterns, drawbridge, and other interesting features of the fort are visible.

Map 31: The Tybee Island area.

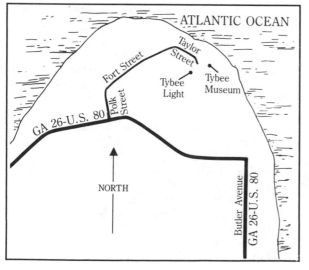

Return to GA 26-U.S. 80 and turn left. Just across Lazaretto Creek, to the left, is the site where Federal artillery batteries were established to shell Fort Pulaski. After 2.9 turn left onto Polk Street at the small sign for Tybee Museum. After .1 bear right onto Fort Street at another small sign for the museum. After .2 continue straight at the intersection onto Taylor Street. After .3 Tybee Museum will be to the left and Georgia's famed Tybee Light to the right.

The museum is situated in a casemate of Fort Screven, which was a series of coastal artillery positions built during the Spanish-American War. Several other concrete emplacements, used for clubs and as private residences, were passed on the way to the museum. Tybee Museum offers a fascinating variety of exhibits relating to coastal Georgia. In the Civil War Room are artifacts and displays that illustrate Fort

The Savannah River today. Hardee's improvised pontoon bridge spanned the river in this area.

Pulaski's bombardment, Sherman's March, and the occupation of Savannah.

Across the street is Tybee Lighthouse. It was established in 1736 and has been destroyed and repaired several times since. It is open to the public.

Return to GA 26-U.S. 80, and turn left for the beaches, which begin to the left about a mile down the highway. Tybee Island is a typical coastal resort area, featuring many hotels and gift shops. ∎

248

The Carolinas

At Sister's Ferry Slocum's wing crosses the Savannah River to invade South Carolina in January 1865.
[HARPER'S WEEKLY]

CHAPTER 18

"The Streets Were Full of Crouching, Despondent, Weeping, Helpless Women and Children"

A fter occupying Savannah for a month, Sherman and his army were ready to continue the campaign. This was an army of action, and it could not long countenance a peaceful occupation when there was an enemy still to be whipped and property to be appropriated and destroyed. The soldiers chaffed under the restrictions of camp, where officers tried to instill a modicum of discipline. There were even periodic attempts to stop gambling and excessive drinking. The men firmly believed that Sherman's soldiers were destined to end the War, and it was time to resume the March.

"I was quite impatient to get off to myself," Sherman wrote, "for city life had become dull and tame." In the field, Sherman's authority was supreme and paperwork was almost nonexistent. In Savannah, government and military officials arrived to question his practices and motives. Northern businessmen contrived to enrich themselves, and Southerners begged for supplies and protection. The monotonous routine that had driven Sherman from the peacetime army hurried his departure from Savannah.

Sherman had a chilling thought for the people of South Carolina. His men had borne no particular malice toward Georgians, but they felt South Carolina was the cradle of secession. That state had forced the war and all the death and destruction that attended it on the country; and it now would suffer. As one Union soldier wrote, "If we don't purify South Carolina, it will be because we can't get a light." That possibility seemed unlikely. Rumor circulated that Kilpatrick's men spent five thousand dollars on matches in Savannah.

Howard's half of the army was placed on ships and transported to Beaufort, South Carolina. They would feint on Charleston before driving directly toward Sherman's true objective in that state: Columbia, the state capital. Sherman joined them on January 21. Slocum pushed one corps across the Savannah River and advanced on both sides of the stream for forty miles to threaten Augusta; then he marched for Columbia. The two columns would be a considerable distance apart, at the onset separated by over fifty miles. The city of Savannah remained occupied by General John Foster and a division sent from Grant in Virginia.

General John Schofield, part of the force that had annihilated Hood at Nashville six weeks earlier, had been dispatched to occupy Wilmington, situated halfway between Savannah and Richmond. His thirty-thousand-man Army of the Ohio would repair the railroad between Wilmington—the South's last functioning port—and Goldsboro. He would wait there with fresh reinforcements and supplies until Sherman arrived.

So desperate was the condition of the Confederacy that little had been done to defend South Carolina or to prepare her citizens for the horrors that were to come. The ruin of Georgia had been warning enough, but the people of South Carolina did not wish to believe that Sherman would venture into their beloved state.

President Davis and the state had little enough with which they could oppose the movement. Wade Hampton was allowed to leave Virginia with a

Union troops slog through South Carolina's lowland swamps. [HARPER'S WEEKLY]

division of horse soldiers to protect his home state, and Wheeler's troops, under a cloud from their depredations in Georgia, joined in the defense. Of the soldiers who had evacuated Savannah, Hardee retained control of nine thousand men in Charleston—the Georgia militia had immediately left for Augusta after Savannah's evacuation. Most of the remaining eleven thousand soldiers in the decimated Army of Tennessee were ordered rushed to the defense of the Carolinas, but the state of transportation in the deep South sorely slowed their movement. Ultimately, only five thousand arrived. All the manpower the Confederacy could muster was mobilized, but the force was pathetic. Sherman wrote of his "contempt for these scattered and inconsiderable forces." They scarcely delayed his advance.

A manpower shortage was not the only problem facing the Confederates. Believing the War was beyond salvation, men were returning home in droves, deserting the Army of Tennessee, the Army of Northern Virginia, and the state militias. Many responded to pleas from wives and mothers, who had so proudly packed them off to war, to protect their homes. Sherman had accomplished this disintegration of Confederate morale and military forces, and the effect accelerated as he ravaged the Carolinas.

Hardee was instructed to stop Sherman at South Carolina's wide rivers. The Rebels were to defend Charleston, but to abandon it if necessary and protect Columbia.

The weather was Sherman's only immediate obstacle. It had rained for several weeks, and Carolina's lowlands were flooded. Pontoon bridges were washed away, and columns could trudge only a few miles a day through knee-deep mud. While pickets stood duty in boats, men slept in foot-deep water. A newspaper reporter found General Williams and his entire staff sleeping among the branches of a large tree like so many chickens. Sherman's wheeled vehicles—70 cannon, 2,500 supply wagons, and 600 ambulances—were heartily cursed by the soldiers who had to bring them through the mud.

Howard approached the first barrier in his path, the Salkehatchie River, whose fifteen channels and vast swamps presented a formidable five-mile-wide obstacle. Hardee had ten thousand men defending the crossing with heavy artillery support, but the Federals brushed aside the resistance. Two divisions waded through the swamp, a feat that took three hours. They found the Confederates outflanked by a Union force that had crossed upstream.

Howard bridged the streams, corduroyed the remainder of the path through the morass, then continued his advance; the Confederates were astounded. Joseph Johnston decided Sherman had the greatest army "since the days of Julius Caesar." Hardee, on the scene, barely believed the evidence of his own eyes.

The first stop for Slocum's Left Wing was Hardeeville. Every building in town was dismantled for shelter or firewood, including the church. His men then crossed the Edisto and North Edisto rivers with barely a pause. Flanking columns had accomplished their accustomed maneuver.

Kilpatrick's cavalry ravaged the nearby town of Barnwell. As it burned,

Federal skirmishers cross the Edisto River on an improvised footbridge.

Kilpatrick danced in a hotel with liberated slaves. When he informed Sherman that the town would have to change its name—to Burnwell, Sherman laughed.

Kilpatrick ranged to the west to destroy bridges and trains on the railroad that led from Columbia to Augusta. At Aiken his old nemesis, Joe Wheeler, had prepared an ambush with two thousand men. The Rebels opened a crashing fire when Kilpatrick's men rode into the streets, and Kilpatrick was almost captured as the Yankees were chased five miles out of town.

Two weeks after the March resumed, Sherman's army camped on the outskirts of Columbia on February 15. They had covered 130 mud-splattered miles. At daybreak the next morning Sherman saw the city in the distance. The Confederates had evacuated without resistance, and the South Carolina state capital, with a population of twenty thousand, lay defenseless.

Columbia's mayor, Thomas L. Goodwyn, rode out to Sherman with a familiar message: "The city is surrendered. I request protection for the innocent civilian population and their property. "It is no small thing to march into the heart of an enemy's country and take his capital," Sherman told Howard. It was becoming a familiar feeling to Sherman. He had just captured his third.

The people of Columbia had long known the fate of Jackson and Meridian, Mississippi; of Atlanta and half a dozen other Georgia cities and towns; and of every community in southern South Carolina. They dreaded what Sherman intended to do to Columbia, even though the General informed Mayor Goodwyn that no private property would be harmed. If Sherman believed that statement, he was alone.

"This is a doomed city," a Federal major told a civilian. "The whole army knows it." Another officer told the ladies at a house, "Leave this town—go anywhere to be safer than here."

A considerable portion of the Union army had found liquor in the conquered city and consumed it in great quantity. As night approached on February 17, they took to the streets with torches. The soldiers were joined by the released inmates of the state penitentiary, escaped Union prisoners from a Columbia pen, and a few newly liberated slaves.

Sherman had fallen asleep during the afternoon. He awoke to find a city block afire and the flames being fanned by a high wind. Sherman and Howard took to the streets to organize men to fight the fire, but as they did so, Conyngham noted, "a hundred fires were lighting all around them."

"I trust I shall never witness such a scene again," Conyngham continued, "drunken soldiers rushing from house to house, emptying them of their valuables, firing them." Finding civilians fighting the conflagration with fire

South Carolina's new capitol in Columbia remained unfinished during the Civil War. Union artillery bounced several cannonballs off its sides for target practice.
[LIBRARY OF CONGRESS]

engines, drunken soldiers cut up the hoses with bayonets and axes.

"A drunken soldier with a musket in one hand and a match in the other is not a pleasant visitor to have about the house on a dark, windy night," Slocum noted. The citizens of Columbia had firsthand evidence of that fact.

Federal soldiers raped a number of black women, and one infantryman was killed by an officer while attemping to rape a white girl. Other soldiers were shot in the act of setting fires and robbing citizens.

Sister Baptista Lynch had expected proper treatment from Sherman's men. She was a friend of Sherman's sister and had taught his daughter Minnie. Now her convent, crowded with young nuns and schoolgirls, was invaded by vulgar Union soldiers. The men stole gold altar vessels and ordered the building evacuated. Quickly and quietly, the women left the church, which was consumed by flames moments later.

Fire destroyed the state capital and spread to the campus of South Carolina College, which was used as a Confederate hospital. Doctors and nurses valiantly fought the flames, but many wounded and sick Rebel soldiers, unable to crawl to safety, were immolated.

Three-fourths of the city was destroyed that night—almost 1,400 structures. It was Atlanta repeated.

Engineer Poe, who was responsible for authorized demolitions, found Columbia's ruin disturbing. "The burning houses, lighting up the faces of shrieking women, terrified children, and frantic, roving drunken men, formed a scene which no man of the slightest sensibilities wants to witness a second time."

The city of Columbia after the devastating conflagration. [LIBRARY OF CONGRESS]

Sherman's victorious entry into Columbia. Flying pieces of cotton fill the air.
[HARPER'S WEEKLY]

"It was a sad sight to witness the smoking ruins of the town, the tall, black chimneys looking down upon it like funeral monuments," wrote Conyngham, "and to see old women and children, hopeless, helpless, all frenzied, wandering amidst the desolation."

"The streets were full of rubbish, broken furniture, and groups of crouching, despondent, weeping, helpless women and children," a Columbia newspaper stated.

Until his death, Sherman heatedly denied responsibility for the fires. Confederate cavalry had set fire to cotton as they left the city, he claimed. When the wind picked up, burning particles of cotton had been carried to every part of the city. Other Federal sources indicated that the cotton in question had been drenched with water and the fires thoroughly extinguished long before the city was burned. The controversy raged for decades. Whatever the initial cause, the fire was undoubtedly spread deliberately by a large number of Sherman's soldiers. They, and their commander, reveled in Columbia's ruin, as indicated by Sherman's postwar statement: "Though I never ordered it and never wished it, I have never shed any tears over the event."

After Howard left Columbia, Slocum joined the column to help in their old pastime—destroying railroads. Sherman would now threaten Charlotte, North Carolina, but he marched to Fayetteville and Raleigh. Receiving word that Hardee had evacuated Charleston and Bragg was giving up Wilmington, Sherman believed the war would conclude within six months.

The conduct of Union soldiers in South Carolina was unconscionable. They had destroyed by fire almost every community in their path, and many isolated farms were torched as well. In Georgia, most habitations had been left standing, but in South Carolina lives were in jeopardy. Citizens were hanged until they revealed the location of valuables, and a number of women were raped.

As a result of these atrocities, many of Wheeler's men lost all control, and bands of Union foragers were captured and killed. Their throats were slashed and the bodies left by the road, usually with signs that read, "Death to all Foragers." One day seven men were found executed together; eighteen on another day; twenty-one on still another. About 110 Federals were killed in such a manner in Carolina. There had been sixty-four such cases in Georgia. Righteously, Sherman announced that his officers were to punish their men for "excesses," but he could not allow the enemy to do so.

In late February Kilpatrick informed Wheeler that Confederates would be executed if the recent killings of foragers was not explained. Wheeler expressed innocence and promised an investigation. The matter was closed for the moment.

Sherman may have been disturbed by the recent executions of his foragers, because after his men destroyed the city of Winnsboro, he was temporarily outraged. He threatened his most hardened pillagers with punishment, but then remembered their unstinting devotion in battle. "I would have pardoned them for anything short of treason," he swore and let them off once again. He did order the wagons checked for loot, and in one division five tons of contraband were discovered. Among the hoard was a golden statue of Jesus taken from a church. "They are too wicked to tell," admitted a Union officer.

Camden was razed on February 23. The depot, a flour mill, a bridge, warehouses packed with meat, and two thousand pounds of cotton were burned. The army was delayed by raging floodwaters that destroyed several pontoon bridges and required the corduroying of over one hundred miles of road.

At Cheraw the soldiers encountered the property of Charleston's monied aristocracy. Besieged throughout the War, Charlestonians thought Cheraw would be a safe storehouse. Fine furniture and artwork was smashed and fine wines eagerly consumed. The Federals found a number of Confederate cannon, including the one that had opened the bombardment on Fort Sumter. A salute was fired with them to honor Lincoln's inauguration, but there were unexpected fireworks as well. Six thousand pounds of gun-

A Harper's Weekly *artist sketched Henry Hitchcock relaxing in front of his tent in the Carolinas.*

powder exploded, killing ten people.

Union soldiers crossed the Pee Dee River into North Carolina, leaving its southern sister the way they had entered. Cheraw was destroyed by fire; it joined a long list of South Carolina communities that had been torched: Hardeeville, Barnwell, Grahamville, Gallisonville, McPhersonville, Blackville, Midway, Orangeburg, Lexington, Columbia, Winnsboro, and Camden.

"The army burned everything it came near in South Carolina," wrote one soldier. "Our track through the state is a desert waste."

Sherman admonished his army to deal fairly with North Carolina. They were more reasonable people than South Carolinians, he argued, and were not so responsible for the War. Heeding his words, the army returned to its Georgia standard of conduct. Food was taken and public property destroyed, but homes and lives were better protected.

As Kilpatrick led the Federal advance toward Fayetteville, he was disturbed to find Confederate cavalry swarming around him. Kilpatrick camped one night at Monroe's Crossroads, where he enjoyed the company of Miss Marie Boozer, a Columbia woman who had accompanied the cavalry chief in a fine carriage.

At dawn, Hampton and Wheeler attacked the Union camp from two directions. Kilpatrick fled his commandeered quarters clad only in drawers, leaping on a horse and fleeing for safety. A Confederate cavalryman glimpsed his beautiful, scantily clad companion calling for help from a window.

"It was the most formidable cavalry charge I ever saw," Kilpatrick grudgingly admitted of the Confederate assault. Wheeler claimed to have cap-

259

tured 350 Union cavalrymen and released nearly 200 Confederates from Federal captivity. As they had at Waynesboro, the Federal infantry was delighted to hear of Kilpatrick's rout.

On March 10 Sherman occupied Fayetteville without resistance. Extensive textile factories in the city were destroyed, and a United States arsenal, which had manufactured arms for the Confederacy, blown up. "I hope the people at Washington have the good sense never to trust North Carolina with an arsenal again," Sherman grumbled.

Two days later a Federal supply ship arrived in Fayetteville. It brought supplies and five hundred bags of mail to the army, their first in six weeks. Before leaving, the Federals shot two thousand unneeded horses and mules and left their rotting carcasses in the city and in the Cape Fear River.

Sherman heard disturbing rumors of Confederate resistance firming to the north of his position. Robert E. Lee, recently promoted by the Confederate Congress to Commander-in-Chief of all southern armies, had reinstated Joseph Johnston to command the Army of Tennessee. The move was against the wishes of President Davis, who had long-standing disputes with Johnston. Even though Johnston's attitude was less than inspiring— "They're only calling me back so that I will be the one to surrender," he complained—Sherman had great respect for his former opponent during the Atlanta Campaign.

Johnston arrived in Smithville in March to concentrate his troops. He was concerned by Schofield, whose thirty thousand troops were advancing from the coast to join Sherman. When they were united with Sherman's twin columns, the Federal force would number ninety thousand.

Johnston's command would be no match for such an army. He had five thousand men from the Army of Tennessee; Hardee brought ten thousand soldiers; Bragg's unit, withdrawing from Wilmington, totaled five thousand; and the Confederate cavalry consisted of six thousand worn-out troopers. Of nearly equal concern was the fact that he had dozens of generals to contend with.

Johnston's only chance to stop, or even slow, Sherman's movement was to strike exposed portions of the northern army. Action would have to be taken soon, for Sherman was dangerously close to the Virginia border. If he reinforced Grant at Petersburg, the Confederate cause would be crushed.

Approaching Smithville from Wilmington on March 6, Bragg encountered thirteen thousand of Schofield's men near Kinston. On March 8, stiffened by the arrival of two thousand Army of Tennessee veterans, Bragg attacked and routed the Federal troops. Reacting to information that a Federal force was on their flank, the Confederates withdrew. Finding no other threat, the Rebels returned and renewed the attack on March 10. By that time Schofield's entire Army of the Ohio had arrived, and Bragg was forced to disengage. The Confederates had suffered 140 casualties but had inflicted 1,300, most of them as captives.

Sherman left Fayetteville and advanced toward Goldsboro. Johnston desperately wanted to prevent him from reaching the latter, for there Sherman would join Schofield. Unfortunately, Bragg had not yet arrived. As a delay-

Savage fighting marked the last battle between Sherman and Johnston at Bentonville, North Carolina. [LESLIE'S ILLUSTRATED]

ing action, Johnston sent Hardee, with 7,500 men, to slow Slocum near Averasboro.

A good position was selected between an extensive swamp and the Cape Fear River, and on March 16 Kilpatrick's cavalry was brought up short before Hardee. The 20th Corps arrived on the following morning, and a Union battery was advanced to punish the Confederates. Two blue divisions attacked Hardee while a brigade slipped into the Confederate rear. They surprised and drove an unbloodied brigade of garrison troops, but the Rebels soon recovered their composure and rallied. The Union advance was stopped, but Slocum continued to press the position throughout the day.

Realizing that another day of combat might destroy his command, Hardee withdrew during the night. He had lost nearly nine hundred men and inflicted seven hundred casualties on the Federals.

Henry Hitchcock found Sherman's actions during the fighting at Averasboro disturbing. The general and his staff stood around in the woods behind the battle line, listening to the sounds of conflict. No move was made to bring up reinforcements and crush the small Southern force.

The three Federal columns would soon unite at Goldsboro with a force three times the size of Johnston's. To prevent this, the Confederate commander sent word to his scouts—find a good position to attack one of the Federal wings. Hampton immediately reported an advantageous spot near Bentonville that presented a perfect opportunity to strike Slocum.

Hampton skirmished with the Federals on March 18, managing to stop them in front of a ridge that Johnston's men would occupy. Sherman had ridden with Slocum that day, but he left early the following morning to confer with Howard, ten miles to the east. There would be no serious combat for a few days, he assured Slocum.

When a division of Federal infantry advanced to clear the ridge of pesky Confederate cavalry, the soldiers were soundly repulsed by intense cannon and rifle fire. A second assault met the same result. Slocum soon recognized the truth. Johnston had arrived during the night with every man he could muster.

The Confederate right was held by Bragg; the center, by Hardee's large corps; the left, by Alexander Stewart and the survivors from the Army of Tennessee.

Slocum had only one corps on the field, and Johnston temporarily outnumbered the Yankees. The Confederates fumbled away their last golden opportunity for victory by wasting the morning transferring troops from Hardee to Bragg, who believed he was being attacked. When the Confederates advanced at 3:00 P.M., Slocum's entire wing was prepared, waiting behind log barricades.

For a while it seemed like the early days of glory for the Army of Tennessee. With colors flying, the Confederates marched forward. Their lines stretched across open fields and the men screamed and fired as they advanced. They were the South's last hope, men who had never given up in spite of all adversity. Their ranks were decimated, and flags that had once led thousands now led tens. The Yankees had seen no such sight since Atlanta, and they would never see it again.

Stewart's men smashed into the Union flank, routing the Yankees. Hardee's ragtag unit fell upon a gap in the Federal front, but Union reinforcements arrived and blunted the assault. Sherman rushed units of Howard's wing to assist Slocum as the Confederates launched fierce attacks throughout the afternoon. The Confederates were beaten back after fighting that some participants swore rivaled Gettysburg in intensity.

Howard's men were in position at Bentonville by the afternoon of March 20, denying the Confederates any chance of victory. In fact, Johnston was in a perilous situation. His back was against a river, and the Rebels were outnumbered two to one. Sherman could have crushed Johnston, but again he refused. He seemed to be waiting for the Confederates to withdraw. "I would rather avoid a general battle," he commented.

March 21 passed in the same manner. Johnston evacuated his wounded amid scattered skirmishing, and in the afternoon one of Sherman's divisional commanders, Joseph Mower, used the cover of a reconnaissance to launch a slashing attack against Johnston's only line of retreat. When Sherman learned of the assault, he recalled Mower, but later admitted he had made a mistake by not encouraging the movement.

Johnston, a master at withdrawing under difficult conditions, removed his army during the night. He had suffered 2,600 casualties; Sherman, only 1,500. "They abandoned all their cities to get enough men to whip me but did not succeed," Sherman gloated. Johnston agreed. He reported to Lee that he had done all in his power to stop Sherman. "I can do no more than annoy him," Johnston concluded.

Schofield joined Sherman at Goldsboro, bringing the army to a strength of ninety thousand men. A supply line was established to bring in food and mail from the coast; and, for the Union effort, conditions could not have looked better.

After Sherman received a report from Grant advising him that Lee's army was dissolving, he decided to confer with his superior and friend. Sherman boarded a transport and met Grant at City Point, Virginia. Lincoln was present, and the three men, undeniably the most important figures in bringing the war to a close, met several times during the following days.

Lincoln had simple instructions for Sherman: Crush the Rebel military and send the southern soldiers back to their farms and shops. The President even suggested that Jefferson Davis be allowed to escape so the country could quietly reunite and return to normalcy as soon as possible.

In Goldsboro, the army was paid for the first time since leaving Savannah. The ragged, barefooted Union soldiers also drew new issues of clothing and boots, and for the first time in months, they looked like an army.

Sherman left Goldsboro on April 10 to march within twelve miles of Raleigh. While skirmishing with Confederate cavalry, a few unfortunate Union soldiers were killed. They were the last men lost in combat by Sherman. In camp that afternoon, word filtered in that Lee had surrendered. For all practical purposes, the war was over.

The men reacted with predictable excitement. Whooping and cheering, they threw all manner of articles into the air and smashed their rifles. "All

Sherman and Johnston thrash out details of the surrender. [HARPER'S WEEKLY]

Johnston surrendered to Sherman in the modest Bennett farmhouse. [HARPER'S WEEKLY]

glory be to God," Sherman wrote in a rare invocation to that source of power. In a few more days, he contended, "the great race is won."

Late on the afternoon of April 13, Sherman entered Raleigh, the third state capital he had occupied on the March.

In the southern camp, only Johnston had heard the news of the Confederate collapse. He concealed it from his army until Lee's paroled men started drifting into camp.

Jefferson Davis had evacuated Richmond on April 2, the day Lee's lines at Petersburg were irretrievably broken. The government entrained for Greensboro, North Carolina, and there Davis received word of Lee's surrender. He called for an emergency conference with Johnston and Beauregard. On April 12 the generals stared silently at each other as Davis outlined plans for raising new armies and continuing the struggle.

On the following day, Davis asked Johnston's opinion of the situation. "My views are, sir, that our people are tired of war, feel themselves whipped, and will not fight," Johnston replied bluntly. "Our country is overrun, its military reserves greatly diminished, while the enemy's military power and resources were never greater, and may be increased to any extent desired." His own forces were "melting away like snow." The war is over, he concluded.

Davis turned to Beauregard, who agreed. "I concur in all General Johnston has said," he said simply.

When Johnston asked permission to open surrender negotiations with Sherman, Davis approved the request. The President of a disintegrating nation soon resumed his flight south.

Sherman was quite receptive to Johnston's initiative when it arrived on April 14, and the generals arranged to meet near Hillsboro on April 17. Before leaving headquarters that morning, Sherman was informed of Lincoln's assassination. He revealed the shocking news to no one.

Johnston and Sherman met in a small room belonging to Daniel Bennett, a country farmer. Johnston had worn his finest gray uniform and was immaculately groomed. Sherman, as usual, was rumpled in dress and appearance. Sherman handed Johnston the message announcing Lincoln's murder and watched for a reaction. Johnston's face broke out in sweat, and he said, "It's a disgrace to the age. The greatest possible calamity to the south. I hope you don't charge this to the Confederate government," he appealed to Sherman.

Sherman agreed the Confederate military had no hand in the outrage, but he believed it possible that President Davis may have been responsible.

Johnston announced that he had authority to surrender all remaining Confederate forces, a prospect that excited Sherman. The generals agreed to continue the discussion on the following day.

On April 18 Johnston agreed to surrender Confederate troops, but he

After the successful conclusion of a history-making campaign, Sherman posed with his commanders. [LIBRARY OF CONGRESS]

demanded assurance of political rights for former Confederates. Sherman's volatile mood was now focused on ending the war, and that led him to exceed his authority in the surrender document. State and local government officials would be permitted to continue in office after an oath of loyalty was signed, it stated. Political rights and property were guaranteed and amnesty granted to southern soldiers.

Sherman was astonished by the violent reaction in Washington against his agreement with Johnston. With Lincoln's assassination, the northern mood demanded punishment for the rebellious South. Secretary of War Edwin Stanton denounced Sherman, and newspapers fostered the belief that Sherman was somehow responsible for Lincoln's death. Charges flew that Sherman had allowed Jefferson Davis to escape, and rumors circulated that he would use his army to take control of the United States government.

After Johnston's surrender, Sherman's troops marched quickly to Washington, D.C., to be reviewed by President Johnson. [LESLIE'S ILLUSTRATED]

Grant moved quickly to put the matter to rest. He traveled to North Carolina and met with his friend, and Sherman publicly admitted he had made a mistake by indulging in matters beyond an immediate military surrender. When he met with Johnston on April 26, the commanders committed themselves to a new agreement. The Army of Tennessee would surrender its arms, and the soldiers would take an oath of loyalty and return home. The men were given rations and allowed to keep horses and mules and enough weapons to fend off the bushwhackers who prowled the southern countryside in the wake of defeat.

Sherman had always maintained that he would be as charitable in peace as he had been vindictive in war, and he set about to prove his word. He returned to Savannah by ship to supervise the distribution of rations to the impoverished people of Georgia. In one week the Federal army distributed 55,000 pounds of meal and flour in Atlanta.

During Sherman's absence, his armies began marching north to Washington, D.C. The officers were in a hurry, and many men died of exhaustion and sunstroke on the way. They covered thirty-two miles in one day and were forcibly prevented from foraging. It hardly seemed like the old days. The troops marched through Richmond, where Sherman rejoined the army, and inspected many of the Virginia battlefields. At Mount Vernon they saluted George Washington's grave, then continued into the capital.

On May 23, 1865, the Army of the Potomac marched in review through Washington. Sherman's veterans showed open contempt for the Easterners. It had taken them four full years to cover one hundred miles and capture one city. Sherman's men had conquered Tennessee, Mississippi, Georgia, and both Carolinas. In the past six months alone they had marched one thousand miles.

The people of the northeast had only heard of the exploits of Sherman's Western armies, but May 24 was their day to shine. Some had secured new uniforms, but most had not. The marched ragged, shoeless, and bareheaded. Their dirty faces and long hair and beards were worn with pride, as they followed standards so tattered that the tens of thousands of spectators could not identify individual units. The lean, hard, tough army was not pretty; but it was impressive, and it had been effective.

After the 15th Corps marched past the reviewing stand, the German ambassador to the United States was heard to say, "An army like that could whip all Europe." When the 20th Corps passed, he added that they could "whip the world." After the 17th Corps filed by, he commented, "An army like that could whip the devil." Undoubtedly they would have tried, and many in the South thought they had been in league with that same fellow. ■

A DRIVING TOUR
■ The Carolinas ■

From Savannah, Sherman's army marched an additional four hundred miles through South and North Carolina. On this second stage of the March, the Federal columns were often widely separated. Following Sherman's route through the Carolinas is difficult, but there are several important sites that should be visited.

Near Ehrhardt, South Carolina, not far from U.S. 601, is Rivers Bridge State Park, at a swampy site along the Salkehatchie River where Confederates made a brief attempt to halt Sherman's advance. Confederate trenches and graves are preserved in the park, which has an Interpretive Center with Civil War displays.

In Columbia is the magnificent State House, a three-story granite structure built between 1851 and 1907. For amusement, Union gunners bounced solid shot off its unfinished walls before they entered the city, and scars left by the projectiles are marked by bronze stars. In a Confederate museum on the corner of Sumter and Pendleton streets are several of the cannonballs that the Federals threw at the State House, as well as other Civil War exhibits.

The Bentonville battlefield, scene of the last major battle between Sherman and Johnston, has been preserved by the state of North Carolina. It is found near U.S. 701, twenty miles south of Smithfield. Earthworks thrown up by Union soldiers have been preserved, and 360 Confederates are buried in a mass grave in a small cemetery. On the grounds is a house that belonged to John and Amy Harper. It was used as a field hospital and is furnished as it would have been when casualties were carried in from the fighting.

The March to the Sea, and the Civil War, ended at the Bennett Place, were Sherman accepted Johnston's surrender. The site, located east of Durham off U.S. 70, is operated by the state. The Bennett house, which burned in 1923, has been faithfully reconstructed, and it is surrounded by farm outbuildings and a split rail fence. Beside the house is the Unity Monument, which has two columns capped by a single stone. It signifies the reunification of the country. A Visitors Center presents exhibits of the Confederate surrenders here and at Appomattox and of the massive destruction suffered by the South. ■

Conclusion

William T. Sherman wrote a new chapter in military history. We call it "Total War," although sometimes it is known as "Modern War." No longer is it sufficient to destroy an enemy's army; military authorities are convinced that the apparatus that arms, feeds, and clothes—in short, supports—an army must be destroyed. Unfortunately, most of that support translates into civilians. Farmers are civilians. So are factory workers. But the concept of "Total War" goes far beyond that.

A *nation,* a *people,* wage war. They allow, even encourage and sometimes demand, that their government fight. Therefore, they are responsible for the war; their citizenship makes them responsible. Civilians should be punished for allowing the war to be fought by their government, and by their sons.

Whether total war is morally justifiable can be argued endlessly. The only factor that enters into its implementation is whether it is effective. Sherman proved that it is. His men destroyed the agricultural and industrial support of Confederate military forces.

"Starvation, literal starvation," is how Confederate General John B. Gordon, himself a Georgian, described the Army of Northern Virginia's winter in Petersburg's fetid trenches. Vast amounts of food, much of it intended for Confederate use, had been destroyed by Sherman. Worse yet was the ruin of the railroad network in the deep South, and it became physically impossible to transport food to Lee. The starving Confederates manning those mean pits at Petersburg were freezing in threadbare uniforms and bare feet, and their munitions were barely replenishable. Sherman's unrelenting assault on the Confederacy's civilian sector was largely responsible for that situation.

We sometimes forget that soldiers are human beings. They have mothers, sisters, wives, children, and sweethearts. They have homes. In Georgia and the Carolinas those people were burned out of their homes in the dead of winter, left hungry and destitute. Some were raped and killed. What soldier could stay at his post, knowing this was happening to his loved ones in his home? Who could continue fighting for a government so weak that it allowed these things to occur? By the time Grant crashed through Lee's lines at Petersburg, the Confederate army had melted away. Men deserted by the thousands, and who could blame them?

Total war was brutal and barbaric, but it was certainly successful. ∎

Appendix A ■ Brick Walls and Rifled Cannon

Tiny Cockspur Island commands the twin channels of the Savannah River near its mouth at the Atlantic Ocean, twenty miles downriver from the port city of Savannah. Expecting trouble from their Spanish neighbors in Florida, the English built a large blockhouse surrounded by a stockade on Cockspur in 1761 and named it Fort George. The fortification was occupied by the patriots during the Revolution and dismantled when they determined the site was indefensible. In 1794 the United States built Fort Greene on Cockspur. It was a six-gun earth and log battery enclosed by a palisade, but in 1804 an enormously powerful hurricane struck the coast and monstrous waves erased all traces of the fort. Many of the garrison were drowned.

During the War of 1812, British fleets ranged at will along the Atlantic seaboard, little hampered by the United States' weak coastal defenses. As a result of this humiliation, President James Madison decided the country needed a system of fortifications extending along the Atlantic and Gulf coasts. In 1821 Cockspur Island was chosen as the site of a powerful fort that would protect the approaches to Savannah.

Simon Bernard was a famed military engineer under Napoleon who sought American employment following the Battle of Waterloo. He was commissioned a general in the United States Corps of Engineers and assigned the task of designing the Cockspur installation. His original plan called for a two-story brick fort that would mount three levels of guns, but the island, a soft mudball, could not have supported the weight. The top story was eliminated, and a foundation of crossed timbers and wooden piles driven seventy feet into the soil was added as a foundation for the masonry.

Construction, which began in 1829, was not completed until 1847. Work was halted each summer because of the danger posed by malaria and other diseases, and workers were brought to the site each fall. Progress was further delayed by hurricanes, freezing winds, and occasional lack of funding. Skilled workers were recruited from across the United States, and the manual labor was supplied by slaves hired from nearby rice plantations.

All the materials used in this enormous project were shipped to the island. They included 25,000,000 bricks and staggering quantities of iron, lead, and heart-of-Georgia pine lumber. Most of the bricks were made near Savannah and shipped in lots of several million, but a sturdier brick for vital arches was

271

In April 1862, Fort Pulaski is battered by a furious Union bombardment.
[LESLIE'S ILLUSTRATED]

imported from Maryland and Virginia. Stone was brought from New York.

One of the first men to work on the project in 1829 was Robert E. Lee. He was a green lieutenant fresh out of West Point when he surveyed the site and established an extensive dike system for drainage. In 1833 the fort was officially named for Count Casimir Pulaski, a Pole who had fought valiantly for the Americans during the Revolution. Wounded during an unsuccessful American and French assault to recapture Savannah from the British, Pulaski was taken aboard a ship, where he died. Legend states that the hero was given up to the sea near Cockspur Island.

After eighteen years of exhausting work, Fort Pulaski was completed at a cost of one million dollars. The fort's five sides have a circumference of 1,580 feet, and the enclosed parade ground is two and one-half acres in size. The walls are seven to nine feet thick and rise twenty-five feet above a moat, which is forty-eight feet wide and seven feet deep. Although intended to be armed with 146 cannon, half on top of the fort, the remainder in brick casemates below, Pulaski received only 20 long 32-pounder naval guns.

Fort Pulaski was never intended for defense against surprise attack. The government expected months of mounting tensions before a war broke out, so for thirteen years the only inhabitants of the masonry mountain were a caretaker and a sergeant who tended the guns.

The news of South Carolina's secession in December 1860, was met by the people of Savannah with great enthusiasm. In a show of solidarity for the actions of their neighbors, they paraded through the city with torchlights.

The occupation of Fort Sumter, situated in Charleston Harbor, by Federal troops on December 26 caused Savannahans to react with fear and anger. They believed that a similar action would threaten Savannah's security. Popular opinion was further inflamed by a telegram from Georgia's fiery U.S. Senator Robert Toombs. He expressed the opinion that war was inevitable and that Fort Pulaski would soon receive Union reinforcements.

On January 1, 1861, Colonel Alexander R. Lawton sent a telegraphic message to Governor Joseph Brown, asking him to review the situation in Savannah. Brown arrived later that day and consulted with Lawton, then authorized the Georgia militia to occupy Pulaski. A day was spent requisitioning supplies and arranging transportation for 134 men and 6 pieces of field artillery. On January 3 the soldiers marched through cheering throngs to board the steamboat *Ida,* which, ironically, was the property of the United States Government.

Landing at Cockspur around noon, the men disembarked and formed ranks. To the beat of drums, they marched unopposed into the fort, where Colonel Lawton raised the Georgia flag. When Captain William Whiting, the officer in charge of United States forts in Georgia and Florida, arrived several days later, Lawton entertained him "with great civility." He signed a receipt for the fort, and Whiting laid off the caretaker. Unfortunately, the next change of ownership would not be so polite.

The Georgians found Fort Pulaski in terrible condition. The parade ground was choked with underbrush, the quarters were unfit for habitation,

Union batteries on Tybee Island concentrated their fire at a single angle of Fort Pulaski.
[HARPER'S WEEKLY]

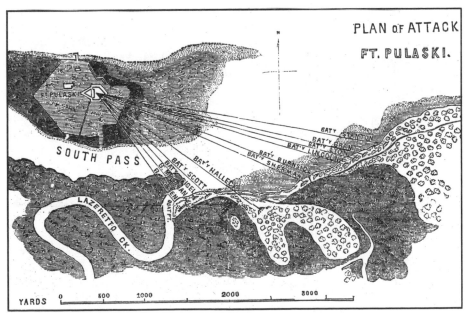

273

and the moat was filled with mud. The guns were useless with rust, and their carriages were rotten. Captain Francis S. Bartow, who assumed command of the fort, faced a great deal of work, but his men attacked the duty with great enthusiasm.

The guns were cleaned, and new carriages were built for them. Soldiers cleared the parade ground, and slaves dug out the moat. The powder magazine was dried out and provisioned, and cannon were remounted around the walls. With the fort returned to fighting trim, the 650-man garrison began training in the use of heavy artillery.

Similar work progressed all along the southern seaboard. Earthen forts were prepared on nearby Hilton Head, South Carolina, on Tybee Island, only a mile and a half south of Cockspur, and on the remainder of Georgia's sea islands. To patrol the numerous coastal waters, a Georgia navy had also been formed. It consisted of five steamers, each armed with one or two guns, and was led by Commodore Josiah Tattnall, a famed but aged officer.

When a British observer, William Howard Russell, was shown around Fort Pulaski, he was impressed with the spirit and activity he witnessed. Privately, he believed the Georgians did not fully comprehend the realities of modern war. "They do not understand the nature of the new shells and heavy vertical fire or the effect of projectiles from great distances falling into works. . . . What I saw did not satisfy me that Pulaski was strong, or Savannah very safe." His observations of southern naiveté was confirmed by a Georgia private who wrote his mother that "the boys are in good spirits. 'Spilin' for a fight."

On May 27 the first Federal blockade ship appeared off the bar. Captain Francis Bartow missed the sight, having left a week earlier to defend the southern frontier in Virginia. Two months later, after preserving the Confederate line at Manassas until Thomas "Stonewall" Jackson arrived, Bartow was killed. He became Georgia's first hero of the Civil War, albeit posthumously.

On November 7 a massive Federal amphibious force smashed Confederate resistance and captured Hilton Head and Port Royal. This event panicked many Georgians, who believed it was the first move to capture Savannah. The Union action was so traumatic that Robert E. Lee was sent to command the coastal forces of South Carolina and Georgia. Convinced that the barrier islands could not be held, Lee ordered batteries razed and guns and crews moved to reinforce defenses on the mainland. Pulaski would remain a Confederate bastion, but a supporting battery established near the lighthouse on Tybee Island was withdrawn.

Lee inspected Fort Pulaski twice during November 1861 and ordered a number of improvements in its defense. He had the parade ground trenched to prevent enemy solid shot from rolling destructively inside the fort, and several guns were remounted to defend the fort's rear. Barricades of heavy timbers were erected against the casemates to protect gunners from shell fragments, and Lee directed earthen traverses to be constructed between the guns on the exposed parapet for the same purpose.

Feeling secure behind their presumably impregnable walls, Fort Pulaski's garrison spent a pleasant Christmas. Several weeks earlier, a last blockade runner had slipped past Pulaski into Savannah. Additional Federal warships sealed the river tight, and Rear Admiral Samuel Francis DuPont, commander of the South Atlantic Blockading Squadron, sank stone-laden ships in the channel as a final precaution.

At Port Royal, Union General Thomas W. Sherman (no relation to William T.) requisitioned siege guns and made plans to subdue Fort Pulaski. The U.S. Navy ordered James Wilson to map the numerous rivers and creeks in the area to determine whether the fort could be bypassed, but Wilson reported that it would not be possible. Curiously enough, Wilson would return to Georgia at War's end as a highly respected cavalry leader. His troops were credited with capturing Confederate President Jefferson Davis near Irwinton.

On November 24 the Federals occupied abandoned Tybee Island. The Federal fleet now anchored in sheltered water just beyond the reach of Pulaski's guns. With his pitiful fleet, Tattnall gamely tried to chase the blockaders away two days later, but he was driven off and failed to entice the enemy closer to Pulaski.

The Federals continued to slowly close a noose around Pulaski during the winter of 1862. They labored four days to drag a battery of guns across eight hundred yards of marsh to set up a position at Venus point. When the *Ida,* carrying supplies for Pulaski, headed down the river on February 13, the Federal guns opened fire, but the little steamer managed to escape to Cockspur. On the following day Tattnall led four ships to attempt a rescue, but superior numbers forced them to retire. The little *Ida* did not need Tattnall's assistance, for on February 15 she executed a daring maneuver and ran back into Savannah by way of the second channel of the Savannah River.

A union mortar battery fires at Fort Pulaski.

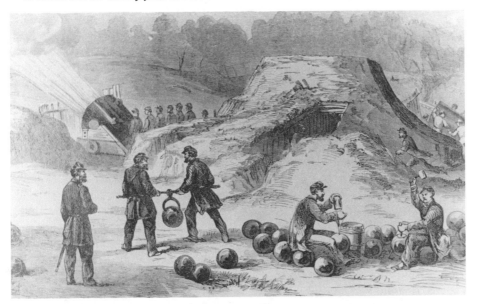

The Federals soon built a battery to command that channel, then placed a barrier across Tybee Creek. When they established infantry and gunboat patrols of the water passages, Pulaski was isolated.

Trapped inside the fort were 385 men commanded by Colonel Charles H. Olmstead. Their situation was certainly serious, but far from desperate. They had 48 cannon with which to defend themselves and 120 rounds for each piece, and there was food enough to last until late summer. It would require a lengthy siege to force Pulaski's surrender, but the Federals decided not to wait. On February 19 General Sherman sent Captain Quincy A. Gillmore to Tybee Island with orders to prepare for a bombardment.

Military science held that Fort Pulaski could not be reduced by bombardment. Cannon could breach Pulaski's defenses if located within a half mile of the thick walls, but Tybee was one to two and one-half miles distant. The U.S. Chief of Engineers declared that Pulaski was solid as the Rocky Mountains and that the fort "could not be reduced in a month's firing with any number of guns of manageable calibers." Lee, recently standing on Pulaski's ramparts, had pointed toward Tybee Island and assured Olmstead, "They can't breach your walls at that distance."

Because Gillmore had been following the development of a new weapon, the rifled cannon, he believed these experts were mistaken. Until this point in military history, cannon had been cast solid, and smooth bores had been drilled into them; and the guns fired round shot, which had a limited range and velocity. The rifled gun featured grooves inside the barrel that sent bullet-shaped shells farther and with greater accuracy and power. Gillmore proposed to combine the strengths of rifled guns, smoothbore cannon, and mortars to reduce Fort Pulaski.

Sherman approved Gillmore's plan, but he wrote that the bombardment would merely "shake the walls in a random manner." He set about preparing his infantry to storm the fort after the shelling had sufficiently rattled the Confederate gunners.

In late February, Gillmore began preparations for the bombardment. Large amounts of material were unloaded in the surf and manhandled ashore, then moved over miles of road that had been hastily constructed across sand and swamp. Sufficient timbers and planking to construct eleven batteries, supporting magazines, and shelter for the soldiers were hauled to the shore and transported inland. For the final mile, work could be managed only at night because Fort Pulaski's gunners had a perfect view of the beach.

Hidden by a ridge of sand, men labored many nights to prepare the gun emplacements. Then the hard work started. Mortars, each weighing eight and one-half tons, and the heavy cannon were loaded on sling carts and pulled across the island by teams of 250 men in harness. Through great exertion, and with considerable injury, they dragged 16 mortars, 10 regular cannon, and 10 rifled guns into the line of batteries which extended for 2,500 yards along the shore. The guns were provided with 900 rounds apiece, and a store of 9,600 pounds of gunpowder was stashed near Tybee Light.

During February, Colonel Olmstead in Fort Pulaski heard the night work progressing, but he could not see targets on which to fire. The garrison gamely readied the fort for action, and on the morning of April 10, 1862, a

Heavy artillery face the sea at Fort Pulaski National Park.

young lieutenant perched on Pulaski's walls noticed that the ridge on Tybee Island had been leveled, and the mouths of numerous cannon were peeking from the sand.

Olmstead was alerted. As he scanned the ominous new features on Tybee, a small boat left the island and bore James Wilson to Cockspur. Olmstead's reply to Wilson's surrender demand, "I am here to defend the Fort, not to surrender it," was returned to Gillmore as the Confederates confidently cleared their positions for action.

At 8:10 A.M. the Federals opened the bombardment with a mortar shell that exploded beyond the fort. A second mortar round fell short. Union guns on the right of their line opened fire first, and smoke rippled along the beach to the left as other batteries joined the fray.

The guns of Fort Pulaski that faced Tybee Island quickly and energetically returned fire, but with little effect. The Federal batteries were shielded by the ridge and by sandbags, and Confederate shot fell before and behind the Union guns, inflicting only one casualty during the entire siege.

The Federal cannon concentrated their fire on three embrasures (gun ports) at Pulaski's southeastern angle, and hits by Union cannon on the brick face caused the entire fort to shake. One projectile entered a gun position and wounded every member of the crew. Shrapnel severed the ropes that secured the Confederate flag to a pole, and the standard fluttered to the parade ground; under fierce enemy fire, Lieutenant Christopher Hussey and Private John Lathan heroically raised it aloft on a ramrod. Throughout the day Pulaski reverberated with the sounds of thunderous explosions and shattering bricks.

By noon, Pulaski had absorbed nearly fifty heavy blows, and the targeted gun ports were noticeably larger. The bombardment continued for ten and one-half hours and diminished only as darkness fell. Gillmore had a shot fired every ten minutes or so to deny the fort's garrison sleep. In any event, the Confederates would have been unable to get much rest that night. Most of the fort's guns had been dismounted by enemy fire or recoil, and crews labored to restore them to action.

Taking stock on Tybee, the Federals were discouraged by the day's work. They believed that the bombardment was having little effect on the monstrous brick fortification, and certainly the mortars were causing little damage. Most of their shells exploded high above the fort or outside the walls. A few plunged into Fort Pulaski, but before exploding they burrowed into the sand and harmlessly spewed enormous quantities of mud in all directions.

Inside the fort, Olmstead was worried. His twilight inspection showed the southeastern angle had lost two to four feet of its brick protection. The Columbiads' heavy balls battered and loosened the brick, while Parrott shot shattered layers of masonry. It was left to the James rifles to do most of the damage. They hurled shells that bored up to two feet into the walls and caused greate quantities of brick to cascade into the moat.

At dawn the battle was renewed with fresh fury. Pulaski's guns fired rapidly, but with virtually no effect. The gunners on Tybee, joined by a navy gunboat, an artillery-laden barge, and other nearby land batteries, concentrated on piercing Pulaski's walls. Most of the Confederate guns were silenced—dismounted, covered with mounds of collapsed bricks, or teetering on the edge of battered walls. Most telling were the two huge holes that were battered into the fort by noon. As Union gunners on Tybee peered through the gaps into the parade ground, ten thousand Federal infantry prepared to assault the fort.

Inside Fort Pulaski, Olmstead gave the gunners a rest and examined his situation. A dozen men had been wounded, one fatally, and rifled shells were whistling through the gaps in the wall. Olmstead wrote that the most alarming development was that "projectiles had access in a straight line to the traverse that protected our magazine." That was what Gillmore had intended when he initiated the bombardment.

At 2:00 P.M. a rifled shell flew across the fort and exploded against an earthwork thrown up against the magazine. The chamber was filled with smoke and a work party decided to flee; the magazine contained forty thousand pounds of gunpowder. This incident convinced Olmstead that it was only a matter of time before the Federal fire breached the magazine and the entire garrision was annihilated in a blinding flash. Hoping to save his men, the twenty-five-year-old Colonel lowered the Confederate flag and ran up a white sheet.

Gillmore boarded a boat to take possession of Pulaski. As he passed his men, they cheered and danced on the beach. Olmstead met the victorious Federal at the fort's gate, and for an hour they discussed Pulaski's surrender in Olmstead's quarters. The two men decided that Confederate officers

Federal artillery battered these gaping holes in Fort Pulaski's thick walls. This photograph was taken soon after the bombardment before the fort was repaired.
[LIBRARY OF CONGRESS]

would give up their swords, but enlisted men would be permitted to keep their personal possessions. The United States flag was soon raised over Fort Pulaski.

Colonel Olmstead sat down and wrote his wife, describing in detail the siege and circumstances that had led him regretfully to surrender his command. He praised the conduct of his men and told of the bombardment's ferocity. "Two casemates are completely torn to pieces," he noted, "the outer wall having fallen out into the moat, while the casemates adjoining are . . . cracked and crumbling from top to bottom. . . .

"Guns such as have never before been brought to bear against any fortification have overpowered me, but I trust to history to keep my name untarnished. Good night, God bless you," he concluded.

A Savannah newspaper provided further information about Fort Pulaski's surrender. It stated that most of her guns had been dismounted and that the holes at the angle were six feet wide. "The moat outside was so filled with brick and mortar that one could have passed over dry-shod," the paper revealed. "The protection to the magazine in the northwest angle of the fort had all been shot away; the entire corner of the magazine next to the passageway was shot off, and the powder exposed, while three shots had actually penetrated the chamber."

The fall of Fort Pulaski had little impact on the final outcome of the Civil War, and it did not affect Savannah beyond a panic of short duration. The Federals decided that it was impractical to assault the city from the sea, but the lessons learned here caused a revolution in coastal defense. In thirty hours of bombardment, the Federals threw over five thousand projectiles at Fort Pulaski. Most of the damage was accomplished by three rifled guns—a sixty-four-pounder and two eighty-four-pounders. These rifled cannon spelled the end of brick and stone fortifications, which guarded most of the world's ports.

Olmstead's men were initially imprisoned at Governor's Island in New York Harbor. Then they were transferred to Fort Delaware and Johnston's Island, Ohio, where some joined the northern war effort and others succumbed to disease. The remainder were exchanged during the summer and fall of 1862 near Richmond, Virginia, and Vicksburg, Mississippi, and made their way back to Savannah.

The Federals expended a great deal of effort in repairing the damage they had taken such pride in inflicting. The gaps in the wall were repaired, and some guns from Tybee were mounted in the fort. Pulaski was garrisoned throughout the War, but boredom was the greatest threat to the Union soldiers. To help pass time, they organized the first baseball games played in Georgia.

In October 1864, the garrison became jailors when five hundred Confederate prisoners of war were housed in several barred casemates. The prisoners suffered severely through the winter, lacking blankets, firewood, and adequate food. As a result of this cruel treatment, many died. During their ordeal the captives trapped and ate an estimated sixty cats that wandered into their cells. The surviving prisoners were transported to Fort Delaware in March 1865.

On April 29, two hundred shots were fired from Fort Pulaski's guns to celebrate the end of the Civil War, but the installation's usefulness was not yet ended.

After Jefferson Davis was captured near Irwinton, he was taken to Macon and Augusta, then down the Savannah River to spend a night aboard ship in sight of Cockspur. Pulaski was soon a pen for political prisoners as the Federals rounded up southern "war criminals" and housed in its casemates Confederate cabinet members, state governors, and other luminaries of the late rebellion. Pulaski, active before the Civil War erupted, saw service long after hostilities ceased. ∎

Appendix B ■ The Gallant Defense of Fort McAllister

The southernmost Confederate defense of Savannah was Fort McAllister, located twelve miles below the city on the south bank of the Ogeechee River at Genesis Point. Built seven miles upriver from the Atlantic Ocean on the first high ground, it was surrounded by protective marshes and was intended to guard the mouth of the Ogeechee, a back-door route into Savannah. It had been placed to protect an important bridge over the Atlantic and Gulf Railroad and to spare river plantations from Federal raids.

Named for a local landowner, the fort was begun in 1861 and expanded throughout its life. McAllister was an outstanding example of the new age in earthen fortifications, perfectly reflecting the lessons learned at Fort Pulaski. Designed by Captain John McCrady, it consisted of a number of gun emplacements separated by large earthen walls called traverses. Wooden frames were constructed, and men used shovels and wheelbarrows to fill them with earth and sand. When the soil was tamped into place, the frames were removed, and the desired shape of the earthworks had been easily attained.

Within the perimeter were large bombproofs, timber-supported shelters covered with a heavy layer of earth, housing ammunition magazines, a hospital, and supply rooms. Each cannon had a bombproof magazine to supply it with ammunition and powder, and a hot shot furnace provided one gun with heated cannonballs designed to set wooden warships on fire.

The fort was initially armed with a large siege gun, twelve field guns, and a ten-inch mortar. To keep enemy ships at a safe distance, the river below the fort was obstructed with piles and torpedos.

A Federal officer observed that McAllister was a "truly formidable work, so crammed with bomb proofs-traverses as to look as if the spaces were carved out of solid earth."

The first of seven attacks against the fort occurred when Union gunboats unsuccessfully tested McAllister's defenses twice in July 1862. They were trying to pass the fort to destroy the blockade runner *Nashville*. Damage done to the earthworks by their shells was quickly repaired.

On November 18, 1862, a Federal ironclad had a crack at McAllister. The *Wissahicton* and her escorts fired over a hundred shells into the fort before the ironclad was struck below the waterline by Confederate gunners and

Abatis made of tangled tree limbs protect the rear of Fort McAllister.
[LIBRARY OF CONGRESS]

forced to withdraw.

On January 27, 1863, after reconnoitering the Rebel obstructions at night in small boats, the *Montauk,* the second monitor-class ironclad constructed, led a five-ship flotilla up the Ogeechee to within 1,500 yards of McAllister. Her captain was John Warden, who had fought the CSS *Virginia* in the original *Monitor* at the classic battle in Hampton Roads, Virginia. He intended to try her new Dahlgren guns, an eleven-inch and a powerful fifteen-inch, on the fort's earthen walls. The *Montauk* hurled sixty-one fifteen-inch shells, the largest yet made, at the fort over a span of five hours. The shells blew huge craters into McAllister's walls, but that night the damage was easily filled in with sand. The Confederates suffered no casualties.

Braving the deadly fire, McAllister's gunners stood by their pieces and peppered the *Montauk* with fifteen hits. The cannonballs caused no damage except minor dents in the thick armor. A northern newspaper reporter who accompanied the expedition had expected the *Montauk* to make short work of the fort, but he later confided, "We failed to estimate the power and durability of that fort."

The *Montauk* and her gunboats returned four days later, on February 1, and McAllister's gallant defenders bounced forty-eight additional shots off the monitor's armored hide during a five-hour exchange. The *Montauk* was able to approach closer than before because sailors had surreptitiously removed many of the threatening mines, and she concentrated her fire against a front section of the earthworks. Two heavy shells that struck the wall simultaneously blew away a third of the barrier and buried two members of the gun crew, John Mahan and William Barber. They were dug out unharmed and continued to serve the gun even though subsequent explosions leveled the wall and left the crew with no protection. Major Robert H. Anderson noted their heroic stubbornness, recording that they "fought to the close of the action, refusing to be relieved," even when one of the fearful fifteen-inch shells plowed completely through the parapet.

The ten-inch mortar, commanded by Captain Robert Martin, continued to return fire after the wooden support platform collapsed from the concussion of repeated firings. "My men were frequently covered with sand, and shells and fragments of shells frequently fell around us," Martin noted.

It was during this assault that Fort McAllister suffered its only fatality: Major John B. Gallie, a 55-year-old native Scotsman who was the commanding officer of the fort. Although he reserved the gun closest to the enemy fleet as his own, Gallie moved among his crews with words of praise and encouragement. While visiting one gun, an enemy shell exploded and wounded him in the face, but Gallie continued his rounds. He was inspecting a thirty-two-pounder when a fifteen-inch shell struck the gun. A fragment of shell (or a piece of the cannon) killed the Major.

Inside the monitor, casualties were confined to broken limbs and bruises. Most of those wounds were caused by bolts from the armor plating, which often popped off and flew like bullets when a Confederate solid shot impacted on the turrent.

After the enemy ships withdrew, Major Anderson praised his stalwart men. "I think that the brave and heroic garrison of Fort McAllister have, after a most severe and trying fight, demonstrated to the world that victory does not, as a matter of course, always perch itself on the flag of an ironclad when opposed even to an ordinary earthwork manned by stout and gallant hearts."

The history of Fort McAllister is intertwined with that of the CSS *Nashville*, a two-masted side-wheel steamer that ran the blockade into Savannah in July 1862, with a cargo of arms from Europe. She attempted to return to England with a load of cotton, but was almost captured by the

This ditch and palisade surround Fort McAllister's land approaches.
[LIBRARY OF CONGRESS]

vigilant Federal fleet and was forced to return hastily. Admiral Francis Du-Pont was informed that the *Nashville* expedited her escape by dumping a million dollars' worth of cotton overboard and stoking her fires with pork and every piece of timber not necessary to keep the ship afloat. Even then she was barely saved by sailing into a storm that obscured her from sight.

In Savannah, the *Nashville* was fitted as a raider and armed with two twelve-pound cannon. Renamed the *Rattlesnake,* she crept down the Ogeechee to Fort McAllister and watched for an opportune moment to escape into Ossabaw Sound and run to sea. There her captain hoped to imitate the exploits of the famed Rebel raider *Alabama.* The Federals kept a close watch on the Ogeechee and discussed ways to keep the *Nashville* bottled up permanently. One suggestion was to sink stone-filled ships in the channel, but earlier attempts to obstruct the Savannah River in this manner had failed dismally. It was decided that perhaps ironclads could pass Fort McAllister and destroy the raider as it lay at anchor.

The *Nashville* tried to escape on February 27, but her route was blocked by Federal ships. She returned and was grounded fast at Seven Mile Bend, just upstream from Fort McAllister. Sharp eyes on the blockading vessels saw the *Nashville*'s plight, and an immediate expedition was planned to sink her.

The *Montauk* and two gunboats started upriver at 4:00 A.M. on February 28, discovering the *Nashville* hopelessly grounded. The gunboats attempted to occupy McAllister, while the fort vainly fired at all three vessels. Although only the masts and stacks of the raider were visible, the *Montauk*'s fifth shot plowed into the *Nashville*'s hull. Three additional shells followed in rapid succession. After the firing paused to let the smoke settle, the newspaper correspondent wrote, "We saw to our great joy a dense column of smoke rising from the forward deck of the stranded vessel. Our exploding shell had set her on fire. A few minutes more, and flames were distinctly visible, forcing their way up, gradually creeping aft until they had reached nearly to the base of the smokestack."

The *Nashville*'s crew had abandoned ship when the monitor started shooting, and they watched helplessly from a distance as the fire spread to her magazine. At 9:45 A.M. the ammunition exploded with a roar that rattled windows in Savannah.

Throughout this action, the Confederates had been frustrated by the failure of their torpedos to destroy a Federal vessel. Many of the mines were defective, while the powder in some had become sodden and others had been removed at night by Union work parties. As the *Montauk* proceeded stately down the river, she hit a torpedo that exploded. The *Montauk*'s engineer described it as "a violent, sudden, and seemingly double explosion." He dashed about the ship trying to determine whether the monitor had been holed by a cannon shot or if a boiler had exploded.

The pilot, who had ignored a feeling of danger moments earlier by plowing over a piece of cloth, which apparently marked the location of the torpedo for the Confederates, quickly beached the *Montauk* on a sandbar. That maneuver covered the hole in her hull with mud and stopped the leak. As the crew made hasty repairs to the ship, they noticed cotton and planks from

Following Fort McAllister's capture, Confederate prisoners are forced to remove deadly torpedos. [LESLIE'S ILLUSTRATED]

the *Nashville* floating past. The debris, the reporter thought, "seemed to show a determination that, if we would not allow the *Nashville* to go to sea as a whole, she was going to run the blockade in pieces."

If Admiral DuPont was proud for having bottled the *Nashville* up for eight months, he was delighted with her destruction, particularly since the press fostered a belief that she regularly ran the blockade every few weeks. "I feel extremely gratified at being rid of her," he confided.

On March 3, 1863, three Union monitors, the *Passaic,* the *Nahant,* and the *Patapsco,* accompanied by three wooden gunboats and three mortar boats, made a concentrated attack against stubborn McAllister. The *Montauk,* undergoing permanent repairs, was unable to participate. Near 9:00 A.M. the Confederates opened the duel by throwing a shot at the *Passaic,* and a general exchange was soon underway. Two hundred and fifty Union shells—about 70 tons of iron—were thrown against the works during a seven-hour bombardment. Only the fort's mascot, Tom Cat, was killed, and three men were wounded. In return, the ironclads were struck forty-five times, with predictably little effect.

The Union bombardment was so furious that it was deemed a miracle that no Confederates died in the assault. When an eleven-inch shell exploded in the midst of ten men in a gun position, shrapnel shrieked in all directions and shattered the gun carriage; but the crew escaped unscathed. Although several guns were dismounted by enemy fire, the garrison of Fort McAllister seemed charmed.

Valor was the order of the day for the Confederate gunners. When a Federal shell smashed the traverse wheel of a cannon, rendering the gun useless, Private Carroll Hanson found a spare wheel in the rear of the fort. He rolled it to his gun through the intense shelling so the piece could rejoin McAllister's magnificent defense.

The fort absorbed a great deal of punishment during this heavy bombardment. Exploding shells and bouncing solid shot made the parade ground a dangerous place to be. The largest bombproof, located in the center of the fort, housed a hospital and supply center. During the attack, it was a shelter for men not needed to man the guns. It seemed safe enough until a huge, fifteen-inch shell hit the top of the bombproof, rolled down the slope, and exploded in front of the entrance, where Confederate officers were huddled in conference. Miraculously, the men were not wounded and suffered only burns.

One massive round from a Federal mortar boat exploded atop the wall that protected the path to the Confederate mortar position. It left a hole four feet in diameter and two feet deep.

McAllister's reply to the monitors was carried primarily by two guns: a thirty-two-pound rifle and a huge forty-two-pound smoothbore. The mortar was also capable of reaching the ironclads, and some shells were filled with sand in hopes that they would crash through the lighter deck armor of a monitor. Several of these shells were seen to hit, but they burst on impact. Federal crews clearing the decks afterward must have puzzled over the scattered piles of sand.

The Confederate infantry had felt useless during earlier Federal naval bombardments, but Lieutenant E. A. Ellarbee found a use for his men. Noticing that the ironclads anchored at the same spot each time they appeared to shell the fort, Ellarbee took his sharpshooters across the river to dig rifle pits in the marsh.

When the Union flotilla steamed up on March 3, the snipers started blazing away at the gun ports. They ignored occasional shells from Fort McAllister that overshot the monitors and came dangerously close to their position. Smoke inside the ironclads made it difficult for Federal officers to see what effect their fire was having on the fort, and one man who left the protection of the *Passaic*'s turret, spyglass in hand, to view the action was killed by fire from the marsh. Sailors within the monitor dragged their comrade inside as Ellarbee hurriedly repositioned his men. Moments later the turret whirled to face the marsh, and charges of grapeshot shredded the vegetation where the sharpshooters had been lurking.

McAllister's garrison was grieved by Tom Cat's death. The pet's demise was noted in the official reports of the battle, which were sent to General P.G.T. Beauregard in Charleston. A Savannah newspaper mentioned the heroic Confederate feline in its account of the battle.

After this assault, the Union Navy decided that McAllister was impregnable and did not molest the fort for the remainder of the War. DuPont had hoped to capture McAllister, but the squadron commander, Captain Percival

As Sherman prepared to march into the Carolinas, Union soldiers dismounted Fort McAllister's heavy cannon for shipment north. [LIBRARY OF CONGRESS]

Drayton, confessed that the damage they inflicted could be repaired with "a good night's work." Horace Greeley later wrote, "From this time the Union fleet saved their ammunition by letting McAllister alone." The Federals would shortly appear in Charleston Harbor and batter Fort Sumter into rubble, but their efforts would prove about as useful as the McAllister episode.

On May 1, 1863, the Confederate Congress passed an act that applauded the "gallantry and endurance" of McAllister's defenders.

Expecting further action from the aggressive Union navy, the Confederates brought in additional powerful guns. They repositioned some cannon to more advantageous positions and expanded the earthworks, particularly in the rear, to protect against infantry assault. There they placed field pieces. The garrison did not see another Yankee for over twenty months; but when they returned, it was in overwhelming force. ■

Appendix C ■ The Saga of Savannah's Ironclads

After the Civil War erupted with the bombardment of Fort Sumter, one of President Abraham Lincoln's first actions was to blockade southern harbors. Realizing that the occupation of Rebel ports would be a priority of the Union navy, the Confederates moved to augment coastal forts with armored warships. Savannah was one of many ports quickly transformed into a shipbuilding center. By the end of 1864, three ironclads, the *Georgia,* the *Atlanta,* and the *Savannah,* had been launched and commissioned, and a fourth, the *Milledgeville,* was nearly complete.

Construction on the Savannah ironclads was slowed by a lack of iron plating and engine parts, problems that plagued the entire Confederate navy. Most of the armor consisted of flattened railroad rails bolted to a thick backing of oak and pine. The propulsion machinery, which was manufactured in Columbus, Georgia, was generally of good quality, but it proved inadequate to move such massive ships. A drawing of the *Savannah*'s engine, penned by Confederate Chief Engineer James Warner, is preserved at the Columbus Museum of Arts and Sciences. It is the only original plan that survived the Confederacy's destruction. The *Atlanta* was unique for having vertical engines.

The completed ironclads were so slow, unstable, and difficult to maneuver that they were rendered useless as rams and ocean raiders. Excursions across the calm harbor were adventurous enough, leaving the behemoths useful only as floating batteries, and they were used to augment Fort Jackson and newly constructed earthworks in the defense of Savannah. Although failures at their intended purpose, the presence of the ironclads was a serious deterrent to Union forays.

Even if the ironclads had been fit for extensive travel, they would have been hampered by a chronic lack of fuel. Only forty-five coal cars were available to support the needs of ships at Charleston, Savannah, and Columbus, where nine ironclads and numerous smaller vessels eventually were in operation.

Because the ships were constructed with green timber and caulked with cotton, they had severe leakage problems, and pumps operated continuously to keep them afloat. In time the situation worsened as ravenous worms weakened the wooden hulls.

The C.S.S. Georgia, *the first Savannah-made ironclad, became a floating battery.*
[LESLIE'S ILLUSTRATED]

A sailor stationed on an ironclad called her a "box (for she is not a vessel)," and added that conditions were "horrible. She is not fit command for a sergeant of marines."

The *Savannah,* a floating sieve, was a miserable place to live and work. Designed to be impervious to heavy enemy shells, the armor denied men working below deck light and ventilation, and survival in the stifling Savannah summer heat was nearly impossible. The ironclad was so hot that the crew lived on a tender. Deserters who reached Fort Pulaski described the sailors as being very unhappy with conditions aboard. A crewman wrote, "I would defy anyone in the world to tell me whether it is day or night if he is confined below without any means of marking time. . . . I would venture to say that if a person were blindfolded and carried below and turned loose he would imagine himself in a swamp, for the water is trickling in all the time and everything is so damp."

Savannah's first attempt at building an ironclad produced the *Georgia,* known as the Ladies' Gunboat because women in cities across the state raised $115,000 for its construction. Work on the *Georgia* increased furiously when Fort Pulaski fell, an incident that Savannahans believed was a prelude to an attack on the city from the sea. That threat never materialized, but the ship was hurriedly completed by May 1862.

The workmen started with an old barge and built a thick wooden gun deck with a steep slope to deflect enemy shot. It was covered with 8 inches of iron that weighed one thousand tons. The *Georgia* was a trial-and-error experiment by people with little shipbuilding experience, and they left no plans, drawings, or records of the ironclad's construction. As a result, estimates of her dimensions range from 260 feet in length and 60 feet in width, to 160 feet by 50 feet. The ship was probably twelve feet high, and her sides extended below the waterline. The *Georgia* was armed with three thirty-two-pounder rifled cannon, two nine-inch smoothbores, and other guns that could be fired out ten armored gun ports, one in either end and four in each broadside. Lieutenant Washington Gwathmey commanded 13 officers and 109 sailors assigned as her crew.

A newspaper writer in 1863 described the *Georgia* as "a monstrous creature . . . with sides and ends sloping to the water at an angle of 45 degrees and covered with large slabs or strips of railroad iron."

As a ram, or even as a movable vessel, the *Georgia* was an abject failure. In a class of ships famous for their lack of propulsive power, the *Georgia* ranked dead last, and her inadequate engines were unable to withstand the tide, much less were capable of making headway. Part of the problem could be attributed to a timber from the stocks which was accidentally attached to the *Georgia*'s hull during construction.

The *Georgia* soon became a pathetic joke, variously described as a "marine abortion," a "splendid failure," and a "nondescript marine mon-

In February 1863, the Union monitor Montauk *destroys the C.S.S.* Nashville, *while Fort McAllister fires on the ironclad.* [LESLIE'S ILLUSTRATED]

ster." Towed to a specially prepared log pen near Elba Island, the ship was positioned to fire a broadside toward both channels of the Savannah River. The proud ship was reduced to the status of a defensive floating battery.

While the *Georgia* was taking shape, construction on a second ironclad, the *Atlanta,* began. Her first incarnation was as the steamship *Fingal,* newly launched when she became one of the first vessels secured by the Confederacy to run goods past the blockade. Purchased in Scotland in September 1861, she was immediately loaded with a priceless cargo of ten thousand rifles, one million cartridges, and numerous cannon, pistols, swords, and medical supplies. Her uneventful maiden cruise for the South took the *Fingal* from Scotland to Bermuda and into Savannah on November 12. The coal shortage delayed a return trip to England for a month. Before the *Fingal* was finally fueled and packed with cotton intended for hungry English textile mills, a Federal blockading fleet had appeared and sealed the harbor tight.

Unable to escape as a blockade runner, the *Fingal* was converted by Confederate officials into an ironclad of the *Virginia* class. She was cut down to the deck, which was widened and strengthened with three feet of wood and iron plate, and a casemate, sloped thirty degrees to deflect shot, covered a gun deck. The armor consisted of two layers of two-inch-thick, seven-inch-long railroad iron secured to three inches of oak and fifteen inches of pine. Two seven-inch guns and two six-inch rifled cannon were

The C.S.S. Atlanta *was captured on its initial cruise and was used to reinforce the Union blockading fleet.* [LIBRARY OF CONGRESS]

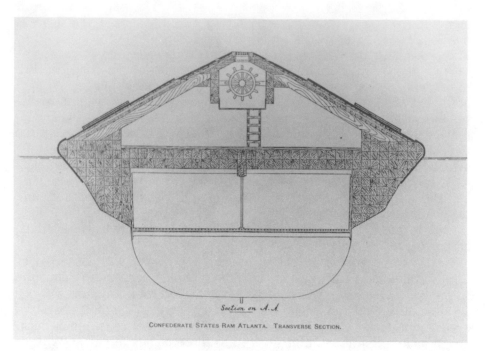

Cross section plan of the C.S.S. Atlanta. *Note the extensive wook backing.*
[OFFICIAL RECORDS OF THE WAR OF THE REBELLION]

placed on pivots so they could be swiveled to fire out eight steel-shuttered gun ports, one at bow and stern, and three on each side. An iron-sheathed ram was added to the bow, along with a spar that would hold a contact torpedo. The formidable-looking craft was 204 feet long and 41 feet wide. Because of her oceangoing hull and the additional weight of armor, the *Atlanta* drew sixteen feet of water, twice what she drew as an ordinary steamer.

After six months of work, the ship, rechristened the *Atlanta,* was completed in July 1862. With her iron hull and efficient English machinery, she was the most mechanically reliable Confederate ironclad yet built. Unfortunately, the armor reduced her former twelve-mile-an-hour speed to six, and of course she leaked. A midshipman called the officers' quarters "the most uncomfortable I have ever seen." He complained that his only personal possessions were two hooks from which his hammock hung.

The *Atlanta*'s initial cruise near Fort Pulaski threw the Federal garrison into alarm. A New York *Herald* correspondent wrote that without Union monitors to counter the threat, the blockading fleet "have before them an excellent opportunity of learning what it is to be blown out of the water."

They need not have feared yet, for the *Atlanta* endured four additional months of shakedown cruises in vain attempts to correct steering and leakage problems. By January 1863, the ironclad had been commissioned, but several chances to accomplish a victory against an all wooden blockading fleet were lost. When the *Atlanta* crept up the Savannah River to attack the Federal fleet in January, its path was barred by obstructions—stone-filled wooden cribs placed by the Confederates to prevent a Federal attack on the city, which officials had failed to remove.

The *Atlanta* could clear the river only at high tide. Her next attempt to attack the Federal fleet in February was thwarted by winds that prevented the tide surge. When Admiral Samuel F. DuPont, in command of the South Atlantic Blockading Squadron, was alerted by sources inside Savannah that the *Atlanta* was about to attack his blockaders, he had the monitors *Montauk* and *Passaic* towed to Savannah in late January.

The *Atlanta*'s captain, Josiah Tattnall, was subjected to intense criticism from several quarters—the public, the South's vocal newspapers, and other military commanders. They blamed him for failing to lift the Federal blockade, relieve pressure on besieged Charleston, and recapture nearby Port Royal, which had been occupied by Union troops early in the war. A sailor expressed the fear that the navy would be "branded as cowards by the unthinking portion of the citizens of Savannah."

In March, Tattnall sailed to Wassaw Sound and prepared to strike the enemy base at Port Royal. He then intended to steam to Key West, Florida, and destroy other blockading vessels. Unfortunately, two Confederate draftees deserted to Fort Pulaski and revealed his plan, and the Federal commander ordered three monitors to take station off Savannah. Tattnall felt that his crudely cobbled ship could not defeat the monitors, and he also feared that the Federals would attack Savannah during his absence, so he canceled the foray until the monitors returned to Charleston.

When Fort McAllister was attacked during the winter of 1863, the understandably concerned citizens of Savannah urged the *Atlanta* to aid those

Side and top-view plans of the C.S.S. Atlanta. [OFFICIAL RECORDS OF THE WAR OF THE REBELLION]

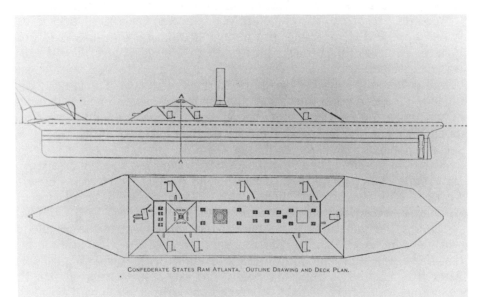

CONFEDERATE STATES RAM ATLANTA. OUTLINE DRAWING AND DECK PLAN.

gallant defenders, but the ironclad was unable to operate in such shallow river waters.

Tattnall was soon relieved of command for his perceived shortcomings in the belief that his replacement, Richard L. Page, was a more aggressive officer. Page spent a month attempting to repair the *Atlanta*'s steering, but found himself removed in favor of William A. Webb, who had a reputation for reckless aggressiveness.

When Charleston was threatened by a massive monitor attack in April 1863, Confederate General P. G. T. Beauregard requested that the *Atlanta* make a diversionary attack to relieve the pressure, but he was informed by Savannah authorities that it was not possible. This incident prompted Beauregard to write angrily, "None of these Confederate vessels or ironclads were seaworthy, and, beyond river or harbor defense, none of them rendered effective service."

The Confederate Navy Department also faced criticism from the public. It was fueled by newspaper accounts that fostered a belief that the *Atlanta* was the most powerful ship afloat. The Federals shared this opinion, but the ironclad was still a primitive, makeshift gun platform.

Although a third Confederate ironclad, the *Savannah,* was nearly complete, Webb dismissed the suggestion that he wait and execute an attack with two ships. Facing several monitors alone did not intimidate him. The boastful Webb proclaimed that "the whole abolitionist fleet has no terror for me," and a week after assuming command he steamed off to attack. An engine soon failed, and he was forced to delay his planned triumphal cruise for yet another month. Hearing rumors of Webb's activity, DuPont confided, "We have a ram fever on again." He promptly dispatched two monitors to Savannah, the *Weehawken* and the *Nahunt*. They were both protected by ten inches of turret armor and armed with an eleven-inch and a fifteen-inch cannon. They would face the *Atlanta*'s four inches of iron and inferior guns.

According to Webb, his grandiose plan was to "raise the blockade between here and Charleston, attack Port Royal, and then blockade Fort Pulaski. Afterwards, he might turn south to Florida waters. The *Atlanta* was provisioned with ammunition and food for an extended voyage, and before dawn on June 16 her bunkers were filled with coal. The ironclad cast off and proceeded down the Wilmington River to Wassaw Sound with hopes of surprising the patrolling monitors at dawn. Webb intended to sink one monitor with his spar torpedo, then concentrate solid shot at the base of the second monitor's turret to jam it.

At 4:00 A.M. the night watch aboard the *Weehawken* shouted an alarm—the *Atlanta* was coming. After Captain John Rodgers ordered his crew to stations, they cleared for action as the monitor steamed directly for the *Atlanta*. John Downes on the *Nahunt* followed.

Sighting the monitors, Webb immediately turned out of the channel to engage them. According to later accounts, Webb's pilots had assured him that there was sufficient water, but the *Atlanta* ran aground on a sandbar. After five minutes of frenzied activity, she was able to back off, but the ponderous battleship could not be steered properly. She ran hard aground a second time, her gun ports poorly positioned to fire on the enemy ships.

At six hundred yards the *Atlanta* sent a shot that splashed between the monitors. The *Weehawken* held her fire and deliberately stalked to three hundred yards, then fired her fifteen-inch gun. The huge solid shot, propelled by thirty pounds of powder, smashed into the *Atlanta*'s side and dislodged large iron and wooden splinters from the bulkhead, wounding sixteen men and rendering forty senseless from concussion. The impact drove the *Atlanta*'s shot out of their racks, adding to the destruction. An eleven-inch shell followed. It crashed into the lightly armored knuckles, springing a seam and starting a serious leak. A third shot struck a gun shutter as it was opening to fire, wounding half the gun crew. A final shell ravaged the pilot house, incapacitating both pilots and a helmsman and stunning a second.

Webb saw no alternative but ignoble surrender. After fifteen minutes of battle, he had gotten off only seven badly aimed shots that failed to hit a target, and the *Nahunt* was pounding up to join the *Weehawken* in battle. Their massive shells were certain to penetrate the *Atlanta*'s thin iron and wreak destruction on her crew, so Webb raised a white flag and addressed his crew: "I have surrendered our vessel because circumstances over which I had no control have compelled me to do so. . . . You all know that if we had not run aground, the result would have been different, and now that a regard for your lives has influenced me in this surrender, I would advise you to submit quietly to the fate which has overtaken us."

Webb surrendered 165 officers and crewmen, most of them converted infantry. They were imprisoned at Fort LaFayette in New York Harbor.

The C.S.S. Savannah *is destroyed on the night following Savannah's evacuation. The blast rattled windows many miles away.* [HARPER'S WEEKLY]

When the crew was exchanged, forty men chose to fight for the North.

The *Atlanta* eventually found its way to sea, although not in the manner Webb had anticipated. The ironclad was taken to the Philadelphia Navy Yard for repairs, and in February 1864, she sailed to Fortress Monroe, Virginia, and became part of the James River Federal blockading fleet. The *Atlanta* appeared later in the war as watchdog over the sinking Confederate raider *Florida,* which had been illegally captured while in a Brazilian port. The ship was brought to Hampton Roads, where it was "accidentally" struck by a Federal transport ship. The *Atlanta* helped isolate Richmond during the War's final year and was scrapped in 1866.

Loss of the *Atlanta* stunned the people of the South. For months they had read glowing accounts of her invincibility in the Confederate press and expressions of fear in northern papers. Rumors abounded that her surrender was the result of incompetency, treason, and even mutiny among the crew.

Captain Rodgers of the *Weehawken* was thanked by Congress for his easy victory and promoted. This resounding victory prompted the production of additional monitors to completely seal the southern ports.

The *Savannah,* begun in 1862 and completed in mid-1863, was commanded by William W. Hunter. She was 174 feet long and 45 feet wide and was armed with five rifled guns, her engines and boilers constructed at the Columbus Naval Iron Works. She was considered a powerful vessel, but the blockade had grown ever stronger; and with evidence of the *Atlanta*'s fighting ability before them, Confederate naval officials refused to send the *Savannah* out to battle.

A year and a half passed without any Federal attempt to capture Savannah from the sea, but in December 1864, the city's fall to Sherman seemed certain. Plans were made to keep the *Savannah* from falling into Union hands. Preparations had already begun for the destruction of the navy's material, and a requisition had been made to equip the sailors with packs and canteens. They were about to join the infantry.

On December 10 Secretary Mallory sent these instructions to Tattnall: "Should Savannah fall, do not permit our vessels . . . to fall into the hands of the enemy. Destroy everything necessary to prevent this." On the 18th, Beauregard traveled to Savannah from Charleston and met with Commander T. W. Brent, who was in charge of the fleet. They determined that the *Georgia* would be sunk, while the *Savannah* would cover the Confederate army's evacuation from Savannah, delay Sherman's pursuit, then fight through the blockade and steam for Charleston.

General William Hardee requested that the *Savannah* and the *Georgia* be sent up the Savannah River to protect vital bridges. However, the plan was not implemented because the *Savannah* drew too much water, and towing vessels were not available for the *Georgia,* which had lain useless in its log pen for two years. Until this point—while the city anticipated an attack from the sea—these vessels had done little but rust.

When the withdrawal began two days later, the *Savannah* cruised up the river to Hutchinson Island and joined Confederate land batteries there in shelling the left of the Federal line to divert their attention from what was occurring in the city. During the night, the *Georgia*'s guns were spiked, and

A rather fanciful rendering of the destruction of an unfinished Confederate ironclad in Savannah.
[LESLIE'S ILLUSTRATED]

she was scuttled at her moorings. When sailors opened her sea cocks, the *Georgia* sank like the rock she was, so quickly that many men were forced to scramble for safety without their belongings. The *Georgia* had never fired her guns in anger.

The ironclad *Milledgeville,* recently launched but not completed, was burned to the waterline and sank in mid-river. After their ceaseless labor, it deeply hurt the shipbuilders to fire the ship, which had been expected to be the most powerful ironclad produced in Savannah. She carried four heavy guns, and although armored with six inches of iron rather than the standard four, the ship was not top heavy and was considered to be extremely seaworthy. Her adequate propulsion system featured English boilers.

A fifth ironclad under construction was burned on the stocks, along with the Navy Yard, shipbuilding facilities, steamers, and an unfinished torpedo boat.

When the sun rose over a smoke-shrouded city on December 21, only the *Savannah* remained. Stung by mounting criticism of the navy's poor performance, Mallory asked Brent to fight the ironclad to the last.

"Under any circumstances, it is better that these vessels should fall in the conflict of battle . . . than that they should be tamely surrendered to the enemy or destroyed by their own officers. If fall they must, let them show neither the weakness of submission nor of self-destruction, but inflict a blow that will relieve defeat from discredit."

Mallory's plea notwithstanding, a sailor aboard the *Savannah* remarked, "If we are attacked, we will follow the course of the other ironclads and either blow up or get captured."

By war's end, the Confederate navy would have destroyed thirty uncompleted ironclads. Of the twenty-two that were finished, four were captured, one destroyed by enemy action, and the remainder sunk by their crews.

Brent's attempt to flee via Wassaw Sound through the Wilmington River was thwarted by Confederate torpedos that were impossible to remove quickly. That was just as well, because Admiral John A. Dahlgren, who had designed the devastating guns mounted on the monitors, had heard of the planned escape and ordered monitors to patrol every channel.

At sunrise on December 21, Federal troops gleefully occupied Fort Jackson and climbed the ramparts to raise the United States flag. Looking across the river, they were startled by the sight of the CSS *Savannah* lying at anchor near Screven's Bluff. A battery of field artillery was unlimbered and opened fire on the ironclad. In reply the *Savannah* defiantly ran up her Confederate flag and returned fire, briefly driving the Federals from their guns. The Yankees responded by harmlessly bouncing numerous shots off the *Savannah*'s thick hide. One shell entered a smokestack, but fortunately, it failed to detonate. Otherwise, the *Savannah* would have indeed gone out in a blaze of glory. The exchange lasted throughout the day. If the Federals had intended a close pursuit of Hardee, at least the *Savannah* discouraged them.

After dark, Brent ran the *Savannah* to the South Carolina side of the river, and his men joined the Confederate army marching to Hardeeville, where they entrained for Charleston. The crew set a slow match to the magazine, and at 11:30 P.M. the ironclad died in a magnificent explosion that was seen and felt over a wide area.

"It lit the heavens for miles," wrote one soldier. "We could see to pick up a pin where we were [several miles distant] and the noise was awful." Ships anchored in Tybee Roads felt the tremors, and windows rattled on Hilton Head.

Now that the uncomfortable, but familiar, ship no longer existed, one marine formerly stationed on her recorded: "You have no idea what a sad blow it was to me. Thinks I, there goes my pleasant quarters, my good clothes, my good warm overcoat, and I am forever cut off from Savannah and the hope of making myself agreeable to the Savannah girls." The young man cheered up somewhat. He had filled his new canteen with whiskey, and several swigs imbued him "with fresh strength and spirit." ■

Appendix D ■ Chronology

1864

September 1. Confederate forces evacuate Atlanta.

September 2. Federal General Henry Slocum's 20th Corps occupies Atlanta.

September 3. President Abraham Lincoln declares September 5 a national day of celebration for the fall of Atlanta.

September 4. Federal General William Sherman orders all civilians evacuated from Atlanta, leading to an angry exchange of notes between the Union commander and Confederate General John B. Hood.

September 10. U. S. Grant urges Sherman to initiate a new offensive against Hood.

September 11–22. Sherman and Hood observe a truce to allow 446 civilian families to leave Atlanta. Some travel south to Rough and Ready, others up the rails to the North.

September 25. Confederate President Jefferson Davis confers with Hood in Palmetto about future operations against Sherman. Davis addresses the Army of Tennessee.

October 1. Hood moves northwest around Atlanta to draw Sherman out of the city.

October 4. Hood strikes at Acworth and Big Shanty while Sherman moves to Kennesaw Mountain to direct a pursuit.

October 5. Federal forces under John Corse heroically repulse a determined Confederate attack on Allatoona.

October 9. Confederate and Federal soldiers skirmish at Dallas.

October 10. Blue and Gray infantry clash at Rome.

October 12. Fighting occurs at LaFayette, near Rome, and Resaca.

October 13. Confederates seize the railroad from Resaca to Tunnel Hill.

October 22. Hood reaches Gadsden, Alabama; Sherman camps at Gaylesburg, near the Georgia border.

November 9. Refusing to abandon the initiative to Hood, Sherman has shifted to Kingston, where he prepares to march to Savannah.

November 10. Federals destroy railroad property in Kingston and around Atlanta.

November 11. War material is destroyed in Rome as occupying Union forces move down the railroad to Atlanta.

November 14–15. Federal soldiers in Atlanta destroy the railroad and burn material and structures of military worth in the city. Most of the city is consumed by fire after soldiers go on a rampage of arson.

November 15. Union troops begin leaving Atlanta for the coast. The Left Wing (LW) along the Georgia Railroad toward Augusta; the Right Wing (RW) down the Macon Railroad.

November 16. LW, accompanied by Sherman, advances through Decatur and Stone Mountain to the Yellow River. RW moves through Jonesboro, Lovejoy, Stockbridge, and McDonough.

November 17. LW crosses Alcovy River and passes Lithonia, Conyers, and Social Circle. RW marches through Jackson, Flovilla, Worthville, and Indian Springs. As Sherman's actions become apparent, Jefferson Davis appoints William J. Hardee to command Confederate forces in Georgia.

November 18. LW through Social Circle, Rutledge, and Covington. President Davis, visiting Macon, urges the commander of the Georgia militia, Howell Cobb, to oppose Sherman with every available man.

November 18–20. RW crosses Ocmulgee River to Monticello, Blountsville, and Clinton.

November 19. LW destroys railroad property in Madison, Buckhead, and Swords. Sherman burns Shady Dale and Newborn.

November 20–22. LW advances through Eatonton and the outskirts of Milledgeville. Federal cavalry skirmishes on the outskirts of Macon.

November 21. RW closes on Irwinton and Gordon. Hardee, in Macon, determines that Sherman's objective is Savannah or Augusta and shifts his troops east.

November 22. Foolish assault by inexperienced Georgia militia against Federal infantry at Griswoldville is repulsed with considerable loss.

November 23. LW occupies Milledgeville, the capital of Georgia, after the legislature flees in panic. RW reaches Oconee River through McIntyre and Toombsboro but is delayed at Ball's Ferry for two days by stiff Confederate resistance.

November 24. Kilpatrick leaves the RW to feint on Augusta with the LW, which moves through Hebron. Hardee, at Oconee, decides the Confederate line on the river must be abandoned.

November 25. LW continues toward Sandersville, fighting through constant resistance.

November 26. LW enters Sandersville after sharp cavalry clash and moves to Tennille and Davisboro. RW occupies Oconee.

November 27. LW crosses the Ogeechee River at Fenns Bridge.

November 28. LW enters Louisville and Bartow. RW occupies Riddleville and Wrightsboro.

November 30. RW crosses Ogeechee River at Midville.

November 27–December 4. Fierce cavalry battles rage around Waynesboro as Sherman feints on Augusta. LW supports Kilpatrick, camping between Millen and Waynesboro.

December 1. RW operates around Herndon and Birdville.

December 2. RW concentrates at Millen.

December 3. LW passes through Buckhead, Lumpkin Station, and Millen. RW marches past Scarboro.

December 4. LW passes Jacksonboro. RW moves through Cameron, Statesboro, Mill Ray, and Summerville. Line entrenched by Georgia militia at Oliver is outflanked.

December 5–7. RW marches through Bulloch County, crosses the Great Ogeechee River at Jenks Bridge, passes Blitchton, and crosses the Canoochee River.

December 8–10. LW marches to Springfield and Ebenezer. RW advances through Eden and Pooler, meeting increased resistance.

December 10–21. Sherman arrives outside Savannah and besieges the city. Artillery exchanges become a daily occurrence.

December 12–19. Kilpatrick crosses the Great Ogeechee to scout approaches to Fort McAllister, then rides to Midway and Sunbury to contact the Federal fleet. Union cavalry scouts and forages throughout Liberty County, but an expedition farther south is turned back at the Altamaha River.

December 13. After a gallant assault, Union forces overwhelm Fort McAllister, isolating Savannah.

December 17. In response to an urgent request, Jefferson Davis informs Hardee that Robert E. Lee can spare no men to relieve Savannah. Sherman sends Hardee a surrender demand. Hardee rejects the ultimatum.

December 20. Confederate forces quietly slip out of Savannah.

December 21–February 1, 1865. Sherman's army occupies Savannah.

1865

January 21. Sherman steams to Beaufort, South Carolina, to join Howard.

February 16. Union soldiers capture and destroy Columbia, South Carolina, by fire.

February 23. Camden, South Carolina, is razed by Sherman's men.

March 10. The Federal army occupies Fayetteville, North Carolina.

March 8–10. Bragg attacks Schofield near Kinston, North Carolina, slowing the Union advance.

March 16. Hardee attempts to delay Slocum at Averasboro, North Carolina.

March 19–21. The last major battle between Western armies occurs at Bentonville, North Carolina. After Sherman blunts Johnston's attack, the Confederates retreat.

April 2. Lee's lines at Petersburg, Virginia, are broken. Jefferson Davis and the Confederate government flee Richmond for North Carolina.

April 9. At Appomattox, Virginia, Lee surrenders to Grant.

April 12–13. In Greensboro, North Carolina, President Davis urges Johnston to continue the war, but is finally convinced that the Army of Tennessee must surrender.

April 13. Sherman enters Raleigh, North Carolina.

April 17–18. Sherman and Johnston meet to arrange a surrender, which is repudiated by the U.S. government.

April 26. Sherman and Johnston conclude a final surrender. The Confederate Army of Tennessee is disbanded.

May 24. Sherman's victorious Western veterans parade in review through Washington, D.C.

Appendix E ■ Resources

Each segment of the March to the Sea tour can be easily completed in two or three days, depending on how many sites or attractions the visitor wishes to enjoy. An exploration of the entire campaign and of eastern Georgia's many historic and natural sites can occupy a full vacation. *To the Sea* has been designed to accommodate either approach. Before setting out, you may want to contact some of the following sources of information. From them you can discover many other fascinating places to see and things to do along the way.

We advise the adventurous traveler to secure county maps from the state. They are currently available for $1.50 each from the Department of Transportation, 2 Capital Square, Atlanta, Georgia 30334. The counties covered in the tour are Baldwin, Bibb, Bryan, Bulloch, Burke, Butts, Chatham, Clayton, DeKalb, Effingham, Emanuel, Henry, Jasper, Jefferson, Jenkins, Jones, Lamar, Liberty, Long, Monroe, Morgan, Newton, Putnam, Rockdale, Screven, Washington, and Wilkinson. A good map of Savannah is also essential. These will enable you to keep up with the tour on maps and will be invaluable if you decide to stray off the tour route.

Other sources of help are listed below for your convenience. If you have particular problems or questions, it is likely that one or more of these sources will be able to provide you with what you need.

Federal

Forest Supervisor, 601 Broad Street, Gainesville, GA 30501.

District Ranger, 349 Forsyth Street, Monticello, GA 31064 (404) 468-2244.

Fort Pulaski National Monument, P. O. Box 98, Tybee Island, GA 31328. (912) 786-5787.

Savannah National Wildlife Refuge, P. O. Box 8487, Savannah, GA 31212.

State

Classic South Information, P. O. Box 657, Augusta, GA 30903.

Coastal Area Planning and Development Commission, P.O. Box 1917, Brunswick, GA 31521.

Fort McAllister Historic Park, P. O. Box 198, Richmond Hill, GA 31324.

Georgia Department of Industry and Trade, P. O. Box 1776, Atlanta, GA 30301. (404) 656-3590.

Georgia Department of Natural Resources, Office of Information, 270
    Washington Street, SW, Atlanta, GA 30334. (404) 656-3530.
Georgia's Antebellum Trail Association, P. O. Box 6354, Macon, GA 31208.
    (912) 743-3401.
Georgia's Historic Heartland, P. O. Box 697, Milledgeville, GA 31061.
Hamburg State Park,. Route 1, Box 233, Mitchell, GA 30820.
    (912) 552-2393.
High Falls State Park, Route 5, Box 108, Jackson, GA 30233.
    (912) 994-5080.
Indian Springs State Park, Indian Springs, GA 30231. (404) 775-7241.
Jarrell Plantation, Route 1, Box 40, Juliette, GA 31046. (912) 988-5172.
Magnolia Springs State Park, Route 5, Box 488, Millen, GA 30442.
    (912) 982-1660.
Panola Mountain Conservation Park, 2600 Highway 155 SW, Stockbridge,
    GA 30281. (404) 474-2914.
Richmond Hill State Park, P. O. Box 347, Richmond Hill, GA 31324
    (912) 727-2242.
Skidaway Island State Park, Savannah, GA 31406. (912) 356-2523.
Sunbury Historic Park, Route 1, Box 236, Midway, GA 31320.
    (912) 884-5999.
Wormsloe Historic Park, P. O. Box 13852, 7601 Skidaway Road, Savannah,
    GA 31406. (912) 352-2548.

Local

BALDWIN COUNTY

Milledgeville-Baldwin County Chamber of Commerce, 130 South Jefferson
    Street, Milledgeville, GA 31061.
Milledgeville-Baldwin County Tourism and Trade, P. O. Box 219, 200 West
    Hancock Street, Milledgeville, GA 31061. (912) 452-4687.
Museum and Archives of Georgia Education, 131 South Clarke Street, Mil-
    ledgeville, GA 31061. (912) 453-4391.
Old Capital Historical Society, P.O. Box 4, Milledgeville; GA 31061.
    (912) 453-4293.
Old Governor's Mansion, 120 South Clarke Street, Milledgeville, GA 31061.
    (912) 453-4545.
Old State Capital, 201 East Greene Street, Milledgeville, GA 31061.
    (912) 453-3481.

BIBB COUNTY

Old Cannonball House, 856 Mulberry Street, Macon, GA 31201.
    (912) 745-5982.
Macon-Bibb County Convention and Visitor's Bureau, P. O. Box 6354, 200
    Coliseum Drive, Macon, GA 31208-6354. (912) 743-3401.
Macon Heritage Foundation, Inc., 652 Mulberry Street, Macon, GA 31208.
    (912) 742-5084.

BULLOCH COUNTY
Bulloch County Historical Society, P. O. Box 42, Statesboro, GA 30458. (912) 764-3047.

Georgia Southern Museum, Rosenwald Building, Georgia Southern College, Statesboro, GA 30458.

Statesboro-Bulloch County Chamber of Commerce, 323 South Main Street, Statesboro, GA 30458. (912) 764-6111.

Statesboro Convention and Visitor's Bureau, P. O. Box 1516, Statesboro, GA 30458. (912) 489-1869.

BURKE COUNTY
Burke County Chamber of Commerce, 241 East Sixth Street, Waynesboro, GA 30830. (404) 554-5451.

Burke County Historical Society, 536 Liberty Street, Waynesboro, GA 30830. (404) 554-4889.

BUTTS COUNTY
Butts County Chamber of Commerce, 464 West Third Street, Jackson, GA 30233. P. O. Box 142. (404) 775-3178.

Butts County Historical Society, P. O. Box 215, Jackson, GA 30233.

CHATHAM COUNTY
Coastal Heritage Center, Inc., 1 Fort Jackson Road, Savannah, GA 31404. (912) 232-3945.

Great Savannah Exposition, 303 West Broad Street, Savannah, GA 31499. (912) 238-1779.

Green-Meldrin House, St. John's Church, 1 West Macon Street, Savannah, GA 31401.

Historic Savannah Foundation, 324 East State Street (Davenport House), 41 West Broad Street (Scarbrough House), P. O. Box 1733, Savannah, GA 31402. (912) 233-7787.

Oatland Island Education Center, 711 Sandtown Road, Savannah, GA (912) 897-3773.

Savannah Area Convention and Visitors Center, 222 West Oglethorpe Avenue, Savannah, GA 31499-5902. (912) 944-0456.

Savannah Science Museum, 4405 Paulsen Street, Savannah, GA 31405. (912) 355-6705.

Savannah Visitors Center, I-95, Savannah, GA 30408. (912) 964-5094.

Tybee Museum, P. O. Box 366, Tybee Island, GA 31328. (912) 786-4077.

Tybee Island-Savannah Beach, P. O. Box 491, Tybee Island, GA 31328. (912) 236-8284.

University of Georgia Marine Extension Service, P. O. Box 13687, Savannah, GA 31416. (912) 356-2496.

CLAYTON COUNTY
Clayton County Chamber of Commerce, P. O. Box 774, 8712 Tara Boulevard, Jonesboro, GA 30237. (404) 478-6549.

Historical Jonesboro-Clayton County, Inc., P. O. Box 922, Jonesboro, GA 30237.

DeKalb County
DeKalb Convention and Visitors Bureau, 750 Commerce Drive, Suite 201, Decatur, GA 30030. (404) 378-2525.
DeKalb Historical Society Old Courthouse on the Square, Decatur, GA 30030. (404) 373-1088, 373-3076.
Georgia's Stone Mountain. (404) 498-6500.
Stone Mountain Village, Main Street, Stone Mountain, GA. (404) 498-8984.

Effingham County
Effingham County Chamber of Commerce, P. O. Box L, C & S Bank, Laurel Street, Springfield, GA 31329. (912) 754-3301.
Guyton Historic Preservation Commission, P. O. Box 128, Guyton, GA 31312.
Historic Effingham Society, P. O. Box 999, Springfield, GA 31329.

Emanuel County
Emanuel County Historic Preservation Society, P. O. Box 1101, Swainsboro, GA 30401.
Swainsboro-Emanuel County Chamber of Commerce, 124 North Main Street, Swainsboro, GA 30401. (912) 237-6426.

Fulton County
Atlanta Convention and Visitors Bureau, 233 Peachtree Street, Suite 2000, Atlanta, GA 30303. (404) 521-6600.
Atlanta Local Welcome Centers:
  3393 Peachtree Road, NE, Lenox Square Mall, Atlanta, GA 30326. (404) 266-1398.
  Peachtree Center, 233 Peachtree Street, NE, Atlanta, GA 30303. (404) 521-6688.

Henry County
Henry County Chamber of Commerce, 1310 Highway 20 West, McDonough, GA 30253. (404) 957-5786.
Henry County Landmarks, Inc., P. O. Box 455, McDonough, GA 30253.

Jasper County
Jasper County Historical Foundation, 267 College Street, Monticello, GA 31064.
Monticello-Jasper County Chamber of Commerce, P. O. Box 133, West Green Street, Monticello, GA 31064. (404) 468-8994.

Jefferson County
Jefferson County Chamber of Commerce, P. O. Box 630, 211 East 7th Street, Louisville, GA 30434. (912) 625-8134.

Jenkins County
Jenkins County Chamber of Commerce, 200 Southside Cotton Avenue, Millen, GA 30442. (912) 982-5595.
Jenkins County Historical Society, P. O. Box 67, Perkins, GA 30822.

JONES COUNTY
Old Clinton Historical Society, Inc., P. O. Box 1262, Gray, GA 31032. (912) 986-3384.

LAMAR COUNTY
Barnesville-Lamar County Chamber of Commerce, 109 Forsyth Street, City Hall, Barnesville, GA 30204. (404) 458-2732.
Barnesville-Lamar County Historical Society, 201 Main Street, Barnesville, GA 30204.

LIBERTY COUNTY
Hinesville-Liberty County Chamber of Commerce, P. O. Box 405, 100 Commerce Street, Hinesville, GA 31313. (912) 368-4445.
Liberty County Historical Society, P. O. Box 797, Hinesville, GA 31313.
Midway Museum, Inc., P. O. Box 195, Midway, GA 31320. (912) 884-5837.
Old Liberty County Jail, 3025 Main Street, Hinesville, GA 31313. (912) 876-5500.
24th Infantry Division and Fort Stewart Museum, ATT: AFZP-PTO-PM, Fort Stewart, GA 31314. (912) 767-7885.

MONROE COUNTY
Monroe County Chamber of Commerce, P. O. Box 811, 91 West Johnston Street, Forsyth, GA 31029. (912) 994-9239.
Monroe County Historic Society, P. O. Box 401, Forsyth, GA 31029.

MORGAN COUNTY
Madison-Morgan Chamber of Commerce, P. O. Box 826, 120 South Main Street, Madison, GA 30650. (404) 342-4454.
Madison-Morgan Cultural Center, 434 South Main Street, Madison, GA 30650. (404) 342-4743.
Morgan County Historical Society, Inc., P. O. Box 207, 277 South Main Street, Madison, GA 30650. (404) 342-9614.
Morgan County Landmarks Society, Inc., 373 West Central Avenue, Madison, GA 30650.

NEWTON COUNTY
Newton County Chamber of Commerce, P. O. Box 168, 1121 Floyd Street, Covington, GA 30209. (404) 786-7510.
Newton County Historical Society, P. O. Box 1155, Covington, GA 30209.
Oxford Historical Shrine, Inc., P. O. Box 1, Oxford, GA 30267.

PUTNAM COUNTY
Eatonton-Putnam County Chamber of Commerce, P. O. Box 656, 105 Sumter Street, Eatonton, GA 31024. (404) 485-7701, 485-4875.
Eatonton-Putnam County Historical Society, Inc., P. O. Box 331, 114 North Madison Avenue, Eatonton, GA 31024.
Uncle Remus Association, Inc., P. O. Box 184, Highway 441 South, Eatonton, GA 31024. (404) 485-6856.

ROCKDALE COUNTY
Conyers-Rockdale County Chamber of Commerce, P. O. Box 483, 1186 Scott Street, Conyers, GA 30207. (404) 483-7049.

Rockdale County Historical Society, P. O. Box 351, 957 Milstead Avenue, Conyers, GA 30207. (404) 483-7323.

SCREVEN COUNTY

Screven County Chamber of Commerce, 101 South Main Street, Sylvania, GA 30467. (912) 564-7878.

Screven County Historical and Genealogical Society, 239 Sylvan Circle, Sylvania, GA 30467.

Sylvania Visitors Information Center, Highway 301, Sylvania, GA 30467. (912) 829-3331.

WASHINGTON COUNTY

Washington County Chamber of Commerce, P. O. Box 582, 119 Jones Street, Sandersville, GA 31081. (912) 552-3247.

Washington County Historical Society, P. O. Box 692, Sandersville, GA 31081.

Bibliography

Andrews, Eliza F. *The Wartime Journal of a Georgia Girl*. New York: D. Appleton, 1906.

Barnard, George N. *Photographic Views of Sherman's Campaign*. New York: Dover Publications, 1977.

Barrett, John G. *Sherman's March Through the Carolinas*. Chapel Hill: University of North Carolina Press, 1956.

Battey, George. *A History of Rome*. Atlanta: Webb and Vary, 1922.

Bonner, James C. *Milledgeville: Georgia's Antebellum Capital*. Athens: University of Georgia Press, 1978.

Bradley, Rev. G. S. *The Star Corps*. Milwaukee, 1865.

Brookman, Charles J., ed. "The John Van Duser [Duzer] Diary of Sherman's March from Atlanta to Hilton Head." *Georgia Historical Quarterly*. June, 1969.

Bull, Rice. *Soldiering*. Jack Bauer, ed. San Rafael, California: Presidio Press, 1977.

Carter, Samuel, III. *The Siege of Atlanta*. New York: Ballantine Books, 1973.

Catton, Bruce. *Never Call Retreat*. Garden City: Doubleday and Company, 1965.

Commager, Henry S. *The Blue and the Gray*. New York: Fairfax Press, 1982.

Connolly, Thomas C. *Autumn of Glory: The Army of Tennessee*. Baton Rouge: Louisiana State University Press, 1971.

Conyngham, David P. *Sherman's March Through the South*. New York: Sheldon and Company, 1865.

Corley, Florence Fleming. *Confederate City: Augusta, Georgia, 1860–1865*. Columbia: University of South Carolina Press, 1961.

Cox, Jacob B. *The March to the Sea*. New York: Scribner's, 1906.

Cumming, Kate. *Gleamings from Southland*. Birmingham: Roberts and Sons, 1895.

Davis, Burke. *Sherman's March*. New York: Random House, 1980.

Davis, William C. *The Orphan Brigade*. Baton Rouge: Louisiana State University Press, 1980.

Dyer, John P. *"Fightin' Joe" Wheeler*. Baton Rouge: Louisiana State University Press, 1941.

DuBose, John W. *General Joseph Wheeler and the Army of Tennessee*. New York: Neale, 1912.

Evans, Clement A., ed. *Confederate Military History,* Volume VI. Atlanta: Confederate Publishing Company, 1899.

Foote, Shelby. *The Civil War, A Narrative: Red River to Appomattox*. New York: Random House, 1974.

Garrett, Franklin M. *Atlanta and Environs,* Volume I. Athens: University of Georgia Press, 1969.

Gatell, Frank Otto, ed. "A Yankee Views the Agony of Savannah." *Georgia Historical Quarterly*. December, 1959.

Gay, Mary. *Life in Dixie During the War*. Atlanta: Darby Publishing Company, 1979.

Georgia: A Guide to Its Towns and Countryside. Athens: University of Georgia Press, 1940.

Georgia Civil War Markers. Atlanta: Georgia Department of Natural Resources, 1982.

Gibson, John M. *Those 163 Days*. New York: Coward and McCann, 1961.

Glattboar, Joseph T. *The March to the Sea and Beyond*. New York: New York University Press, 1985.

Green, Anna Maria. *The Journal of a Milledgeville Girl*. James C. Bonner, ed. Athens: University of Georgia Miscellanea Publications Number 4, 1964.

Griffin, James D. *Savannah, Georgia, During the Civil War*. Ann Arbor: University Microfilm, 1963.

Hitchcock, Henry. *Marching with Sherman*. M. A. DeWolfe Howe, ed. New Haven: Yale University Press, 1927.

Hoehling, Adolf A. *Last Train from Atlanta*. New York: Thomas Yoseloff, 1958.

Hood, John B. *Advance and Retreat*. Bloomington: Indiana University Press, 1952.

Horn, Stanley F. *The Army of Tennessee*. Norman: University of Oklahoma Press, 1952.

Howard, Frances Thomas. *In and Out of the Lines*. New York: The Neale Publishing Company, 1905.

Hughes, Nathaniel C. *General William J. Hardee: Old Reliable*. Baton Rouge: Louisiana State University Press, 1965.

Johnson, Robert U., and Buel, Clarence C., eds. *Battles and Leaders of the Civil War: The Way to Appomattox*. New York: Castle Books, 1956.

Johnston, Joseph E. *Narrative of Military Operations*. Bloomington: Indiana University Press, 1959.

Jones, Katharine M. *When Sherman Came*. New York: Bobbs-Merrill, 1964.

Jones, Mary Sharpe, and Mary Jones Mallard. *Yankees a' Coming*. Haskell Monroe, ed. Tuscaloosa: Confederate Publishing Company, 1959.

Jones, Virgil C. *The Civil War at Sea,* Volume II: *The River War*. New York: Holt, Rinehart, Winston, 1961.

Kerksis, Sydney, compiler. *The Atlanta Papers*. Dayton: Morningside Press, 1980.

King, Spencer B., ed. "Fanny Cohen's Journal of Sherman's Occupation of Savannah." *Georgia Historical Quarterly*. December, 1957.

Knapp, David. *The Confederate Horsemen*. New York: Vantage Press, 1966.

"Letter of a Confederate Surgeon on Sherman's Occupation of Milledgeville." *Georgia Historical Quarterly*. September, 1948.

Lewis, Lloyd. *Sherman: Fighting Prophet*. New York: Harcourt, Brace and Company, 1932.

McInvale, Morton R. "'All That Devils Could Wish For': The Griswoldville Campaign, November, 1864," *Georgia Historical Quarterly*. Summer, 1976.

McInvale, Morton R. *Macon, Georgia, During the War Years*. 1973.

McKee, Gwen, ed. *A Guide to the Georgia Coast*. Savannah: The Georgia Conservancy, 1984.

Major Connelly's Letters to His Wife, 1862–1865. Transactions of the Illinois State Historical Society, Pub. 35, Part III. Springfield, 1928.

Miers, Earl S. *The General Who Marched to Hell*. New York: Alfred A. Knopf, 1951.

Miller Francis T, ed.-in-chief. *The Photographic History of the Civil War: Forts and Artillery*. New York: Castle Books, 1957.

Mitchell, Ella. *History of Washington County, Georgia*. Atlanta: Byrd Printing, 1924.

Nevin, David. *Sherman's March*. Alexandria: Time-Life Books, 1986.

Nichols, George Ward. *The Story of the Great March*. New York: Harper and Brothers, 1865.

Official Records of the War of the Rebellion, Volume XLIV, and Volume XXXIX. Series I. Washington, D.C.: Government Printing Office, 1898.

Osborne, Thomas W. *The Fiery Trail.* Knoxville: University of Tennessee Press, 1986.

Our Women in the War. Charleston: News and Courier Press, 1885.

Pepper, George W. *Recollections of Sherman's Campaigns in Georgia and the Carolinas.* Zanesville, Ohio: Hugh Dunne Publications, 1866.

Harvey J. Powell, ed. *The Experiences of Erasmus H. Jordan.* Monticello, Georgia, 1972.

Reiter, Beth L., and Martin, Van J. *Coastal Georgia.* Savannah: Golden Coast Publishing, 1985.

Reminiscences of Confederate Soldiers. Volumes VIII, IX, XII. Georgia Department of Archives and History. Atlanta, 1924.

Scruggs, C. P. *Georgia During the Revolution.* Norcross, Georgia: Bay Tree Grove Press, 1975.

—————. *Georgia Historical Markers.* Norcross, Georgia: Bay Grove Press, Norcross, 1973.

Sherman in Georgia. Edgar L. McCormick, Edward G. McGehee, and Mary Strahl, eds. Boston: Heath and Company, 1961.

Sherman, William T. *Memoirs of General William T. Sherman.* New York: D. Appleton, 1875.

Starr, Stephen Z. *The Union Cavalry in the Civil War,* Volume III: *The War in the West.* Baton Rouge: Louisiana State University Press, 1985.

Stember, Sol. *The Bicentennial Guide to the American Revolution,* Volume III: *The War in the South.* New York: Saturday Review Press, 1974.

Symonds, Craig L. *A Battlefield Atlas of the Civil War.* Baltimore: Nautical and Aviation Publishing Company of America, 1983.

Upson, Theodore F. *With Sherman to the Sea.* Oscar Osburn Winther, ed. Baton Rouge: Louisiana State University Press, 1943.

Walters, John B. *Merchant of Terror.* New York: Bobbs-Merrill, 1973.

Warner, Ezra J. *Generals in Blue.* Baton Rouge: Louisiana State University Press, 1964.

Warner, Ezra J. *Generals in Gray.* Baton Rouge: Louisiana State University Press, 1959.

Index

Brown, Joseph, 139, 143, 244, 273. Sends militia home, 13, 26; flees Milledgeville, 72; Joe Brown pikes, 79; **75**
Bryan Court House, Georgia, 165
Buchanan, Georgia, 36
Buckhead Creek, 111, 117, 119, 189; **109**
Buckhead, Georgia, 128, 171, 301
Buffalo Creek, 86
Bulloch County, Georgia, 163–64, 301
Bull, Rice, 30, 41, 51, 53, 60, 67, 80, 114, 124
Bummers, *See* Foraging
Burge, Dolly Sumner Lunt, 44–6, 234
Burnt Country, 84
Burr, Aaron, 131; **131**
Burton, Georgia, 161, 167
Byers, Samuel, poem "When Sherman Marched Down to the Sea," 205

Cabins, Emma, 153–54
Calhoun, James M. Surrenders Atlanta, 5; protests civilian evacuation, 7
Camden, South Carolina, 258, 302
Cameron, Georgia, 174, 192
Camp Lawton, 112, 120–21; **112, 113**
Canning, Nora M., 98–102
Canoochee, Georgia, 189
Canoochee River, 165–66, 189, 199
Canton, Georgia, 35, 36
Cape Fear River, North Carolina, 260, 261
Cartersville, Georgia, 20, 35, 36
Cassville, Georgia, 35, 36
Catterson, K. J., 146
Cedartown, Georgia, 36
Cemeteries, Confederate, 126, 127, 128, 130, 132, 182, 184, 186, 192
Central of Georgia Railroad, 164, 166, 172, 175, 189, 190, 199–200, 236
Chambers Mill, Georgia, 48
Chancellorsville, Virginia, 30, 55
Charleston & Savannah Railroad, 198, 220, 226
Charleston, South Carolina, 118, 122, 172, 220, 239, 252, 253, 258. Destruction, 254–58, 302
Charlotte, North Carolina, 258
Chattahoochee River, 9, 20
Chattanooga, Tennessee, 15, 33, 35, 36
Chattooga County, Georgia, 32
Cheraw, South Carolina, 258, 302
Chicago Times, 93
Church of the Immaculate Conception, 25
City Point, Virginia, 263
Clark, John G., 225
Clinton, Georgia, 144, 151, 185

Clyde, Georgia, 165
Clyo, Georgia, 135
Cobb, Howell, 66–8, 135, 143
Cobb, Thomas R. R., 125
Cockspur Island, Georgia, 271–72
Cohen, Fanny, 237
Coit, USS, 214
Cold Harbor, Virginia, 241
Coleman Lake, 189
Columbia, South Carolina, 216. Capture of, 252, 234, 254, 264, 265, 268, 302; **255, 256, 257**
Columbus, Georgia, 9, 11, 263
Commissioner's Creek, 158
Confederate Congress, 73, 287
Connolly, James, 215, 240. On destruction in northern Georgia, 18–9; on Stone Mountain, 41–2; at Conyers, 43–4, 51–2; at Shady Dale, 64; on looting, 66; on Milledgeville, 74–5; on destruction in Milledgeville, 76; on piney woods, 85; on Confederate resistance, 87–8; approaches Fenn's bridge, 95–6; supports Kilpatrick in feint against Augusta, 104–10; anxious in swamps, 116–24; on Ebenezer Creek incident, 118–21; on hunger in the army, 200; writes letter concerning Ebenezer Creek, 201.
Contrabands, **119**
Conyers, Georgia, 43–4, 126
Conyngham, David, 255, 257. On destruction of Atlanta, 21–2; on destruction of Madison, 59–60; on Union occupancy of mill, 77–8
Cooper, A. C., 69, 70, 72
Cooperville, Georgia, 192
Cornwell, Louise Caroline Reese, 155–56
Corse, John, 36, 145, 164, 166, 179, 299. Destroys Rome, 17–8
Cotton, 153, 242
Cotton River, 151, 183
Covington, Georgia, 44–8, 300
Cox, Jacob, 18, 197, 203, 204, 232
Cross Roads, Georgia, 166
Customs House, Savannah, 230, 245
Cuyler, R. R., 166, 198

d'Alvingy, Dr. Peter Paul Noel, 25–6
Dahlgren, John, 213–15, 222, 298
Dallas, Georgia, 14, 299
Dalton, Georgia, 15, 17
Dandelion, USS, 209, 213
Davis, Jefferson, 172, 195, 260, 264–65, 266, 277, 280, 299, 302. Addresses Army of Tennessee at Palmetto, 12–3
Davis, Jefferson C., 29, 57, 65, 66, 74, 75, 117,

Honey Hill, South Carolina, 196–98; in evacuation of Savannah, 232; seizes Fort Pulaski, 273
Georgia Penitentiary, **78**
Georgia Railroad, 243
Georgia Southern College, 190
Georgia State House, **81**
Georgia State Legislature flees Milledgeville, 69–71
Gettysburg, Pennsylvania, 30, 55
Gibson, Georgia, 103
Gillmore, Quincy A., 276–79
Girl Scouts of America, 236
Glidden, John M., 238
Goldsboro, North Carolina, 252, 260, 263
Gone With the Wind, 182
Goodwyn, Thomas I., 254
Gordon, Eleanor Kenzie, 236–37
Gordon, Georgia, 145, 156–59, 186–87, 195, 300; **187**
Gordon, John B., 269
Goshen Church, 135
Governor's Island, New York, Prison, 280
Governor's Mansion, Milledgeville, 75, 129; **75**
Grange, Georgia, 97
Grant, U. S., 5, 10, 11, 34, 178, 213, 216, 231, 232, 239, 240–41, 266, 302. Gives permission for March, 15
Gray, Georgia, 186
Green, Anna Marie, 70, 71, 72, 75, 79, 82–3, 84
Green, Charles, 231, 234, 243, 245, 251; **235, 243**
Greene, Nathaniel, 240
Greensboro, Georgia, 103
Greensboro, North Carolina, 264, 302
Griffin, Georgia, 142, 184
Griswold, Samuel, 186
Griswoldville, Georgia. Skirmishes near, 145; Battle of, 146–49, 158, 186, 300; **148**
Guyton, Georgia, 192

Haddock, Georgia, 151
Hafford, J. H., 144
Halayondale, Georgia, 175
Halleck, Henry, 9. On Ebenezer Creek incident, 121, 214, 216
Hamburg State Park, Georgia, 131
Hampton, Georgia, 142
Hampton, Wade, 252, 259, 260, 262
Harbridge, A. L., 159
Hardee, William J., 143, 160, 253, 260–61, 262, 296, 301, 302. Blamed for loss of Atlanta and reassigned, 14; organizes defense of Savannah, 166, 197; in Macon, 143; at Oconee, 160–61;

assumes command in Savannah, 195; biography, 197; rejects Sherman's surrender demand, 220–21; **197**
Hardeeville, South Carolina, 220, 226, 228, 253
Hardee, Willie, 197
Harris, Iverson, 76
Harris, Joel Chandler, 65, 129
Harvest Moon, USS, 214, 222
Hatch, John P., 197
Hawley, William, 78
Hazen, William B., 164–66, 208, 210, 212, 217; **210**
Hebron, Georgia, 130, 300
Herndon, Georgia, 170
High, Emma, 60–1
High Falls State Park, Georgia, 184
Hight, John, 120
Hill, Benjamin, 73
Hill, Joshua, 60, 128
Hill, Legare, 60, 128
Hillsboro, Georgia, 151, 155–56, 185, 301
Hillsboro, North Carolina, 265
Hilton Head, South Carolina, 274, 298
Hinesville, Georgia, 224
Hitchcock, Henry, 41, 44, 48, 68. On destruction of Marietta, 18–9; on Atlanta's destruction, 21; in Covington, 51; on lack of discipline among troops, 52–3; on foragers, 65; on indiscriminate destruction, 66, 186; in Milledgeville, 74; at Birdsville, 171–72; on Millen's destruction, 172–73; on use of torpedos, 179, 181; Fort McAllister, 210, 212; **171, 259**
Honey Hill, South Carolina, Battle of, 197
Hood, Arthur, 218
Hood, John B. Evacuates Atlanta, 5; drives North, 11–5; fate in Tennessee, 13, 97, 139, 252, 299
Hooker, Joseph, 30
Howard, Frances Thomas, 236–37
Howard, O. O., 29, 38, 57, 151, 153, 157, 158, 159, 160, 162, 164, 178, 180, 204, 212, 222, 236–37, 242, 252, 258, 262, 302. Biography, 55; **55**
Howard University, 55
Howard, W. P. Surveys Atlanta's ruins, 26–7
Huntington, Dr. D. C., 156
Hutchison Island, Georgia, 225, 298

Ida, CSS, 273, 275
Indian Springs, Georgia, 149, 152, 161, 184, 300; **141, 153**
Ironclads, Confederate, 288–98; **289, 290, 291, 292, 293, 295, 297**

McDonough, Georgia, 151, 185, 191, 300; **183**
McIntosh, Chief William, 184
McIntyre, Georgia, 159, 187
McKay, G. H., 172, 217
McLaws, LaFayette, 172, 176, 196, 199, 227, 233
McPherson, James B., 29, 38, 53
Mead, Rufus, 59, 92
Melville, Herman, Poem "The March to the Sea," 91
Meridian, Mississippi, 35
Merrill, Jesse, 212, 213, 214
Middle Ground Road, 122, 124, 134
Midville, Georgia, 189
Midway Church, **203**
Midway, Georgia, 135, 211, 218, 224, 301; **203**
Mill Creek, 116, 164–65
Mill Creek Community, 191, 192
Milledgeville, CSS. Destruction of, 297
Milledgeville, Georgia, 9, 10, 32, 66, 128–29, 158, 300. Legislature evacuates, 69, 71; Union occupation, 71, 72–84; **71, 81**
Millen, Georgia, 10, 11, 111, 172–73, 190, 192, 301. Destruction of, 122; **112, 113, 114**
Millen, Georgia, Prison, 85, 88, 106, 111–16, 190
Mill Ray, Georgia, 163, 301
Mitchell, Ella, 88–9
Mitchell, Margaret, 182
Mobile, Alabama, 9, 11
Monitor, USS, 282
Monitors, 281, 282, 284, 285, 286, 293–97; **237**
Montauk, USS, 282, 284, 285, 293, 298
Monteith, Georgia, 124, 135, 220
Monteith Swamp, 180, 199
Montgomery, Alabama, 9, 11
Monticello, Georgia, 151, 154, 185, 300
Morgan Lake, Georgia, 217–18
Morris, B. F., 185
Mount Vernon, Virginia, 267
Mower, 217, 262
Mrs. "LFJ", 90
Munnerlyn, Georgia, 132

Nahant, USS, 294–95
Nashville, CSS, 212, 224, 281, 283, 284–85, 298
Nashville, Tennessee, 13, 253
Nemaha, USS, 225; **217**
New Ebenezer, Georgia, 134, 142; **134**
New York Herald, 292
New York Times, 37
Newborn, Georgia, 51–2, 63, 127, 135, 300
Newington, Georgia, 134
Newton County, Georgia, 127

Nichols, George Ward, 15, 20, 24, 63, 120, 176, 209, 210, 212. On marching, 66; at Cobb Plantation, 68; on Millen's destruction, 174; on capture of Fort McAllister, 234–36.
Nichols, Kate Latimer, 79
North Carolina. Sherman's invasion of, 259–67

Oakey, Daniel, 33
Oakland Cemetery, 27
Ocmulgee River, 144, 145, 152, 300
Oconee, Georgia, 157, 159, 160, 188, 300
Oconee National Forest, 128
Oconee River, 62, 75, 81, 82, 89, 157, 159–61, 188, 300
Ogeechee Canal, 164, 204, 215, 223
Ogeechee Church, 174–76, 192
Ogeechee River, 96–7, 105, 108, 131, 160, 162, 163–64, 172–73, 178, 189, 190, 192, 207, 208, 209, 211, 212, 213, 214, 215, 222, 223, 224, 281, 282, 284; **97, 100**
Ogeechee Shoals, Georgia, 103
Oglethorpe, James, 122, 134, 245
O'Reilly, Father Thomas, 25
Old Savannah Road, 163
Old State Capitol, Milledgeville, 89, 130. Occupied, 76; Ordinance of Secession repealed, 77–9
Olmstead, Charles H., 276–79
Orphan Brigade, 139, 145, 151, 220
Osborne, Thomas, 151–52, 153, 154, 155, 158, 161, 162, 202, 221, 240
Ossabaw Sound, 195, 216, 224
Osterhaus, Peter J., 29, 143, 144, 160, 163, 164–65. Biography, 143
Oxford, Georgia, 50, 126, 300

Page, Richard L., 294
Palmetto, Georgia, 13, 299
Panola Mountain State Park, Georgia, 183
Paramore Hill, Georgia, 173
Paris Academy, Georgia, 174
Passaic, USS, 286, 293
Patapsco, USS, 285
Patter, John, 114
Pendergast, Harrison, 121
Pensacola, Florida, 11
Pepper, George W., 9, 53. On destruction of Atlanta, 23, 24
Perkerson, Lizzie, 26
Petersburg, Virginia, 213, 240–41, 264, 269, 302
Pets, 115
Philadelphia Navy Yard, 296
Philips, P. J., 146–49

Numbers in **boldface** indicate an illustration